MW01088597

The First Vietnam War

Shawn McHale explores why the communist-led Resistance in Vietnam won the anticolonial war against France (1945–54), *except* in the South. He shows how broad swaths of Vietnamese people were uneasily united in 1945 under the Viet Minh Resistance banner, all opposing the French attempt to reclaim control of the country. By 1947, Resistance unity had shattered and Khmer-Vietnamese ethnic violence had divided the Mekong Delta. From this point on, the war in the south turned into an overt civil war wrapped up in a war against France. Based on extensive archival research in four countries and in three languages, this is the first substantive English-language book focused on southern Vietnam's transition from colonialism to independence.

Shawn F. McHale is Associate Professor of History and International Affairs, George Washington University. His first book, *Print and Power: Confucianism, Communism, and Buddhism in the Making of Modern Vietnam* (University of Hawaii Press, 2004), was a finalist for the Benda Prize in Southeast Asian Studies.

The First Vietnam War

Violence, Sovereignty, and the Fracture of the South, 1945–1956

Shawn F. McHale

George Washington University, Washington DC

CAMBRIDGE
UNIVERSITY PRESS

CAMBRIDGE
UNIVERSITY PRESS

University Printing House, Cambridge CB2 8BS, United Kingdom

One Liberty Plaza, 20th Floor, New York, NY 10006, USA

477 Williamstown Road, Port Melbourne, VIC 3207, Australia

314–321, 3rd Floor, Plot 3, Splendor Forum, Jasola District Centre, New Delhi – 110025, India

103 Penang Road, #05–06/07, Visioncrest Commercial, Singapore 238467

Cambridge University Press is part of the University of Cambridge.

It furthers the University's mission by disseminating knowledge in the pursuit of education, learning, and research at the highest international levels of excellence.

www.cambridge.org
Information on this title: www.cambridge.org/9781108837446
DOI: 10.1017/9781108936002

First published 2021

A catalogue record for this publication is available from the British Library.

ISBN 978-1-108-83744-6 Hardback

Contents

Part III: Endgame, 1953–1956

Figures

Tables

Acknowledgments

This book has been long in the making, and I have concluded its writing in the shadow of a global pandemic. My debts to individuals and institutions in the United States and around the globe are many. I was introduced to the study of Vietnam by professors Trương Bửu Lâm and Nguyễn Đăng Liêm. I would also like to thank those individuals who modeled a life of intellectual curiosity and inquiry, beginning with my father, Thomas McHale, continuing to Swarthmore College, with professors like Don Swearer, the eminent scholar of Theravada Buddhism, and on to graduate school, where I would single out Keith Taylor at Cornell.

I am grateful to the institutions that funded or hosted my work. This book would not have been possible without a Fulbright-Hays research fellowship from the US Department of Education, repeated summer funding from the Sigur Center for Asian Studies at George Washington University, and a sabbatical from the same university. The Center for Vietnamese and Southeast Asian Studies at Vietnam National University – University of Social Sciences and Humanities in Ho Chi Minh City hosted my research stay. Particular thanks to its director, Professor Trần Đình Lâm, PhD. I would also like to thank archivists at the Service Historique de la Défense (Vincennes), particularly Mme. Bertrand; the Archives Nationales d'Outre-Mer (Aix); The Vietnam National Archives-II (Ho Chi Minh City); and the Cambodian National Archives (Phnom Penh).

The *Journal of Vietnamese Studies* and the *Journal of Asian Studies* have both allowed me to reuse parts of articles I wrote for those eminent publications.

A wide range of scholars have helped me on particular parts of this book or shaped the whole. Two graduate students, Ron Leonhart and Ithi Sophonpanich (now deceased), carried out research for me in Cambodia and the United States. My greatest debt is to Chris Goscha, whose work on the First Indochina War has deeply influenced my own. Chris has also provided key sources, commented on the work, and even once provided a place to stay in Vincennes, France when I was carrying out research. Stathis Kalyvas's work has sharpened my understanding of the logic of civil war violence. Two anonymous reviewers gave superb and critical feedback on the manuscript. If I resisted a few of their suggestions, I have spent much time trying to address their concerns. For comments over the years that have shaped this book, or help on particular issues, I would like to thank, in no particular order, Tuong Vu, Li Tana, David P. Chandler, Philip Taylor, Liam Kelley, Christina Firpo, Ben Wilkinson, Eckard Michels, Jérémy Jammes, Pascal Bourdeaux, François Guillemot, Haydon Cherry, Alasdair Bowie, Olga Dror, Hue Tam Ho Tai, Nguyễn Điền, Phạm Quỳnh Phương, David MacKenzie, Nhung Tuyet Tran, Ed McCord, Châu Huy Ngọc, Patrick Gubry, Mike Montesano, and Charles Keith. (Given the controversies sure to be elicited by this work, I will not provide the names of some Vietnamese interlocutors, whom I thank profusely.) The maps were made by Richard Hinton and Chris Robinson. Lucy Rhymer, Emily Sharp, and the rest of the editorial and production staff at Cambridge University Press have shepherded this book from acquisition through to completion.

My spouse, Diane McHale, and children, Vanessa and Kate, have often interrupted my thinking about destruction and war. My heartfelt thanks!

Abbreviations

ANOM	Archives Nationales d'Outre-Mer
CP	Conseiller Politique
DRV	Democratic Republic of Vietnam
ECPAD	L'Établissement de Communication et de Production Audiovisuelle de la Défense, Ministère de la Défense (Ivry-sur-Seine, France)
HCI	Haut-Commissariat en Indochine
ICP	Indochinese Communist Party
NAC	National Archives of Cambodia (Phnom Penh, Cambodia)
NARA	National Archives and Records Administration (College Park Maryland, USA)
PTHNV	Phủ Thủ Hiến Nam Việt
RSC	Résidence Supérieure au Cambodge
SHD	Service Historique de la Défense (Vincennes, France)
SPCE	Service de Protection du Corps Expéditionnaire
UMDC	Unités Mobiles de Défense de la Chrétienté
VNA-II	Vietnamese National Archives (Ho Chi Minh City, Vietnam)

Introduction: Sovereignty, Violence, and Institutional Collapse at the Edge of France's Empire

After the Geneva Accords on Indochina were signed in 1954, Vietnam was temporarily broken into two parts, with the communist-led Democratic Republic of Vietnam (DRV) in the north and the non-communist State of Vietnam in the south. While many cadres and soldiers in the Resistance that fought the French regrouped to the north, Trần Bạch Đằng, a Resistance intellectual who covertly stayed behind in the south, set out for Saigon. Leaving the Resistance zone, he felt disoriented. In Đằng's eloquent words:

> After July 20, 1954, I left the liberated area of Zone Nine, where I had worked and lived for many years, to return to Saigon. I set foot in the Phụng Hiệp market one morning. On the other side of the river was the liberated zone. Facing the market was the Joint [Ceasefire Committee for the South] headquarters, flying the flag of the Land of our Ancestors. Phụng Hiệp was small, but was abuzz with activity. For me, everything was strange. The bus station was noisier, people getting off and on vehicles, bustling to and forth. From the riverbank, I had to walk past many onlookers, and as I passed them, I felt the cold stares in the back of my neck, as if prying eyes were boring into me. Climbing onto the bus, I glanced at the person next to me. He was young, wearing dark glasses – "he looks like he's from the secret police," I thought to myself. Who was behind me? Several times I looked around, then stopped. These mixed-up thoughts put me on edge. The bus moved quickly through more villages and markets than I could remember. When we passed over roads that had been damaged, and reached good roads and did not bounce around anymore, I felt far from Zone Nine, and felt more and more abandoned and alone.[1]

Trần Bạch Đằng's remembrance of his 1954 journey from the Resistance liberated zone to that under control of the State of Vietnam underscores the experiential importance of the internal borders that had shaped the Mekong Delta during the First Indochina War. But it also emphasizes a bitter reality for the communist-led DRV: having failed to win in the South, it was forced to accept the temporary division of the country at the Seventeenth Parallel during the Geneva negotiations. Only covert

---

[1] Trần Bạch Đằng, *Kẻ sĩ Gia Định* (Hanoi: Quân Đội Nhân Dân, 2005), 19–20.

operatives like Trần Bạch Đằng would stay behind to continue the revolutionary struggle.

Why did the communist-led Resistance in Vietnam win their anticolonial war against France and its Vietnamese allies (1945–54) in the rest of Vietnam, but fail in the South? This book, based on extensive archival and secondary research on three continents, eventually answers that question. I confess, however, that when I began my research, that question was not even on my mind. After all, the DRV defeated France resoundingly at the Battle of Điện Biên Phủ in 1954, heralding France's exit from Vietnam. Why quibble over details about the southern third of the country? Communist historians have stated that the Resistance *won* the war in the South. Western analysts vaguely implied the same. In his canonical province study *War Comes to Long An*, Jeffrey Race explained that the Second Indochina War was lost by the South Vietnamese government even before the United States committed massive numbers of troops to Vietnam in 1965. This failure was "conceptual": while the South Vietnamese government focused on not losing, communists had a *"comprehensive view of revolution as a step-by-step process"* with a goal of winning.[2] Where did this strategy come from? Apparently, from the struggle in southern Vietnam against the French and their Vietnamese allies. I beg to differ. Communists would win the Second Indochina War in the South by *recognizing their mistakes* from the First Indochina War. Failure was a learning experience.

When I began this project, and as I end it, my mind has been less focused on who "won" and who "lost," and more about the massive transformations of the South from 1945 to 1954. Fundamental questions still beg to be addressed. How does violence shape and reshape societies? How in war do institutions shatter, and then get reassembled out of the fragments left behind? What does it mean to speak of sovereignty, and its "transfer," in situations of tremendous upheaval and fragmented rule? How exactly did the French empire end in southern Vietnam, and how was a new State of Vietnam born?

In trying to answer such questions, I examine the genesis, unfolding, and conclusion of the First Indochina War, usually called (in Vietnam) the War of Resistance against the French. Specifically, while the book discusses events in Saigon, and touches on Cambodia and the broader French empire, the heart of the book focuses on the Mekong Delta in today's southern Vietnam. This was a war in which the empire played a key role. A slight majority of the regular soldiers and sailors who

---

[2] Jeffrey Race, *War Comes to Long An: Revolutionary Conflict in a Vietnamese Province* (Berkeley: University of California Press, 1972), xvi, 141.

served in French Indochina (256,093 out of 489,560) were not French nationals. These numbers do not even include paramilitary and self-defense forces, who were overwhelmingly non-French. And the estimated 400,000 military and civilian dead? Of the regular and irregular soldiers on the French side who died, five-sixths were not French. If we cast our net wider to look at all the estimated civilian and military dead, the picture is starker. I estimate that those who were not French nationals probably made up approximately nineteen out of twenty of the dead in this conflict. These dead came from over sixty different political units and countries.

Before laying out my argument in depth, it helps to understand the foil against which it has been written. In modern Vietnamese history, the First Indochina War (1945–54), inaugurated with the so-called "August Revolution" of 1945, occupies a privileged place. At a global level, it forms a key part of the struggles for independence that marked the end of European empires in Asia and Africa. In the standard narrative of this war, a resolute, initially outmatched, and broad-based Vietnamese revolutionary nationalist Resistance fights against a powerful French military, ultimately triumphing against great odds. The story always begins with the Việt Minh seizure of power during the "August Revolution" of 1945, in the north, an act whose effects ripple southwards all the way to the Mekong Delta, and culminates, back in the north, with Hồ Chí Minh's proclamation of independence on September 2, 1945, at Ba Đình Square, Hanoi. Communist historians (and many others) often insist that the war broke out, in the north, on December 19, 1946, after diplomatic negotiations between the DRV and France broke down. The war effectively concluded with the 1954 battle of Điện Biên Phủ in the north. With this defeat, France was forced to end the war and depart from Indochina. This is a very 'northern' story, one in which a northern template frames our understanding of what turns out to be a messy whole.

One of the problems of much writing on the First Indochina War is that it locates the ultimate victory of the Vietnamese in 1954 in either the founding of the Indochinese Communist Party (ICP) itself, or in the events of the communist-led August Revolution of 1945, which are seen, in some way, to serve as the template for future victory. But was it? What if we centered our account of the First Indochina War on the plural South, with its own particular history, overlooked in the northern-centered narrative mentioned above? This book tries to avoid inventing new "chimeras of the origin." After all, as Foucault has penetratingly observed, the inherited past is "an unstable assemblage of faults, fissures, and heterogeneous layers" that play out across time.[3] The search for an "originary moment," such as the August Revolution of 1945, encapsulating in embryo the promise of the future victory, is doomed to failure. Not only did the war have multiple strands that do not easily weave together, but its character cannot be defined by one master strand that links beginning to end.

In the South, the Resistance lost the first phase of the thirty-year military and political struggle for the South. But who "won"? Ironically, none of the contestants who actually fought. The war actually began in the South in September 1945, and over 3,000 French, British, and Japanese (now under Allied command) died fighting the Việt Minh before December, 1946 – the "official" month of the beginning of the war.[4] The great majority of these casualties occurred in Cochinchina. I roughly estimate that at least 10,000 civilians and armed members of the Việt Minh, and probably more, were killed in this initial period. "It is in Cochinchina and southern Annam," General Valluy stated in 1946, "that the future of the French in Indochina and the Far East is playing out,"[5] a view echoed that same year by Admiral Thierry d'Argenlieu, High Commissioner for Indochina. It was in the South that the French had the greatest success at turning back the communist-led Việt Minh after 1947 and in transferring power to a non-communist regime. Overlooked in the literature is that the Resistance had failed to win the war for the South by 1953, paving the way for a series of anti-communist states to rule the South until 1975. But this history is rushed over, and the reader can be forgiven for believing that nothing fundamentally important happened in the South from September 1945 to July 1954, when Ngô Đình Diệm became prime minister, opening a new chapter in southern Vietnamese history.

Looking at the war from the South underlines the extent to which the standard approach to the war curiously tends to ignore both empire and local history and frames modern Vietnamese history in terms of

---

[3] Michel Foucault, "Nietzsche, Genealogy, History," in Michel Foucault, *Language, Counter-Memory, Practice: Selected Essays and Interviews*, edited by Donald F Bouchard (Ithaca: Cornell University Press 2012), 144, 146.

[4] For an articulate argument over the December 1946 beginning of the war, see Stein Tønnesson, *Vietnam 1946: How the War Began* (Berkeley: University of California Press, 2010). French losses from September 1945 through November 1946 of 2896 are based on Commandant Gilbert Bodinier, *Le retour de la France en Indochine (1945–1946): textes et documents* (Château de Vincennes, SHAT, 1987), 81–82. I include here the statistic for "disappeared," which seems to mean not confirmed dead. I do not include the statistic for deserters in my calculation. A further 108 Japanese died while fighting under British or French forces from September 26, 1945 to December 4, 1945.

[5] Letter from Général Valluy, Commandant supérieur par intérim les troupes françaises en Extrême-Orient, October 29, 1946, in Bodinier, *Le retour de la France en Indochine (1945–1946)*, 274.

nationalism, revolution, and the Cold War.[6] Frederick Logevall has modified this standard view: he argues that "the Franco-Viet Minh war was simultaneously an East-West and North-South conflict, pitting European imperialism in its autumn phase against the two main competitors that gained momentum by mid-century – Communist-inspired revolutionary nationalism and U.S.-backed liberal internationalism."[7] Yet even this elegant modification has its downsides. Logevall invokes nationalism as a political *deus ex machina* to explain communist Vietnamese success. Take Logevall's statement that by 1954, the side opposing the French, "led by the venerable 'Uncle Ho,' had opposed the Japanese and driven out the French and thereby secured a nationalist legitimacy that was, in a fundamental way, fixed for all time."[8] This is hyperbole. It assumes that from the level of the village to the state, from rural areas to urban, a shared "nationalism" is the glue that binds the inhabitants of Vietnam together, drawing together disparate people into a terminal community of allegiance, the nation. Rather than take nationalism and the nation for granted, shouldn't the task of historians be to *substantiate* how, exactly, the inhabitants of Vietnam belonged to larger groups? The inhabitants of the South, after all, belonged to all sorts of communities after 1945.

These short comments on the standard narratives and their drawbacks raise the question: how should we understand this contentious conflict, particularly when it has become so iconic? As Shahid Amin astutely observes, "when historical significance is attached to an occurrence independent of the event, the facts of the case cease to matter."[9] This insight amply fits Vietnam, where official histories of the "Resistance War" pile facts upon facts to narrate key moments in the triumph of the communist-led Resistance. Historians praise righteous "revolutionaries" and "martyrs" (*liệt sĩ*) and condemn "reactionaries" (*phần tư phản động*) who engage in "deceptive ploys" (*thủ đoạn*) or "plots" (*am mưu*), aided by "lackeys" (*tay sai*) and "hooligans" (*lưu manh*). This language "at the service of judgment"[10] pervades Vietnamese accounts of the war. It is also

---

[6] For examples of major exceptions to my comments, see Christopher Goscha, *Un État né de la guerre* (Paris: Armand Colin, 2013); François Guillemot, *Dai Việt, indépendance et révolution au Viêt-Nam. L'échec de la troisième voie, 1938–1955* (Paris: Indes Savantes, 2012).

[7] Frederick Logevall, *Embers of War: The Fall of an Empire and the Making of America's Vietnam* (New York: Random House, 2014), xvi.

[8] Logevall, *Embers of War*, xxii.

[9] Shahid Amin, *Event Metaphor Memory: Chauri Chaura 1922–1992* (Berkeley: California, 1995), 10.

[10] Paul Ricoeur, "The Hermeneutics of Testimony," quoted in Amin, *Event Metaphor Memory*, 85.

the language of exculpation, the attempt to skip over unsettling details of what happened long ago. The most troubling events of the war are treated elliptically, passed over in silence, or not placed against contradictory evidence.[11] Analogous issues shape most French narratives, dominated by an impulse to explain why France "lost" Indochina. French studies tend to pass over in silence the war crimes that were an integral part of this conflict, as well as the central contribution to the war effort of those who were not French nationals.

The Argument of This Book

The war for the Mekong Delta was both a civil war and a war pitting Vietnamese against the French. It was not, in other words, a simple two-sided conflict. To understand this complexity and its dynamics, the book focuses on arguments over sovereignty, violence, and institutions in a regional context – the Mekong Delta. By looking at issues regionally, it contrasts with single-province studies, which offer great depth but can be unrepresentative of a larger region, or national-level studies, which show some variation across space, but by their design, tend to homogenize. The book is organized into two sections and a conclusion. The first section (Chapters 1 through 4), entitled "Fracture," focuses on the contested history of the Mekong Delta, and how it shaped the upheavals there and in Saigon from mid-1945 to late 1947. Because these years were so pivotal in modern Vietnamese history, this section makes up almost half the book. At the beginning of the First Indochina War, a broadly supported but internally split Việt Minh confronted the French. Vietnamese military units, while often full of ardor, remained disorganized and badly trained. A surprisingly weak French military tried to subdue these ragtag forces, with limited success. Meanwhile, the communists in the Việt Minh tried to bend the organization to their will, alienating their non-communist allies. The French did their part to encourage these divisions. The result was the "double fracture" of the political system that occurred in 1947. The Việt Minh fractured: one wing stayed with the communists, who opposed the French, while the other one tactically collaborated with the French with the aim of achieving independence. At the same time, Khmer-Vietnamese ethnic violence broke out, following its own logic. This messy double fracture deeply shaped southern politics up to 1975 and beyond.

---

[11] For an example of such factual wealth combined with charged language, see Hội Đồng Chỉ Đạo Biên Soạn Lịch Sử Nam Bộ Kháng Chiến, ed., *Lịch sử Nam bộ kháng chiến* [History of the Southern Resistance] (Hà Nội: Chính trị quốc gia, 2010), Vol. 1.

The second section of the book (Chapters 5 to 9), entitled "Disassemblage/Reassemblage," examines the war from mid-1947 up to 1953. Rather than pen a simple chronological approach to these developments, I divide this section into thematic chapters that address key themes of the book, including the shifting use of race; the issue of sovereignty from the level of the empire down to the village; the variegated character of violence; and the collapse and rebuilding of institutions. The title of this section gets at a general truth about war: while war often destroys institutions, it also gives rise to a parallel recombination and reassemblage of their fragments in innovative ways.

By late 1947, the conflict, no longer a binary contest between two sides, was settling into a complicated stalemate. Despite the "double fracture," the Việt Minh, now increasingly dominated by the communists, pursued a clear strategy for victory. The French countered it in the South with a "pacification" strategy, and managed to gain the cooperation of a range of Vietnamese and Khmer Krom (Khmer of the lower Mekong Delta). These groups included the Tây Ninh branch of the Cao Đài, militias claiming to defend the Buddhist Hòa Hảo, as well as a sprinkling of other armed groups, such as Catholic militias and village self-defense forces. Slowly, the French-led alliance, aided by Việt Minh mistakes, gained the upper hand. From 1950 onwards, with the coming of the Cold War (and American funding to the war in Indochina) the war in the South tilted in favor of France, the State of Vietnam, and local anti-communist groups. By 1953, the Franco-Vietnamese anti-communist alliance in the South had effectively defeated the Resistance in most of the delta. The South, in other words, differed sharply from the Center and the North.

Chapter 10 looks at the endgame of empire and its legacies. By late 1953, the French clearly realized that they could not delay the birth of a truly independent South Vietnam. Furthermore, by 1954 the Resistance was marginalized in the South. But the alternative to the Resistance was unclear. Into 1954, the balkanized parastates and militias of the Mekong Delta which had confronted the Resistance still relied on French funding to make this system work. As this system fell apart in 1954, and the Americans pushed aside the French, the South entered a new tumultuous phase. In essence, the French and a motley, assorted group of parastates and militias had cleared a path for the rise of a new non-communist Vietnamese state. Such was the context of the rise of Prime Minister Ngô Đình Diệm in 1954. While this book does not go into detail on the Diệm regime, it does trace overlooked legacies from the war that had impacts and aftershocks from the local level all the way to the far reaches of the French empire. But let us first return to look in depth at the issues of sovereignty, institutions, and violence, as this discussion helps to frame the book as a whole.

Empire and the Problem of Sovereignty

Sovereignty is a core political concept of the modern world. In Daniel Philpott's pithy definition, sovereignty is the "supreme authority within a territory."[12] Benedict Anderson adds that "[i]n the modern conception, state sovereignty is fully, flatly, and evenly operative over each square centimetre of a legally demarcated territory."[13] But how well do such definitions capture the situation of people in southern Vietnam at the end of empire? This book will bring together what at first seem like incommensurate approaches to the study on sovereignty: ones that focus on legal claims to define a territory, and which are propounded by states or their agents, and others that look at the de facto practice of sovereignty in rural areas. It is only by combining attention to both that we can understand how sovereignty was debated, articulated, and practiced, and how seemingly incommensurate approaches, put together, help us understand the strange end of the French empire in southern Vietnam.

Recent studies of empire have reoriented our attention away from bilateral relations of imperial powers with particular colonies in order to fathom the nature of imperial sovereignty in general.[14] Burbank and Cooper refer to such rule as "layered sovereignty"; Will Hanley, writing on the Ottoman Empire, calls this phenomenon "multiple, overlapping sovereignties."[15] Sovereignty was not simply layered, or fragmented, but interpenetrated in quirky ways. The same could be said of French Indochina during the war. Natasha Wheatley adds to a new twist to such arguments: she shows how experts in international law debated, between the two world wars, the emergence of new legal subjectivities, as in mandates and minorities, which were endowed with real or potential

---

[12] Daniel Philpott, *Revolutions in Sovereignty: How Ideas Shaped Modern International Relations* (Princeton: Princeton University Press, 2001), 16.

[13] Benedict Anderson, *Imagined Communities* (London: Verso, 1991), 19.

[14] Mark Atwood Lawrence, *Assuming the Burden: Europe and the American Commitment to War in Vietnam* (Berkeley: University of California Press, 2005) draws on American, British, and French sources to provide a transnational perspective of the diplomatic struggle to pull the United States into the war.

[15] Jane Burbank and Frederick Cooper, *Empires in World History: Power and the Politics of Difference* (Princeton: Princeton University Press, 2011), 17; Will Hanley, "When did Egyptians Stop Being Ottomans? An Imperial Citizenship Case Study," in Willem Maas, ed., *Multilevel Citizenship* (Philadelphia: University of Pennsylvania Press, 2013), 90–91.

legal personhood.[16] "Trading in analogies that spanned slaves and unborn children, interwar jurists labored to uncover (or create) conceptual space around the edges of state sovereignty. In so doing, they generated a remarkable catalogue of new legal species."[17] Similar activity shaped the "end" of the French empire and its "replacement" by a new creature, the French Union: the end of one real entity and its replacement with another entity, whose sovereign reach was ambiguous, and whose reality, fictionality, or legal personhood was not clear. Understanding such oddities is key to understanding the halting transfer of power from France to the State of Vietnam.

If empires at their end were sometimes puzzling in legal terms, how was sovereignty expressed and practiced within the boundaries of political units such as French Indochina or Cochinchina? Internally, sovereignty claims are made real through territorialization: the process by which a territory is made and remade as part of a political unit. "Always in the making," Christian Lentz argues, "territorial relations are continually generated through material and symbolic contests, landscape transformations, and spatial practices."[18] Yet even in times of peace, such processes can be undermined by a lack of capacity to extend a state's reach into peripheral regions. Territorialization can be hemmed in by "friction of terrain." That is, the more difficult it is to reach an area from the center of state power, the less likely that area is to come under effective state control. State authority can fade and even stop at marshes and mountains.[19]

So far, so good. But as Lentz and others have implied, the particular *texture* of sovereignty in a time of decolonization and war is different. In such times, violence overtly shapes its nature and practice.[20] Thomas Blom Hansen and Finn Stepputat argue that de facto sovereignty is "a tentative and always emergent form of authority grounded in violence that is performed and designed to generate loyalty, fear, and legitimacy from the neighborhood to the summit of the state."[21] Stepputat has further argued that the practice of sovereignty is fragmented through

[16] Natasha Wheatley, "Spectral Legal Personality in Interwar International Law: On New Ways of Not Being a State," *Law & History Review* 35 (August 2017), 753–788.
[17] Wheatley, "Spectral Legal Personality," 786.
[18] Christan Lentz, *Contested Territory: Điện Biên Phủ and the Making of Northwest Vietnam* (New Haven: Yale University Press, 2019), 4.
[19] On "friction of terrain," see James Scott, *The Art of Not Being Governed: An Anarchist History of Upland Southeast Asia,* (New Haven & London: Yale University Press, 2009) in Chapter 3.
[20] Achille Mbembe, *Necropolitics* (Chapel Hill: Duke University Press, 2019), 66.
[21] Thomas Blom Hansen and Finn Stepputat, "Sovereignty Revisited," *Annual Review of Anthropology* 35 (2006), 296, 297.

different "registers of sovereign power" including, for example, states, companies, and illegal networks.[22] Achille Mbembe is more blunt: "The ultimate expression of sovereignty resides, to a large degree, in the power and the capacity to dictate who may live and who must die. Hence, to kill or to allow to live constitute the limits of sovereignty, its fundamental attributes." Wars against reoccupiers, and civil wars, are at the extreme of the practice of such violence. The preceding observations underline that conceptualizing and "making" sovereignty are shaped by one's place in a hierarchy that stretches from the global to the local level. It ranges from legal claims in the international arena to practices, in local areas, that make real the claims to sovereignty. It involves territorialization and violence.

Of course, every historical trajectory is shaped by contingent events. When we turn to the First Indochina War in southern Vietnam, we can see that it involved the entirety of the French empire. The five constituent "countries" (*pays*) of French Indochina (Cochinchina, Cambodia, Annam, Tonkin, and Laos) formed part of the larger French Union after 1946. As I will argue in Chapter 6, this legal reality was far more important (and perplexing) than much of the scholarship recognizes. Membership in the French Union was also crucial in a very practical way: the reconstituted French empire provided soldiers to fight the war. As earlier noted, a slight majority of all "regular" soldiers sent by France to Indochina were born outside of France. Recruits hailed from Europe, Africa, North Africa, the Middle East, the Caribbean, North, Central and South America, and South and Southeast Asia. These new soldiers were integrated into an empire-spanning military, shipped across the globe, and deployed in Mekong Delta villages. To the above we can add all the local militia and self-defense members who fought in the conflict. In the south, these were mostly Vietnamese, but also included a large number of Khmer.

If the war was shaped by empire, it unfolded at regional and local levels. Going local allows us to think through what it meant to be part of an empire, and how that affected fundamental issues of sovereignty and belonging at the ground level. The South was the site of an epic contest over sovereignty. The inhabitants of the Mekong Delta entertained, at different times, five possible sovereignty outcomes for the region: to remain part of a larger "federal" Indochina (whether under the French Union or "Indochinese" control); to become part of an independent Vietnam (whether of a South Vietnam or a unified Vietnam); or, for the

---

[22] Hansen and Stepputat, "Sovereignty Revisited," *Annual Review of Anthropology* 35 (2006), 297, 302.

Khmer parts of the delta, to be attached to Cambodia. Clearly, only one of these possibilities triumphed. When French Indochina split up into three parts, some administrative borders were transformed into national borders demarcating territories. But far from being a neat split, the dismantling of the structure of French Indochina was messy, halting, and protracted. It was a "long partition" that, arguably, did not end until 1989, when Vietnamese troops withdrew from Cambodia. While some claim that the border between Cambodia and Vietnam was definitively determined in 2005, trifling border issues were not resolved as of 2018. Understanding this long partition, which can be compared to that of Palestine, India, or French West Africa, is a minor theme of this book. It sheds light on how some Khmer Krom (ethnic Khmer from the lower Mekong Delta) as well as Cambodians still argue that Cambodia "owns" some of this territory.

France claimed full legal sovereignty over the entirety of the Vietnamese state and territory up to 1949 and de facto paramount power up to 1954. Nonetheless, during the First Indochina War, large chunks of the delta escaped the control of any French or Vietnamese central state. National-level claims over sovereignty confronted de facto sovereign practices on the ground by a welter of groups – aspirational states, parastates, militias, and self-defense forces – with contesting notions of what, exactly, they were claiming. In some parts of Vietnam, undisputed French rule disappeared forever on March 9, 1945. Thus, Father Lê Tiền Giang notes that in the Mekong Delta, there were congregations [họ đạo] under Catholic forces living under DRV authority that were never seized by the French.[23] Similarly, after 1949, many Cao Đài and Hòa Hảo areas were outside the de facto control of France or the anti-communist State of Vietnam. Finally, Cambodia still claimed parts of the Mekong Delta, even though it had exercised no effective rule over these areas since the early nineteenth century. The contestation over this claim during the First Indochina War, which led to significant violence between Vietnamese and Khmer, is so significant that this book will pay sustained attention to it.

Violence and Institutional Collapse

Since you left, the war has bequeathed to our country a trail of misfortune and grief. A day never passes without arson and death. And I assure you that such scenes will forever be burnt into our minds and can never be erased: atrocities, rapes, homes set on fire, decapitated heads at the

---

[23] Lê Tiền Giang, *Công giáo kháng chiến Nam Bộ*, 26.

ends of sticks, bodies of the drowned clogging the rivers, strewn along roads... To illustrate this for you, a single example: every day, two processions of two horse-drawn wagons laden with corpses goes down General Lizé Street towards the Chí Hòa cemetery. The two drivers, wearing Chinese clothing, wide-brimmed hats, and sunglasses, whip the horses. One of them, I am not sure why, clangs cymbals in sudden bursts. On the wagon are heaped dozens of corpses, some intact, others horribly mutilated, with no coffins or mats to cover them. And thus each and every day, a procession of two wagons in the morning, and two more in the evening. Two years of war have brought nothing but destruction and bloodshed.[24]

As Âu Trường Thanh suggests above, wars upend societies and leave trails of destruction. His view echoes one pole of the scholarship, which focuses on war's destructive side. As China historian Diana Lary argues: "The hallmark of war is chaos. War attacks the social fabric and brings loss of cohesion and fragmentation to systems and institutions that seemed solid and resistant to change."[25] While this view is usually true, war can both destroy and transform. The anthropologist Stephen Lubkemann, writing on the Mozambican civil war, has argued that wars have both "generative" and "destructive" sides. War is a "social condition" in which "warscape living was shaped not solely, incessantly, or even predominantly with reference to violence."[26] This latter view aptly fits the Mekong Delta during the First Indochina War, where violence was episodic and varied across space.

Reading French or Vietnamese works on the First Indochina War, we often get the sense that coercion is instrumental: that is, it flows top-down from French or Việt Minh political decisions. The best literature addressing ethnic, mass, and civil war violence, however, rejects an instrumentalist rendering of the causes and dynamics of violence.[27] In a penetrating study on civil war, the political scientist Stathis Kalyvas has argued that

---

[24] ANOM. HCI. Conseiller Politique 107. [Intercepted letter from Au Truong Thanh, Saigon, to Dang Ngoc Chi, Paris. June 6, 1947]. Is this the twenty-two-year-old Âu Trường Thanh, who would eventually rise to high positions in the Republic of Vietnam? A deep thanks to Charles Keith for providing me with this letter, and many others, from this dossier.

[25] Diana Lary, *The Chinese People at War. Human Suffering and Social Transformation, 1937–1945* (Cambridge: Cambridge University Press, 2010), 2.

[26] Stephen Lubkemann, *Culture in Chaos: An Anthropology of the Social Condition in War* (Chicago: University of Chicago Press, 2008), 13, 15.

[27] On ethnic violence, see, for example, Ashutosh Varshney, *Ethnic Conflict and Civic Life: Hindus and Muslims in India* (New Haven: Yale University Press, 2002); on mass violence, see Geoffrey Robinson, *The Killing Season: A History of the Indonesian Massacres, 1965–66* (Princeton: Princeton University Press, 2018); on civil war, see the pathbreaking book by Stathis Kalyvas, *The Logic of Violence in Civil War* (Cambridge: Cambridge University Press, 2006).

"violence needs to be analytically decoupled from war." More specifically, "the causes of violence in civil war cannot be subsumed under the causes of civil war."[28] They have, in other words, different logics: for one, civil war violence is a "joint production" of higher-level political actors and local inhabitants,[29] and the latter bring their particularistic biases, antipathies, and histories into the process. At first, this argument might seem perplexing: after all, do not movements, parties, and armies initiate war? Don't they cause the violence? Does not the scholarship on Vietnam frame the entire logic of the First Indochina War in terms of the struggle between the communist-led Việt Minh and the French and their allies?

To frame the issues in such a way is to believe the accounts of the major actors, and to remain stuck at the macrolevel. When (following Kalyvas, and many anthropologists) one descends to the level of districts and villages, another – sometimes startlingly different – picture emerges. Civil war violence often has a logic that is particular to a specific place. In the case of the western Mekong Delta, for example, national political movements intersected with a world of local grievances, feuds, political and religious differences, and ethnic antagonisms.

With war comes a pervasive uncertainty, one that can ebb and flow over time. Norms and practices that had once been taken for granted were now contested. Boundaries once considered commonsensical – such as those between ethnic groups, domains of action, genders, or between right and wrong – are now shaken up. Many people lacked adequate knowledge of the situations into which they were thrust. "Doxic" knowledge – which Bourdieu defines as "the tacitly assumed presuppositions that give the social world its self-evident, natural character"[30] – is turned upside down.

Uncertainty shapes violence. Arjun Appadurai has contrasted two approaches to ethnic violence, one that sees collective violence as a product of "heightened conviction," and the other that "focuses on doubt, uncertainty, and indeterminacy." This second view examines what happens when "there is a growing sense of radical social uncertainty about people, situations, events, norms, and even cosmologies."[31] Here, uncertainty is seen as a factor in its own right that can trigger violence. John Lonsdale echoes this insight: commenting on the 1950s Mau Mau revolt in Kenya, he argues that, analytically, a sense of disorientation should be at the core of our research: "intimate unease... must surely

[28] Kalyvas, *Logic of Violence in Civil War*, 20.
[29] Kalyvas, *Logic of Violence in Civil War*, 6.
[30] Pierre Bourdieu, *Outline of a Theory of Practice* (Cambridge: Cambridge University Press, 1977), 3.
[31] Arjun Appadurai, "Dead Certainty: Ethnic Violence in the Era of Globalization," *Development and Change* 29 (1998): 905, 906.

be our quarry. It makes normal behavior perilous and abnormal action a possible deliverance... a pervasive sense of unease makes collective protest, even violence, thinkable."[32] Such formulations are ways of saying that social trust has either eroded or broken down, and individuals no longer believe in authoritative norms, institutions, or even particular leaders. This breakdown varies across space. Temporally, violence ebbs and flows. Appadurai's and Lonsdale's insights apply best to the initial phase of the war, as institutions are collapsing without strong ones to replace them. They do not apply as well to later phases, when ethnic and political cleavages harden.

Violence reshaped institutions. In war, institutions are destroyed and reassembled, and these institutions range from the state down to the family. In times of peace, of course, the French colonial state had provided the skeleton apparatus that held French Indochina together and preempted alternative states from arising. Institutions like the state also reinforce norms and practices that allow people and groups to function effectively. Further down in the village, institutions ranging from the council of notables to kin networks shaped local society. Some of these institutions, such as local kin networks, are hard to research today, as little recorded information is available on them. Much of the literature on institutions, unfortunately, analyzes them in times of peace. It is less helpful at shedding light on societies in times of extreme transition or upheaval.

In late 1945, the inhabitants of Indochina were facing what Andrew Walder, in his study of the Red Guards in Beijing, has referred to as "institutional collapse." Walder argues that when institutions fall apart, many norms and practices, such as those about relations with authority, are up for renegotiation. In this context, the microdynamics of inter-actions among different factions, and not preexisting institutional or social identities, can come to shape new norms.[33] How do we theorize the nature of such dramatic "transitions"? David Stark has argued: "Change, even fundamental change, of the social world is not the passage from one order to another but rearrangements of the patterns of how multiple orders are interwoven. Organization innovation in this view is not replacement but recombination."[34] Expanding on this idea, Stan

---

[32] John Lonsdale, "Authority, Gender, and Violence: The War within Mau Mau's Fight for Land and Freedom," in E. S. Atieno Odhiambo and John Lonsdale, eds., *Mau Mau and Nationhood: Arms, Authority and Narration* (Oxford: James Currey, 2003), 51.

[33] Andrew Walder, *Fractured Rebellion: The Beijing Red Guard Movement* (Cambridge: Harvard University Press, 2012), 12–13.

[34] David Stark, "Recombinant Property in East European Capitalism," *American Journal of Sociology* 101(4) (January 1996), 995.

B. H. Tan has argued that the state at the Central Highlands frontier of Vietnam changed in a similar manner: it was a "assemblage of institutions" where state formation was "a dynamic process of recombination of different layers and groups of society, or extra-societal influences." Out of this process, a variety of ideas and practices "are redefined and recombined to produce a hybrid or even possibly something new."[35] This is what the overlooked Vietnamese intellectual Lương Đức Thiệp once called the "revolution in zigzags," where old jostled with new, creating new amalgams.[36]

This book draws on these arguments, but with a twist: it underscores that violence, upheaval, and social dislocation in particular often drove such change, and shaped the shifting assemblage of institutions that underwent collapse and recombination. Old institutions, or fragments of them, were repurposed and recombined to craft new ones.[37] Beyond institutions, practices and ideas (such as about race) "morphed" in new directions. In the end, new contenders for power in rural areas often ended up with flimsy institutions, such as militias that depended on French military aid but that also set up local taxation "systems" to acquire revenue. Their often zig-zag development shaped new norms and practices, such as in funding militias and parastates. Such change was not always for the better.

For the communists of southern Vietnam, institutional collapse and reconstruction were key problems. The Party in the South had briefly fallen apart when the French arrested thousands who joined the Nam Ky uprising of November 1940.[38] Many communist cadres, imprisoned during World War II on the islands of Côn Đảo, missed the August General Uprising of 1945 and only arrived on the mainland in late September. For the communists in the Việt Minh, then, the key problem was how few communists there were in the South. Furthermore, factionalism and mistrust between "old" and "new" communists undermined the Party. So began the First Indochina War. In the next nine years,

---

[35] Stan B. H. Tan, "Dust Beneath the Mist: State and Frontier Formation in the Central Highlands of Vietnam, the 1955–61 Period" (PhD dissertation, Australian National University, 2011), 107, 109–110.

[36] Lương Đức Thiệp, *Xã hội Việt Nam. Việt Nam tiến hóa sử* [Vietnamese society. The history of Vietnam's evolution] (Saigon: Liên Hiệp, 1950 [1944]), 457.

[37] This theme – the repurposing of institutions that have lived beyond their original use – is key to Michel Foucault, *Histoire de la folie à l'âge classique* (Paris: Gallimard, 1972), 19. For an application of Levi-Strauss's concept of "bricolage" to the Vietnamese state, see Brett Reilly, "The Sovereign States of Vietnam, 1945–1955," *Journal of Vietnamese Studies*, 11 (3–4) (Summer–Fall 2016), 103–139. On "assemblage" and "recombination" applied to the state at the frontier, see Stan B H Tan, "Dust Beneath the Mist".

[38] See Hộ Đồng Chỉ Đạo Biên Soạn Lịch Sử Khởi Nghĩa Nam Kỳ, *Lịch Sử Khởi Nghĩa Nam Kỳ* (Hanoi: Chính Trị Quốc Gia, 2005).

communists would engage in a massive program of institution building, one that led to the erection of the DRV state and the vast expansion of the ICP. Competing with this project was a French-led one that would ultimately lead to an alternative, the State of Vietnam. Complicating matters, the Cao Đài, Hòa Hảo, Khmer, Chinese, and other contestants all strived to build up their own institutions (political parties, religious networks, military forces, merchant networks) to counter threats from others. They would do so as a civil war, wrapped up in a struggle for independence against France, raged.

It is important to note that ethnic and religious differences, obvious at the beginning of the conflict, did not preempt cooperation. For example, Catholics and Khmer were initially found on both sides of the conflict. As violence spiraled upwards, however, it drove the formation of sharp cultural, ethnic, and religious cleavages that forced those on the fence to take sides. In the worst of times, such as in 1946 or 1947, local violence took on a dynamic of its own unrelated to the official positions of the contending "national" parties. Newly sharpened cleavages then solidified, shaping the rest of the war till 1953 or 1954.

The battle for the delta really was a series of "microwars," differing from province to province, in which local cleavages shaped reaction to "national" level strategies. While rural order in general broke down, there was significant variation. Some villages, for example, were hit hard by catastrophes (like massacres) while adjacent areas emerged unscathed. Temporally, violence, chaos, and terror often punctuated periods of relative peace, giving the war a particular texture. Capturing war's uneven impact is essential, for it helps us explain the way the war was perceived, from the bottom up, in the delta.

Looking at the overall arc of the war, this book contests the conventional arguments about French military strategy in Vietnam. Scholars repeatedly stress that France failed to develop a novel counterinsurgency strategy against what the theorists Charles Lacheroy and David Galula both called "revolutionary war" and Roger Trinquier called "modern war."[39] The problem with this argument about "failure" is that it never fit the south, where the French drew on traditional "pacification" techniques that they had honed in North Africa. The use of these traditional

---

[39] For the official view, see *Les enseignements de la guerre d'Indochine (1945–1954). Rapport du Général Ély*, Vol. 1 (Vincennes: Service Historique de la Défense, 2011 [1955]). Also see Élie Tenenbaum's study of the circulation of new strategic thinking after World War II on insurgency and counterinsurgency. Élie Tenenbaum, "Une Odysée subversive: la circulation des savoirs stratégiques irrégulières en Occident (France, Grande-Bretagne, États-Unis) de 1944 à 1972" (PhD dissertation, Paris Institute of Political Studies, 2015). Many thanks to Christopher Goscha for forwarding me this doctoral dissertation.

techniques, combined with intelligence collection and targeting of communist organizations, eventually led to the defeat of the communist-led Resistance. The South, in other words, is an exception to many generalizations about French strategic failures in the First Indochina War. Who won the war? That is difficult to say, and I will address that issue at the end of this book.

A Final Point

For marketing purposes alone, the title of this book is *The First Vietnam War*. For historical accuracy, however, the text of the work uses the term "First Indochina War." This complex conflict, which combined features of imperialism, resistance, and civil war, was not restricted to Vietnam, but played out throughout "Indochina" and its successor countries of Vietnam, Laos, and Cambodia.

In this work, I use the term "Việt Minh" to refer to the loose coalition, led by communists but including many non-communists, that opposed the French from 1945 to Spring, 1947. For the period from late Spring 1947 onwards, I abandon that terminology and use the term "Resistance" to refer to the anti-French organization, under the communist-led DRV, now shorn of many of its non-communist members. This change in terminology reflects the impact in the South of what I call, in this book, the "double fracture" of 1947 that split the nationalist movement.

Part I

Fracture, 1945–1947

1   A Plural Mekong Delta under Stress

This book focuses on a region the Vietnamese call by a variety of names, including the Delta of the Nine Dragon River, the Mekong Delta, or simply "the West" (*miền Tây*). This region, defined by the Mekong River and its tributaries, is one of the great deltas of the world. In the period under discussion in this book, this region extended to the north to the outskirts of Saigon (today's Hồ Chí Minh City); to the west, it actually extended across the Cambodian-Vietnamese border; and it was bounded to the south and east by the Gulf of Thailand and the South China Sea (see Figure 1.1).

The Mekong Delta has only recently been fully integrated into Vietnam. Its contested and complex history has shaped it up to the present. Historically, the entire zone from Phnom Penh down to the lower Mekong Delta was a multiethnic zone of contact in which Khmer, Chinese, Malay, Cham, Vietnamese, and assorted others circulated. It was a periphery, far from the core of the Cambodian or Vietnamese polities, a place in between the port, coastal, and sea-oriented "water frontier" and "littoral society" discussed by Li Tana and Charles Wheeler and the plains-oriented "geo-body" discussed by Thongchai Winanchakul.[1] It was once a wet, lowlands version of the highlands "Zomia" discussed by Willem Van Schendel and popularized by James Scott.[2]

---

[1] Li Tana, "The Water Frontier: An Introduction," in Li Tana and Nola Cooke, eds., *Water Frontier: Commerce and the Chinese in the Lower Mekong Region, 1750–1880* (Landover, MD: Rowman & Littlefield, 2004), 1–20; Charles Wheeler, "Re-Thinking the Sea in Vietnamese History: Littoral Society in the Integration of Thuận-Quảng, Seventeenth-Eighteenth Centuries," *Journal of Southeast Asian Studies*, 37(1) (February 2006), 123–153; Thongchai Winichakul, *Siam Mapped: A History of the Geo-body of a Nation* (Honolulu: University of Hawaii Press, 1994).

[2] Willem van Schendel, "Geographies of Knowing, Geographies of Ignorance: Jumping Scale in Southeast Asia," In P. Kratoska, R. Raben, and H. Nordholt, eds., *Locating Southeast Asia: Geographies of Knowledge and Politics of Space* (Singapore: Singapore University Press, 2005); James Scott, *The Art of Not Being Governed: An Anarchist History of Upland Southeast Asia* (New Haven & London: Yale University Press, 2009).

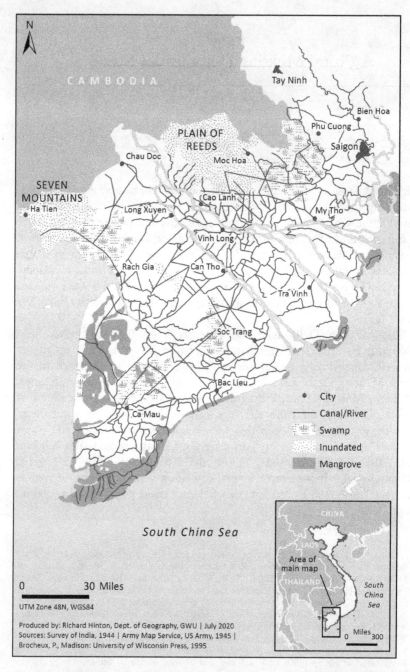

Figure 1.1 The Mekong Delta in the mid-twentieth century

Before the French, if states desired to control this lightly populated "periphery," their ambition foundered on lack of adequate state capacity. This history, and the devastating economic and social dislocation of World War II, shaped this region's response to war.

Today, our cartographic imagination, conditioned by maps demarcating nation-states, places the Mekong Delta in "Vietnam." So it is; but such "mapping" is deceptive. The delta is not oriented northwards towards the rest of Vietnam: its rivers flow out of Cambodia along a northwest-southeast axis, emptying into the South China Sea. When the water level in the Mekong rises too high, excess water flows back into the Tonle Sap Lake in Cambodia, which acts as a giant catchment basin and moderates the extent of flooding downstream. Canals and streams crisscross this delta, wedged between Vietnam and Cambodia, straddling land and sea.

1.1 Ethnicity, Place, and Space in Historical Perspective

By the end of the seventeenth century, a new political actor entered the far south: the Vietnamese Nguyễn lords. They expanded southwards to Cambodian Prey Nokor (Saigon), and in the eighteenth and nineteenth centuries pushed further south and west into the Mekong Delta. Cambodian and Vietnamese kingdoms thus collided, mixing together Vietnamese newcomers, Siamese expansionists, remnants of a defeated Cham polity, Ming refugees from the Qing empire, Malay and possibly some Javanese, and longstanding populations of ethnic Khmer. The result was a complex ethnic, religious, linguistic, and political mosaic. Nguyễn rulers worked hard with limited means to consolidate control over this unruly Mekong Delta frontier. They asserted their power over the preexisting populations of Chinese in Mỹ Tho, Sóc Trăng, and Hà Tiên (some of the main areas of settlement), and Cham in Châu Đốc and Tây Ninh. They also moved into lands traditionally claimed by the Cambodian monarchy that were lightly populated by Khmer.

This legacy of contestation would shape the later unraveling of French Indochina during the First Indochina War. For this reason, this chapter pays special attention to the Khmer, who long predated the Vietnamese in the delta. Modern Vietnamese accounts minimize the significance of Khmer sovereignty claims and routinely emphasize that in 1757, Cambodia supposedly ceded their rights to this territory. As one work states, "from 1757 onwards, the entire region from Đồng Nai to Hà Tiên was completely part of Vietnam's national territory and [this] was recorded clearly on our administrative maps. The border between our country and Cambodia [Chenla] had been demarcated clearly."[3] Such is the dominant interpretation in Vietnam.

In fact, the historical record of Cambodian "cession" of territory is quite contested. The term "cession" implies a formal agreement, but none has come to light. In 1904, Étienne Aymonier argued that the cession of Preah Trapeang (Trà Vinh) and Basak (Sóc Trăng) in the mid-eighteenth century, carried out by a contender to the Cambodian throne during an internal Cambodian struggle for power, was virtually forced upon the Cambodians: "the term *cession* poorly characterizes these incessant [Vietnamese] encroachments, which did not ratify any formal act." Aymonier prefers the term "usurpation" to describe this process.[4] It is perhaps most accurate to state that in 1757, a Cambodian contender to the Cambodian throne traded away rights to govern peripheral territories and peoples that he did not control, and that the Vietnamese had barely settled, so that he could gain Vietnamese support and seize power at the center of his future realm. Aymonier further argues that immediately after 1758, while most Khmer of the lower Mekong Delta were theoretically subject to Vietnamese rule, "the Khmer still occupied the interior of these vast territories, apparently retained their national leaders, recognized the authority of their own kings, but did not have to submit any less to the influence and power of the Annamite mandarins."[5]

This "cession" was not accepted by many Khmer of the delta. Tạ Chí Đại Trường notes that at the end of the eighteenth century, Nguyễn Ánh, who went on to defeat the Tay Son "rebels" and unite Vietnam, allowed the Khmer of Bassak to rule themselves.[6] Choi Byung Wook concludes that in the late eighteenth century, "the basic policy of the Gia Định regime [i.e. the Vietnamese rulers over the area surrounding Saigon] toward the Khmer people guaranteed the Khmer self-government and co-existence."[7] Indeed, from the Tây Sơn uprising and rule (1771–1802) through the Lê Văn Khôi rebellion (1833–35), many southerners escaped the tight control of any monarch.

The rule of Emperor Minh Mệnh (also referred to as Ming Mạng) (1820–41), however, marked a turning point in Vietnamese-Khmer relations, as Minh Mệnh pursued a far more aggressive policy towards Cambodia proper. He forced all Khmer in the lower Mekong Delta to

---

[3] Phan Đại Doãn et al., *Một số vấn đề về quan chế triều Nguyễn* (Huế: Thuận Hóa, 1998), 70.
[4] Aymonier, Étienne. *Le Cambodge. Le groupe d'Angkor et l'histoire* (Paris: Leroux, 1904), 787,788.
[5] Ibid., 788.
[6] Tạ Chí Đại Trường, *Lịch sử nội chiến ở Việt Nam từ 1771 đến 1802* ([Saigon]: Văn Sử Học, 1973), 241.
[7] Choi Byung Wook, *Southern Vietnam under the Reign of Minh Mạng: Central Policies and Local Response* (Ithaca, NY: Southeast Asia Program, 2004), 33.

adopt the Vietnamese family names Thạch, Sơn, Kim, Lâm, or Danh.[8] Nguyễn actions provoked Khmer animosity and resistance. As Minh Mệnh complained, perhaps about the situation in Cambodia proper:

The Thổ people [Cambodians] are incontrollable: at times they submit; at times they rebel, they are unpredictable. Last year, they endured several sackings and massacres by Siamese troops. Their land was bare. [I] look after them; the court dispatched an army to repel the enemy, saved them from despair and issued them blankets. Why then did they become hostile and turn into enemies of the Kinh [Vietnamese], and carry out massacres?[9]

From the 1820s onwards, the Nguyễn monarchy pushed the Khmer to become loyal subjects by adopting the names, language, clothing, and civilizational practices of the Vietnamese. To Vietnamese rulers, the different customs and beliefs of the Khmer were not an essential barrier to eventual assimilation.[10] To borrow David Howell's formulation for Tokugawa attempts to make the Ainu Japanese, the Nguyễn rulers "were more concerned with exteriority – the visible compliance with norms – than with the internalization of the principles behind these norms."[11] The Nguyễn dynasty, however, did not stop at "assimilation lite." Emperor Minh Mệnh occupied eastern Cambodia from 1835 to 1841. As one Vietnamese source stated, "Now that our country is changing things [in Cambodia] in a significant way and registering [Khmer] households, the day of transforming old [Khmer] customs into *Hoa* [Vietnamese] has come!"[12]

Cambodians deeply resented this occupation. In late 1840, faced with a threat to their continuing existence as a country, they rose up in widespread revolt. French missionary M. Miche wrote that in that year:

From letters that I have just received from Bangkok, Tonkin is in full revolt, civil war is ravaging Cochinchina, and Annamite Cambodia is in flames. Here is what has given rise to the troubles that have bathed Cambodia in blood. The king of Cochinchina, motivated by who knows what sense of vertigo, has gotten into his mind that everyone in the realm has to wear the same kind of dress. Hearing this, people were vexed, to the point that a general uprising took place throughout Annamite Cambodia. Cambodians, who constituted a majority of the population

---

[8] Choi, *Southern Vietnam*, 129.
[9] Emperor Minh Mệnh, quoted in Vũ Đức Liêm, "Vietnam at the Khmer Frontier: Boundary Politics, 1802–1847," *Cross-Currents: East Asian History and Culture Review* 5 (2) (November 2016), 553.
[10] See "'Trấn Tây phong thổ ký': The Customs of Cambodia" [1838], translated by Li Tana, in *Chinese Southern Diaspora Studies* 1 (2007), chl-old.anu.edu.au/publications/cs ds/csds2007/Tran_Tay.pdf (accessed July 18, 2020).
[11] David Howell, *Geographies of Identity in Nineteenth-Century Japan* (Berkeley: University of California Press, 2005), 16.
[12] "Trấn Tây phong thổ ký," 156. In this context, "Hoa" refers to Vietnamese.

in most areas, pillaged the Cochinchinese, massacred the mandarins and those who put up resistance.[13]

Vietnamese annals record an armed force of 2,000 coming down from the Thất Sơn mountains, straddling today's Cambodia-Vietnam border, to attack Kiên Giang province, where Vietnamese mandarins and inhabitants "fled in fear."[14] The Vietnamese mandarin Nguyễn Công Trứ wrote to the court that "now the Cambodian [Thổ] rebels are rising up all over" in the lower Mekong Delta.[15] Khmer living in Hà Tiên, An Giang, Kiên Giang, Sóc Trăng, Trà Vinh, and Vĩnh Long all participated in this revolt, which dragged on into 1843.[16]

    To resolve the dissension, Siam and Vietnam signed a treaty in 1846 that put the Cambodian king Ang Duong back on his throne. The Nguyễn dynasty, overextended and pressured by Siam, finally withdrew from Cambodia. But the damage had been done. Anne Hansen cites a searingly evocative Cambodian memoir from 1848 on the situation:

The country was shattered. In every village, [people] struggled to find sources of income but could not. None of the rice farms or garden crops had been planted because everyone had been too afraid of Vietnamese and Siamese soldiers coming into the rice fields... Entire villages were devastated, abandoned, deathly quiet. It was sorrowful and heart wrenching beyond description seeing the misery of widows with tiny children, their heads resting in their laps, whom they were powerless to feed.[17]

If Vietnam "lost" its protectorate in eastern Cambodia, it retrenched in order to consolidate its hold on the lower Mekong Delta.

    Where, then, was the border between Cambodia and Vietnam? As Vũ Đức Liêm comments, earlier borders on maps had played multiple functions – as defensive frontiers, administrative limits, state borders, and boundaries of Vietnameseness. "Over the nearly one hundred years since five Khmer prefectures were annexed to Hà Tiên in 1755, Vietnamese political boundaries moved westward. Frequent rhetorical shifts between civilizational frontier and state boundary characterized the Nguyễn intervention in Cambodia. Each time the language changed, so did the

---

[13] *Annales de la Propagation de la Foi*, Vol. 14 (Lyon: Chez L'Éditeur des Annales, 1842), 148–149.
[14] Quốc Sử Quán Triều Nguyễn, *Quốc Triều Chính Biên Toát Yếu* (Hue: Thuận Hóa, 1998), 315.
[15] Ibid., 315.   [16] Ibid., 312–336.
[17] *Rýan Padam Ta Mas* [1908?], in Anne Hansen, *How to Behave: Buddhism and Modernity in Colonial Cambodia* (Honolulu: University of Hawai'i Press, 2011), 45. For two moving Khmer poems on the impact of Vietnamese warmaking and subjugation on the Khmer, see Khin Sok, translator, *L'annexation du Cambodge par les Vietnamiens aux XIXè siècle d'après les deux poèmes du Vénérable Bâtum Baramey Pich* (Paris: Éditions You Feng, 2002).

imagined geography."[18] By 1847, Vietnam had defined for itself an unambiguous state border. Labussière, writing in 1880, stated that it was "barely forty years ago [i.e. around 1840] that the Annamese court finally succeeded in substituting its authority for that of the Cambodian king."[19] Adhémard Leclère has written that after the 1846 treaty, "Cambodians began to flee the provinces that now form part of Cochinchina and that the *Yuon* [Vietnamese] had annexed in the past. The plots of lands they abandoned were subsequently occupied by Annamite farmers."[20] Bitter struggles broke out. Khmer retaliated against dispossession using arson, even murder; the Vietnamese judges, in turn, fined entire villages of Khmer for such acts. In the end, more Khmer fled for Cambodia.[21] Today, we might refer to Nguyễn dynasty actions as "ethnic cleansing."

The French invasion of Vietnam in 1858 catalyzed "long-simmering" tensions. In 1859, Cham and Khmer communities in the An Giang province border region rose up in rebellion; "by the end of that year it was spreading out of control."[22] In 1860, Cambodia invaded An Giang and Hà Tiên.[23] Under relentless pressure, the Nguyễn court formally ceded three provinces of southern Vietnam to France in 1862, followed by the three westernmost ones in 1867. This complicated history should drive home the simple point that the Khmer, whether in Cambodia or in the lower Mekong Delta, were still contesting Vietnamese claims to the delta in the 1860s.

The arrival of the French radically transformed the contest between Cambodians and Vietnamese. The French declared Cochinchina a directly ruled colony, and after a series of agreements, the Nguyễn dynasty signed a treaty ceding this region to France. All Vietnamese sovereignty claims over the area were rendered null and void. In contrast, the French made Cambodia a protectorate in 1863. Over twenty years later, as I have stated elsewhere:

the creation of a new "superspace" of French Indochina (1887–1945) pre-empted conflicts over sovereignty and territory from breaking out. This large entity of

---

[18] Vũ Đức Liêm, "Vietnam at the Khmer Frontier," 96.
[19] M. Labussière. "Étude sur la propriété foncière rurale en Cochinchine et, particulièrement, dans l'inspection de Soctrang," *Excursions et Reconnaissances* 3 (1880), 333.
[20] Adhémard Leclère, *Histoire du Cambodge depuis le 1er siecle de notre ère, d'après les inscriptions lapidaires, les annales chinoises et annamites et les documents européens des six derniers siècles* (Paris: Librairie Paul Geuthner, 1914), 434.
[21] Leclère, *Histoire du Cambodge*, 434.
[22] Jacob Ramsay, *Mandarins and Martyrs: The Church and the Nguyen Dynasty in Early Nineteenth-Century Vietnam* (Stanford, CA: Stanford University Press, 2008), 151.
[23] Quốc Sử, *Quán Triều*, 423.

French Indochina, joining all five *pays* or countries of Tonkin, Annam, Cochinchina, Laos, and Cambodia, was a *non-national* space with ambiguous internal borders. It offered some protection for Khmer, in the sense that French rule prevented Vietnamese from encroaching on Cambodian sovereignty. In this superspace, a wide variety of imagined and actual communities could co-exist without entering into conflict over actual territorial spaces.[24]

In theory, if not in fact, France accepted the Cambodian monarchy's claim to sovereignty over Cambodia proper. *Left unsettled until 1949 was the resolution of Cambodian sovereignty claims over parts of the lower Mekong Delta.*

Under French rule, the population of Cambodia and the Mekong Delta underwent transformation. Vietnamese migration to Cambodia and to the lower Mekong Delta shot up. Vietnamese, not Khmer, came to staff much of the French colonial apparatus in Cambodia.[25] By 1945, roughly 300,000 Vietnamese made Cambodia their home.[26] The situation in the lower Mekong Delta sharply differed. Chinese emigration to Cochinchina, including the Mekong Delta, surged from the late nineteenth century.[27] Vietnamese in-migration to the lower Mekong Delta upended the ethnic balance. If the Khmer probably formed the majority of the delta in the very early nineteenth century, by 1944 they had turned into a small minority in a Vietnamese sea.

While promoting Vietnamese in-migration to the delta, the French reversed the Nguyễn dynasty's attempt to assimilate the Khmer to Vietnamese norms and civilization. The French were contradictory: even as they saw themselves as "protecting" the Khmer, they packed the ranks of the Cambodian and Cochinchinese administrations disproportionately with French and Vietnamese, and shunted the Khmer into lower-level positions. The French encouraged Cambodians and Vietnamese to stay apart. Writing in 1907, Judge Edgar Mathieu observed "how rare are the marriages between Annamites and Cambodians" in Cochinchina, adding that relations between the two groups were "unfriendly."[28] Little had changed forty years later: one

---

[24] Shawn McHale, "Ethnicity, Violence, and Khmer-Vietnamese Relations: The Significance of the Lower Mekong Delta, 1757–1954," *The Journal of Asian Studies* 72 (May 2013), 367–368.

[25] Lê Hương, *Việt kiều ở Kampuchea* (Saigon: Trí Đăng, 1971), 82.

[26] This is a common estimate, and a reasonable extrapolation from the 1930 census. See NAC. RSC. Dossier 3061. "Tableau récapitulatif de la population non-blanche. Année 1930."

[27] See Tracy Barrett, *The Chinese Diaspora in Southeast Asia* (London: I.B. Tauris, 2012), 22.

[28] Edgar Mathieu, "Le type du Cambodgien de Cochinchine," *Revue Internationale de Sociologie*, 15(1) (1907), 596.

1948 report suggested that one in ten Khmer marriages in the Mekong Delta were with Vietnamese.[29] The same low rate of Khmer-Vietnamese intermarriage was found on the Cambodian side of the border. Separation between ethnic groups was encouraged by the educational system. In addition to allowing temple schools, the French set up a limited number of Franco-Khmer schools to complement the Franco-Vietnamese ones.

Under the French, the Khmer of the Mekong Delta (the Khmer Krom) strengthened their religious ties to Cambodia. From the 1920s onwards, the Buddhist Institute in Phnom Penh reached out to the Khmer Krom in Cochinchina, trained their monks, and supplied the populace with printed Khmer materials.[30] In 1944, the French placed the *Mekhon* (heads of the Khmer Buddhist sangha in Cochinchina) under "the spiritual authority of the Leaders of the Sects in Cambodia."[31] These developments encouraged more Khmer Krom to travel: "a new spirit has arisen which makes them more willing to return to their country of origin [*sic*]. They maintain rather close relations with the Mother Country, and monks in particular regularly take their leave there to improve themselves spiritually, and students travel to Phnom Penh to continue their studies."[32]

I close this section with a captivating fragment of the *Bangsavatar Basak* [Chronicle of Bassac], one unlike the usual Vietnamese narratives. Chandler calls this work "a popular history collected in the 1940s in a Cambodian-speaking area of southern Vietnam":

In former times there was little dry land here, and people would go everywhere in boats but never farther than the sounds of dogs barking in their village could be heard. There were no canals then, and no paths; there were only forests with tigers, and elephants, and wild buffaloes; no people dared to leave their villages.

For this reason, hardly anyone went to the royal city [*krung sdach*]. If anyone ever reached it, by poling his canoe, the others would ask him about it. 'What is the king's appearance like? Is he like an ordinary man?' And the traveler, seeing all these frightened ignorant people, asking questions, would say: the king has an elegant beautiful appearance, unstained by dust, or sweat, and he has no scars. He's neither short nor tall, neither too young nor too old.' Now dishonest travelers would tell lies about the king, and would exaggerate...

---

[29] Charles Vavasseur, "Étude sur les minorités khmères en Cochinchine." Saigon, October 30, 1948, in VNA-II, *Phủ thủ hiến Nam Việt* [hereafter PTHNV] F.1–48.
[30] Penny Edwards, "Making a Religion of the Nation and Its Language: The French Protectorate (1863–1954) and the Dhammakay." In *History, Buddhism, and New Religious Movements in Cambodia*, eds. John Marston and Elizabeth Guthrie (Honolulu: University of Hawai'i Press, 2004), 75–78.
[31] Vavasseur, "Étude."   [32] Ibid.

People would ask what the realm was like, the older people would say that being there meant there was always plenty to eat – soup, rice, and meat, and that everyone was happy.[33]

Reading these lines, it is clear that the Khmer of the delta once lived far outside the control of the Nguyễn court in remote, even wild, areas. They

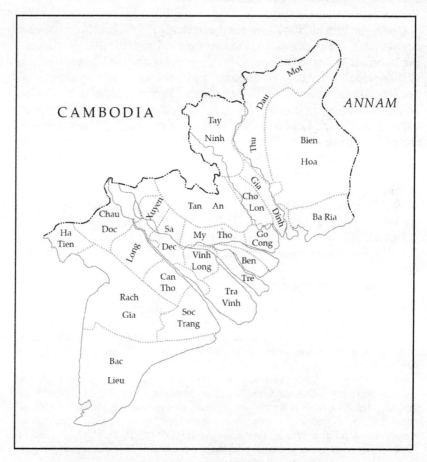

Figure 1.2 Provinces of southern Vietnam, 1945
Source: Chris Robinson, 2020. Based on Pierre Gourou, "La population rurale de la Cochinchine," *Annales de géographie* 51(285) (1942), 11.

---

[33] Quoted in David Chandler, "Going Through the Motions: Ritual Aspects of the Reign of King Duang of Cambodia (1848–1860)," in David Chandler, *Facing the Cambodian Past: Selected Essays 1971–1994* (Chiang Mai: Silkworm Books, 1996), 17.

were only tenuously connected to the Cambodian monarchy. This autonomy and isolation was destroyed as new migrants – Chinese, Vietnamese, then French – refashioned the delta. The long transformation of the Mekong delta would set the stage for the violence of the post-1945 years. But the creation of the superspace of French Indochina, in which no Vietnamese ruled over the Mekong Delta or Cambodia, blocked the final Vietnamese attempt to claim the lower Mekong Delta for an emerging Vietnamese nation. It allowed the Khmer to keep alive their claim to the delta while strengthening ties to Cambodia. The final struggle between Khmer and Vietnamese for the lower Mekong delta, in other words, was put on hold from 1862 to 1945. It would have to be resolved from 1945 onwards.

1.2 The Mottled Delta in 1945

The Mekong Delta is one of the great rice deltas of the world. It features marshes and forests, plantations and rice fields, mangrove forests and seacoast. While dominated by flat expanses, the region also includes hills, sand dunes, limestone karsts, and small mountains. Some authors divide the delta into coastal, riverine, and mountainous zones. Philip Taylor goes further, dividing the Khmer-settled parts of the Mekong Delta, plus Tây Ninh province, into eight different environmental subregions.[34] These eight zones cover the area at the core of this book.

Not all of the delta was easily accessible. It was unevenly settled, with densely populated areas mixed with sparsely inhabited ones. The heart of the western Mekong Delta, the "rice basket" centered around the Mekong River and its tributaries, was packed with people: it had a population density of 162 persons per square kilometer in 1942. In contrast, Hà Tiên province was thinly settled, with a population density of only three persons per square kilometer. It was hard to traverse large zones, such as the U Minh Forest/Point of Cà Mau or the Plain of Reeds, with respective densities of only 11 and 6.6 persons per square kilometer.[35] Those fighting against the French would exploit them as zones of refuge during the war. The U Minh Forest was then a giant tropical wetlands forest, edged with mangroves, bordering the Gulf of Thailand; the densely vegetated Plain of Reeds (with large expanses of tall reeds) was flooded for much of the year. Besides these zones, other areas, such as the tropical forests of Tây Ninh province or the mountains along the Cambodia-Cochinchina border, also offered sanctuary.

[34] Philip Taylor, *The Khmer Lands of Vietnam: Environment, Cosmology, and Sovereignty* (Singapore: NUS Press, 2014), 11–13.
[35] Pierre Gourou, "La population rurale de l'Indochine," *Annales de Géographie* 51(285) (1942), 12, 13, 11.

Historically, the Khmer had settled the Mekong Delta early, followed by Chinese, Cham, Malays, and others. The Vietnamese had arrived relatively late. By 1945, the Mekong Delta, although approximately 90 percent Vietnamese, was mottled: ethnically, linguistically, politically, religiously, and in terms of place of origin. Traces of earlier settlement patterns remained. While the 350,000 Khmer formed only 6 percent of Cochinchina's population, they concentrated in the provinces of Trà Vinh (85,000), Rạch Gía (65,000), Sóc Trăng (80,000), and Châu Đốc (45,000).[36] (Trà Vinh province alone counted 108 Khmer temples in 1948, with 520 resident monks.[37]) Lesser numbers scattered in Bạc Liêu provinces Cần Thơ, Rạch Gía, Châu Đốc, and Tây Ninh provinces. Most areas of Khmer settlement were close to branches of the Mekong or canals. This pattern of Khmer concentration would shape the war.

Significant numbers of Chinese (as well as Sino-Khmer and Sino-Vietnamese) lived in the Mekong delta. But who, exactly, were the Chinese? Some delta inhabitants were creole in culture, mixing Chinese, Khmer, and Vietnamese practices. *Minh Hương* had Sino-Vietnamese ancestry and kept their ties to Chinese culture. Many belonged to Chinese congregations. While most Chinese lived in the main city of Cholon, significant clusters of Chinese lived in the western Mekong Delta provinces of Cần Thơ, Rạch Giá, Sóc Trăng, and Bạc Liêu. Some Chinese, such as those in Mỹ Tho and Hà Tiên, could trace their ancestry back several hundred years to Ming loyalists who fled China with the rise of the Qing dynasty. Chinese aside, other populations existed in much smaller numbers. Small pockets of Cham were found in Tây Ninh and Châu Đốc provinces. Malays were found in and around Châu Đốc.

Ethnic and political diversity aside, the dominant Vietnamese were themselves split on religious lines. Catholic congregations had been established in the delta since the late sixteenth century.[38] Cao Đài temples were scattered across the region. The Cao Đài embraced a new religion, founded in 1926, drawing on Western spiritism, Chinese secret societies, and Vietnamese practices, and incorporating a broad range of Western, Vietnamese, and East Asian spirits into its pantheon. Perhaps one in five persons in the delta belonged to this religious group by 1945.[39] The Hòa

---

[36] Vavasseur, "Etude."   [37] Ibid.

[38] Jacob Ramsay, *Mandarins and Martyrs: The Church and the Nguyen Dynasty in the Nineteenth Century* (Stanford: Stanford University Press, 2008), 25.

[39] Hoskins suggests that one-fourth or one-fifth of Cochinchina in 1940 followed the Cao Đài. See Janet Hoskins, *"God's Chosen People": Race, Religion, and the Anti-Colonial Struggle in French Indochina*. Asia Research Institute Working paper 189 (September 2012), 4.

Hảo was a heterodox branch of Buddhism dating from 1939 with a charismatic leader, Huỳnh Phú Sổ. They comprised somewhere between 200,000 to one million followers.[40] While often portrayed as an exotic sect, the Hòa Hảo actually combined beliefs particular to the western Mekong Delta with a peasant householder orientation found from the earliest days of Buddhism, as well as teachings from the broad salvationist Pure Land tradition that has been one of the major poles of East Asian Buddhism. Added to these religious streams were many other teachings, from Protestantism to Pure Land Householder [Tịnh Độ Cư sĩ] and Strange Scent of the Precious Mountains [Bửu Sơn Kỳ Hương]. The delta, in other words, was a religiously dynamic and complex region in 1945. The link between religious allegiances and politics, however, was up for negotiation.

1.3 Economic and Social Uncertainty in the Delta

At the core of the upheaval in the Mekong Delta was its particular economic structure, which was susceptible to exogenous shocks. From the late nineteenth century onwards, the French colonial state "developed" the delta, digging canals, draining marshland, and expanding the area that could be planted with rice and other agricultural commodities. The delta would come to depend on strong export markets in rice to sustain its growing population. In areas settled by Vietnamese the longest, such as those close to the city of Saigon, landholdings were smaller. Even so, a large number of farmers still rented the land they tilled. Areas that had come under recent exploitation, such as the core of the western Mekong Delta today, boasted more large landowners and plantations. Here, plantation owners and other landowners took a higher cut of the harvest from tenants,[41] and thus exploited landless renters more. In prosperous times, a large "floating population" of landless laborers could find work, sometimes on the large French, Vietnamese, even Chinese estates; but in downtimes they faced difficulties.[42]

---

[40] As Pascal Bourdeaux shows, statistics on the size of the Hòa Hảo vary widely, from 200,000 on up. Basing himself on a 1949 study, Bourdeaux suggests that there were 600,000 to 700,000 in 1950. Huỳnh Phú Sổ himself claimed over a million adepts. See Bourdeaux, "Approches statistiques, de la communauté du bouddhisme Hòa Hảo," in Goscha and de Tréglodé, eds., Naissance d'un État-Parti, 293–299.

[41] J. Decaudin, "Un essai d'économie dirigée: le marché du paddy et le marché du riz en Cochinchine 1941–1944" (special issue of the Bulletin de l'Économie Indochinois, 1944, Fascicules III and IV), 10.

[42] David Biggs, Quagmire: Nation-Building and Nature in the Mekong Delta (Washington: University of Washington Press, 2010), 148.

On the eve of World War II, Cochinchina's economy had recovered from the Great Depression of 1929–30. It was producing, on average, about 3,100,000 tons of rice and exporting half (1,500,000), making it one of the top three rice exporters in the world.[43] World War II, however, would be transformative. The Japanese conquest of Southeast Asia in 1941 and 1942 broke some of the economic bonds that linked the region. Rice-rich Burma, Thailand, and southern Vietnam had once exported to India, Malaya, and central and northern Vietnam. Interregional transportation dropped, and finally came to a halt, when the Americans began air raids on shipping routes and railways after 1943. When war severed these economic links, Bengal and north-central Vietnam suffered major famines, and Malaya endured acute food shortages.[44]

As the economy crumbled, economic infrastructure did as well. In September 1945, the journalist André Blanchet noted that "plantations, from which the Japanese had expelled the French on March 9, were abandoned, rubber trees untended, and rail equipment rusted."[45] Transportation routes had broken down. Railroads had deteriorated. Blanchet observed that "wherever you go in Indochina, whether it be Cochinchina, Phnom Penh, Pakse or Hanoi, [one finds] vast graveyards of cars and trucks."[46] Few individuals had access to working motorized transport. From 1945 onwards, canals and rivers became the transportation routes of choice in the delta.

Economic degradation during the war hurt rural dwellers. By 1945, Mekong Delta peasants were wearing tattered clothes. They had to scramble to find basic commodities, like salt or lamp oil. To travel long distances, they often walked, as many cars, buses, and trains had broken down, been destroyed, or lacked fuel. Roads and waterways were often in pitiful shape. One Mekong delta farmer complained of the lack of fuel and noted that "no one could buy new clothes, and our old clothes were worn and torn after two or three years. Mosquito nets were used to make outfits for women while men just wore shorts. We also washed sacks to wear as a shirt without sleeves."[47] Vương Liêm, a boy during World War II from Tập Rèn, Sóc Trăng province, stated that "daily life was essentially one of hardship, there was not enough work to feed oneself, and so one could not

---

[43] Decaudin, *Essai d'économie dirigée*, 5.

[44] On such economic and food disruptions, see, for example, Christopher Bayly and Tim Harper, *Forgotten Soldiers: The Fall of British Asia, 1941–1945* (Cambridge, MA: Harvard University Press, 2005), especially 327–335.

[45] André Blanchet, *Au pays des ballila jaunes: relation d'un correspondant de guerre en Indochine* (St. Étienne: Dorian, 1947), 24.

[46] Ibid., 149.

[47] Bảy Long, interviewed in David A. Biggs, *Quagmire: Nation-Building and Nature in the Mekong Delta* (Seattle: University of Washington Press, 2010), 116.

get enough clothing, mosquito nets and blankets, pillows, and other things... Soap was seen as a luxury, even though the famous 'Cô Ba' soap was sold everywhere."[48] A communist party history of Tiền Giang province noted that even landlords and administrators had become poor and their clothes were threadbare [xơ xác]. The French Vichy regime fretted about these issues: in February 1942, for example, it censored articles on the difficulty of finding potatoes and on the poor rice harvest in Gò Công province.[49] "Goods were critically short and prices soared," but the purchasing power of inhabitants was weak: "daily life for people, once difficult, became worse."[50]

In the long run, the decade from 1944 onwards would devastate the export-oriented Mekong Delta far more than the Great Depression of the 1930s. The Depression, lasting from 1931 to 1934 in the South,[51] led to social, economic, and political upheavals, with many peasants losing their land and being thrown out of work. Rice exports dropped 46 percent from a peak in 1928 to their nadir in 1931.[52] The period from 1944 to 1954 would be even more calamitous, leading to even more severe contraction of land under cultivation, more joblessness, more depopulation of parts of the delta, far higher levels of migration, and – of course – more violence and more dead. The downturn began at the end of World War II. By 1944, exports from the Mekong Delta, once one of the world's major rice baskets, had plunged to their lowest level since 1912.[53] By 1945, with American air attacks, overall exports from Indochina – including rice – had plunged even further, to 1.4 percent of 1940 levels.[54] In the western Mekong Delta in particular, provincial rice cultivation dropped, depending on the province, between 20 and 85 percent in 1945.[55]

By 1945, then, delta inhabitants had to cope with dramatic economic shocks. Problems cascaded: with little rice slated for export, less was planted; with less planted, landowners had less need for harvest labor, thereby throwing many landless laborers out of work; in response, some of them turned to banditry, others to politics. The Chinese rice millers had

---

[48] Vương Liêm, *Đồng quê Nam Bộ (thập niên 40)* (Ho Chi Minh City: Văn Nghệ Thành Phố Hồ Chí Minh, 2003), 89.

[49] Vietnam National Archives-II [hereafter VNA-II]. Thông Đốc Nam Kỳ. II.A 45 file 243(12), "Censure de la presse française du 1er janvier au 31 mars 1942."

[50] Ban Nghiên Cứu Lịch Sử Đảng, *Lịch sử Đảng Bộ tỉnh Tiền Giang* (s.l., Tiền Giang, 1985), 139–40.

[51] Pierre Brocheux, *The Mekong Delta: Ecology, Economy, and Revolution, 1860–1960* (Madison, Wisconsin: Center for Southeast Asian Studies, 1995), 153.

[52] Brocheux, *Mekong Delta*; percentages calculated from statistics on p. 164.

[53] Decaudin, *Un essai d'économie dirigée*, 128.

[54] Jean Delvert, "Quelques problèmes indochinois en 1947," *L'information géographique* 12, 2 (1948), 51–2.

[55] Quoted in Pascal Bourdeaux, "Approches statistiques," 287.

no rice to mill; landowners could not pay off their creditors; moneylenders acquired land they did not want and became cash-poor. This unfolding economic disaster primed rural inhabitants for the political upheavals that followed. Plantations were breeding grounds of discontent, as the landless workers in places such as the LaBatsche plantation (Sóc Trăng province) were pulled into ethnic and political violence.

1.4 Conclusion

By the summer of 1945, the Mekong Delta was under enormous stress. Rice production had plummeted. Thousands of laborers were out of work. Migrants were flowing in and out of the delta, and from the countryside to the cities of the delta. By September, France was sending troops back to the South, promising to retake the colony of Cochinchina that it had lost. The delta was being primed for a massive level of violence. To this priming, and its eventual release, we now turn to understand the fractious August General Uprising of 1945, the spark for the war that followed.

On September 22, 1945, rearmed French soldiers, recently released from
Japanese internment camps, shabbily dressed and lacking any discipline,
rampaged through Saigon, abusing the Vietnamese populace. The
next day, September 23, would go down in history: Trần Văn Giàu,
a key communist leader of the southern Việt Minh, announced that
"the war of Resistance has begun!"[1] Vietnam's armed struggle against
the French had started. It would last nine more years. The morning of
that same day, another event happened that has tumbled into obscurity.
An unidentified Vietnamese assassinated Lê Văn Vững, Secretary of the
Trotskyist Saigon-Cholon Committee, in front of his house on Albert the
First Street.[2] The juxtaposition of these two events is jarring: why, on
the day that the war of Resistance against the *French* is declared, are
Vietnamese killing *Vietnamese*?

This assassination clues us in to the enduring divisions at the heart of
the August General Uprising [*Tổng Khởi Nghĩa*], which kicked off over
a month earlier. The August General Uprising, commonly referred to as
the August Revolution, refers to a complex series of events, unfolding in
the north, center, and south of the country, to seize power from the de
facto Japanese rulers of Vietnam and establish, before the French military
returned, that the Vietnamese were the rightful rulers of Vietnam. The
titular leader of this uprising was the Việt Minh, a front organization led
by communists. The uprising began when, on August 16, Hồ Chí Minh
issued a call to all Vietnamese: "the decisive hour in [our] people's destiny
has arrived... We cannot delay. Advance! Advance! Heroically
advance!"[3] A series of events, leading to seizures of power, rippled
through Vietnam from north to south. The uprising culminated with

---

[1] Trần Văn Giàu and Trần Bạch Đằng, eds., *Địa chí văn hóa thành phố Hồ Chí Minh* (Ho Chi
Minh City: Thành phố Hồ Chí Minh, 1987), Vol. 1, 356.
[2] Trần Ngươn Phiêu, *Phan Văn Hùm: thân thế và sự nghiệp* (Amarillo, TX: Hải Mã,
2003), 122.
[3] Hội Đồng Chỉ Đạo Lịch sử Nam Bộ Kháng chiến, *Lịch sử Nam Bộ Kháng chiến*, Vol. 1,
(Hanoi: Chính trị quốc gia, 2010), 145.

declarations of Vietnamese independence in cities and towns throughout the country on September 2, 1945. In Vietnam, accounts of this iconic series of events emphasize Vietnamese unity against both the Japanese and the French. Vietnamese from all walks of life organized protests on a scale never before seen in modern Vietnamese history. Taken together, the August uprisings marked a turning point in twentieth-century Vietnamese politics, and would deeply shape the war to come.[4] They would become an iconic moment in the long global struggle against imperial rule.

Today, the dominant interpretation of the August General Uprising emphasizes the leading role of the Indochinese Communist Party (ICP) at the head of the Việt Minh, and emphasizes the national framework of the upheavals. We immediately face a problem, however, when trying to force the August General Uprising in Saigon, and the violence that followed a month later, into the conventional revolutionary nationalist narrative. Saigon was stubbornly different. While virtually all southerners opposed the return of the French, this shared sentiment papered over what François Guillemot has called the "fracturing" of Vietnamese politics.[5] Nowhere were divisions deeper than in the South. Uncertainty, division, and violence shaped the *aftermath* of this mass event: the rampant settling of scores, ethnic and political profiling, gang-style violence, imprisonment, and executions. The ultimate failure to create a unified front – and the animosity engendered by the uprisings themselves – shaped the war in the countryside as well. Intriguingly, one division is almost never mentioned in accounts of the mass uprisings: the ethnic one. The August uprisings and the beginnings of resistance in September were an ethnic *Vietnamese* event. They failed to include any significant participation of Chinese, Khmer, Cham, or other minorities of the South.

---

[4] The literature on the "August Revolution" is enormous, with David Marr, *Vietnam 1945: The Quest for Power*, the most prominent work in English. Tuong Vu has argued that "we can... distinguish two revolutions in Vietnam: a nationalist revolution in 1945–46 and a socialist revolution in the four subsequent decades (1948–88)." See Tuong Vu, "Triumphs or Tragedies: A New Perspective on the Vietnamese Revolution," *Journal of Southeast Asian Studies* 45 (2014), 236–257. This suggestive argument doesn't quite fit the South. François Guillemot rhetorically poses the question: [was] "the August Revolution of 1945 an uprising or a coup d'état?" See François Guillemot, *Viêt-Nam, fractures d'une nation. Une histoire contemporaine de 1858 à nos jours* (Paris: La Découverte, 2018), 114.

[5] François Guillemot, "Au coeur de la fracture vietnamienne: l'élimination de l'opposition nationaliste et anticolonialiste dans le nord du Việt Nam (1945–1946)." In Christopher E. Goscha and Benoît de Tréglodé, eds., *Naissance d'un État-Parti: le Viêt Nam depuis 1945* (Paris: Les Indes Savantes, 2004). 175–216. The two key leaders in the Saigon uprising, the communists Trần Văn Giàu and Phạm Ngọc Thạch, were not allowed to publish, under official imprimatur, their uncensored memoirs of what had happened.

Needless to say, my view, emphasizing division, conflicts with the orthodox view of the impact of what scholars usually call the August Revolution of 1945. Labels are significant: in calling this event a "revolution," authors link it to the October Revolution of 1917 and the French Revolution of 1789, implying that the event itself was equally transformative. I will assert, following Charles Tilly's argument about revolutions, that while a *revolutionary situation* existed in the South in August 1945, leading to extensive uprisings, this was not followed by a successful *revolutionary outcome* in which the contestants gained undivided control of the state apparatus.[6] The outcome was more complicated. In calling this event the "August General Uprising," I am putting aside the implicit comparison to past revolutions and simply returning to the name the protagonists themselves initially gave their insurrection.

Understanding what happened in August and September 1945 in Saigon helps us understand the fractures that shaped the war as a whole. The August General Uprising was shaped by its preconditions, and this chapter will therefore look at the slow disintegration of the economy and the collapse of the French and Japanese regimes in the spring and summer of 1945. It will also focus on those Vietnamese groups which tried to take advantage of this opportune moment. I call this the parallel and intersecting mobilizations in the quest for power, as different religious and political groups jockeyed for political control, sometimes in alliance, sometimes at loggerheads. If they joined in unity at key moments, the process was marked by sharp divisions as well, as a discussion of the violence of this uprising will underline. When the British, then the French, arrived, they simply pushed this contestation out of Saigon and into the Mekong Delta. I now turn to this story, which is pivotal to understanding the overall arc of the war in the South.

2.1 The Slow Collapse

Vietnamese communists often state that the August General Uprising succeeded because the Việt Minh seized the "opportune moment" to launch their insurrection. But this moment was months in the making, enabled by the slow collapse of French, then Japanese, ruling institutions, and the long-term degradation of the economy during World War II. This collapse, and the accompanying economic and social upheavals, would "prime" the uprisings that followed. The uprising itself burst forth right after Japan surrendered to the Allies, the remnants of the Japanese empire

---

[6] Charles Tilly, *Regimes and Repertoires* (Chicago: University of Chicago Press, 2006), 159.

were crumbling in Southeast Asia, and economic collapse was accelerating.

Japan's conquest of Southeast Asia during World War II threw the region into turmoil. The war placed tremendous strain on the French colonial state in Indochina. The conflict accentuated centrifugal tendencies already at work. Cochinchina, for example, vastly increased its autonomy from Hanoi. Increasingly, Vietnamese, like other Southeast Asians, had to fend for themselves. By August 1945, when World War II officially ended, the southern part of the country had been drifting away from centralized rule for more than four years.

Chapter 1 touched on the slow economic collapse of the Mekong Delta, particularly from 1943 onwards. Here I will just note that shortages reached the cities as well. In 1943, Saigon radio announced a reduction in soap rations; in 1944, cloth was becoming scarce, and old clothing was being donated to the poor.[7] According to Thiếu Mai, after the Japanese seized power in March 1945, "daily necessities like rice, meat, sugar, milk, charcoal, soap, matches, etc... suddenly became scarcer than ever before" in Saigon.[8] Nguyễn Hiến Lê noted that inflation hit hard: "In 1939, a lượng of gold cost 160 piasters, but at the beginning of 1945 the price had climbed to 1,000 piasters, so the piaster was now at a sixth of its value; life was very difficult."[9] Dinh Minh Cao, a Chinese from Saigon, complained in a July 20, 1945 letter that:

Products are extremely expensive. One can only buy them with purchase vouchers provided by the Supply Service. Most merchants engage in the black market despite severe sanctions imposed by the local government. Fabric sells for 33 to 50 piastres a meter, cigarettes from one and a half to eight piastres a packet, towels are more than ten piastres each, wooden clogs [sabots] around two piastres a pair and shoes from fifty to sixty piastres a pair.[10]

As the economy collapsed, the French, then Japanese, rule crumbled as well. Indochina's de facto dual system of governance had been an oddity in the Japanese empire: the French Vichy regime continued to rule at the pleasure of the Japanese for most of World War II. Then, before the United States defeated Japan in the Battle of Manila in March 1945,

---

[7] On soap and cloth, see American intercepts of Saigon radio broadcasts in Research and Analysis Branch, Office of Strategic Services, *Programs of Japan in Indo-China With Index to Biographical Data. Assemblage # 56* (Honolulu: Office of Strategic Services, August 10, 1945), 120–121.

[8] Thiếu Mai [Mrs. Vũ Bá Hùng], *Ngược gió: Hồi ký* (Saigon: Đồng Nai, 1972), 315.

[9] Nguyễn Hiến Lê, *Hồi ký Nguyễn Hiến Lê* (Ho Chi Minh City: Văn Học, 2006), 295.

[10] National Archives of Cambodia [hereafter, NAC]. Résidence Supérieure au Cambodge [hereafter, RSC]. File 34,189. [Intercepted letter from Dinh Minh Cao, Saigon, to Man Hong Sen, Bangkok. July 20, 1945. Translated from Chinese into French.]

General Terauchi shifted the headquarters of the Southern Army, responsible for all of Southeast Asia, back to Saigon. On March 9, 1945, anxious about the allegiances of the French administration, the Japanese military seized power. That evening, at 6 p.m., Japanese Ambassador Matsumoto issued an ultimatum to Governor-General Decoux: hand over power to the Japanese within two hours. Caught off guard, Decoux stalled for time. He failed. At five minutes to eight, the French military received news of attacks on garrisons in the provinces. Soon thereafter, the Japanese military attacked and routed the unprepared French military garrisons in Hanoi. In two days, the Japanese wrested full control of Indochina away from the French.[11]

The French were stunned by their rapid defeat. Their military seemed completely unprepared for this possibility. Most French garrisons surrendered after limited fighting. The Japanese interned or imprisoned almost all French soldiers. French residents in Saigon and the Mekong Delta were shell-shocked by the Japanese seizure of power. They had clung to the fiction that France still remained in charge, and felt humiliated when the Japanese finally overthrew the French regime. From March to mid-September 1945, the French watched, helplessly, as others determined the fate of Indochina.

While many French lost their jobs, some continued to work for the new government after March 9, 1945, particularly those with technical expertise in areas like power generation. In Hoàng Tấn's words, "On its face, it did not seem that Saigon changed much. The Japanese set up a puppet administration, spreading their Greater East Asia demagoguery. They kept intact the administrative apparatus, or if not then nearly the same. Everyone kept their original posts, including the French [Tây] heading offices."[12] On the prison island of Côn Đảo, the French, including the Legionnaires, stayed in charge until the Japanese military arrived and tossed them into prison.[13] The Japanese relocated French living in the countryside to major cities like Saigon, Hue, Hanoi, and Phnom Penh. They interned (or placed under house arrest) French civilians. Members of the French military, utterly surprised by the Japanese coup d'état, were traumatized by their internment. In his memoir, Marcel Gaultier conveys how he and other

---

[11] Here I combine elements from an eyewitness, Paul Mus, and a secondary source. See Paul Mus, *Le Vietnam chez lui* (Paris: Centre d'Études de Politique Étrangère, 1946); Vu Ngu Chieu, "The Other Side of the 1945 Vietnamese Revolution: The Empire of Viet-Nam (March–August 1945)," *Journal of Asian Studies* (February 1986), 294.

[12] Hoàng Tấn, *Nguyễn Bính: một vì sao sáng* (s.l., Đồng Nai, 1999), 80.

[13] Nguyễn Hải Hàm, *Từ Yên Báy đến Côn Lôn (1930–1945): Hồi ký* (Falls Church, VA: Nha Sach The He, 1995), 197.

military prisoners, "dirty, unshaven, half-naked," were constantly hungry, often sick, and whipsawed by emotions.[14]

The Japanese seizure of power marked the end of French rule. But what replaced it? And did Japan allow "independence" to the Vietnamese or not? The answer is complicated. The Japanese took over the top echelon of the Indochina administration, but allowed a new entity – the Empire of Vietnam – a degree of autonomy. Under the watchful eye of the Japanese military, Vietnamese moved into positions of authority in local administration. The Vietnamese-led Empire of Vietnam, in existence from March to August 1945, abrogated the nineteenth-century treaty with France that imposed a "protectorate." On March 11, Emperor Bảo Đại announced cryptically that "Vietnam will, by its proper efforts, develop to the point to merit the condition of an independent state," and promised to "collaborate" with Japan to reach this goal.[15] Japan, in other words, was still the boss.

The former French colony of Cochinchina, however, was a special case. Here, the Japanese military was at sixes and sevens. In a Tokyo broadcast on March 13, Japan announced that it would "extend wholehearted support to healthy racial movements which are based on the Joint Declaration of the GEA [Greater East Asia] nations." "The important thing now," the new Governor of Cochinchina Minoda stated on April 9, "is to establish the prestige of an independent people by conducting ourselves in order and discipline." Independence under Japanese military rule – that was Japan's odd formula.[16]

Japan's victory, however, would be shortlived. Japanese power crumbled throughout Southeast Asia in early August 1945, but Japan was busy trying to shape the endgame of empire. On August 9, 1945, Sukarno and Mohammed Hatta, the two leaders of the Indonesian nationalist movement, flew into Saigon on a Japanese military plane. They continued on to Dalat: on August 11 they met with Field Marshal Terauchi, commander of Japanese military forces in Southeast Asia, to work out the timetable and details of Indonesia's declaration of independence. Sukarno and Hatta then returned to Saigon, and on August 13 flew out of the country.[17] The two men would declare

[14] Marcel Gaultier, *Prisons japonaises. Récit vécu* (Monte Carlo: Regain, 1950), 235.

[15] For the proclamation text, see Philippe Devillers, *Histoire du Viet Nam de 1940 à 1952* (Paris: Éditions du Seuil, 1952), 125.

[16] For Japanese proclamations, see American intercepts of Japanese radio broadcasts in Research and Analysis Branch, Office of Strategic Services, *Programs of Japan in Indo-China with Index to Biographical Data. Assemblage # 56* (Honolulu: Office of Strategic Services, August 10, 1945), 88, 87.

[17] Benedict O'Gorman Anderson, *Java in a Time of Revolution* (Ithaca: Cornell, 1972), 63–64.

Indonesia's independence four days later. Japan clearly was working hard to shape post-war Southeast Asia.

On August 15th, after the United States had relentlessly bombed its cities and dropped atomic bombs on Hiroshima and Nagasaki, Emperor Hirohito announced Japan's surrender. This date usually marks the effective end of World War II in Asia. Yet the Japanese empire in Southeast Asia lingered on beyond August 15. Saigon became a transit point in the drama of this empire's death throes. Subhas Chandra Bose, the fiery Indian nationalist leader fighting the British, touched down in Saigon on the morning of August 17. Later that afternoon, he flew off to Taipei on a Japanese bomber, eventually dying in a plane crash in Taiwan.[18]

2.2 Parallel and Intersecting Mobilizations to Seize Power

The Japanese seizure of power on March 9, and their openness to some forms of Vietnamese self-assertion, would give rise in the South to parallel and intersecting mobilizations on the part of Vietnamese organizations with the ultimate aim of gaining political power. The mobilizations occurred in parallel: different groups wanted to build on different core areas of strength, such as the Cao Đài around Tây Ninh province, or the Hòa Hảo in the western Mekong Delta, and mobilize actual and potential followers in these areas to their cause. Many of these mobilizations happened "off-stage," on the periphery, outside of the center of power in Saigon and thus less subject to repression. They often operated according to different logics, ranging from apocalyptic millenarianism, as with the Hòa Hảo Buddhists, to strictly following the Party line, as with the "Liberation" faction of communists. But as no one contestant had the institutional capacity to seize and hold power at the center on their own, these organizations tactically allied with others. Their mobilizations intersected in August, in Saigon, towards a common goal. As we shall see later in this chapter, if organizations tried to mobilize from the top down, they had no control over many individuals and bands who took matters into their own hands.

These mobilizations were jumpstarted by Japan's own statements. Vương Hồng Sển of Sóc Trăng, in the Mekong Delta, first heard about Japan's coup d'état on March 9, 1945, over the radio. Three days later, he listened to the radio when the Japanese announced the peoples of Indochina were now "independent" – but "what was funny was that this

---

[18] Mihir Bose, *Raj, Secrets, Revolution: A Life of Subhas Chandra Bose* (London: Grice Chapman, 2004), 19–21.

independence would take place under the Protectorate of Great Japan!"[19] Nonetheless, Vietnamese became thrilled at the possibility of true independence.

From March 1945 onwards, as the endgame of World War II came slowly into focus, time seems to have accelerated. On March 18, 50,000 Vietnamese participated in a demonstration in Saigon to "celebrate the ouster of the French" and to create the Vietnam National Independence Party (*Việt Nam Quốc Gia Độc Lập Đảng*).[20] From the historical capital of Huế, in central Vietnam, Emperor Bảo Đại issued edicts on July 5 and 9 granting freedom of assembly and freedom to form unions. One newspaper exulted: "The first ten days of July 1945 could be called ten days of freedom."[21] Within the constraints of Japanese military rule and endemic paper and ink shortages, the press flourished. But change was not simply top-down. An openness to mass participation – from youth movements to the press – shaped public life. Vietnamese political and social agitation multiplied, as groups previously indifferent to politics were now pulled into it.

The communist-led Việt Minh was determined to seize this opportunity. It faced a severe challenge: if it was the dominant non-governmental force in the north and center of the country, it was weak and divided in the South. A key reason was that the French had hunted down, arrested, imprisoned, or executed leaders and followers in the South who participated in the abortive Nam Kỳ uprising of 1940. As a result, most of the key southern communist cadres ended up in prison for the duration of the war.

Remaining communists reconstituted the Party Committee for the South in 1943. Unfortunately, they had split into "Liberation" and "Vanguard" factions. The Liberation faction claimed to follow the Party line closely, including total rejection of collaboration with the Japanese. The Vanguard faction would eventually pursue tactical collaboration with the Japanese and Trotskyists at the end of the war. Significant as well, as David Elliott notes, the "Vanguard group represented urban sectors and the upper strata of rural society, while... [the] Liberation group was dominated by people from more modest rural backgrounds."[22] Such differences led to bitter conflicts.

Against this backdrop of division, on April 21, 1945, with Japanese approval, Phạm Ngọc Thạch and others founded the Vanguard Youth

[19] Vương Hồng Sển, *Hơn nửa đời hư* (Westminster, CA: Văn Nghệ, 1995), Chapter 20.

[20] Guillemot, *Dai Viet et révolution*, 247.

[21] "Đời sống Đông Dương. Mấy đạo dụ về tự do," *Thanh Nghị* 117 (July 21, 1945), 23.

[22] David Elliott, *The Vietnamese War: Revolution and Social Change in the Mekong Delta 1930–1975* (Armonk, New York: M. E. Sharpe, 2003), 46–48, 49.

Movement.[23] Thạch would later be identified as a person who had joined the ICP, but the movement itself was not formally linked to the communists. Two weeks later, Phạm Ngọc Thạch appointed the apparent Trotskyist Nguyễn Thị Sương (wife of the probable Trotskyist Hồ Vĩnh Ký) as the head of the Vanguard Women's Movement.[24] The significance of this fact is enormous. The single largest organization that would take part in the August General Uprising, the Vanguard Youth, brought together Trotskyists, Stalinists, nationalists, Catholics, and a host of other groups into one organization.

It is worth pausing here to consider the origins of such a capacious understanding of how to build a movement. Thạch's intriguing collaboration with Trotskyists and the Japanese reminds us of earlier collaborations, dating from the 1930s, between so-called "Stalinists" and "Trotskyists." Southern political allegiances, in general, had been quite fluid: parties flitted in and out of existence and, as Hồ Tấn Vinh suggests, individuals, ever "pragmatic," "jumped" from one group to another.[25] Individuals often joined entourages in which friendship and commitment to vague and general beliefs trumped strict adherence to ideological orthodoxy. People of very different political beliefs interacted with each other, became acquaintances and even friends, and visited each other in their homes.

Many political leaders in the South came out of a Westernized and French-speaking cosmopolitan elite. A surprising number of the leading participants in the uprising, like the communist Trần Văn Giàu, had attended the prestigious Lycée Chasseloup-Laubat in Saigon and studied in France. The early revolutionary Thái Văn Lung had studied at this lycée and in France and held French citizenship.[26] The Vanguard Youth leader Phạm Ngọc Thạch, a doctor from a wealthy landowning family,

---

[23] The nature of the Vanguard Youth and its leader, Dr. Phạm Ngọc Thạch, has been shrouded in mystery. Histories of the Indochinese Communist Party routinely note that Thạch was a member of the ICP. Indeed, he appears to have become an ICP member in 1944, but refused to get dragged into disputes between Stalinists and Trotskyists. Deep thanks to Hue Tam Ho Tai, who provided information from Hồ Hữu Tường's unpublished diary, and Nguyễn Điền, who pointed me to information in Trần Văn Giàu's memoir. Published sources in Vietnam avoid mentioning that Phạm Ngọc Thạch was sacked from his position as leader of the Vanguard Youth after the August General Uprising.

[24] Thiếu Mai, Ngược gió, 314. The author was a high-ranking militant in the Vanguard Women's Movement. Trần Văn Giàu states that Hồ Vĩnh Ký, "a friend of [Phạm Ngọc] Thạch," was a Trotskyist. Hồi ký Trần Văn Giàu, Chapters 10, 11, www.diendan.org /tai-lieu/hoi-ky-t-v-giau (accessed February 25, 2021).

[25] Hồ Tấn Vinh, "Viết về Hồ Văn Ngà". https://namkyluctinh.org/a-lichsu/hotanvinh-hovannga.pdf.

[26] Thiếu Sơn, "Bài học" in Thiếu Sơn, Nghệ thuật và nhân sinh (Hanoi: Văn Hóa thông tin Hà Nội, 2000), 387.

had studied in France and married a Frenchwoman.[27] The lawyer Diệp Ba, a non-communist member of the Vanguard Youth, would, surprisingly, go on to head the Democratic Republic of Vietnam (DRV)'s Public Security Service of the South (*Công An Nam Bộ*) from 1949 to 1954. Hoàng Xuân Nhị, a French-educated intellectual from Huế, who had veered from Trotskyism to Stalinism to Nazi collaborationism (when he was in France) and back to the left, all in the short period from 1937 to 1947, would direct an early Việt Minh organ in the Mekong Delta, the *Voix du maquis*, written, oddly, in… French.[28] One could list many others. At the beginning, with few communist cadres, the southern Việt Minh relied heavily on such educated non-communists. In this, it differed sharply from its northern and central counterparts, which moved quickly to purge non-communists from the ranks.

Indeed, the southern Việt Minh was culturally different from its analogues elsewhere in the country. The journalist Germaine Krull, speaking to Việt Minh leader Dr. Phạm Văn Bạch in Saigon, noted his impeccable French: indeed, he had spent years in Lyon, France studying law. Bach said to Krull that "we like the French and our culture is French. I, myself, not only speak the language but think in it. But we will not be a colony anymore."[29] When the French journalist André Blanchet asked the communist Trần Văn Giàu why all the Việt Minh leaders appeared to be intellectuals, doctors, and teachers, Trần Văn Giàu is quoted as saying: "I myself blame our movement for being bourgeois. But to rebuild a country, one needs intellectuals, they are the ones that must guide the masses. I myself am a bourgeois who has become a communist."[30]

Given such backgrounds, and fluidity of political allegiances, it was perhaps not surprising to see friendships and even collaborations in 1945 among leading Trotskyists, Stalinists, Catholics, and non-communist nationalists. When Phạm Ngọc Thạch organized a four-person delegation to meet an incoming British delegation at Tân Sơn Nhứt airfield on

---

[27] Nguyễn Thanh Sơn, *Trọn đời theo Bác Hồ. Hồi ức của một người con đồng bằng sông Cửu Long* (Ho Chi Minh City: Trẻ, 2005), 149.

[28] Huỳnh Minh Hiền, "Từ Đông Tháp Mười đến Cà Mau, hai thủ phủ của Nam Bộ trong Kháng Chiến chống Pháp," in Thăng Long, ed., *Nhớ Nam Bộ và cực nam Trung Bộ buổi đầu Kháng chiến chống Pháp* (Ho Chi Minh City: Trẻ, 1999), 515. Hoàng Xuân Nhị would rise in the DRV hierarchy despite his past flirtation with Nazism. See Charles Keith, "Vietnamese Collaborationism in Vichy France," *Journal of Asian Studies* 76(4) (November 2017), 992–1003.

[29] Krull, "Dairy [*sic*], Following the Allied Occupation in September 1945," [2], entry for September 17, 1945, p. [12], Folder 07, Box 02, Douglas Pike Collection, The Vietnam Center and Archive, Texas Tech University, www.vietnam.ttu.edu/reports/images.php?img=/images/241/2410207001.pdf.) (accessed December 27, 2018).

[30] André Blanchet, *Au pays des ballila jaunes: relation d'un correspondant de guerre en Indochine* (St. Étienne: Dorian, 1947), 198. The interview took place in February 1946.

September 6, "a strange fact" was that all members of the delegation –
Trần Văn Thạch, Huỳnh Văn Phương, Phan Văn Chánh, and Mrs Hồ
Vĩnh Ký – "belonged to the Fourth International" of Trotskyists.[31] The
high-ranking Trotskyist leader of the Saigon police (Sûreté), Huỳnh Văn
Phương, is said to have supplied arms for the uprising and allowed
Vanguard Youth members to practice marksmanship at the Sûreté firing
range.[32] Such collaboration was perhaps a necessity: the ICP needed
allies in Saigon itself, and were weak in the countryside.

While the ICP was weak in southern Vietnam, a range of non-
communist groups had taken advantage of the Japanese seizure of
power to expand their influence in the region. From March to August,
the Cao Đài religious group may have organized the most potent
Vietnamese armed force. As Werner notes, "Cao Đài paramilitary groups
and perhaps guerrilla forces were trained in the Nitinan shipyard under
the auspices of the Japanese army just before the coup [of March 9] took
place." Furthermore, 3,000 Cao Đài "troops" played a very minor role in
the coup itself.[33] The de facto political leader of the Tây Ninh branch of
the Cao Đài, Trần Quang Vinh, claimed that by 1945, the sect had 20,000
volunteers in its Cao Đài militia, which seems an exaggeration.[34]

The Vanguard Youth, with Japanese blessing, dramatically expanded
its influence throughout much of the delta, building up the single most
important mass-based organization that would later take part in the
August General Uprising. In Rạch Gía, Vanguard Youth organized
youth of all ethnic backgrounds with a simple message: promote unity,
defend the villages and their property, and produce food.[35] The Hòa Hảo
religious group entrenched itself in the far west as its leader, Huỳnh Phú
Sổ, toured the region, encouraged farmers to plant crops, and preached
his millenarian message of salvation. Closer to Saigon, the Bình Xuyên,
patriotic toughs, also vied for influence. A wide range of parties also tried,
under the constraints of Japanese rule, to mobilize followers.

As the Japanese empire crumbled in August 1945, these parallel mobilizations by different Vietnamese groups to seize power eventually

---

[31] Nguyễn Kỳ Nam, *Hồi ký 1925–1965*, Vol. 2, 224. Three of these delegation members
belonged to the Foreign Affairs Committee of the Provisional Government of Nam Bộ.
See NAC. Carton 55. *Thời báo* (Phnom Penh) 39 (September 15, 1945), "Nam Bộ."

[32] See Hồ Hữu Nhựt, *Trí thức Sài Gòn-Gia định, 1945–1975* (Hanoi: Chính Trị Quốc gia,
2001), 60; Trần Ngươn Phiêu, "Nỗi lòng Huỳnh Tấn Phát," https://nghiencuulichsu
.com/2015/03/25/noi-long-huynh-tan-phat/ (accessed November 1, 2015).

[33] Jayne Werner, "The Cao Đài: The Politics of a Vietnamese Syncretic Religious
Movement" (PhD dissertation, Cornell University, 1976), 242.

[34] Trần Quang Vinh, *Hồi ký Trần Quang Vinh*, 242.

[35] Nguyễn Ngọc Lầu, "Tôi tham gia cách mạng tháng tám ở Hà Tiên," in Trần Bạch Đằng
et al, eds, *Mùa Thu rồi. Ngày hăm ba.* (Hanoi: Chính trị Quốc gia, 1995), 400–401.

intersected, albeit tentatively, under a Việt Minh umbrella. In Saigon, they faced no French or Japanese armed opposition. It is important to underscore this point: the Vietnamese did not overthrow the Japanese or French. French administrators, military and police, after all, were interned or under house arrest. And the Japanese? Initially, they were in a quandary. General Terauchi, commander of Japanese forces in French Indochina, pleaded for food for his 70,000 soldiers on the ground. Dr. Phạm Ngọc Thạch, the leader of the Vanguard Youth who would play a pivotal role in the August General Uprisings, agreed to help. Thạch made two requests: that the Japanese military not intervene in any Việt Minh uprising, and that it supply "necessary" weapons. General Terauchi agreed.[36]

Did the Việt Minh need to seize power in August? No. Its leaders could have negotiated a de facto peaceful transition of power from the Japanese. But the communist leaders of the Việt Minh "needed" an uprising for two reasons. First, they wanted to present the Allied Forces and the French, whose forces were expected to land in French Indochina, with a fait accompli: the Vietnamese seizure of power. Second, and perhaps equally important, it wanted to preempt other Vietnamese groups and come out on top in the internal Vietnamese power struggle. In the words of Trần Văn Giàu, the leading revolutionary in the South at the time:

The most important thing was not to be absent from the South, and not to delay the general revolutionary uprising for all of Vietnam and Indochina. But we had to face a reality: we were weak. Little time remained. When expressing myself before the Regional Committee, I often used the French phrase "course contre la montre" [race against the clock] to [speak of the need to] build, strengthen and develop a unified party, a unified anti-imperialist front, and to build a very large "political army" (words borrowed from Stalin: Armée politique); and to do so in a short time, so that our Party could become the strongest party in the South.[37]

Trần Văn Giàu touches on the crux of the matter: the greatest immediate challenge to the communist leadership of the Việt Minh came not from the French or Japanese, but from rival Vietnamese groups. Given communist weakness, particularly outside Saigon, this was the key structural problem of the proposed revolution. Structural divisions could only be overcome if rivals, on the successful seizure of power, fell in behind communist leaders, and the communist leaders in turn reached out and addressed their concerns. This did not happen, and the rivalry between

[36] Hội Đồng Chỉ Đạo, *Lịch Sử Nam Bộ Kháng Chiến*, Vol. 1: 1945–54, 149.
[37] Trần Văn Giàu, *Hồi ký*, Chapters XIV and XVI, www.diendan.org/tai-lieu/hoi-ky -t-v-giau.

communists and others would endure for the duration of the First Indochina War.

Divisions and problems manifested themselves early in urban and rural areas. In the provinces, after March 9, the Japanese had arrested the remaining French bureaucrats such as province chiefs, as well as any notoriously pro-French Vietnamese in the administration. The Japanese rural administration was short-lived: it collapsed in mid-August 1945, unmooring bureaucrats, soldiers, and police in the provinces from any larger state structure and any higher guidance. The state, in other words, was "decapitated." Vương Hồng Sển noted that the administration of Sóc Trăng province after March 1945 was "like a snake that has lost its head" – the province chief and his deputy had fled to Cà Mau, so things fell apart.[38] As links broke between the Japanese colonial state and the provinces, links between rural and urban areas also were severed, as this story from Sóc Trăng province suggests:

Once, after my father and some relatives had boarded the bus to Saigon a few days earlier, they didn't return. The whole family waited and waited. Nearly ten days later, after walking and walking, they returned. They looked downbeat, worn out, exhausted, and hungry. No buses had been running so they had had to walk more than two hundred kilometers, losing nearly a week. That was in August 1945. My father said to me:
—War has broken out there! Allied planes were dropping bombs on the Japanese in Saigon...[39]

Sơn Nam, who would become a Việt Minh cadre, observed the social and religious effervescence before the Japanese stepped down from power in August 1945:

In the markets outside of Rạch Giá, many people from the border area of the Seven Mountains, sometimes in colorful clothes with flowing long hair, or clothed like actors in the hát bội opera, preached about the "changing of the times" or the "end of the age." It seemed as if these sects could not agree with one other.[40]

One event from central Vietnam must be mentioned, as it influenced the uprisings in Saigon and affected the Mekong Delta: the Cao Đài contention that Việt Minh units massacred almost 3,000 Cao Đài believers and others in Quảng Ngãi province, central Vietnam, in August 1945. The extent and character of this massacre is hotly debated, but the Cao Đài have collected evidence in support of this claim.[41] This attack drove

---

[38] Vương Hồng Sển, *Hơn nửa đời hư*, 261. (online version)
[39] Vương Liêm, *Đồng quê Nam Bộ (thập niên 40)*, 101.
[40] Sơn Nam, *Hồi ký*, Vol. 2. *Ở Chiến khu 9* (Ho Chi Minh City: Trẻ, 2002), 45.
[41] One source states that the Việt Minh massacred "8,000" in Quảng Ngãi province in August 1945: see "Những [sic] hành vi khủng bố và phá hoại làm lộ chân tướng của Việt

a wedge between the communists in the Việt Minh and the Cao Đài, making collaboration between the two difficult.

On August 14, the National United Front – a rickety coalition composed of the Cao Đài, Hòa Hảo Buddhists, Buddhist Pure Land lay followers, an association of state employees, the "Struggle" group of Trotskyists, Vanguard Youth, but excluding the communists – formed to oppose the return of the French. Perhaps exaggeratedly, Nguyễn Kỳ Nam, present at that meeting, wrote about their key rival: "People talked about the Việt Minh. But who were the Việt Minh? Where were they? No one knew."[42] After the Japanese announced their surrender to the Allies, the National United Front mobilized a large demonstration on August 21.

The National United Front had gained the upper hand over the Việt Minh, but this advantage was fleeting. The Việt Minh leaders were organizing their own front. They convinced the Vanguard Youth, the single largest movement, to switch its allegiance to the Việt Minh coalition. This change of heart was not difficult: although the Vanguard Youth leader, Phạm Ngọc Thạch, had collaborated with the Japanese military, he had clandestinely joined the ICP. The Việt Minh organized a demonstration on August 25 in which "several hundred thousand" took part, followed by a huge event to declare Vietnamese independence on September 2 in which 300,000 to one million participated.[43]

And the French? Lost in the tumult of August 1945 were the interned French soldiers. After Emperor Hirohito announced Japan's surrender on August 15, 1945, the Allies, in a fit of irony born of necessity, entrusted the Japanese troops to protect prisoners of war that the Japanese had interned in French Indochina. In Marcel Gaulthier's prison, French soldiers, under Japanese eyes, raised the French Tricolor in a prison in which Japanese wardens had engaged in mindless brutalities; "we gazed upon these colors, gripped by what may have been the most beautiful emotion of our lives."[44] Such emotions would soon cede their place to despair, then elation, then disorientation, as the Vietnamese seized the moment to take back their city before Allied forces arrived.

Minh," *Bạn Dân*, số 2 (Sunday) (February 3, 1946). Other sources suggest a much smaller death toll. Janet Hoskins, citing a Cao Đài source, gives the number of 2,791 Cao Đài victims. See Hoskins, "Colonial Caodaists" (unpublished paper), 21. Given that the names of the killed were inscribed on a Cao Dai memorial, Hoskin's number seems the most accurate.

[42] Nguyễn Kỳ Nam, *Hồi ký 1925–1965*, Vol. 2, 28–29.

[43] Trần Văn Giàu, *Hồi ký*, Part 14; Werner provides the estimates that 300,000 to one million took part. Jayne Werner, "The Cao Đài," 261.

[44] Gaultier, *Prisons japonaises*, 250.

The French were angered and humiliated during the "independence" celebrations of September 2. While the Vanguard Youth strived to assure order on that day, chaos still broke out amidst the massive demonstrations. Thiếu Mai has given a precise eyewitness account: "With my own eyes I saw three or four French in ordinary clothes appear and shoot out of an opening in the window [of the Jean Comte building], then hide. Bricks also came off of the Cathedral, where many people saw the bullets raining down from the steeple."[45] This testimony is curious: no one can see bullets flying through the air, the French had earlier been stripped of all weapons by the Japanese, and most French were under the protective guard of the Japanese. Other Vietnamese, however, made similar claims about French shootings.[46]

Thiếu Mai called the Vietnamese reaction to this attack a "riot": "as the simmering hatred boiled up, getting more fervent by the minute," Vietnamese attacked the buildings from which the shots were supposed to have come. A Japanese army or police unit intervened to calm down spirits.[47] The journalist and eyewitness Nguyễn Kỳ Nam noted how a crowd, thinking it heard gunfire from the offices of a lawyer named Paris, "broke down the doors, threw countless folders and pieces of paper into the street, arrested some French on the upper story, men and women – tied their hands, had them walk from Bonard Street to Catinat to bring to the police [Công An]: –'Here are the people who fired on the demonstration.'" The author wryly added, "outside, the sounds of gunfire continued."[48]

These French denied to the police that they had shot on the crowd. Nguyễn Kỳ Nam eventually concluded that all these conflicting stories about gunshots could not all be accurate.[49]

During this day, Vietnamese, French, and British were killed and wounded. Nguyễn Kỳ Nam stated that five French were killed, and thirty wounded French ended up in hospitals.[50] Gaultier writes that one eighty-year-old Catholic Father was savagely beaten and another had his throat slit. Crowds also attacked the camp of Dutch POWs, but they were deterred when the Japanese guards fired back.[51] Caught up in a frenzy,

---

[45] Thiếu Mai, *Ngược gió*, 322. Thiếu Mai participated in the demonstration as a leader in the nationalist Women's Vanguard Youth, part of the movement founded by Dr. Phạm Ngọc Thạch.
[46] For another account, see Trần Quang Vinh, *Hồi ký*, 248.
[47] Thiếu Mai, *Ngược gió*, 323.   [48] Nguyễn Kỳ Nam, *Hồi ký*, Vol. 2, 221.
[49] Ibid., 221.
[50] See the reprint of the official announcement of the Provisional Administrative Committee – i.e. the Việt Minh – in Nguyễn Kỳ Nam, *Hồi ký*, Vol. 2: 221, 223; and Thiếu Mai, *Ngược gió*, 323.
[51] Gaultier, *Prisons japonaises*, 276.

the crowd even attacked the French wife of Vanguard Youth leader Phạm Ngọc Thạch; she escaped with a swollen and bloody face and eight broken teeth.[52] The Nam Bộ Resistance Committee also stoked discord: on September 2, 1945, it made the incendiary comments: "From this moment, our foremost task is to wipe out the French enemy and its lackeys."[53]

Despite the violence that marred the September 2 demonstration in Saigon, it had begun in a peaceful and disciplined manner. Demonstrations this large had never happened in Vietnam. Together with the mass demonstrations held in other Vietnamese cities that day, they telegraph a key point: masses of Vietnamese opposed the French return. Behind the scenes, however, it was clear that unity was extremely fragile.

2.3 Allied and French Assertions of Power, and the Vietnamese Response

Up until September 13, while Vietnamese groups struggled among themselves for political dominance, the trend seemed clear: to try to come together under a loosely organized Việt Minh. Japanese troops stood by, protecting former POWs, but keeping above the fray. The looming arrival of Allied occupation forces changed the calculus of contestants. Saigon and all of Indochina beneath the Sixteenth Parallel came under the operational authority of South East Asia Command (SEAC), which was in charge of accepting the surrender of the Japanese in Southeast Asia at the end of the war.

On September 13, "part of a brigade" of the 20th Indian Division under British General Douglas Gracey, accompanied by a small number of French troops, flew in to Saigon.[54] The British were to supposed to accept the Japanese surrender and repatriate prisoners of war. Accompanied by the Recovered Allied Prisoners of War and Internees organization of the Allies, the British liberated the Indonesian "romusha" laborers as well as the other prisoners of war and other internees in Cochinchina (1,700 Dutch; 265 Australians; 57 Americans, as well as

---

[52] Trầm Hương, "Người mẹ thầm lặng bên người cha anh hùng," [Mothers working alongside heroic fathers] *An Ninh thế giới* [Global Security], March 3, 2009, https://antg .cand.com.vn/Tu-lieu-antg/Trai-khoay-va-nghiet-nga-293935/ (accessed August 13, 2020).

[53] Hội Đồng Chi Đạo, *Lịch sử Nam bộ kháng chiến*, Vol. 1, 237.

[54] F. S. V. Donnison, *British Military Administration in the Far East 1943–1946* (London: Her Majesty's Stationery Office, 1956), 408.

British and French).[55] General Gracey then expanded their duties to "secure the key area of Saigon" and "to maintain order."[56] British troops carried out sweeps; secured arms depots, and arrested "suspicious" Vietnamese. Gracey did not set up a formal military administration, however, as SEAC expected that the French would assume that role when they arrived.

Gracey also had to deal with the dispirited, bitter, and angry French community. As one former prisoner said, "the new arrivals exhibited a frostiness towards us, manifesting their ignorance of our situation during the four years of Japanese occupation."[57] Writing on October 19, 1945, the French journalist André Blanchet, speaking of the "old" French inhabitants, wrote that "what afflicts them is the impression they have, whether justified or not, that the new arrivals see them as somewhat degenerate Frenchmen, shabby, and mangy, from whom arise all of the ills of Indochina."[58] The Franco-Dutch journalist Germaine Krull, who had landed in Saigon in mid-September, described the French of Saigon as:

a frightened people, starved for news, who knew little and understood less of what had happened: in short, people who had lived in a vacuum. To them, the 9th of March [when the Japanese seized power] was a black day that marked the beginning of the war and of all their woes.... They complained bitterly that since that date the Japanese had forced them all to remain in Saigon. They said: if only you knew how much we have suffered since the riots of September second! You cannot imagine how dreadful the Annamites are. They are nothing but thieving, lying, deceitful scoundrels without a shred of gratitude or decency.[59]

And what about these Vietnamese? Colonel Jean Cédille, the highest-ranked French representative in Saigon, wrote on September 17 that:

The arrival of the French has, above all, worked up the Annamites who are now proclaiming that they are all willing to fight to the last. They even talk about collective suicide to oppose our return. Those who are worked up practically don't obey the Executive Committee anymore. The latter is riven by internal squabbles. Since my arrival, I have seen three different flags flying in the streets. I cannot list the number of ministerial reshufflings that have taken place in the past four weeks. Right now, there is an acute struggle between Trotskyists and Stalinists. The former, much more xenophobic and less conciliatory, seem to have the upper

---

[55] Most of my information on the POWs comes from John Kleinen, "The Dutch Diplomatic Post in Saigon: Dutch – Vietnamese Relations (1945–1975)," in *Lion and Dragon: Four Centuries of Dutch – Vietnamese Relations* (Amsterdam: Boom, 2008), 128–130. Most of the 265 Australians were survivors of work on the Burma-Thailand railway. On the Australians, there is an audio file of a broadcast from Saigon in August 1945: www.awm.gov.au/collection/C1255512 (accessed March 15, 2019).
[56] Donnison, *British Military Administration*, 407.   [57] Gaultier, *Prisons japonaises*, 280.
[58] Blanchet, *Au pays des Ballila jaunes*, 44–45.   [59] Krull, "Dairy [*sic*] of Saigon," [3].

hand at present, especially towards the other nationalist and anti-French factions: in a word, everywhere disorder rules...[60]

The Việt Minh Executive Committee strived to avoid conflict with the British but promoted massive non-cooperation with the French. In early September, the General Secretary of the General Federation of Southern Labor Unions, Nguyễn Lưu, called on all inhabitants in Saigon to refuse to join French military units, work with the French, sell foodstuffs to the French, or act as their guides.[61] On September 19, the People's Committee of Nam Bộ declared a general strike, calling on everyone to refuse all military, administrative, or economic collaboration.[62] In this charged atmosphere, where Krull describes the French population as in a "panic," the 20th Indian Division under General Gracey struggled to assert Allied authority. Gracey's force, composed mostly of Punjabis, Sikhs, and Nepalese Gurkhas, was only part of a brigade. Given his lack of manpower, it is not surprising that Gracey soon mobilized the surrendered Japanese to maintain order.

The Vietnamese, however, could not be contained by French, British, or Japanese arms. Writing about the events of September 21 through the 23rd, a Vietnamese from Phú Nhuân, adjoining Saigon proper, wrote that:

Saigon is consumed by a strange effervescence that it has never before experienced. It's as if there is a force impatiently pushing people into the streets. In the information offices, people stand shoulder to shoulder under the statements, appeals, and directives that the [Vietnamese] Government has pasted to the walls. We are as thirsty for news as we are for water.[63]

In the section that follows, I want to underline that much is at stake in how we interpret the violence of August and September 1945. On the one hand, one could assume that the Vietnamese, following their political leaders, expressed their politically motivated interests in a "rational" way, and that the British and French, opposing them, also acted out their interests as well. But violence is not always instrumental. It does not always flow from the political positions. The actions from September 23 to the 25th – like earlier ones – devolved, at times, into vendettas, rioting, and destruction. While in some cases, violent acts may have been directed from on high, in others, they welled up from below as a range of

---

[60] Rapport de Cédille au Général Leclerc, Saigon, September 17, 1945, reprinted in Bodinier, *Le retour de la France*, 177.
[61] Hội Đồng Chỉ Đạo, *Lịch sử Nam Bộ kháng chiến*, 222.
[62] Nguyễn Việt, *Nam Bộ và nam phần Trung Bộ trong hai năm đầu Kháng Chiến* [(1945–1946) (Hanoi: Văn Sử Địa, 1957), 27.
[63] Nguyễn Việt, *Nam Bộ và nam phần Trung Bộ*, 24.

individuals and groups took matters into their own hands. Some persons were attacked simply for being French, or foreigners; others because they were suspected collaborators, or from rival parties; yet others in reaction to French provocations.

On September 23, French POWs, technically free but still living in their camps, demanded to be rearmed to help take back the city. The British General Gracey agreed. The result was a disaster. Doidge Estcourt Taunton, an officer with the 20th Indian Division at the time, noted the result: "the French were, just sort of, rampaging, may I put that word, the French were rampaging down the streets and letting off shots quite unnecessarily."[64] Guy de Chézal, who had parachuted into Indochina earlier that year as a French military liaison, witnessed Frenchmen, "drunken with revenge," abusing Vietnamese left and right: "The crowd was despicable. The soldiers amused themselves by tying the natives to trees, trussing them up, and whipping them."[65] As the historian Ronald Spector describes it, "gangs of French soldiers and civilians roamed the city, assaulting Vietnamese, including women and children, at random. Any Vietnamese found on the streets was in danger of being kicked, beaten, and hauled off to a police station."[66]

The journalist Krull was scathing about French soldiers, contrasting the orderly and disciplined British troops with the woefully undisciplined 11th Colonial Army, composed of newly liberated internees: "The officers of the 11th were filthy and unshaven, and the men resembled a rioting civilian population." In her account, the French soldiers tortured Vietnamese, burned down their houses, abused the population in myriad ways. Speaking of September 23, the day that the 11th tried to take back City Hall, Krull wrote that "I remember the horror and shame that I felt in June of 1940 when Vichy was established, but never in my life had I felt such utter sadness and degradation as on this night."[67]

The former French internees saw their rampages in a far different light than Krull: "the soldiers rejoice: their morale, so low during the captivity, now redeemed all past failures... Despite their rags, [they reclaimed] their dignity... Their fervor is so ardent that the Annamites, terrorized, fled without a fight."[68] This author goes so far as crediting French troops with saving the French from getting their throats slit. Whatever the

[64] Interview with Doidge Estcourt Taunton for "Vietnam: A Television History," https://openvault.wgbh.org/catalog/V_FFA5A0F537504A9A9945BF9EC7CC22FE (accessed May 30, 2019).
[65] Guy de Chézal, *Parachuté en Indochine*, 270.
[66] Ronald Spector, *In the Ruins of Empire: The Japanese Surrender and the Battle for Postwar Asia* (New York: Random House, 2008), 127.
[67] Krull, "Dairy" [*sic*], [22].   [68] Gaultier, *Prisons japonaises*, 286.

explanation, the French colonials reasserted their authority over the Vietnamese in such a disorderly way that they undercut any possible French legitimacy. Aggravated by French brutalities that undermined the Allied effort, the British, in an irony lost on no one, replaced French in the furthest guard posts with Japanese![69]

Rearming the interned French troops was a turning point. It antagonized the Vietnamese and hastened the breakdown of a fragile order. Thiếu Mai aptly characterizes the resulting violence as a French-Vietnamese "feud to the death."[70] On September 23, 1945 – the same day as the assassination of Lê Văn Vững that opened this chapter – groups of Vanguard Youth in Saigon were in a frenzy, looking for "Vietnamese traitors" who had killed Vietnamese. Thiếu Sơn recounts his encounter with youth out for blood that day. They found a suspect on his street – his neighbor, the writer Thái Phi, who had made the fateful mistake of joining a pro-Japanese organization. The Vanguard Youth team accused Thái Phi of shooting a youth with his gun. Thiếu Sơn defended Thái Phi as he knew him innocent of the crime. "A youth raised his voice: 'The blood of my brother was spilled out there. Don't make excuses for a traitor [*Việt gian*].' I was frightened, averted my eyes, and allowed them to take him away." Thái Phi would never be seen again.[71] This mob justice repeated itself again and again in 1945. One can assume that time and again, fearful bystanders stood by as the innocent were killed. As Thiếu Sơn observed, "Bullets killed many individuals unjustly."[72]

By September 24, bands of Vietnamese roamed the streets on the lookout for Europeans. Some individuals escaped harm through luck. The métis doctor Huỳnh Văn Thương was arrested on his way home from work on the evening of September 24, but was soon freed: a Binh Xuyên gang member recognized that the doctor had given him medical care months earlier at Cholon's Lalung-Bonnaire hospital.[73] Others met worse fates. On the morning of September 24, "Si Tali Hari Sin" [Sithali Hari Singh?], a watchman, saw a large mob attack his French boss, Dumarest; armed with sticks, and crying "Hit him!! [*Đánh đánh đập đập*], they knocked him to the ground. From later reports, Dumarest was killed by a brick to the head and thrown in the river.[74] A Chinese witness

---

[69] Gaultier, *Prisons japonaises*, 292.   [70] See Thiếu Mai, *Ngược gió*, 327.
[71] Thiếu Sơn, "Nam Bộ Kháng Chiến," in Thiếu Sơn, *Nghệ thuật và nhân sinh*, 447.
[72] Thiếu Sơn, "Sau ngày 9–3–1945" [After March 9,1945] in Thiếu Sơn, *Nghệ thuật và nhân sinh*, 447.
[73] ANOM. HCI. SPCE 379. Service de la Sureté. Entrevue avec le Docteur HUYNH VAN THUONG. Saigon, July 3, 1946.
[74] ANOM. HCI. SPCE 33. Commissariat de la Police Mobile de Saigon. [Document beginning "L'an Mil Neuf Cent ..." Saigon, October 19___[unreadable]. [This is a copy of a document from September 28, 1945].

at the Kitchener Bridge that morning saw seven Europeans attacked and killed between 8 a.m. and 10 a.m. At 8:20 in the morning, for example, he saw:

Two westerners attacked by the mob. One was killed immediately and his body thrown from the bridge. The other, dressed in a white short-sleeved shirt, of average height, rather large with chestnut hair that fell over his rather round face, was wounded and his shirt covered in blood. He was tied up and brought, alive, to the bridge. At that moment, a Japanese walked by, and the European cried out for help. The Japanese left without providing any aid, and after he left, the wounded man was thrown, alive, from the bridge.[75]

Lucien Félixine had a similar experience: walking down rue Paul Blanchy towards the Tân Đinh market on September 25, he was attacked by a mob of Vietnamese, who kicked and punched him and knocked him down, injuring him; Félixine was only saved by the intervention of Japanese troops.[76]

Such random violence was the context for an event that particularly shocked the French, the massacres on September 24–25 at the Cité Hérault, a small neighborhood housing French and Eurasians of modest means. One trigger for the killings may have been the rumors that seemed to have been flying around Saigon. A year after the Cité Hérault massacres, during a commemoration of these events, Dr. Thinh (the puppet President of the Autonomous Republic of Cochinchina) noted how "rumors had been maliciously spread in the city [of Saigon], alluding to massacres in France of Indochinese students or the possible poisoning of the public fountains."[77] Whatever the cause, the result was horrific. Eyewitnesses testified that on September 25, bands of Vietnamese engaged in a methodical, house-by-house search for French and Eurasians, many of whom were taken away to be killed, violated, or mutilated in some way.[78] Phạm Duy had some sobering reflections on this event:

...the saddest was the attack on the Cité Hérault in the Tân Định neighborhood, where approximately two hundred Frenchmen were killed and another one hundred arrested and taken away. At that time I was living in Tân Định, so I witnessed this massacre from beginning to end. For the first time in my life,

---

[75] ANOM. HCI. SPCE 33. "Déposition du 7 Février 1946 de TCHUONG DUC."
[76] Lucien Félixine, *L'Indochine livrée aux bourreaux* (Paris: Nouvelles Éditions Latines, 1959), 75–76.
[77] ANOM. HCI. SPCE 96. Service de la Sûreté Fédérale de l'Indochine. Speech of Dr. Thinh, in *Le Populaire* (Saigon), September 25, 1946.
[78] French collected testimonies from survivors of this tragedy. See Marcel Augoyard, "Le massacre de la cité Hérault." Saigon, January 10, 1946. Held by the Service Historique de la Défense. Thanks to Chris Goscha for forwarding me this material.

I saw people kill others. I saw people who had been as gentle as my neighbors in the past, so how is it that they could dismember and drink the blood of their enemies so easily? I realized a truth: one only has to nurture resentment a great deal for people to be brave enough to kill without pity. And the resentment of a colonized people towards the French penetrated deeply into the hearts of the Vietnamese over eighty years. Afterwards, I saw individuals like Bửu Dương, in charge of the secret police in Tân Bình, boast of having disemboweled people, tied them at the neck, and thrown into the river [cho mò tôm] those that he thought were traitors.

From these days, terrorism in our country began.[79]

The remaining French and Eurasian inhabitants were rescued when a Cambodian servant managed to smuggle out a message to the English forces alerting them that massacres were taking place.[80] All in all, at least 135 French citizens were kidnapped or disappeared on September 24 and 25 in Saigon and Cholon.[81]

As the Cité Hérault case suggests, those perceived to be foreigners, such as Eurasians, Indians, and Chinese, often came under suspicion. For one, Indians, Arabs, Malays, and Pathans served on the Saigon police force.[82] Bayly and Harper note that "half a dozen local Indians were murdered during the September outbreak and nearly seventy were kidnapped by militants."[83] A Vietnamese woman reported that her Bengali husband, a watchman, had been abducted that night and was in a makeshift Việt Minh prison.[84] The Chinese Chamber of Commerce of Nam Kỳ, in addition to noting extensive property losses, stated that from September 23 to November 4 1945, eighty-one Chinese were killed by both French and Vietnamese.[85] Ngô Vân mentions that a black acquaintance from Antilles living with his Vietnamese wife in Thủ Đức (adjoining Saigon) was taken away by the Việt Minh and killed.

---

[79] Phạm Duy, Hồi ký, Book 2, Chapter 3. The phrase "mò tôm" [catching the shrimp??] appears to refer to the practice of killing people, tying them together, and throwing them in the river. https://phamduy.com/vi/van-nghien-cuu/hoi-ky-2/5598-chuong-3 (accessed June 15, 2020).

[80] Augoyard, "Le msssacre de la cité Hérault," 7.

[81] ANOM. HCI. SPCE 33. Liste chronologique des Français disparus ou enlevés par les rebelles Viet Minh de Septembre 1945 à Fevrier 1949.

[82] In 1952, the 4,800 police employees included 3,300 Vietnamese, 1,100 Cambodians, Malays, Arabs, and Pathans, and 440 French, including those from French overseas territories abroad. See ANOM. HCI SPCE 68. Dossier F.III.6.13 "La tâche ingrate et périleuse de la police préfectorale gardienne de Saigon-Cholon," Journal d'Extrême-Orient, May 21, 1952, p. 1.

[83] Christopher Bayly and Tim Harper, Forgotten Wars: Freedom and Revolution in Southeast Asia (Cambridge: Harvard University Press, 2007), 156.

[84] ANOM. HCI. SPCE 33. Dosier "1945." Bulletin de renseignements. Activités annamites (No. 9). 8.12.45.

[85] Cited in Shiu Wentang, "A Preliminary Inquiry into the Wartime Material Losses of Chinese in Vietnam, 1941–1947," Chinese Southern Diaspora Studies, Vol. 4, 2010, 123.

To this ethnic violence was added destruction. Gaultier notes after one night, "huge fires ravaged the port"; another night, "the ruins of the [central] market were in flames; the Michelin and Labbé warehouses, as well as the Customs building, burned, giving off an intense red smoke." Yet a different night, speaking of attacks to the north of the city, he wrote of "large fires whose glow illuminated to immense heights fantastic clouds." Vietnamese fled the city in great number; leaving behind many dead: Gaultier reports, again, that "700 bodies were collected at the main Saigon market"[86] – a number that seems to be a gross exaggeration.

Faced with heightened passions and fragmented control, the Việt Minh stoked passions further, but then seemed surprised by the results. If violence against outsiders could unite Vietnamese against a common enemy, violence against Vietnamese split the Việt Minh. The search for "traitors" within, building for months, spiraled out of control. On September 29, 1945, the Cứu Quốc newspaper exhorted the populace: "We call upon our compatriots to denounce dangerous traitors."[87] Given such incitement in an already charged environment, it is no surprise that the "traitors" were found everywhere. A 1948 work notes that "in Saigon, Vietnamese traitors were often arrested who were selling Japanese weapons to the French."[88] (Left unstated is why the French would buy guns that they could take for free.) Such arrests aside, the Việt Minh imprisoned, or tried to imprison, numerous perceived threats to its rule. In October 1945, French forces "liberated" the Saigon central prison. Jean Leroy, a Eurasian fighting with the French forces, freed from jail Nguyễn Văn Tâm, a brutal anti-communist who would go on to become one of the first presidents of the State of Vietnam.[89]

Nguyễn Việt justifies the summary justice meted out in the streets of Saigon in September 1945:

In the streets of Saigon, a large number of active Vietnamese traitors were arrested by youths. In order to get rid of reactionary traitors, The People's Committee of the South issued the order to punish them by shooting them on the spot; because of that, the French faced many difficulties in finding individuals who would collaborate with them.[90]

Who, exactly, were these perceived "traitors"? Some had undoubtedly collaborated with the Japanese or French. Others had not. Stalinists targeted Trotskyists, even those who collaborated with Việt Minh leaders

[86] Gaultier, Prisons, 289, 293, 294, 295.
[87] Cứu Quốc newspaper, quoted in Nam Bộ và Nam Phần Trung Bộ (1957), 32.
[88] Ngô Hà, Cách mạng tháng tám (Bangkok: Tủ Sách Tin Việt Nam, [1948]), 19. Parts of this book were written in 1947.
[89] Jean Leroy, Fils de la rizière (Paris: R. Laffont, 1977), 85.
[90] Nguyễn Việt, Nam Bộ và Nam phần Trung Bộ, 33.

in the uprisings. The killing of Lê Văn Vững on September 22, earlier noted, was but one example. A few days later, the teacher Nguyễn Thi Lợi, in charge of the Trotskyist "Struggle" group's newspaper, was assassinated.[91] Tạ Thu Thâu, the well-known southern Trotskyist activist, was arrested in Quảng Ngãi city in August 1945, detained in Xuân Phổ, a village nearby, and executed in December.[92] Trần Văn Thạch and Phan Văn Hùm, well known as Trotskyist journalists and public figures, were executed in October 1945; so were the Trotskyists Phan Văn Chánh, Huỳnh Văn Phương, Hồ Vĩnh Ký, and his wife Nguyễn Thị Sương. Showing how far the "revolution" had veered off course, one of these individuals (Phan Văn Hùm) had been elected as an alternate to the People's Committee of Nam Bộ on September 7,[93] and three of these individuals had served on the Foreign Affairs Committee of the Provisional Government of Nam Bộ. And Nguyễn Thị Sương? Phạm Ngọc Thạch had appointed her to lead the women's branch of the Vanguard Youth, perhaps the major mass organization taking part in the August General Uprising. But we should not jump to conclusions that every killing of a Trotskyist was by Stalinists: Hồ Vĩnh Ký and his spouse may have been killed for their wealth.[94]

To these killings we can add many others. Bùi Quang Chiêu, a longtime southern politician, collaborator with the French, and major landlord, was assassinated in late September.[95] Việt Minh assassins targeted politicians associated with the National United Front [Mặt trận Quốc gia Thống Nhứt], a key rival to the Việt Minh before the August General Uprising. They would also wipe out the nationalist leaders of the minor and curious Vietnam National Independence Party [Việt Nam Quốc gia Độc Lập Đảng].[96] Its nationalist leaders – Hồ Văn Ngà, Dương Văn Giáo, and Nguyễn Văn Sâm – would be assassinated in 1946 and 1947.

This violence clues us in to an essential point: the August General Uprising had not led to a decisive victory that unified the Vietnamese.

[91] Trần Nguơn Phiêu, "Những nhân chứng cuối cùng," Đàn Chim Việt (October 6, 2011).
[92] I follow Professor Hoàng Ngọc Thành, "Những ngày cuối cùng của nhà ái quốc Tạ Thu Thâu tại Quảng Ngãi," in Nguyễn Văn Đính, Tạ Thu Thâu: Từ Quốc gia đến Quốc Tế ([Amarillo, TX]: Hải Mã, [2005?], 104, 109, Appendix I. Many thanks to Professor David MacKenzie for sending me this book. Compare Phương Lan, Nhà cách mạng Tạ Thu Thâu (Saigon: Khai Trí, [1972?]), 436–441.
[93] NAC. Carton 55. "Uỷ ban nhân dân Nam Bộ đã thành lập" [The Nam Bộ People's Committee has been formed]. Thời báo (Phnom Penh), September 13, 1945.
[94] On their death, see Nguyễn Kỳ Nam, Hồi ký, 2, 302–304.
[95] Bùi Quang Chiêu, a French citizen and reformist, was most likely imprisoned then killed at the end of September or October 1945. See the folders on him in ANOM. Indochine. SPCE. Carton 380.
[96] Marr, Vietnam 1945, 110–112, 381.

Instead, Vietnamese were fracturing, and no one was working to tamp down emotions. Why? One answer is suggested by a Party newspaper from the end of September 1945. Appalled at collaboration with dubious elements, a hardliner thundered:

We cannot fail to call attention to the softness of heart of a number of Việt Minh cadres. They misunderstood the Front's policy. They endorsed the policy of "forgiving" [xi xoa] the enormous crimes of the Việt traitors who had betrayed their nation as well as those of the professional agitators [khieu khich]. They assumed that in doing so [we] would "enlarge the Front," "avoid sectarianism," "unify the people," "recruit talented men" [and] "settle down our domestic affairs in order to confront the foreigners."

Liberation Flag [Cờ Giải Phóng] rebuked those who collaborated with elements such as the Đại Việt Party or the Trotskyists. It advocated one solution to dealing with these "criminals": "we must raise our arms as high as possible in order to strike down the leading Việt traitors with all our strength, and draw their followers to the revolutionary side."[97] In other words: kill traitors, but welcome their followers.

Hardline leaders, displeased with the unfolding of the revolution, went after their rivals. Hoàng Quốc Việt, the representative of the Party Central Committee in the South, took Trần Văn Giàu, the leader of the August uprisings, to task in September. By mid-September, he was trying to rein in Giàu. In Giàu's words, he stated: "Do not issue, on your own whim, the call for resistance. Wait for the directive of President Hồ Chí Minh. Do not be hot-headed, wait for the directive of the Party Central Committee."

Trần Văn Giàu ignored the advice. He launched a call on September 23 for armed resistance to the French before hearing from Hồ Chí Minh or the central committee. In Giàu's words, "Việt condemned me for lacking discipline and being anarchistic." Indeed, Giàu and Việt came to logger-heads on a series of issues. Việt forced the dissolution of the Vanguard Youth, previously so important in the uprising, perhaps because the organization had developed outside of central Party control. He disagreed with Giàu on whether or not Trotskyists should be allowed to have a role in the revolution, and on how to deal with the Hòa Hảo. "One person had to go. The person who had to go at that time was me (and Phạm Ngọc Thạch), as Thạch had also resisted Việt over the dissolution of the Vanguard Youth and the issue of issuing a call for armed resistance."[98] Trần Văn Giàu, forced out of his leadership role, was sent packing to the

---

[97] Cờ Giải Phóng, September 30, 1945, quoted in Vu Ngu Chieu, 434–434. I have edited the translation slightly.
[98] Tran Van Giau Hồi ký, Chapter XVII.

north to meet with the Central Committee. Also forced out, for unclear reasons, was Kiều Đắc Thắng in the Eastern Zone. The Party recalled Thắng to the north, replaced by Nguyễn Bình, who would soon become the best-known southern general.[99]

By October, Saigon had radically changed. "Saigon was like a dead city," Nguyễn Việt observed, with only French and British soldiers and "traitors" on the streets. "The markets were deserted, workplaces bereft of workers."[100] When Thiếu Sơn came back to the city, it was as empty as a "desert," except for the Western and Gurkha soldiers.[101] For October 27, young Jacques Vautibault recorded:

Yesterday evening, the Gurkhas suffered two killed near their encampment. Today they retaliated – they encircled the neighborhood and set fire to it. In these thatched huts, the fire had its fun and so did the soldiers. The huts crackled, bamboo burst like firecrackers. It was very impressive. The neighborhood was mercilessly burned down by the soldiers. The natives living in the area fled with some belongings on their backs. Soldiers shot some individuals in front of the populace.[102]

The French journalist Henri Estirac, arriving in Saigon on November 2, 1945, was struck by the empty streets: "In Saigon, there are no Annamites: or, if they are there, we don't see them. Most of them, for safety, have followed the Viet Minh [out of the city]. Only the French, the Chinese, the freshly arrived English and some Americans remain." But if most Vietnamese had fled the city, Estirac noted that "planters and Europeans living near the city took refuge in Saigon."[103]

2.4 Conclusion

The Việt Minh attempt to seize power in the South in August 1945 marked a turning point: anti-French sentiment crystallized among broad groups of Vietnamese. The demonstrations and events in Saigon and the delta underlined that the populace overwhelmingly

---

[99] Vương Liêm, *Huỳnh Văn Một, người con trung dũng của Đức Hòa-Chợ Lớn* (Hanoi: Quân đội nhân dân, 2006), 129. Kiều Đắc Thắng, a controversial figure suspected in a variety of deaths, including that of the Trotskyist Phan Văn Hùm, was expelled from the Party, judged by a military tribunal, and executed in 1947. See Lê Hoàng, "Đại tướng Lê Đức Anh và những phiên tòa xét xử gián điệp," *Công lý* [Justice], April 13, 2012.

[100] Nguyễn Việt, *Nam Bộ và Nam phần Trung Bộ*, 45.

[101] Thiếu Sơn, *Nghệ thuật & nghệ sinh*, 449.

[102] Diary of Jacques de Vautibault, a soldier in Leclerc's Deuxième Division Blindée, the first French division to land in Saigon. See https://2db.forumactif.com/t3277-groupement-de-marche-en-indochine (accessed June 6, 2016).

[103] Henri Estirac, *Je reviens de l'Indochine*, 40, 39.

opposed the French return and supported independence. These groups, however, could not agree on a common vision of a nationalist revolution. Indeed, understanding this event only in terms of a unified "revolution" leads to an interpretive impasse. It makes more sense to think of this event as a series of parallel mobilizations of disparate groups that sometimes intersected, sometimes diverged, and sometimes devolved into chaos. It was a turning point that generated multiple visions of the future, some revolutionary, some not – visions that were set in motion in the years that followed. Seeing the events in such a way underlines what should be obvious: the South had its own particularities and divisions, ones that profoundly shaped the years from 1945 to 1954.

The absence of a common Vietnamese vision was linked to organizational rivalries. The lack of strong centralized control had significant consequences. Initially, the populace often used nonviolent approaches to achieve their goal. But along with a rational, disciplined approach to struggle came a very different kind of contestation. The emotions of the time sometimes got out of hand, and protest could devolve into rioting, mayhem, and indiscriminate violence. This should be no surprise: all major uprisings in history have been shaped by such turmoil.

I am loath to speculate unduly about the past. But in this particular case, there seems to be a marked shift in the anti-French Việt Minh between August and October 1945. In the first half of August, despite the rough and tumble of Saigon politics and clear rivalries and animosities, nationalists, communists, and Trotskyists could all reach across Party lines and tentatively collaborate in large and small ways. But I believe that this "Saigon" style of doing politics was an anathema to the Party Center in the North. Pushing aside Trần Văn Giàu and Phạm Ngọc Thạch, turning definitively on the Trotskyists and nationalists with whom they had collaborated, the ICP went after the leaders of potential rival parties in September and October 1945 with a vengeance. To triumph, the ICP believed that it first had to destroy its one-time allies. The beginnings of the war in the South, then, began amidst severe internal dissension, some of whose wounds have festered until the present.

Looking retrospectively, knowing the winners and losers in struggles, we can easily discern patterns to the past and structure our narratives accordingly. Our task here, however, is to "bracket" that retrospective knowledge as much as possible, and try, instead, to write history looking forward. We need to be attentive to both dissension welling up from below and that driven by major actors. Seen in such a light, what strikes the analyst is the significance of the radical social uncertainty defining Vietnamese worlds in 1945. World War II was over: but the future for the inhabitants of French Indochina was as uncertain after August 15, 1945 – the date of Japan's surrender – as it had been before. These issues would play themselves out in the countryside, only in deadlier form. To this topic we now turn.

3 Priming Upheavals in the Mekong Delta

Gazing at the people and the land, the heart aches.

Shedding the monk's robe, assuming the warrior's garb

Chasing invaders from the country,

The independence flag flies high.
    –Hòa Hảo Prophet Huỳnh Phú Sổ, "Shedding the Monk's Robe," 1946.

In August 1945, after the French and then Japanese states collapsed in the countryside, a space opened up for alternative groups to seize power. With the imminent arrival of French troops, many southerners, like Huỳnh Phú Sổ quoted above, shed one peacetime identity and adopted a new wartime one. In fact, almost all southerners opposed the French and supported the Việt Minh, a rickety coalition of rival forces that included religious groups, such as Catholics, Cao Đài, and Hòa Hảo Buddhists, as well as a variety of nationalists. By the end of 1947, however, this coalition was in tatters. Its leaders' attempt to unify the nationalist Resistance through force had backfired. Key rival groups, attacked by the Việt Minh, either joined forces with the French or staked out a grey zone between collaboration and resistance. Mekong Delta politics fractured along ethnic and political lines, leaving a legacy that shaped the South up to the final communist triumph in 1975 and beyond.

Why did this happen? Previous scholarship has relied on a mix of three arguments to explain what I call the "double fracture" of the Mekong Delta. It has underlined the hamfisted and failed attempts of the communists in the Việt Minh to squash potential allies, leading to resistance; it has pointed to the skill of anti-communist nationalists in playing off the French against their rivals; and it has shown how the French skillfully exploited ethnic and "nationalist" divisions in the South for their own ends.[1] These three arguments are implicitly instrumentalist: that is,

---

[1] See Jayne Werner, "The Cao Dai: Politics of a Vietnamese Syncretic Religious Movement" (PhD dissertation, Cornell University, 1976), especially p. 278.

different groups make conscious political and military decisions in a bid to either seize power, hold on to it, or ally with one side in a bid to defeat the other. There is little room for the role of contention from below as a driver of division in its own right. Furthermore, the story of Khmer-Vietnamese antagonisms, violence, and irredentism tends to get forgotten – or subsumed under this larger narrative of Vietnamese actions.

This chapter presents an alternative argument for what I call the "double fracture," one that builds on these earlier – and incomplete – contributions. It centers the argument on the transformative impact of a dynamic of violence on the delta. Violence hardened social and political cleavages, thus shaping contestation. Targeted and indiscriminate violence worsened antagonisms between rival groups in the delta, some of whom, in a bid for survival, turned to the French for help. Rivals did not simply use violence instrumentally to achieve political goals. On the contrary, a dynamic of violence created a pervasive sense of uncertainty that profoundly shaped daily life in the delta.

As has been noted in other contexts, collective violence – whether of riots or mass murder – does not come out of nowhere. It is "prepared" or "primed."[2] Chapter 2 showed the beginning of this process at work in Saigon. This chapter focuses on the "priming" phase in Mekong Delta, while Chapter 4 will examine the double fracture itself. Sometimes this violence and uncertainty was linked to "national"-level issues; much of the time, it welled up from below. This violence was not uniform in intent or in logic, which is why this chapter takes pains to distinguish between inter-Vietnamese fractures along political lines and Khmer-Vietnamese splits along ethnic lines.

The diverse patterning of violence in the Mekong Delta confirms the observation by Stathis Kalyvas: "a central feature of civil wars is the breakdown of the state monopoly of violence and its replacement by locally segmented monopolies of violence."[3] Discrete events, such as massacres, often initiated cascade effects, such as extensive migration, that undermined the resilience of the broader society. This radical uncertainty and attendant violence became a driver of social and political dynamics on its own terms.[4] To understand this eventual violent "double

---

[2] Paul Brass calls the first stage of an ethnic riot "preparation" or "rehearsal"; Alexander Hinton calls the run-up to the Khmer Rouge massacres and deaths "genocidal priming." See Paul Brass, *The Production of Hindu-Muslim Violence in Contemporary India* (Seattle: University of Washington Press, 2003), 15; Alexander Hinton, *Why Did They Kill? Cambodia in the Shadow of Genocide* (Berkeley: University of California Press, 2010), 29.

[3] Stathis Kalyvas, "Wanton and Senseless? The Logic of Massacres in Algeria," *Rationality and Society* 11(3) (1999), 259.

[4] On how violence generates or deepens political cleavages, see Kalyvas, *The Logic of Violence in Civil War* (Cambridge: Cambridge University Press, 2006), and

fracture," with splits along ethnic as well as political lines, we first sketch out the conditions and processes that allowed large-scale violence to break out, as well as the French, Vietnamese, and Khmer actors involved.

3.1 France's Challenge: Institutional Collapse and Reconstruction

As Janet Flanner wrote from Paris in January of 1945:

Parisians are colder than they have been any other winter of the war. They are the hungriest they have been since the Prussian siege of Paris [1870–71], when their grandparents ate mice. Because there is still a lack of coal to transport anything, even coal, the citizenry is still waiting, muffled to its ears, for its single sack per person due last August. Electricity has been ordered turned off all over France from morning till evening, except for an hour at noon.[5]

This was the France that, in eight months, would begin its attempted reconquest of Indochina. If liberation in 1944 eased the trauma of Germany's 1940 invasion, it did not change the fact that the war devastated France. Germany imprisoned a million and a half French soldiers in 1940. It sent many off to Germany to be exploited as forced labor; at the end of the war, two-thirds of them still remained in captivity.[6] More than two million French were driven from their homes.[7] France suffered steep material losses from war and occupation: two million buildings destroyed, most rail stock gone, industrial production at half the level of 1938, and a plunge in government revenue. War losses were "in constant francs, an amount three times greater than the total damage found after the First World War."[8] Approximately 400,000 French died in the conflict.[9]

And the French military? Speaking of the young soldiers who went off to war in Indochina, Laurent Beccaria has observed that:

Nothing, first of all, can be understood without reference to the shock of the 1940 defeat and the trauma it inflicted on youth aged fifteen to twenty, who saw crumble, in several days, the world of their parents, official and institutional

---

Daniel Branch, *Defeating Mau Mau, Creating Kenya: Counterinsurgency, Civil War, and Decolonization* (Cambridge: Cambridge University Press, 2009).
[5] Janet Flanner, January 17, 1945 entry, in *Paris Journal 1944–1965* (New York: Harcourt Brace Jovanovitch, 1977), 12.
[6] Pieter Lagrou, "Les guerres, les morts, et le deuil: bilan chiffré de la Seconde Guerre mondiale," in Stéphane Audoin-Rozeau, et al., *La violence de guerre 1914–1945* (Paris: Éditions complexe, 2002), 318.
[7] Lagrou, "Les guerres, les morts, et le deuil," 325.
[8] Olivier Feiertag, "Le nerf de l'après-guerre: le financement de la reconstruction entre l'Etat et le marché (1944–1947)," *Matériaux pour l'histoire de notre temps*, 39–40 (July–December 1995), 47.
[9] Pieter Lagrou, "Les guerres, les morts, et le deuil," 320.

France, with its prefects and local government, panicking, at the heart of the debacle. To be eighteen in 1940 was to feel like an orphan... Thousands of boys and girls stepped into life in the midst of a complete social breakdown, a collapse of the social order.[10]

World War II shattered the French armed forces. France's surrender to Germany in 1940 plunged the French military into its deepest crisis since 1870, when Prussia defeated it. It struggled to recover: the journalist de la Gorce noted the "extreme poverty" of the armed forces in 1944 and 1945.[11] As the war ended, the Allies abruptly cut off funding to French forces. In 1945, France was rebuilding its bifurcated military: a metropolitan force built to fight conventional war in Europe and a colonial force to suppress internal rebellions in the empire. World War II had added a new fracture: the military split into Resistance and Vichy wings. The war in Indochina transformed this model again, throwing together colonial and metropolitan, ex-Vichy and Resistance, into a new and unstable amalgam.

Weakness manifested itself not simply in terms of men and materiel, but in the command of the army itself, deeply marked by the after-effects of Vichy. The high command refused to draw on officers who had served in Indochina during World War II: it considered them Vichy collaborators. Those interned in German camps were shunted aside, as were many who had served in the Armée d'Afrique or under the Vichy regime of Maréchal Pétain. The military would eventually purge 131 generals. By 1948, 12,679 officers of all ranks had been dismissed or forced to retire, forcing the military to keep inept but politically safe officers.[12] These decisions shaped the Expeditionary Corps that landed in Indochina in 1945, an army that faced critical shortcomings in leadership, materiel, logistics, and training.[13]

Curiously, however, writers repeatedly emphasize the strengths of the French military. The historian Fredrik Logevall, echoing much of the scholarship, correctly notes that France was "prostrate" after its defeat in

---

[10] Laurent Beccaria, "Soldats perdus des guerres orphelines," *Vingtième Siècle. Revue d'histoire*, 22 (April–June 1989), 103.

[11] Paul-Marie de la Gorce, *La République et son armée* (Paris: Fayard, 1963), 435.

[12] Bodin, *La France et ses soldats, Indochine,1945–1954* (Paris: L'Harmattan, 1996), 26–7. Cf. a 1950 study, stating that 985 active-duty officers, 1,845 reserve officers, and 818 non-commissioned officers had been punished during purges, and that 7,833 officers [*cadres*] had been affected in some way. See Julie Le Gac, *Vaincre sans gloire: le Corps Expéditionnaire français en Italie (novembre 1942-juillet 1944)* (Paris: Les Belles Lettres, 2014), 175. General de Lattre de Tassigny pushed hard to get rid of particularly incompetent officers. See SHD. 10 H 4656. Dossier "1810." J. De Lattre. "DECISION." Saigon, November 13, 1951.

[13] On France's attempt to wage war in Indochina on the cheap, see Hugues Tertrais, *Le piastre et le fusil* (Paris: Comité pour l'histoire économique et financière de la France, 2002), Chapter 1.

1940 and "humiliated" in 1945 by Japan at a time when "the European imperial system was crumbling" – but then, one page later, referring to the French military in Indochina, states that "The French had a massive superiority in weapons and could take and hold any area they really wanted."[14] As the early years of the war would show again and again, this was not true.

Vietnamese recognized French challenges at the same time they faced their own. As one Vietnamese wrote, "many cadres optimistically believed that 'because the French were weak, they had to negotiate. With the situation in France, and their weak forces... we would only have to resist for several months.'"[15] A recent Vietnamese history notes that despite its strengths, "the enemy also had its weaknesses. From the start it lacked enough troops, and aid from France was limited. Therefore, it could only seize the cities and towns and could not deploy throughout the rural areas."[16]

So who served in these French forces? Recruits would eventually come from at least sixty territories, colonies, and countries in Asia, Europe, Africa, and the rest of the globe. As Michel Bodin notes, "from September 1945 to the cease-fire of July 1954, 488,560 men landed in Indochina (233,467 French, 72,833 Legionnaires, 122,920 North Africans, and 60,340 Africans)."[17] From January 1950 on, French nationals, including the PFAT (Personnel Féminin de l'Armée de Terre; female non-combatant auxiliaries), always formed a minority of all regular soldiers.

As the table above indicates, France sent no Africans and North Africans to Indochina before 1947. At first, it recruited only French and other Europeans. Few heeded the call: "After 1945, recruitment took place in a situation of continuous crisis."[18] In January 1946, over 67,000 soldiers were concentrated in the south. By January 1947, this number had dipped by nearly 5,000, as soldiers were sent north. Volunteers were of poor quality. Recruits were less schooled than the average Frenchman: only one in seventeen had a high school diploma. Bodin notes a category of "compelled volunteers," such as juvenile delinquents who had their records erased if they joined, or minor Nazi collaborators who could "redeem themselves by joining special units."[19]

---

[14] Fredrik Logevall, *Embers of War: The Fall of an Empire and the Making of America's Vietnam* (New York: Random House. 2014), xvi, xvii.

[15] Nguyễn Việt, *Nam Bộ và Nam phần Trung Bộ* 39, quoting from a 1949 Resistance newspaper.

[16] Hội Đồng Chỉ Đạo, *Lịch Sử Nam Bộ Kháng Chiến*, Vol. 1: 1945–54 (Hanoi: Chính trị quốc gia, 2010), 301.

[17] Bodin, *La France et ses soldats*, 7.   [18] Bodin, *La France et ses soldats*, 26.

[19] Michel Bodin, "Le combattant français du Corps Expéditionnaire en Extrême-Orient, 1945–1954," *Guerres mondiales et conflits contemporains* 168 (October 1992), 180.

Table 3.1 *National origin of French regular soldiers*

Year	French	Foreign Legion	North African	African	PFAT	Total
January 1946	59,985	7, 121				67,106
January 1947	51, 175	11,131				62,306
January 1948	51,530	12,259	10,787	2,260	713	77,549
January 1949	43,633	11,741	13,591	5, 813	757	75,535
January 1950	46, 767	17,868	25, 478	12, 015	868	102,996
January 1951	48, 145	16, 664	22,892	13,281	1,018	102,000
January 1952	56,917	19,893	32, 861	17,445	1,294	128,410
January 1953	56,158	19, 224	29,553	17,072	1,629	123,636
January 1954	53,109	18,224	36,720	19,731	2,080	129, 864

Source: CHETOM (France). 15H113. "Forces Françaises Terrestres en Extrême Orient, 1946–1953." Table in Sarah Zimmerman, "Living Beyond Boundaries: West African Servicemen in French Colonial Conflicts, 1908–1962," (Dissertation, University of California at Berkeley, 2011), 101.

France was forced to turn to other Europeans. From 1944 to 1947, blatantly violating the 1929 Geneva Convention on prisoners of war,[20] the French military "recruited" Axis prisoners. In March 1944, the Legion began recruiting Italian prisoners of war in North Africa. Later that year, it began enlisting Austrian POWs, then finally, in 1945, German POWs.[21] Eckard Michels estimates that 3,000 to 5,000 German POWs joined the French Foreign Legion in 1945 and 1946.[22] A good number of recruits came from other countries on the Axis side, such as Hungary.

Recruitment problems aside, the French Expeditionary Corps was initially disorganized, unprepared, undisciplined, and too small. The first French Commissioner of Cochinchina, Colonel Cédille, arrived in Cochinchina in September 1945 with almost no staff. He was forced to scrounge for pens, paper, and desks.[23] General Leclerc, named commander of the French Expeditionary Forces in Indochina by de Gaulle,

[20] See the Convention relative to the Treatment of Prisoners of War, Geneva, July 27, 1929, https://ihl-databases.icrc.org/applic/ihl/ihl.nsf/Article.xsp?action=openDocument&doc umentId=8B7B7425B25A2A4CC12563CD00518F29 (accessed January 2, 2018).
[21] Eckard Michels, "L'Allemagne et la Légion Étrangère" [Germany and the Foreign Legion] *Cahiers du CEHD* 18 (2002), 158–159. Thanks for Professor Michels for sending me his essay.
[22] Eckard Michels, personal communication, June 28, 2013.
[23] Krull, "Dairy [*sic*] of Saigon, Following the Allied Occupation in September 1945." Folder 07, Box 02, Douglas Pike Collection, The Vietnam Center and Archive, Texas Tech University www.vietnam.ttu.edu/virtualarchive/items.php?item=2410207001 (accessed August 13, 2020).

did not arrive in Saigon until October 5 – and on a British ship.[24] He also had to "make do." As Delmas commented, "Improvisation: we know the lack of intellectual preparation with which Leclerc, like his principal collaborators, tackled the Indochinese problem."[25] Leclerc commanded few troops: "the weakness of French power was symbolized by the fact that when he drove from the airport to the centre of the city, the route was lined with Japanese and Gurkha troops, acting as guards in both the ceremonial and practical sense."[26] (The 70,000 Japanese troops still in the south, some pressed into service by the British, far outnumbered the new British and French forces.) Indeed, after Japan's surrender, Japanese troops were asked to carry out logistical tasks and wage combat in the Mekong Delta.[27] France was fashioning its approach to Indochina on the fly.

The United States appears to have initially refused to arm French troops destined for Indochina. Nonetheless, the entrepreneurial French travelled to Manila, Bangkok, and other parts of Asia awash in surplus war materiel to snap up landing craft, jeeps, guns, ammunition, and even British Pacific Compo and American K-Rations.[28] The British, sympathetic to the French colonial cause, supplied French forces with food, fuel, and even munitions until June 1946.[29] The French also requisitioned local supplies. Yannick Guiberteau, for example, commanded a river gunboat in 1945 and 1946 that had been converted from a Compagnie Gressier rice barge.[30] But French entrepreneurship and "making do" had its limits. In 1947, the military still had a glaring lack of radio receivers, vehicles, and tires for vehicles. And, "while 3,682 vehicles had been requested from the Metropole, only 210 had been received; as for tires, of the 76,639 requested, 10,843 had arrived." Lacking spare parts, some combat vehicles were useless; new trucks were placed on blocks because they lacked tires.[31]

---

[24] Jean Lacouture, "Pourquoi l'espoir? Pourquoi l'échec?" in Fondation Maréchal Leclerc de Hautecloque, *Leclerc et l'Indochine 1945–1947: Quand se noua le destin d'un empire* (Paris: Albin Michel, 1992), 261–262.

[25] General Jean Delmas, "Les moyens militaires," in Fondation Maréchal Leclerc de Hautecloque, *Leclerc et l'Indochine 1945–1947*, 94.

[26] Peter Denis, *Troubled Days of Peace: Mountbatten and South East Asia Command, 1945–46* (Manchester: Manchester University Press, 1987), 146.

[27] Between August 15 and December 4, 1945, 109 Japanese soldiers died in southern Vietnam. Masaya Shiraishi, "Présences japonaises," in Fondation Maréchal Leclerc de Hautecloque, *Leclerc et l'Indochine*, 45.

[28] See, e.g., Yannick Guiberteau, *La Dévastation cuirassé de rivière* (Paris: Albin Michel, 1984), 311.

[29] Delmas, "Les moyens militaires," 99.   [30] Guiberteau, *La Dévastation*, 341.

[31] Gilbert Bodinier, *La Guerre d'Indochine 1945–1954: Textes et documents.* Vol. 2: *Indochine 1947: règlement politique ou solution militaire?* (Vincennes: SHAT, 1989), 44–45, 49, 37.

Poor organization and training worsened the French lack of materiel and personnel. Initially, France sent experienced units to Indochina, ones that had taken part in the liberation of France. After them, however, the French military was woefully unprepared for the war it would face. Adjutant Henri Meysonnet, whose troopship left for Indochina on October 12, 1945, noted that "it was only right before our departure [from France] that we came across scraps of information on the Viet Minh."[32] Soldiers came from diverse military backgrounds, ranging from Resistance guerrillas to regular Army soldiers who had fought in Italy. To Roger Delpey, who arrived in Cochinchina at the beginning of 1947, the slapdash training of his own "hastily assembled"[33] battalion beggared belief:

Six days were devoted to the training of this "battailon de marche" for Indochina. It was formed from both enlistees and re-enlisted, from the Resistance, the 1st Army, and the former French Expeditionary Corps in Italy. They came from regiments and battalions stationed in every province of France... How could anyone seriously believe that six days would be sufficient to set up a unit of several hundred men that had to be equipped and armed? [The unit contained] hundreds of men who held different, if not opposed, conceptions of war.[34]

This military began to transform itself in 1947, when the first Africans and North Africans arrived in Vietnam. "Reinforcements have arrived in Saigon. Others will be coming soon," Lâm Lê Trình wrote to an acquaintance in Paris in March 1947. "Saigon is becoming a military city. On the streets – Bonard, Charner – you see spahis, Moroccans, Arabs, Legionnaires, everything. A colorful mob, smelling of gunpowder and war."[35]

Looking at the war as a whole, three broad categories of soldiers stood out. French nationals – overwhelmingly volunteers – made up nearly half of all regular soldiers and officers. The second major source of recruits, almost 73,000, streamed into the French Foreign Legion from countries once under Axis rule, such as Germany, Hungary, and Ukraine. More than 40 percent of Legionnaires in French Indochina were ethnic Germans. Of these Germans, 8 percent had served in the Waffen-SS.[36] A small number of Legionnaires had fled the Nazis, such as Rudolf

---

[32] Henri Meysonnet and Bernard Meysonnet, ed., "Indochine 1945–1947," Unpublished manuscript, [2011?], 11.

[33] Roger Delpey, Soldats de la boue (Paris: Maison des Écrivains, 1949), 37.

[34] Ibid., 49.

[35] ANOM. HCI CP 107. [Letter from Lam Le Trinh, Saigon, to Lam Trong Thuc, Paris. 7 March 1947.]

[36] Pierre Thoumelin, L'ennemi utile; des vétérans de la Wehrmacht et de la Waffen-SS dans les rangs de la Légion étrangère en Indochine ([Giel-Courteilles]: Schneider, 2013), 79; 96–99. Thoumelin sampled 390 German military archive files cross-checked with French military records.

Schröder, a former sociology student from Cologne, Germany.[37] Other young Europeans who had not fought in World War II also volunteered for the Legion. In 1953, for example, a Swiss diplomat estimated that 600 Swiss had served in Indochina after 1945.[38]

The third and largest stream of non-French manpower came from the colonial global south: the African, Maghreb, and Asian possessions of France. Africans and North Africans only began arriving in April 1947.[39] From this point onwards, their numbers grew inexorably. They hailed from places like Morocco, Algeria, Guinea, and Senegal. Their motivations for joining the French military varied. After interviewing African veterans, Yao Kouassi concluded that for the roughly 30% who volunteered, material advantages, such as ability to support family and save money, were key. Employment in the army was seen as a "springboard" to post-army employment, as the colonial state reserved jobs for army veterans.[40] Some soldiers expressed pride in fighting for France. Ahmadou Kourouma, a Senegalese who left for Indochina in 1952, stated: "I am a soldier and I served the France that colonized us... I felt that I had to fight on the side of France."[41] A surprising number of the officers would later play prominent military and political roles in Africa and the Maghreb.

In southern Vietnam, if these regular troops played a critical role for the French, their numbers were dwarfed by those of Vietnamese and Cambodians. By 1954, according to Vietnamese sources, the total number of soldiers on the French side in Vietnam, Laos, and Cambodia – a number that included French and "Indochinese" regular armed forces as well as "supplétif" or paramilitary forces – had reached 445,000. Thirty-three percent of these, or 146,000, were European or African. The other 299,000 came from Vietnam, Laos, or Cambodia.[42] Of the estimated 112,032 who died on the French side, only 18,015, or 16%,

---

[37] Heinz Schütte, "Les Doktors germaniques dans le Viet Minh," *Aséanie* 15 (2005): 61–85.
[38] Schweizerisches Bundesarchiv (Bern). E-2800 1967/59/41. Conseil national. "Réponse aux interpellations Boner du 23 mars 1953 et Schütz du 24 mars 1953 concernant la Légion étrangère. September 16, 1953," https://dodis.ch/10697 (accessed on October 27, 2013).
[39] Michel Bodin, *Les Africains dans la guerre d'Indochine* (Paris: Harmattan, 2008), 16, 19.
[40] Yao Kouassi, "La participation militaire de l'Afrique noire à la guerre d'Indochine (1947–1955)" (Doctoral thesis, Pantheon-Sorbonne University, 1986), 37, 41.
[41] Issa Sembène oral interview, February 1, 1991, quoted in Aissatou Diagne, "Le Sénégal et la guerre d'Indochine," 40.
[42] See Võ Nguyên Giáp, *Điện Biên Phủ, điểm hẹn lịch sử: hồi ức* (Hanoi: Quân đội nhân dân, 2001), 14. Jacques Dinfreville, *L'opération Indochine* (Paris: Éditions Internationales, 1953), states that there were 525,000 regular and irregular soldiers in all of Indochina in 1953.

were French nationals.[43] The "face of battle" was overwhelmingly non-white.

3.2 The Việt Minh: Organizing the Disorganized, Hunting Down Enemies

Facing the French was the Việt Minh, struggling to grow in a time of state collapse and social upheaval. When the Việt Minh issued a call for non-cooperation, including a food blockade of Saigon,[44] city inhabitants fled for the countryside by the thousands. Never again would Saigon, and its sister city of Cholon, have populations so small. Many Saigon inhabitants seem to have fled willingly. Thiếu Sơn, a socialist and an avid supporter of the Resistance, nonetheless admitted: "To tell the truth, I only evacuated because I feared being seen as a traitor [Việt gian] or being punished like many other traitors."[45] Like tens of thousands of others, he fled to a countryside almost empty of French citizens.

When urban Vietnamese flowed into the countryside from September 1945 onwards, they entered a realm in which the state and even village government had collapsed. In late September or early October of 1945, Nguyễn Hiến Lê fled from Saigon to a village in Long Xuyên province. "The atmosphere of Tân Thạnh village had markedly changed. Only the young, most from farming families, were found on the roads. Few village notables and landlords remained. Fewer motorized boats were going back and forth, and absolutely no ghe hầu or motorized boats."[46]

As the state collapsed, a climate of fear, suspicion, and uncertainty gripped the delta. New groups, like the Việt Minh, tried to fill the breach.

---

[43] No consensus exists over the number of war dead on the French side. I rely on Michel Bodin's figures, discussed in Christopher Goscha, "Casualties," *Historical Dictionary of the Indochina War* (Copenhagen and Honolulu: NIAS/Hawaii, 2011), https://indochine .uqam.ca/en/historical-dictionary/223-casualties-indochina-war.html (accessed April 6, 2018). See also the French Ministry of Defense database of "Morts pour la France" during the Indochina War (1945–1954), available on the site "Mémoire des Hommes," www.memoiredeshommes.sga.defense.gouv.fr. This resource, based on individual records of all dead, lists every person who was given the designation "Died for France" ("*Mort pour la France*") during the war. It includes foreign soldiers who directly served under French command, but does not include those in irregular militias or in the armed forces of the Associated States of Laos, Cambodia, and Vietnam. As of June 27, 2017, this database lists 15,701 French nationals who served in the armed forces and died in the war. This is still about 2,300 short of what Bodin estimates.
[44] Nguyễn Việt, *Nam Bộ và Nam phần Trung Bộ*, 40–41, 46.
[45] Thiếu Sơn, "Nhớ Vũ Tùng," *Nghệ Thuật và nhân sinh* (Hanoi: Văn Hóa thông tin Hà Nội, 2000), 462.
[46] Nguyễn Hiến Lê, *Hồi ký* (Ho Chi Minh City: Văn Học, 2006), 332–333.

Armed gangs roamed the countryside, including robbers, "knives for hire," and underworld figures. The communist Trần Văn Trà noted the challenge that this posed in the fall of 1945:

many truly wanted to defend the revolution, but some of them wanted to take advantage of the general disorder of the time for their personal gain, to increase their status, take power, or become 'emperors' and 'generals.' Because of this, in and around Saigon and to the Southeast sprouted up many military units [bộ đội] with contradictory aims and under no unified command, no one serving anyone else, all while fighting or stealing weapons from each other.[47]

In this chaos, fear manifested itself in "banal" and even darkly amusing ways. When an illiterate peasant girl with the Vanguard Youth stopped Nguyễn Hiến Lê in Đức Hòa, she opened the books he was carrying:

–"So what are these books you are carrying?"
   I replied:
   –"These are my books on irrigation."
   –"Western books?"
   –"Yes."
   –"So you have Western books? Follow me to the People's Committee."

A member of the People's Committee then told Lê to get rid of any object with the colors of the French flag, as it could be a coded signal to the enemy.[48] This reaction was not isolated: the Việt Minh accused a family of refugees outside of Hóc Môn of being reactionaries who should be killed, all because one person was carrying pencils and a towel in the three colors of the French flag.[49]

As insecurity reigned, trust eroded, and suspicion of others grew, a brutal struggle played out. French memoirs from this period note bodies floating down Mekong Delta rivers and heads impaled on bamboo sticks. At the very end of October 1945, Jean Leroy, leading a French military unit, noticed that "in a canal, mutilated corpses were floating; we found others that had been hastily buried in a common grave: these were local officials and Annamite notables that the Việt Minh had massacred after torturing them."[50] Crossing the Plain of Reeds in October 1945, the Trotskyist Ngô Văn caught sight of "fresh mounds of earth marking graves, some listing the names of the slaughtered persons," and remarked on "the foul odor of the innumerable corpses floating on the current and

---

[47] Trần Văn Trà, "Chiến tranh nhân dân khởi đầu từ Nam Bộ nhu thế" [How did people's war break out in the South?] in *Nam Bộ thành đồng Tổ Quốc* (Hanoi: Chính trị Quốc gia, 1999), 34; Đảng Ủy Bộ Chỉ Huy Quân Sự Tỉnh Vĩnh Long, *Lực lượng vũ trang tỉnh Vĩnh Long 30 năm kháng chiến (1945–1975)* (Hanoi: Quân Đội Nhân Dân, 1999), Vol. 1, 55.
[48] Nguyễn Hiến Lê, *Hồi Ký*, 326–7.
[49] *Hồi ký cuộc đời Quả phụ Mục sư Triệu Nguơn Hên* (s.l. [Vietnam?], s.n., 2007), 15.
[50] Jean Leroy, *Fils de la rizière* (Paris: R. Laffont, 1977), 89.

edging along the riverbanks – some with no faces, some tied up. Who were they? Where had they come from? Who had killed them?" At one point, his group "passed through a village just after the French had been there. Soldiers had lined up all the villagers in squatting positions on the edge of a canal, then machine-gunned them all."[51] On November 8, 1945, cruising up the Vaico river toward Tây Ninh, Henri Meysonnet noticed, two or three times, "swollen corpses floating on the river. Some had their hands tied behind their backs."[52] On December 29, 1945, after his troop ship had tied up at the Saigon port, Henry-Jean Loustau noticed bodies floating down the river. Laborers at the docks "confirmed that they were victims from a Catholic mission located upstream that had been attacked some days before our arrival."[53]

The French contributed amply to this cycle of violence. A few examples will suffice. On November 13, 1945, Jacques de Vautibault blithely noted in his diary: "The patrol took some Viet Minh prisoners and to make them talk, all means have to be used. We shot several." Three days later, near Tây Ninh, he commented that another platoon in his regiment "is frequently taking prisoners who talk after mild tortures [petits supplices] and who then end up either dead or as informants, as they denounce rather easily their family and friends."[54] World War II in Europe, and perhaps traditional French military practices in colonies, shaped French abuses in the Second Indochina War. Henry Ainley, who served in the Foreign Legion in Cochinchina from 1951 to 1953, was scathing:

The next two years were to confirm what I had sensed the first day. Torture and brutality were routine matters in the questioning of suspects, and frequently I was obliged to be an unwilling and disgusted witness, powerless to intervene. Unfortunately, brutality and bestiality were not exclusively reserved for official suspects. Rape, beating, burning, torturing of entirely harmless peasants and villagers were of common occurrence in the course of punitive patrols and operations by French troops, throughout the length and breadth of Indochina; the same measures evidently being applied to bona fide Vietminh as well. Nor were these measures exclusively applied by the men; officers and NCOs assumed an active and frequently dominating role.[55]

[51] See Ngô Văn, "In the Crossfire: Adventures of a Vietnamese Revolutionary," Chapter 7, www.bopsecrets.orgvietnam07.crossfire.htm (accessed January 26, 2012).
[52] Henri Meysonnet, "Indochine 1945–1947," typescript (received from son of author January 3, 2011), 33. The Vaico is now known as the Vàm Cỏ.
[53] Loustau, Les deux bataillons, 59.
[54] Online at https://2db.forumactif.com/t3277-groupement-de-marche-en-indochine (accessed June 6, 2016).
[55] Henry Ainley, In Order to Die (London: Burke, 1955), 29–30. More research is needed on the French use of rape.

Writing from Trảng Bàng, Tây Ninh province in 1946, Trần Văn Phước lamented how Vietnamese were under attack by all sides:

We have known all sorts of misery and still live completely terrorized, first, by bands of pirates who run rampant at night and, second, by the Partisans (former soldiers of Viet Nam who joined the French troops) who themselves terrorize by day; they abduct persons for ransom, engage in searches and seize anything they want, all while threatening the population... Let us not speak of the other abuses that must be endured, like imprisonment and torture... These things are happening in the shadows, the French GOVERNMENT completely ignores them. We live in a state of constant terror.[56]

What could the Việt Minh do? Communists did not dominate the politics of the South, unlike in the North and Center of the country. Indeed, in the western Mekong Delta, communists could only rely on 120 Party members in April 1945.[57] In Sóc Trăng province in 1945, the number of party cadres "could be counted on one's fingertips."[58] As the communist Nguyễn Thanh Sơn observed:

Western Nam Bộ was a remote area, lacking direct leadership of the Party Central Committee or the Regional Committee of Nam Bộ.... The guide for every thought, every action was mainly the most recent resolutions of the Party Central Committee or the Việt Minh program. Given the changing situation, they often were compelled to act independently.[59]

Many seasoned cadres languished on Côn Đảo, the prison island off the southeast coast. Not until September 15 did the new provisional government send a boat out to Côn Đảo to free the prisoners. The liberated included members of the Vietnamese Nationalist Party (*Việt Nam Quốc Dân Đảng*), communists, followers of the Cao Đài religion, and Khmer. On arriving in Sóc Trăng, where a branch of the Mekong River flows into the South China Sea, the former prisoners received a warm welcome. After three days of rest, they travelled upriver to Cần Thơ, where residents welcomed them again. As one political prisoner stated, "the older persons stayed put, whereas the youth in good health, whether communist or nationalist, joined forces in the maquis to oppose the French."[60] As resistance to the French grew in the delta, these skilled cadres would play

---

[56] ANOM. HCI 96. [Intercepted letter sent from Tran Van Phuoc, village de Thanh Phuoc par Tay Ninh – Godauha, Cochinchine, to Dr. Nguyen Van Thinh, Conseiller Consultatif de Cochinchine, May 23, 1946.]

[57] Nguyễn Thanh Sơn, *Trọn đời theo Bác Hồ. Hồi ức của một người con đồng bằng sông Cửu Long* (Ho Chi Minh City: Trẻ, 2005), 149.

[58] Trương Dương Vũ, *Máu trở về tim. Ký sự* (Soctrang [?]: Tổng Hợp Hậu Giang, 1988), 7.

[59] Nguyễn Thanh Sơn, *Trọn đời theo Bác Hồ*, 171.

[60] Nguyễn Hải Hàm, *Từ Yên Báy đến Côn Lôn (1930–1945). Hồi ký* (Falls Church: Nha Sach The He, 1995), 204–205.

a crucial role. Nonetheless, given the lack of communist cadres, the Việt Minh was forced, in the short term, to rely heavily on non-communist volunteers.

Most Việt Minh volunteers lacked experience. Nguyễn Hiến Lê, who had fled Saigon, noted that in his new village of Tân Thạnh, "the head of the village People's Committee was a youth who had gone to high school."[61] At a meeting in October 1945, the Việt Minh focused on building up the "revolutionary armed forces from the bottom up": "The key positions on the committee were nearly all occupied by youths who came into the revolution via the student movement. [They had] little experience in revolutionary campaigns, and did not yet understand how to organize an armed resistance."[62] Of the intellectuals in the governing apparatus of the Resistance in 1947, Trần Bạch Đằng notes that "nearly all were from outside the [Communist] Party."[63]

Communists in the Việt Minh faced internal challenges as well: bitter rivalry between "Vanguard" and "Liberation" factions, already mentioned in Chapter 2. This rivalry – dating to before the August General Uprising of 1945 – had festered, and conflicts continued to flare up. The Party Center, anguished, wrote to its southern members in May 1946 that "it had recently received news that some communists, under the appellations of 'new Việt Minh' and 'old Việt Minh,' had recently had conflicts in some places, even leading to killings, and we are deeply pained by this."[64] In June 1946, these rival groups provisionally united their two networks of provincial party committees.[65] Even so, the revolutionary Nguyễn Thanh Sơn has argued that "up till 1947, in the internal affairs of the southern branch of the Party, prejudices originating from the pre-Uprising period endured... [and] sapped the strength and leadership of the Party."[66] Complicating matters, and to soothe an international audience fearful of communist influence in the Việt Minh, the Indochinese Communist Party (ICP) dissolved itself in November 1945. The move boomeranged. The international communist movement became wary of supporting the Việt Minh and the Democratic Republic of Vietnam (DRV). Self-dissolution also hurt recruitment: in the Mekong Delta, communist cadres avoided speaking publicly about the Party.

---

[61] Nguyễn Hiến Lê, *Hồi ký*, 333.   [62] Nguyễn Thanh Sơn, *Trọn đời theo Bác Hồ*, 163.
[63] Trần Bạch Đằng, *Kẻ sĩ Gia Định*, 242.
[64] "Thư gửi các đồng chí Xứ uỷ Nam Bộ, ngày 30-5-1946," *Văn Kiện Đảng* Vol. 8, https://tulieuvankien.dangcongsan.vn/van-kien-tu-lieu-ve-dang/book/van-kien-dang-toan-tap/van-kien-dang-toan-tap-tap-8-88 (accessed August 14, 2020).
[65] Trần Văn Trà, "Chiến tranh nhân dân khởi đầu từ Nam Bộ như thế," *Nam Bộ thành đồng*, 54.
[66] Nguyễn Thanh Sơn, *Trọn đời theo Bác Hồ*, 192. See also Trần Bạch Đằng, *Kẻ sĩ Gia Định*, 235.

Communists in the Việt Minh faced a range of rivals. Through the late summer and fall of 1945, groups in the delta vied to organize themselves. The comparatively well-armed Bình Xuyên settled in near Saigon. In September, Trotskyists set up the group "Struggle" in Mỹ Tho and put out a newspaper. They competed with communists as well as the Phục Quốc Đồng Minh Hội and elements of the Đại Việt Party. Gò Công boasted the New Democracy Youth group.[67] The Democracy Party, which collaborated with Hồ Chí Minh and was affiliated with the Việt Minh, had party members in the delta, some of whom either died or were arrested early in the war.[68]

Particular thorns in the communist side were the four "Revolutionary militias" (*Dân Quân Cách Mạng*) close to Saigon and in eastern Nam Bộ. A French-trained sergeant who participated in the August General Uprising led the First Division. It included members of the police. This unit "had the most people and guns, and mastered military tactics better than other units."[69] Vũ Tam Anh, a supposedly pro-Japanese landowner member of the Đại Việt Party, led the 1,000-strong Second Division. It "disintegrated and surrendered to the enemy at the beginning [of the uprising]."[70] Nguyễn Hòa Hiệp, the son of a landowner who worked as a postal clerk, was in charge of the Third Division.[71] Trần Văn Trà claimed that Hiệp, a Japanese collaborator, had also worked for the French secret police. Whatever the truth to the latter assertion, Nguyễn Hòa Hiệp had been an early member of the Vietnamese Nationalist Party, opposed to the communists, and had welcomed a Trotskyist "workers militia" into his ranks. Lý Hoa Vinh, an overseas Vietnamese of Chinese ancestry who once lived in Thailand, led the 2,000-strong Fourth Division. Vinh returned to Vietnam during World War II, supposedly as a Japanese spy.[72]

A bewildering assortment of other units rounded out Việt Minh forces, including Bình Xuyên toughs of a nationalist persuasion, militias made up of former policemen and informers, and Hòa Hảo and Cao Đài forces. No central command exerted authority. Some of these forces devolved into banditry: "we joked that it was the era of the modern Twelve Warlords."[73] Of course, one person's gangster is another person's hero,

---

[67] *Lịch sử Đảng Bộ tỉnh Tiền Giang*, 138.
[68] Vũ Đình Hòe, *Hồi ký* (Hanoi: Văn Hóa Thông Tin, 1994), 423–424.
[69] Trần Văn Trà, "Chiến tranh nhân dân khởi đầu từ Nam Bộ như thế," in Trần Văn Trà, *Nam Bộ thành đồng*, 20. This and the next few paragraphs rely heavily on this essay.
[70] Ibid., 20. [71] Vương Liêm, *Huỳnh Văn Một*, 127. [72] Ibid., 127–8.
[73] Trần Văn Trà, "Chiến tranh nhân dân khởi đầu từ Nam Bộ như thế," in Trần Văn Trà, *Nam Bộ thành đồng*, 22. The Era of the Twelve Warlords could refer to a period of upheaval in Vietnam during the tenth century, or to the Twelve Warlords who ruled China during the Republican Period.

and we should take communist judgments on their rivals with some skepticism.

Faced with such organizational chaos, the DRV, based in Hanoi, sent General Nguyễn Bình down south to centralize control over the resistance. He arrived in November 1945. In 1946, Nguyễn Bình struggled to fuse twenty-five different military detachments [chi đội] into a unified armed force. This was easier said than done. As Christopher Goscha has noted, "in theory, these chi đội formed an integral part of the Vệ Quốc Đoàn. In reality, these different military groupings preserved leadership and operational control over their own units."[74] By 1947, fifteen Việt Minh units remained, but autonomy from central command persisted. That year, Nguyễn Văn Sâm, organizing a rival nationalist front to the Việt Minh, argued that while true communists commanded only three militias, Việt Minh agents had heavily infiltrated the other twelve.[75]

To consolidate control over the Việt Minh, the Việt Minh arrested, imprisoned, and executed so-called "traitors" [Việt gian]. The use of targeted assassination was an accepted Việt Minh policy. On May 15, 1945, the Việt Minh in the North formally set up assassination squads (đội Danh dự trừ gian, or "honor squads to eliminate traitors") to kill its rivals. David Marr estimates that "several thousand alleged enemies of the revolution" were abducted and killed in late August and September 1945 alone.[76] The Việt Minh set up similar assassination units in the South. Nonetheless, we should not jump to conclusions: many different groups killed individuals.

The "search for traitors" shaped the early years of the war. David Elliott mentions that the slogan "'better to kill mistakenly than to release mistakenly'" circulated in one southern province.[77] Anyone could fall under suspicion, especially landlords, village notables, Cao Đài, Hòa Hảo, Catholics, and those who had worked for the French or Japanese. A pro-Resistance book on the South in 1945 and 1946 noted that in "free zones" under Resistance control, "the people paid particular attention to

---

[74] Christopher Goscha, "La guerre par d'autres moyens: réflexions sur la guerre du Việt Minh dans le Sud-Vietnam de 1945 à 1951," Guerres mondiales et conflits contemporains 206 (2002), 27.

[75] SHD. 10 H 603. S.E.S.A.G. Bulletin de renseignement No. 12984. Saigon, 29 March 1947. Source: Annamite. Valeur: Très sure. Très secret.

[76] David Marr, Vietnam 1945: The Quest for Power, (Berkeley and Los Angeles: University of California Press, 1995), 519. See also Guillemot, Dai Viet: indépendance et révolution au Viêt-Nam. L'échec de la troisième voie. 1938–1955, (Paris: Les Indes Savantes. 2012), 295.

[77] Dong Chi: Hoi ky cach mang, 56–7, quoted in David Elliott, The Vietnamese War: Revolution and Social Change in the Mekong Delta 1930–1975, (Armonk, NY: M. E. Sharpe, 2003), 91.

exterminating traitors... Many times, women and children also helped to hunt them down."[78]

Christopher Goscha writes that in the South, "the French reported that between 6 March and early July 1946 two hundred Vietnamese 'notables' had been assassinated."[79] Many more assassinations would follow. In short, there seems to have been a generalized fear of "traitors," but also a specifically Việt Minh attempt to target them.

Communists targeted Trotskyists with a vengeance. In October 1945, the newspaper *Liberation Flag* exhorted followers: "To avoid the unfortunate defeat of the revolution, compatriots must not shirk from liquidating the Trotskyists, and above all must fight the policy of some individuals to collaborate with the Trotskyists."[80] When the Trotskyist Ngô Văn fled Saigon to escape capture, he ended up arrested anyhow by Nguyễn Văn Trọng. Trọng, a former police chief under the French, had joined the Việt Minh. Eventually Ngô Văn escaped, rescued by militia friends.[81]

To manage the hunt for "traitors," the Việt Minh developed a legal framework for the arrest, trial, imprisonment, and execution of suspects. On September 13, 1945, the DRV established military tribunals throughout the country through Edict 33C. In early September 1945, its branch in the South, the Provisional Government of Nam Bộ, announced that it was "preparing to set up Investigative Committees in each province whose task is to identify and denounce traitors. The latter will be judged and punished by People's Courts. Their belongings will be confiscated, their landholdings seized and divided among the poor."[82]

In the abstract, this system preserved a form of legality. Huỳnh Thạnh Mậu, a brother of Hòa Hảo leader Huỳnh Phú Sổ, Trần Ngọc Hoành (a son of Hòa Hảo militia leader Trần Văn Soái) and the writer Việt Châu were brought before a tribunal in the Cần Thơ stadium, judged, then executed on October 7, 1945.[83] In Trà Vinh city, the Việt Minh executed

---

[78] Nguyễn Việt, *Nam Bộ và Nam phần Trung Bộ*, 53.

[79] Christopher Goscha, "A 'Popular' Side of the Vietnamese Army: General Nguyễn Bình and the Early War in the South (1910–1951)," in Christopher Goscha and Benoît de Tréglodé, eds., *Naissance d'un etat-parti* (Paris: Les Indes Savantes, 2004) 345.

[80] Tân Trào, "Phải triệt ngay bọn Tơ-rốt-skít" [We must exterminate the Trotskyists], *Cờ Giải Phóng* 23 (October 7, 1945), reprinted in *Cuộc kháng chiến thần thán của nhân dân Việt Nam*, Vol. 1 (từ 23 tháng chín 1945 đến tháng chạp 1947) (Hanoi: Sụ Thật, [1958?]), 17.

[81] See Ngô Văn, "In the Crossfire: Adventures of a Vietnamese Revolutionary," Chapter 7, www.bopsecrets.org/vietnam/07.crossfire.htm (accessed January 26, 2012).

[82] See NAC. Carton 55. "Để bài trừ bọn PHẢN QUỐC" [On eliminating reactionaries], *Thời báo* (Phnom Penh) 37, September 11, 1945, p. 1.

[83] Huỳnh Hữu Thiện, *Tiểu sử ông Huỳnh Thạnh Mậu* (Liên Chính XB, 1954), https://hoa hao.org/p74a4022/tieu-su-ong-huynh-thanh-mau (accessed on September 30, 2018); SHD. GR 10 H 4166. Lieutenant Lacroix, *Phật giáo Hòa Hảo* (sl., s.n., June 1949), 17.

three pro-French personalities in the Trà Vinh Stadium, including the high-ranking administrator Lê Quang Liêm.[84] Such practices were repeated elsewhere in the delta. Nguyễn Ngọc Chương, a former village chief and landlord, describes one such trial. Chương owned a large tract of coconut trees in An Hóa village, Bến Tre province. At the end of October 1945, in Chương's words, "when the French seized Mỹ Tho, the Resistance was still present here. The Việt Minh set up military tribunals; barrister Ch. presided, and clerk Tr. acted as the prosecutor and sentenced me. I was arrested and sent to the jail in Cai Lậy, where I was imprisoned with several hundred others." Chương was jailed for several months, then freed by the French army on January 7 [1946]. He then fled to the delta city of Mỹ Tho.[85]

A legal process serving the needs of revolutionary justice quickly confronted the realities of war. Tellingly, one source states that at trials, few individuals were sentenced to prison: they were either executed or given a warning.[86] Some individuals who ordinarily would have been given long sentences were instead killed. Thus, in 1946, Lê Đình Chi, head of the Board of Military Justice in Zone Seven, authorized the Biên Hòa Police chief to execute prisoners without any legal process: "given the grave situation, any dangerous criminal who deserves to die may be executed by the wardens in case of a [French] terror attack." Ever bureaucratic, he required that a report of such executions be made to higher authorities.[87] If such exceptions undermined justice, it is important to put them in context: some Việt Minh units seem to have failed to set up any judicial process at all.

We have only a sketchy idea of the Việt Minh detention system in the Mekong Delta, one that would operate throughout the war.[88] As territory shifted hands, prisons moved. In September 1945, according to one French report, the Việt Minh took hostage 450 Hòa Hảo members

---

[84] Việt Nam Cộng Hòa [Republic of Vietnam], *Địa phương chí tỉnh Vĩnh Bình* (S.l: s. n.,1973), 44. Thanks to Ben Wilkinson for providing me with this source.

[85] "Phóng sự – tôi đi 'lục tỉnh" [Reportage: I visited the 'six provinces'] *Phục Hưng* [Renaissance] (Saigon), July 4, 1949.

[86] Lê Hoàng, "Đại tướng Lê Đức Anh và những phiên tòa xét xử gián điệp," *Công lý*, April 13, 2012.

[87] ANOM. HCI SPCE 379. Service Judiciaire de la 7ème zone au Camarade Thuong – Sûreté de Bienhoa. March 18, 1945 [sic:1946]. Signed: Le Dinh Chi. On Lê Đinh Chi, see Christopher Goscha, *The Indochina War 1945-1956: An Interdisciplinary Tool*, (Copenhagen and Honolulu: NIAS/Hawai'i, 2011), https://indochine.uqam.ca/en/histor ical-dictionary/760-le-inh-chi-19121949.html (accessed August 27, 2015).

[88] We lack the depth of primary material comparable to what David Marr used to sketch out northern Vietnam's detention system. See David Marr, *Vietnam: State, War, and Revolution (1945–1946)*, (Berkeley: University of California Press, 2013), Chapter 7.

from Long Xuyên and Châu Đốc province and jailed them in Châu Đốc. The French liberated them in December.[89] One large internment camp seems to have been found in Cai Lậy, not far from Mỹ Tho, housing hundreds of prisoners in late 1945. As the French seized the towns of the delta, the Việt Minh moved prisons to inaccessible places, such as the swamps of Cà Mau. In 1947 and 1948, the French repeatedly attacked and burned down a Việt Minh prison in Bình Hòa in the Plain of Reeds. In March 1948, they liberated 200 prisoners kept there.[90] Prisoners came from all backgrounds, including those affiliated with the Hòa Hảo, Cao Đài, Bình Xuyên, and Đại Việt.

This section concludes with a story from Vĩnh Long province that captures the low-level brutality of the struggle to dominate the country-side in 1946 and 1947. In Châu Thành, the French had deployed an Afro-European military unit to guard their newly "pacified" area. Opposing them was Dương, head of the People's Committee of Bình Phước village. The new French-appointed administrator, Xê, "arrested Dương, tortured and killed him, and then brought his head to the Ngã Tư market," presumably as a lesson to the Việt Minh. In response, the People's Committee held a trial, condemned Xê, and an assassination team tracked him down and killed him. Xê was followed by another administrator who arrested members of the Resistance. An assassination team also tried to kill him – while he was only wounded, he fled the area.[91] Such was the nature of war in the delta between 1945 and 1947.

3.3 The Việt Minh's Contentious Relations with the Hòa Hảo and Cao Đài

Because the Hòa Hảo and Cao Đài would prove so central to the fracturing of the Việt Minh, it helps to revisit the summer and fall of 1945, when dissension involving these two religious groups first surfaced. The highest-ranking revolutionary in the western Mekong Delta, Nguyễn Thanh Sơn, has argued that the Việt Minh made crucial early mistakes that, combined with Hòa Hảo bull-headedness, pushed the two groups apart at a critical time. The Việt Minh excluded Hòa Hảo leader Huỳnh Phú Sổ from the Provisional Committee for the uprising in August 1945,

---

[89] ANOM. HCI SPCE 385. Sûreté Fédérale au Cambodge. Rapport du Police Spéciale." Phnom Penh, March 20[?], 1947.

[90] ANOM. HCI SPCE 379. Bulletin de Renseignment No. 1408/2S. Saigon, June 12, 1948.

[91] This paragraph is based on Đảng Ủy Bộ Chi Huy Quân Sự Tỉnh Vĩnh Long, *Lực lượng vũ trang tỉnh Vĩnh Long 30 năm kháng chiến (1945–1975)* (Hanoi: Quân Đội Nhân Dân, 1999), 65–66.

arrested him briefly, then selected him to be a "special member" of a reformed Administrative Committee of Nam Bộ. This incident "hurt Huỳnh Phú Sổ deeply and, obviously, harmed the unity with Hòa Hảo armed forces that already had a complicated internal situation."[92] During the August General Uprising, the Việt Minh arrested thirty-five Hòa Hảo (including Lương Trọng Tường, Huỳnh Phú Sổ's personal secretary) and detained them in Saigon's central prison; they were not released until October. They also attempted to kidnap Sổ.[93] Unsurprisingly, the Việt Minh had rocky relations with the Hòa Hảo.

In the late summer of 1945, the Hòa Hảo, strongest in the western Mekong Delta, "demanded" control of the provinces of Cần Thơ, Long Xuyên, and Châu Đốc. The Việt Minh leadership rebuffed the ultimatum.[94] Communist historians have consistently argued that the Hòa Hảo, who mobilized thousands of followers in Cần Thơ, then tried to seize power in September 1945. The Việt Minh cracked down on Hòa Hảo demonstrators in Cần Thơ, throwing many Hòa Hảo leaders in jail. A contemporaneous pro-Việt Minh account claims that the "uprising... was easily repressed," with only one death and ten wounded.[95] A Chinese who witnessed the clash from his home in Cần Thơ described Hòa Hảo believers, dressed in brown and carrying knives and swords, marching up against Việt Minh with rifles. When the Hòa Hảo refused to halt, the Việt Minh opened fire: "many dead and wounded were scattered across the road."[96] The Việt Minh arrested an estimated 450 Hòa Hảo followers in Cần Thơ during this demonstration, imprisoning them in Châu Đốc until they were liberated in December 1945. Apparently in the same demonstration, they tried (and failed) to arrest the Hòa Hảo leader Huỳnh Phú Sổ.[97] Năm Lửa – the *nom de guerre* of Trần Văn Soái, who would become one of the most famous militia leaders during the war – managed to escape.[98]

---

[92] Nguyễn Thanh Sơn, *Trọn đời theo Bác Hồ*, 158–159, 162.
[93] ANOM. HCI SPCE 385. Note. Arrestation de Huynh Phu So, Chef de la Secte 'Phat giao Hoa Hao." Saigon, ___May 1947. On attempts to kidnap Huỳnh Phú Sổ, see Guillemot, *Đại Việt*, 254, 261.
[94] *Lịch sử Nam Bộ Kháng Chiến*, 229.
[95] NAC. Carton 55. "Tin đồ Hòa Hảo định chiếm châu thành Cầnthơ" [Hòa Hảo believers planned to seize Cần Thơ], *Thời báo* (Phnom Penh), September 18, 1945, 2.
[96] Lưu Khâm Hưng, "Cần Thơ trong ký ức tôi", https://luukhamhung.blogspot.com/2016/12/can-tho-trong-ky-uc-toi.html (accessed June 15, 2017).
[97] ANOM. HCI SPCE 385. Sûreté Fédérale au Cambodge. Rapport du Police Spéciale." Phnom Penh, March 20, 1947; Pasacal Bourdeaux, "Interpretative essay on the 'Hòa Hảo Revolution,'" 8–9, unpublished paper, 2007.
[98] NAC. RSC. Carton 55. "Tin đồ Hòa Hảo định chiếm châu thành Cầnthơ," *Thời báo* (Phnom Penh), September 18, 1945, 2.

The Hòa Hảo have long seen this September conflict as a brazen attempt by communists to seize power, and have claimed a far higher death toll. Evaluating this conflict, the communist cadre Nguyễn Thanh Sơn frankly admitted mistakes: "the violent disturbance was quelled in Cần Thơ. However, the spontaneous action of the Hòa Hảo entailed severe consequences. The blood of many Hòa Hảo believers was unjustly shed. The ringleaders, like Lý Phú Xuân (Việt Châu), Huỳnh Văn Khấu, Từ Linh Hoan... were executed."[99] Việt Minh actions incensed Hòa Hảo in Cần Thơ and in adjoining provinces. In nearby Long Xuyên, an area with many Hòa Hảo followers, the local People's Committee bluntly explained its actions and issued a proclamation:

Because the Hòa Hảo wanted to resort to armed violence to overthrow the government of the South, they engaged in violence in Cần Thơ on September 9th [1945] and were completely defeated. To avoid bloodshed... in Long Xuyên, the government has arrested leaders of the Hòa Hảo to calm these disorders. Several of those leaders have been arrested not because the government wants to kill them, but because the government simply wants to confine them. It will treat them kindly: it just does not want them to incite sincere believers and create disorder at this critical moment.[100]

It is important here to understand the character of the Hòa Hảo and its charismatic leader, Huỳnh Phú Sổ. Huỳnh Phú Sổ, only twenty-five years old in 1945, was steeped in the Bửu Sơn Kỳ Hương (Strange Fragrance from the Precious Mountain) tradition of the western Mekong Delta, an assemblage of Buddhist teachings known since the nineteenth century. Drawing on these beliefs, Huỳnh Phú Sổ preached that Vietnamese were approaching the end times [tận thế], marking the end of one cosmic era and the beginning of a new one, and that only the virtuous true believers could find salvation.[101] As Cồ Việt Tử has written:

Relying on the Sấm giảng [Prophecies of Huỳnh Phú Sổ], many peasants believed that on a day in the near future, out of Sam Mountain in Châu Đốc would emerge vestments and a golden throne for an Enlightened King who comes into existence for the salvation of the world. To Hòa Hảo believers, that Enlightened King is none other than their Master [Huỳnh Phú Sổ], or the reborn Buddha Master of the Western Peace.[102]

[99] Nguyễn Thanh Sơn, Trọn đời theo Bác Hồ, 161. According to Nguyễn Hiến Lê, however, his friend Việt Châu was in Saigon at the beginning of the supposed attempt to seize power.
[100] NAC. RSC. 23,711. Proclamation from Dương Văn Ân and Nguyễn Văn Nhung, Chủ tịch Ủy ban Hành Chính Long Xuyên, Long Xuyên, September 9, 1945.
[101] See Vương Kim, Tận thế và hội Long Hoa (Saigon: Long Hoa, 1953), 102–110, for an analysis of Huỳnh Phú Sổ's writing on the topic.
[102] Cồ Việt Tử [pen name of Nguyễn Duy Hinh], Vụ án Ba Cụt (Saigon: Nguyễn Duy Hinh [1956], 13. The author refers to himself as an advisor to Huỳnh Phú Sổ.

No secular power could hope to rule the western Mekong Delta without obliging Huỳnh Phú Sổ and his Hòa Hảo followers. In November 1946, Huỳnh Phú Sổ offered a religious logic for the foundation of the Social-Democrat Party as an alternative to the Việt Minh:

According to my observations on Buddhist doctrine, for Shakyamuni Buddha after his enlightenment, compassion, universal caring, and great unity of all beings is the core. I recognize Him as a radical revolutionary in thought. "All sentient beings have Buddha-nature" and "The Buddha has the same essential and undifferentiated Buddha nature as all sentient beings." There is equality in essential nature, but sentient beings are not equal to the Buddha because their level of enlightenment is not the same, not because they haven't similarly evolved as the Buddha. If in this world, sentient beings who are advanced exploit those who are backwards, that is contrary to these true teachings. Shakyamuni Buddha did not apply that practical teaching in his lifetime due to the unfavorable Indian social environment. So he just expressed its spirit. Today, the level of progress of humanity has reached a satisfactory level, science has progressed, and it is possible to realize these ideals and create a society that is egalitarian and humane. So with a heart filled with compassion and universal caring that I have absorbed, I will harmonize these beliefs with new social and organizational methods, to practically serve our compatriots and humanity.[103]

This utopian vision of politics would soon be tested by the fires of war.

The Việt Minh also had contentious relations with the Tây Ninh branch of the Cao Đài. As earlier mentioned, the Cao Đài may have possessed the most powerful Vietnamese armed force in the South in the summer of 1945. Despite this fact, and for reasons that remain obscure, local Việt Minh forces in Quảng Ngãi killed nearly 3,000 Cao Đài followers in August 1945, angering the Cao Đài. While Cao Đài participated in the August General Uprising, they soon came into conflict again with communist leaders of the Việt Minh. On October 9, 1945, Việt Minh at a post in Bình Điền, fifteen kilometers from Saigon, arrested the de facto Cao Đài leader Trần Quang Vinh. Vinh was imprisoned with other leaders suspected by the Việt Minh, such as the Trotskyist Hồ Văn Ngà. After the Việt Minh moved these prisoners to Cà Mau, they managed to break out of jail in January 1946.[104] Why was this particular Cao Đài leader seized? As A. M. Savani put it, the Việt Minh "feared a Cao Đài movement that was hierarchical, disciplined, and backed by the Japanese. They proposed to its leaders to integrate it into the Viet Minh, but on the

---

[103] "Ông Hồn-Quyền ở (Saigon) vào chiến-khu phỏng-vấn Đức Huỳnh Giáo-Chủ," in Giáo Hội Phật Giáo Hòa Hảo, Sấm giảng thi văn toàn bộ của Đức Huỳnh Giáo chủ ([Saigon]: Ban Phổ Thông Giáo Lý Trung Ương, 1970), 450.
[104] Trần Quang Vinh, Hồi ký Trần Quang Vinh (S.l.: Thánh thất vùng Hoa Thịnh Đốn, 1997), 11–12, 22–26.

condition that its troops would be disarmed. Trần Quang Vinh refused and was arrested by Trần Văn Giàu."[105]

The tense relations between Cao Đài and Việt Minh continued into 1946. The Cao Đài were increasingly caught in a pincer between their Vietnamese rivals and the French enemy. In the spring of 1946, Việt Minh General Nguyễn Bình pressured the Cao Đài to dissolve their own military units and integrate into Việt Minh ones. As pressure increased on the Cao Đài, the French attacked Cao Đài positions. In May 1946:

> the French captured the entire Cao Dai headquarters in Saigon-Cholon, including twenty-two dignitaries (but not the guerrilla leaders), and raided twelve Cao Đài meeting places. In exchange for the release of these captives and the return of exiled dignitaries, including Phạm Công Tắc [from Madagascar], [de facto leader Trần Quang] Vinh signed an accord on behalf of the Cao Đài army providing for the surrender of the Cao Đài *chi đội* to the French expeditionary corps in June 1946.[106]

Caught between a rock and a hard place, Trần Quang Vinh chose the least bad option – collaboration with the French – in order to protect the Cao Đài. From this point onwards, the Cao Đài leadership shifted slowly into a tactical alliance with the French, a process which would lead to the fracture of 1947.

3.4 The Unraveling of Khmer-Vietnamese Relations

If the struggle only pitted French against Vietnamese contestants, it might have been possible for the Vietnamese to resolve their internal political disagreements and create a unified Resistance. But the struggle involved others. The Vietnamese were blindsided when, after a hiatus of sixty years, extensive Khmer-Vietnamese violence broke out in 1945 and 1946. Vietnamese repeatedly refer to these killings as *"cáp duồn"* – a Khmer term that refers to the beheading of the *Yuon*, or Vietnamese. Whether or not beheading was common, the term *"cáp duồn"* has crystallized, for the Vietnamese who lived through these times, the horror of the experience. Given that Khmer and Vietnamese had overwhelmingly avoided bloodshed since the late 1880s, the task is to explain this sudden change.

---

[105] A. M. Savani, *Notes sur le Caodaisme* (Saigon[?]: 1954), 125.
[106] Werner, "The Cao Đài," 279. It is unclear whether the French placed Phạm Công Tắc on the island prison of Nosy Lava, Madagascar. They had kept him interned in Tsitondroina, in the central highlands of Madagascar, until October 1944, then moved him to house arrest in Ambalavao. See *Journal officiel de Madagascar et dépendances Madagascar*, October 14, 1944, p. 713, https://gallica.bnf.fr/ark:/12148/bp t6k6480054x/f5.item (accessed August 13, 2020).

Cambodian dislike of the Vietnamese is often presented as a constant of Vietnamese-Cambodian interactions since the seventeenth century, and an anti-Vietnamese strain has influenced some foreign scholarship on Cambodia.[107] A common representation of animosity between Khmer and Vietnamese,[108] one that may date from the early nineteenth century, is the story of the cooking pot. In this tale, the Vietnamese are said to have buried three live Khmer up to their necks to make a tripod, lit a fire between them, and placed a pot on the heads of the unfortunate victims to boil water for tea.[109] This story is often said to date from the building of the Vinh Tế canal, on the border between Vietnam and Cambodia, in the early nineteenth century. In the digging of this canal, numerous Cambodians died. What better indication could one have of Vietnamese barbarism?

It turns out, however, that relations between Vietnamese and Khmer have ranged from friendly to hostile. Antipathy has ebbed and flowed. From the late 1880s to 1945, Khmer and Vietnamese engaged in almost no large-scale ethnic violence. Explaining this shift from difficult co-existence to violent antagonism is thus key. A first clue is in the strong ties that have linked the Khmer Krom communities of the lower Mekong Delta to Cambodia. Historians of Cambodia routinely mention the role of key individuals with lower Mekong Delta roots, such as Son Ngoc Thanh, Son Ngoc Minh, Pach Chhoeun, Son Sann, Tou Samouth, or the Khmer Rouge leaders Ieng Sary and Son Sen, in post-1945 Cambodian history. Son Ngoc Thanh, to take up one example, came from Trà Vinh and worked at the Buddhist Institute in Phnom Penh before becoming a famous nationalist leader. Son Sen, who later became the Khmer Rouge Minister of Defense, attended a Franco-Khmer school in Trà Vinh town.[110] Lon Nol, the fiercely anti-Vietnamese general who over-threw Prince Sihanouk in 1970, had similar connections: one grandfather hailed from the province of Tây Ninh (once claimed by Cambodia, now part of Vietnam). Lon Nol himself studied in Saigon.[111] Most of the individuals listed above would become strongly anti-Vietnamese.

---

[107] See, for example, Marie Alexandrine Martin, *Cambodia: A Shattered Society* (Berkeley: California, 1994), particularly 5–44.

[108] This part of the chapter draws heavily on Shawn McHale, "Ethnicity, Violence, and Khmer-Vietnamese Relations: The Significance of the Lower Mekong Delta,1757–1954," *The Journal of Asian Studies* 72 (May 2013), 367–390.

[109] Khmers Kampuchea Krom Federation *The Khmer-Krom Journey to Self-Determination* (Pennsauken, NJ: Khmers Kampuchea-Krom Federation, 2009), 41.

[110] Bunthorn Som, "Thach Chov: A Former Student of Khieu Samphan." *Searching for the Truth* (Phnom Penh), (First Quarter, 2010), 22.

[111] Ian Harris, *Cambodian Buddhism: History and Practice* (Honolulu: University of Hawai'i Press, 2005), 168.

Some Khmer, including those with Mekong Delta roots, initially proposed Vietnamese-Cambodian collaboration. V. M. Reddi states that
Son Ngoc Thanh, briefly Foreign Minister of Cambodia in the summer
of 1945, "had been exhorting the Cambodians to collaborate 'sincerely
and fraternally' with the Vietnamese."[112] Ben Kiernan has noted the role
of Khmer Krom radicals such as Thach Choeun (aka Son Ngoc Minh),
perhaps the first Khmer member of the ICP, and Lam Phay, brother-in-
law of Son Ngoc Thanh, who collaborated with the Vietnamese and,
"under the name Chan Samay later became a senior member of the
Khmer communist movement."[113] The Cambodian political figure
Pach Chhoeun, originally from Cochinchina, also proposed collaboration. He travelled to Sóc Trăng and Trà Vinh provinces in late 1945
and called on Khmer monks and lay followers to work with the
Vietnamese against the French. Working with the Việt Minh, Pach
Chhoeun set up the "Independent Cambodia Committee" – apparently
in Châu Đốc – to fight for Cambodian independence. This group seems to
have fallen apart by February 1946.[114]

Given such attempts at collaboration, why and how did the spiral of
violence begin? The story is complicated. As earlier noted, after the
Japanese seized power from the French on March 9, 1945, the French
administration fell apart in urban and rural French Indochina. In this
context, Cambodians and Vietnamese both took actions in Cambodia
and Cochinchina that antagonized the other. In the summer of 1945,
King Sihanouk claimed that Cochinchina belonged to Cambodia.
Relations between Khmer and Vietnamese predictably worsened.
Writing from Saigon, S. Shirata, affiliated with the Japanese mission,

[112] V. M. Reddi, *A History of the Cambodian Independence Movement 1863–1955* (Tirupati:
Sri Venkatteswara University, 1970), 108.
[113] Ben Kiernan has documented the Khmer Krom roots of these Cambodian political
figures. See, for example, his *How Pol Pot Came to Power: Colonialism, Nationalism, and
Communism in Cambodia, 1930–1975* (New Haven: Yale University Press, 2004), 21,
23-24, 50. See also David Chandler, *Tragedy of Cambodian History: Politics, War, and
Revolution since 1945* (New Haven: Yale University Press, 1991). On the struggle of the
Khmer of Cochinchina during the First Indochina War, see Thomas Engelbert,
"Ideology and Reality: *Nationalitätenpolitik* in North and South Vietnam of the First
Indochina War," in Thomas Engelbert and Andreas Schneider, eds., *Ethnic Minorities
and Nationalism in Southeast Asia* (Frankfurt: Peter Lang, 2000), 105–142; McHale,
"Ethnicity, Violence, and Khmer-Vietnamese Relations," 367–390; Philip Taylor,
"Losing the Waterways: The Displacement of Khmer Communities from the
Freshwater Rivers of the Mekong Delta, 1945–2010," *Modern Asian Studies* 47(2)
(2013), 500–541.
[114] This section on Pach Chhoeun draws on Penny Edwards, "The Tyranny of Proximity:
Power and Mobility in Colonial Cambodia, 1863–1954," *Journal of Southeast Asian
Studies* 37(3) (October 2006), 433; Ban Liên Lạc Cựu Chiến Binh Quân thời kỳ
1945–1954, *Tư liệu lịch sử Quân tình nguyện Việt Nam ở Campuchia (1945–1954)* (Cà
Mau: Mùi Cà Mau, 1998), 45–47.

wrote to Ly Hoa Ung in Phnom Penh that on hearing the news of Sihanouk's claim, "Saigonese, and particularly the young, are very upset and swear that they will fight if necessary."[115] A Phnom Penh resident wrote to a Saigon friend in July 1945 that "despite everything, there is a feeling of loathing between Cambodians and us."[116] Rumors swirled: one Cambodian, hearing that some Cambodians were converting to the Cao Đài religion (founded by Vietnamese), warned that "unless the Cambodian government stopped this, all Cambodians would become Cao Đài."[117]

After Sihanouk claimed that Cochinchina belonged to Cambodia, Việt Minh leaders expressed hope that his statement would not gain traction among Cambodian political leaders. This was wishful thinking. In late August 1945, Nguyễn Thanh Sơn, who was organizing revolutionary forces in the western Mekong Delta, tried to contact the Cambodian government "to suggest that the Cambodian government ally with Vietnam to defend the sovereignty of the two peoples faced with the French colonialists' return to Indochina." But when the Cambodian leader Son Ngoc Thanh met with Dr. Phạm Ngọc Thạch and the Administrative Committee of Nam Bộ to discuss this proposal, he shocked the Vietnamese by proposing that Cambodia should receive the two Cochinchinese provinces of Trà Vinh and Sóc Trăng. (These provinces had heavy concentrations of Khmer.) Talks predictably broke down.[118]

In the fall of 1945, Khmer-Vietnamese relations were marked by contention. First, violence broke out between Vietnamese and Khmer early that month: the People's Administrative Committee of Nam Bộ "was sent scrambling after Son Thai Xuan, a Khmer Krom village elder in Trà Vinh Province, was killed. He was the grandfather of Son Ngoc Thanh, the Cambodian prime minister."[119] Meanwhile, rumors of Khmer-Vietnamese antagonisms circulated on the Cambodian-Vietnamese border near Hà Tiên: "all it would take is for a small fight between a Vietnamese and a Khmer to ignite a bloody conflict."[120] By

---

[115] NAC. RSC. Dossier 34189. [Intercepted letter from S. Shirata, Japanese mission in Saigon, to Ly Hoa Ung, Phnom Pehn. July 18, 1945.]

[116] NAC. RSC. Dossier 34.189. [Copy of letter intercepted from Hien, 3ème Bureau Ministère des Finances, Phnom Penh à Nguyen Van Dat Redacteur des P.T.T. Saigon. Translated from the Vietnamese. July 19, 1945.]

[117] NAC. RSC. Dossier 34.189. [Intercepted letter from Oum in Prey Veng to Pach Chhoun, director of the newspaper *Nagavatta*, Phnom Penh, July 19, 1945.]

[118] Ban Liên Lạc, *Tư liệu lịch sử*, 44.

[119] Brett Reilly, "The Sovereign States of Vietnam, 1945–1955," *Journal of Vietnamese Studies*, 11(3–4) (2016), 116.

[120] NAC. Carton 55. "Tin Cao-Miên" [Cambodia news]. *Thời báo* (Phnom Penh), September 4, 1945.

September 20, the situation had worsened: a Phnom Penh newspaper reported that "recently, some Vietnamese communities in Cambodia have been riled up. Throughout Cambodia, fake and strange rumors circulate that the Cambodian government plans to eradicate all Vietnamese in Cambodia." The Cambodian prime minister, Son Ngoc Thanh, forcefully denied these reports.[121]

Relations between Khmer and Vietnamese in Cambodia continued to worsen. On October 11, the Phnom Penh Chief of Special Police wrote that Cambodians were asking: "What is the government waiting for? The enemy is becoming numerous." The meaning of this enigmatic remark seems clarified by reports that Vietnamese who continued to work for the French "were threatened with assassination."[122] A few days later, "the Annamite colony learned with anxiety about the disappearance of His Excellency the Prime Minister Son Ngoc Thanh." (He was arrested by the French General Leclerc in mid-October.) At that time, the Vietnamese community saw Thanh as a friend. In the Vietnamese quarters [of Phnom Penh], residents organized themselves into self-defense groups under the Việt Minh umbrella.[123] Vietnamese were also forming guerrilla groups in the Cambodian provinces of Prey Veng and Kandal by October 1945.[124] Armed Vietnamese groups were found as far west as Battambang and Siem Reap in western Cambodia.

The situation was spiraling out of control. By the fall, Vietnamese were scrambling to leave Cambodia, with most heading to the Mekong Delta or Saigon. (How many left is unclear, but approximately 300,000 Vietnamese lived in Cambodia in 1945.) At the end of 1945, the Cambodian government eliminated ethnic Vietnamese village chiefs (*mekhum*),[125] thereby depriving themselves of natural intermediaries to the Vietnamese population. The crisis brewing in Cambodia quickly spilled over into the lower Mekong Delta. This was not difficult: news and people traveled easily up and down the Mekong River linking Cambodia and Vietnam. In this chaotic situation, Cambodian military units deployed in the lower Mekong Delta (western Cochinchina) as well as Cambodia. Việt Minh attempts to seize the South, of course, may have also contributed to rifts between Khmer and Vietnamese.

---

[121] NAC. Carton 55. "Chính Đính" [Rectification]. *Thời báo* (Phnom Penh), September 20, 1945, 1.
[122] NAC. RSC. Dossier 23.711. Le Chef de la Police Spéciale. Situation politique du Kampuchea. October 11, 1945.
[123] NAC. RSC. Royaume du Kampuchea. Police Nationale. "Rapport du 16 octobre à 6 heures du matin." October 17, 1945.
[124] Ban Liên Lạc Việt kiều Campuchia Hồi Hương, *Ánh truyền thống Việt kiều Campuchia đối với Tổ quốc (1930–1975)* (Cà Mau: Mũi Cà Mau, 1998), [3].
[125] Lê Hương, *Việt kiều*, 15.

While some accounts present the violence between Vietnamese and Khmer as coming out of the blue, it took long years of "priming." In 1927, Khmer of Ninh Thanh Lợi (then part of Rạch Gia province), rose up in rebellion to protest against their land being stolen from them. Some of the Khmer who participated had themselves been the victims of Vietnamese land-grabs in Cà Mau province.[126] Such practices continued into the 1930s. Suzanne Karpelès, head of the Buddhist Institute in Phnom Penh, who made repeated trips to the lower Mekong Delta in the 1930s, reported on a litany of Khmer Krom complaints about abusive Vietnamese bureaucrats, land dispossession, poor treatment of Khmer monks, and Vietnamese arrogation of power in the provinces of Tây Ninh, Long Xuyên, Trà Vinh, and Rạch Giá.[127] Such local issues intersected with broader ones in the upheavals of the summer of 1945. In at least one province, Sóc Trăng, Khmer youth had been organized into Yuvan units. Yuvan Kampucherath, founded in Cambodia in 1941 with King Sihanouk as the titular head, mobilized the youth in support of the Cambodian nation. These Sóc Trăng Yuvan would later collaborate with the Vanguard Youth in 1945 and participate in the August General Uprising of August 1945.[128]

The youth played a key role. Vương Liêm gives a riveting description of Khmer agitation in Tập Rèn village in Sóc Trăng province. At the time, he was a boy living in the Vietnamese hamlet of a larger village with many Khmer. One day in late November, 1945, a large crowd of Khmer youths and young adults gathered, yelling and getting worked up about fighting the Việt Minh. "Armed with sticks and knives, they marched back and forth in the neighborhood as a provocation." As night fell, tension grew palpably. Vương Liêm's sister had heard that the Khmer were going to "cáp duồng," or behead the Vietnamese. Would the Việt Minh save them?

We anxiously waited, fearful of the unruliness of the crowd of youths with sticks, on tenterhooks, not knowing if the [Vietnamese] soldiers would arrive in time.

---

[126] See the excellent contemporary account: Lê Quang Liêm, "La vérité sur l'échauffourée de Ninh-Thanh- Loi (Rachgia)," *Écho Annamite* (May 19, 1927), 1.

[127] See RSC 22329. Institut Bouddhique à M. l'Administrateur, Chef de la Province de Tayninh. November 7, 1933; RSC dossier 22329. [Lettre de l'ordinant de la Pagode de Vat Khnong à Mlle. le Conservateur de la Bibliothèque Royale à Phnom Penh.] Tra Vinh, December 29, 1933; RSC 17378. Institut Bouddhique à Monsieur le Général de Division BIDON. Phnom Penh, May 30, 1934; RSC 4182. Mlle. Suzanne Karpelès à Mme. Lafuente, Tressalan, La Turballe, Loire Inférieure. October 30, 1939; RSC 22342. Institut Bouddhique. [Letter: Province de Longxuyen. Doléances de Cambodgiens. February 1940?]

[128] See Anne Raffin, Youth Mobilization and Ideology: Cambodia from the Late Colonial Era to the Pol Pot Regime," *Critical Asian Studies* 44(3) (2012), 397; on Yuvan in Sóc Trăng, see Nguyễn Minh Châu and Nguyễn Thanh Hà, *Báo cáo tổng hợp đấu tranh cách mạng của công nhân và công đoàn tỉnh Sóc Trăng* (Sóc Trăng, s.n., 2011), 52–54.

I was so tired I fell asleep, but I can't say for how long. Hearing distant gunfire, my sister shook me awake. The gunfire became clearer, and at times bullets whizzed through the gardens behind the house. I was terrified, trembling all over. This was the first time in my youth that I had heard gunfire and seen the red of bullets flying through the darkness. My sisters and I flattened ourselves against the earth of the kitchen floor. I was shaking so much that my teeth were chattering and I could not stop, so my older sister dragged out some old clothes, wrapped me in them, and hugged me, pressing my feet and hands together.

I was scared out of my wits when I heard the angry outbursts, yells, and cursing of the Khmer. At first, it seemed as if they were calling on each other to go into the hamlet to stop the [Vietnamese] soldiers. Then, on hearing the gunfire, they turned and ran. They were running for their lives – I heard the pounding of the feet, the splashing through the water, and the yells gradually fading away from the *srok* and the village... Suddenly, the sounds of feet from afar gradually became clearer. People burst into talking. It was the Việt Minh![129]

This volatile situation only needed a final catalyst, which would be provided, as Chapter 4 shows, by French attempts to mobilize Khmer against the Vietnamese.

3.5 Conclusion

World War II unleashed a cataclysm in Southeast Asia whose effects were still playing themselves out in 1945 and 1946. As the French and then Japanese state collapsed, nothing comparable replaced it. Economically, the Mekong Delta had once been a rice export powerhouse. By 1946 and 1947, rice cultivation had plummeted, throwing the delta back to a subsistence level, but also throwing many tenants and laborers out of work. In a context of uncertainty, unease, and violence, the fractious Việt Minh and the weak French military and civilian apparatuses vied for control. No one group could dominate the delta. At the same time, political rivalries and Khmer-Vietnamese antagonisms worsened. The delta was primed for more upheaval. It would come in 1947, a watershed in the history of modern southern Vietnam.

---

[129] Vương Liêm, *Đồng quê Nam Bộ (thập niên 40)* (Ho Chi Minh City: Văn Nghệ Thành Phố Hồ Chí Minh, 2003), 104–106.

Violence can be mobilized against an external foe. It can also turn on itself. If the struggle in the South began in order to expel the French, violence ended up transforming the countryside, and ripping Mekong Delta society apart. The delta went through two internal fractures at the beginning of the war. The first, dating from late 1945 and into 1946, split many (but not all) Khmer from Vietnamese. The catalyst of this fracture was France's drive into the delta from late 1945, when it recruited "partisans," and especially ethnic Khmer, to fight Việt Minh forces. By giving Khmer weapons to fight Vietnamese, the French worsened ethnic antagonisms, leading to extensive violence between these two communities. The violence split the Khmer community into factions but set most Khmer on the path of increasing collaboration with the French. The second major fracture split the majority Vietnamese population into different political camps. The catalyst of this second fracture was the Việt Minh's attempt to subdue rivals for leadership of the "nationalist" movement. Primed during 1945 and 1946, this second fracture occurred in 1947.

These two fractures reshaped the South in distinct ways. When Vietnamese fought Vietnamese, they clashed over politics but shared a common goal: an independent Vietnam. The Khmer case sharply differed. Far from fighting for Vietnamese independence, most Khmer Krom supported either French rule, autonomy for Khmer communities, or reversion of Cambodian enclaves in the Mekong Delta to Cambodia. In other words, the Vietnamese and Khmer fractures had far different implications for sovereignty. In the middle were the French, attempting to manipulate both antagonisms in order to extend their power in French Indochina. Together, the intra-Vietnamese struggle for control of the nationalist movement and the Khmer-Vietnamese struggle were foundational. Understanding both is key to grasping decolonization and the strange birth of South Vietnam. There is no better place to start than with the French military's drive into the delta from late 1945 to early 1946.

4.1 Khmer-Vietnamese Antagonism Intersects with France's Attempt to Seize the Delta, 1945–1946

Dusk was falling. Returning home, the road ran through a market area where not a human shadow could be seen – the entire village had fled the disaster. I saw bodies of the dead strewn across the road, houses and belongings in utter disarray, goods in the shops knocked all over by the soldiers. Most heartrending to see was the shop where I had bought potassium permanganate [*thuốc tím*] the other day. It had been smashed up, its owner killed right in front of his door. That was the evil crime of the barbaric French Expeditionary Force, wildly unleashing its rage.

Trembling, panic-stricken, I hurried home.

Khương Mễ on early 1946 in the village of Tân Khánh.[1]

As noted in Chapter 3, a crisis had been brewing in Cambodia since the summer of 1945 over Khmer-Vietnamese relations. As news easily traveled down the branches of the Mekong, this crisis quickly spilled over into Cochinchina and intersected with the French attempt to retake the Mekong Delta, leading to extensive violence.

When I first encountered primary materials on Khmer massacres of Vietnamese in Cambodia and the lower Mekong Delta from 1945 onwards, I was taken aback: these events are little mentioned in the secondary literature, and have rarely been portrayed as significant. The story of this ethnic and political violence had to be pieced together from fleeting mentions in military archives, memoirs, newspapers, and secondary sources. If official secondary sources neglect this series of events, it is not because of their unimportance. The more one studies Khmer-Vietnamese relations in the Mekong Delta, the more one senses that these massacres formed a small part of an evolving dynamic of ethnic animosity, one with roots in the eighteenth and nineteenth centuries, that shaped post-1945 ethnic relations between Khmer and Vietnamese as well as the relations between the states of Cambodia and Vietnam.

The initial French drive into the delta in late 1945 hit some villages and towns hard. A nationalist non-communist called the French attacks, supplemented by raids carried out by local "partisan" troops, a calamity: these were "the darkest nights" for the western Mekong Delta.[2] French attacks on Việt Minh units and sweeps through villages joined with widespread Khmer massacres of Vietnamese. Tracking the resultant conflicts is difficult, as they occurred over a broad region. Khmer-Vietnamese violence occurred in the entire area between Phnom Penh and the South China Sea. Lê Hương notes that the

---

[1] Khương Mễ, *Đời tôi và diên ảnh* (Ho Chi Minh City: Thành phố Hồ Chí Minh, 2003), 19.
[2] Hoành Kim Anh, *9 năm kháng chiến miền tây Nam Bộ* (Saigon: s.n., 1957), 60.

Vietnamese communities hardest hit in Cambodia were in Kandal province, Prey Veng, Takeo, and Svay Rieng. These areas, all with significant Vietnamese population, border Vietnam. In Vietnam, Lê Hương mentions that Khmer pillaged, raped, and killed Vietnamese (and possibly some Chinese) in Trà Vinh, Bạc Liêu, and Sóc Trăng.[3] To these places General Trần Văn Trà adds Rạch Giá and Tây Ninh provinces, as well as the Cambodian areas near the border with Tây Ninh.[4] All of these areas had significant concentrations of Khmer. At least one province with a small Khmer population, Vĩnh Long, also saw notable Khmer killings of Vietnamese.[5] This province bordered Trà Vinh, which had a sizeable Khmer population. Recently opened French archival sources suggest that violence, including Vietnamese reprisals, was found in Châu Đốc, Hà Tiên, and Cà Mau provinces as well.[6]

The killing was catalyzed by the French military's drive to retake the delta in the late fall of 1945. At first, the French could recruit few Vietnamese to help them. One Vietnamese source claims that in the fall of 1945, so few "lackey traitors" volunteered to work with the French military that the French encountered numerous operational difficulties. For the push into the delta, the French relied on a motley assortment of troops, including Japanese soldiers, reconstituted colonial militias, Cambodian troops sent from Cambodia, and what the French oddly called "partisans." ("Partisans" were hired on the spot, and armed, but under very loose French control.) Jean Leroy, who took part in this reconquest of the Mekong Delta, recruited twenty "partisans" from among the Việt Minh prisoners in the Mỹ Tho jail.[7]

As the French drove into the delta, they broke apart Vietnamese forces. In his *Journaux de marche* – the commanding officer's day to day account of combat operations – Colonel Massu is terse and cryptic, speaking frequently of "nettoyage" ("cleansing"). He lists repeated French victories over Việt Minh bands.[8] The French did not seize Trà Vinh city until December 2, 1945.[9] Other major cities were captured by February 1946. The exact temporal and geographical sequence of events rests unclear. In

---

[3] Lê Hương, *Việt kiều ở Kampuchea* (Saigon: Trí Đăng, 1971), 252.
[4] Trần Văn Trà, "Chiến tranh nhân dân khởi đầu từ Nam Bộ như thế," in *Nam Bộ thành đồng*, 59–60; Trần Văn Trà, *Miền Nam thành Đồng đi trước về sau* (Hanoi: Quân Đội Nhân Dân, 2006), 179.
[5] Đảng ủy-Bộ Chỉ Huy, *Lực lượng vũ trang tỉnh Vĩnh Long*, Vol. 1, 56.
[6] See a variety of documents found in SHD. 10H 3825.
[7] Jean Leroy, *Fils de la rizière*, (Paris: R. Laffont, 1977), 90; Bộ Tư Lệnh Quân Khu 9, *Quân Khu 9 30 năm kháng chiến* (Hanoi: Quân đội nhân dân, 1996), 61.
[8] SHD. 10H 5938. Arrivée Ben Cat commencé le 28.12.1945 terminée le 15/2/46. Journaux de marche/ Opérations de Col. Massu. November 1945 – February 1946.
[9] Tinh Ủy ban Nhân Dân tỉnh Trà Vinh, *Lịch sử tỉnh Trà Vinh* (Ban Tư Tưởng Tỉnh Ủy Ttrà Vinh, 1999), Vol. 1, 44.

tracking these events, it is important to note that witnesses sometimes mixed together what happened in August and September 1945 (when French authorities were nowhere to be seen in rural areas) with what probably happened in early 1946 (when the French military seized back control of major towns of the delta, then moved into the countryside). The French still, however, did not control large chunks of the delta outside the main cities, and insecurity reigned through 1946.

After the attacks on Trà Vinh and Sóc Trăng, the French pushed on. By January 4, 1946, the French and their forces had seized the province seats of Trà Vinh and Sóc Trăng, taking Bạc Liêu township by January 29, 1946.[10] Việt Minh forces fled into the countryside and points south. A French source made antiseptic comments about military progress in Rạch Gía province: "The area of Goquao-Giong Rieng–Long My is now being cleared. We find no more indications of large armed groupings; nonetheless, security is precarious because of the presence of Viet Minh, found in small bands, who are resorting to piracy."[11] The French continued on to Cà Mau, where some Việt Minh had retreated. In Giồng Bốm, Cà Mau, they encountered the forces of a Vietnamese Cao Đài landlord, Cao Triều Phát, who wholeheartedly supported the Việt Minh. According to an official Vietnamese military history, the French "massacred thousands of believers" there between April 22 and 25, 1946.[12] Claude Réau, a participant in the retaking of the delta, gave a conflicted assessment of French operations: "I continued to accompany Ponchardier and his 'Tigers'... and it seemed, in his multiple victories, punitive or peaceful, mostly necessary, given the risks run and the losses suffered, but sometimes clumsy, ineffective, and politically incorrect or too brutal."[13]

In fact, the French attacks had two contradictory effects: breaking apart the Việt Minh, but also inflaming the Khmer against the Vietnamese populace. The result was explosive. It is possible that within Cochinchina, the province of Trà Vinh saw the earliest massacres. Thomas Engelbert writes that "Uproar was created first in Trà Vinh, then spread later to Sóc Trăng and Bạc Liêu. Khmer militias used their guns and settled old scores... with their Vietnamese neighbors, especially the poor Khmer tenant farmers with their Vietnamese

---

[10] Trần Văn Trà, *Miền Nam thành đồng di trước về sau*, 191.
[11] SHD. 10H 3825. F.T.S.V. 2ᵉ Bureau. "Situation à Rach Gia." Saigon, March 19, 1946.
[12] Bộ Tư Lệnh Quân Khu 9, *Quân khu 9 30 năm kháng chiến (1945–1975)* (Hanoi: Quân đội nhân dân, 1996), 77.
[13] Claude Réau, "Avec le Corps léger d'intervention de Djidjelli à Tam-Binh," in Jean Clauzel, ed., *La France d'Outre-Mer 1930–1960: témoignages d'administrateurs et de magistrats* (Paris: Karthala, 2004) 531–532.

landlords."[14] A history of the August 1945 uprisings in the south and their aftermath noted that "the greatest difficulty after we seized power [in Trà Vinh] was that reactionaries incited Khmer to rise up and kill Vietnamese cadres."[15] The author blames Khmer animosity towards ethnic Vietnamese on imperialists. One source notes that on or after December 12, 1945, when the French military returned to Trà Vinh, some Khmer rose up: "Amidst the chaos, with people fleeing their homes, some Khmer following the French rose up, looted, set fire to homes, and beheaded Vietnamese."[16] Trương Dương Vũ, in his evocative memoir, explains how the conflict first came to Sóc Trăng in 1945 and 1946. Here he recounts the experiences of Năm Trương:

When in Đại An, Năm Trương witnessed our fellow kin [đồng bào] from Trà Vinh fleeing to Sóc Trăng. Sampans, overflowing with people from the other side of the Bassac [river], were crossing to Sóc Trăng. The stories they told about fleeing made one shudder with fright. Our fellow kin from Trà Vinh took sampans. Those who did not flee in time were beheaded, disemboweled, the young hacked to pieces... Our Trà Vinh compatriots were terror-stricken. Năm Trương was overcome with emotion. Looking towards Ngan Rô, Rạch Gòi, Sóc Vông, he stated that there were many [Khmer] villages and he felt anxious.[17]

Or another account from that time, by the same author:

[They] followed the stream of refugees going from Mây Hắc, on the road through Phú An, Song Phụng, to Cái Cao... to find a place far from the enemy posts, a place with lots of our kinfolk [đồng bào], far from the Khmer villages or Hòa Hảo areas. Every day, corpses of the enemy, of our kinfolk, of carabao, of dogs, bobbed on the Hậu River. Those living along the river banks did not dare eat the shrimp! Everything was permeated by an atmosphere of death, illness, and terror.[18]

Violence soon broke out in Sóc Trăng and Bạc Liêu provinces as well. Commenting on the destruction and killings from December 1945 to early January 1946, the Chinese writer Vương Hồng Sển of Sóc Trăng province lamented the way that the "cruel" Cambodians took advantage of the French desire to repress the Vietnamese (and perhaps others) in his village: "they seized belongings, and set fires so that the sky was darkened in the hamlet of Hòa An. They were without conscience, amusing

[14] Thomas Engelbert, "Ideology and Reality: *Nationalitätenpolitik* in North and South Vietnam of the First Indochina War," in Thomas Engelbert and Andreas Schneider, eds., *Ethnic Minorities and Nationalism in Southeast Asia* (Frankfurt: Peter Lang, 2000), 128–129.

[15] Bùi Công Đặng, "Tổng khởi nghĩa ở Lục Tinh," in Trần Bạch Đằng, et al, eds., *Mùa Thu rồi. Ngày hăm ba* (Hanoi: Chính trị Quốc gia, 1995), 454.

[16] Việt Nam Cộng Hòa, *Địa phương chí tỉnh Vĩnh Bình* (S.l.: s.n.,1973), 44.

[17] Trương Dương Vũ, *Máu trở về tim. Ký sự* ([Sóc Trăng?]: Tổng Hợp Hậu Giang, 1980), 15.

[18] Ibid., 23.

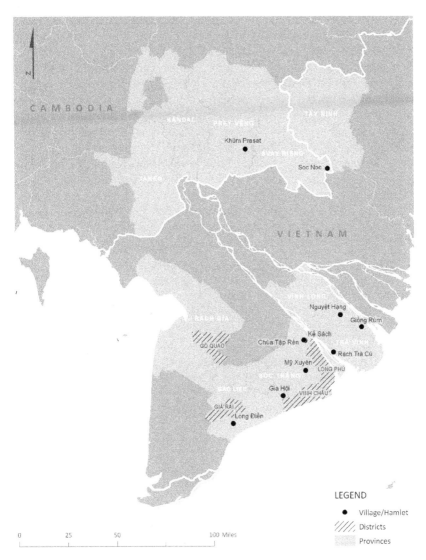

Figure 4.1 Sites of Khmer-Vietnamese violence, 1945–7
The map above is not a comprehensive representation of all the provinces, particular districts, and villages in Cambodia and Vietnam in which Khmer-Vietnamese violence broke out.
Source: Nuala Cowan, creator, based on data from the author. Published in Shawn McHale, "Ethnicity, Violence, and Khmer-Vietnamese Relations: The Significance of the Lower Mekong Delta, 1757–1954," *Journal of Asian Studies* 72(2) (May 2013), 376.

themselves by killing people for no reason."[19] Sển gives us a riveting sense of the brutality, chaos, and fear in the attacks on Sóc Trăng. On January 5, the Sóc Trăng market is set alight; the French troops arrive, the Vietnamese ones withdraw. The next day, the Bãi Xàu market also goes up in flames. In Hòa Tú, where he temporarily takes refuge, he can see the dark smoke from the Nhu Gia market, also on fire. Calamity follows calamity: the next few days, Khmers are on the rampage, sacking and killing. But January 18 and 19 "are the most horrible of all during this evacuation": the sky is "lit up red," and he hears the news that French troops are coming on boats from Bạc Liêu to attack his village, Hòa Tú, and so he flees again. From the 20th to the 25th, he moves from place to place in a boat, for "to flee was to flee death."[20]

Two hundred kilometers up the Mekong, on the Cambodia-Vietnam border, Yannick Guiberteau offers an odd account of the French seizure of Tri Tôn by a combined Franco-Cambodian force on January 24, 1946:

We noted with curiosity the arrival of the Cambodian column, which had marched from Tinh Biên, on the Vinh Tế canal [near the Cambodia-Cochinchina border]. At its head marched the infantry, brave soldiers, led by French officers. They were followed by a column of 2,000 to 3,000 persons: men, women, and children walking behind, or on oxcarts, carrying their meager belongings as well as loot.[21]

It appears – though the evidence is still sketchy – that violence spiked again in February and March 1946. The French military again seems to have acted as a catalyst, but was unable or unwilling to clamp down on violence when it spiraled out of control. Intriguingly, Prince Monireth of Cambodia sent "several hundred" of his troops to Cochinchina in January 1946. They were put under French command to be used in the reconquest of the region.[22] First used in the reconquest of the area northeast of Saigon, these troops then took part in operations around Tây Ninh province. Apparently in January, the French also recruited troops from Sóc Trăng, Bạc Liêu, and Châu Đốc provinces for the second battalion of the B.M.E.O. (Bataillion de marche d'Extrême-Orient).[23] On February 24, 1946, the French military carried out an "urgent and high priority draft [levée]" of one thousand persons in the provinces of Sóc Trăng, Trà Vinh, and Cần Thơ.[24] These untrained paramilitary forces supplemented French units. They included many

---

[19] Vương Hồng Sển, *Hơn nửa đời hư* (California: Văn Nghệ, 1994), 396.
[20] Ibid., 300–302.
[21] Yannick Guiberteau, *La Dévastation: cuirassé de rivière* (Paris: Albin Michel, 1984), 182.
[22] Henry-Jean Loustau, *Les deux batallions: Cochinchine-Tonkin, 1945–1952* (Paris: Albin Michel, 1987), 61.
[23] Ibid., 63.   [24] Bodin, *La France et ses soldats*, 118.

Khmer. In essence, by recruiting Khmer to fight against ethnic Vietnamese, the French stoked an already tense situation.

When General Nyo received reports in February and March of a "struggle" between Vietnamese and Khmer in Châu Đốc, Sóc Trăng, and Trà Vinh provinces, he grew alarmed: "we must avoid, at all costs, that our Cambodian auxiliaries thwart our aims – [we must] try to stifle a well-known racial hatred."[25] Nyo's statement had no impact. By early March, his intelligence services were reporting that "three provinces, at this time, live in fear of the Cambodians. These are the provinces of Travinh, Chaudoc, and Soctrang. Followed by their wives and children, they [the Cambodians] pillage and kill, and in some areas they make all the men disappear." For Trà Vinh province, this source adds, "the Administration and the Army are using Cambodians to continue the 'cleansing' (*nettoyage*). Every Annamite is considered to be 'Viet Minh,' thus criminal, and is shot, most often without due process."[26]

A history of the Việt Minh Public Security forces mentions that in February 1946, a "reactionary clique" of Khmer in Bạc Liêu province incited the youth to violence. These youths, "supported and armed by the French, arrested revolutionary cadres and members of the masses, and tortured and killed them in a very savage manner." They imprisoned others in a Cambodian temple. This group was wiped out by a Vanguard Youth team composed of Khmer but led by a Vietnamese who attacked the temple, released "five thousand" prisoners and dozens of cadres, and uncovered the bodies of twelve "revolutionary fighters" who had been killed.[27] The prisoner numbers seem wildly inflated. Vietnamese sources are too sketchy to pin down overall death tolls. One source, published long after the events had passed, suggested that "there were places like the district of Vĩnh Châu, Giarai [in Bạc Liêu province] where an entire village was killed with more than one hundred lives lost."[28] A third source on Bạc Liêu elliptically states that "around this time" – apparently in January 1946 – "incidents" (*cuộc xô xát*) occurred in the villages of Vĩnh Trạch, Hưng Hội, Vĩnh Châu, Châu Thới, Hoà Bình, Long Điền, Vĩnh Mỹ, and Khánh Bình. These "incidents" appear to have been violent.[29]

[25] SHD. 10H 3825. S.E.S.A.G. "Cambodgiens de Cochinchine." Saigon, February 18, 1946.
[26] SHD. 10H 3825. Deuxième Bureau. "Partisans cambodgiens. Provinces de TRAVINH-CHAUDOC-SOCTRANG" Saigon, March 6, 1946.
[27] Lê Ngọc Bổn, *Biên niên sự kiện lịch sử lực lượng an ninh nhân dân (1945–1954)* (Hanoi: Công An Nhân Dân, 1995), 51–53.
[28] Hoành Kim Anh, *9 năm kháng chiến miền tây Nam Bộ*, 60.
[29] Ban Chấp Hành Đảng Bộ Tỉnh Bạc Liêu, *Lịch sử Đảng bộ tỉnh Bạc Liêu (1927–1975)* (Bạc Liêu: Ban Thường Vụ Tỉnh Ủy, 2002), Vol. 1, 117.

Killings gave rise to counter-reprisals, but it is difficult to know how widespread they were. After blaming French military intelligence for causing "contradictions" between Khmer and Vietnamese that led to Khmer killing Vietnamese, General Trần Văn Trà admitted that the Party "used force to repress, and arrested hundreds of Khmer."[30] A source of uncertain reliability that appears to refer to Sóc Trăng and Bạc Liêu provinces alone presents the Việt Minh reaction as much bloodier:

Cambodians were executed by the hundreds. The number of victims cannot be determined. During the months of December 1945 and January 1946, massacres of Cambodians were particularly common in the provinces of Sóc Trăng (Cai Sach and Go Co regions). In Bạc Liêu province, assassinations were still a daily occurrence until April [1946].[31]

The closest any Vietnamese has come to providing a "smoking gun" is in this revelatory Việt Minh document, captured by the French military in Cà Mau:

The Cambodian Question in Camau – The Party has never called for the massacre of Cambodians. On the contrary, it has always pursued a policy of friendship towards them to gain their sympathy. However, cadres who came from elsewhere gave the order to massacre Cambodians, thus creating diplomatic difficulties given the barbaric attitudes toward ethnic minorities. Comrades are requested to carry out strict inquiries in such cases in order to uncover the agents of such crimes and to report to the regional committee.[32]

Violence between Khmer and Vietnamese endured across the delta and into Cambodia. For example, in the Gò Quao-Long Mỹ-Giồng Riềng area (near the town of Rạch Gía), the French reported that bands of Việt Minh were resorting to small-scale looting, while Khmer were still killing Vietnamese in mid-March 1946.[33] Killing occurred elsewhere as well. One source, apparently speaking of 1946, states that Khmer on both sides of the Cochinchina-Cambodia border near Tây Ninh "rose up against the Vietnamese... From bases in Cambodia, they crossed the border, finding and killing Vietnamese, setting fire to houses, stealing property, causing untold misery, death and grief."[34]

While this early phase, from August 1945 through March 1946, saw numerous killings, there was spatial variation in these deaths. Ethnic

---

[30] Trần Văn Trà, *Nam Bộ thành đồng*, 59–60.
[31] SHD. 10 H 602. Livre Blanc. Atrocités Việt Minh. Saigon, June 6, 1946. Perhaps the author misspelled Kế Sách and Gò Quao.
[32] SHD. 10H 3825. Deuxième Bureau. Le développement de la conférence au commisariat régional de Camau le 15.3.46. [Captured and translated document].
[33] SHD. 10H 3825. 2ème Bureau. Situation à Rach Gia. Saigon, March 19, 1946.
[34] Ban Liên Lạc, *Tư liệu lịch sử*, 92.

violence was concentrated in areas with large numbers of Khmer, but even in these areas, some villages were hit hard while others were spared. Tư Hớn, the representative of the People's Committee in charge of affairs on the Labaste Plantation in Sóc Trăng, noted that:

In Kế Sách, the reactionary Khmer from Kế Sách also flocked to the densely populated areas and Vietnamese gardens to loot and kill, but not to the extent of that in Long Phú district [Sóc Trăng province]. Few of our fellow kin [đồng bào] in Kế Sách living on the border with Cần Thơ province were victims of the reactionary Khmer, but they were apprehensive about the reactionary Hòa Hảo. Reaching Tân Lập, it was as if one had entered a safe area, where people could eat and sleep in peace... Here it seemed utterly calm.[35]

Vietnamese sources often refer to Khmer actions as a "movement" (*phong trào*) to kill Vietnamese, but no central Khmer authority directed the atrocities. Now, it is true that events over the summer of 1945, such as the Cambodian declaration of independence and the rising antagonism against Vietnamese in Cambodia, influenced Khmer Krom in Cochinchina. But the initial violence in 1945 and 1946, while shaped by Cambodian events, was also fueled by a concatenation of localized grievances, such as conflicts over Vietnamese seizures of Khmer land. The French reoccupation of the delta lit this fuel and sparked a series of conflagrations. As the war dragged on, and as a range of outside actors became involved in local affairs, violence became linked to broader ethnonationalist claims. This largely suppressed history has never been adequately described or analyzed, nor has its significance been addressed.

Explanations for the violence tend to diverge along ethnic grounds. Vietnamese almost always portray Khmer massacres of Vietnamese as senseless, brutal, and coming out of the blue. A typical account is the one by Nguyễn Hiến Lê, a writer who opposed the French return but did not join the Việt Minh. Referring to the town of Long Điền, in Bạc Liêu province, he wrote that:

many Thổ [Khmer] would get drunk and pillage, seeking places full of belongings, and whatever Vietnamese they met they would "*cáp duồng*" [cut off the head]. The Thổ tragedy in southern Vietnam was truly catastrophic: in times of peace, they [the Khmer] were docile and courteous, but in times of disorder they became brigands. In Tân Thanh, also in 1946, rumors spread several times that Thổ [Khmer] from Svay Rieng [Cambodia] would be crossing Đồng Tháp with plans to set fire to houses, steal rice, or steal water buffalo from several villages near where I was staying. The populace had to take precautions and organize to resist them.[36]

---

[35] Trương Dương Vũ, *Máu trở về tim*, 41–2.
[36] Nguyễn Hiến Lê, *Hồi ký Nguyễn Hiến Lê*, 348.

Vietnamese communists add a twist to this kind of story, blaming the French military and their intelligence services for inciting the Khmer.[37] In contrast, when Khmer have remembered the events of 1945, they have skipped over the initial Khmer attacks in 1945 and 1946 and focused on subsequent Vietnamese massacres of Khmer and later Vietnamese land-grabs. Philip Taylor has eloquently reported on oral narratives on events in the 1940s: after Khmer fled areas coming under attack, the Việt Minh and Hòa Hảo moved in, seized the land, and redistributed it to ethnic Vietnamese.[38] An American document from 1979, conveying Khmer Krom beliefs, states that in 1945:

> thousands of Khmer Krom were killed in pogroms carried out in various location in the Ca Mau, Soc Trang, and Bac Lieu areas. The most common method of killing was by setting fire to buildings into which Khmer Krom had been herded. Those who tried to flee from the buildings were shot. The stories of these pogroms have been passed down orally through successive generations of Khmer Krom.[39]

If Vietnamese and Cambodians point fingers at each other, and some-times at the French, the French try to absolve themselves of responsibil-ity. French sources repeatedly assert that "a latent animosity" existed between Khmer and Vietnamese under French rule, but "never had a chance to manifest itself." One source pins part of the blame for violence on the Việt Minh: "In 1945, the Việt Minh became all powerful in the provinces and did not fail to demonstrate to its antagonist the superiority of its position. In a natural reaction, at the time when French authority was being reestablished in these areas, numerous Cambodian elements collaborated with our troops and in certain cases took revenge."[40]

These widespread killings and atrocities constituted the first fracture, driving a wedge between many Vietnamese and Khmer. Was France's main intention to foment ethnic hatred? Perhaps not, but it was clearly aware of the dangers of using Khmer "partisans" in a war against Vietnamese. Desiring to defeat Việt Minh forces, France took advantage of ethnic antagonisms to achieve its larger aim. In the years to come, the Việt Minh would strive to reach out to Khmer and convince them that

---

[37] Hướng Tân and Hồng Đức, *Kháng chiến Cao-Miên nhất định* (Việt Bắc [?]: Sự Thật, 1954), 25; Trần Văn Trà, *Miền Nam thành đồng đi trước về sau*, 179.

[38] Taylor, "Losing the Waterways: The Displacement of Khmer Communities from the Freshwater Rivers of the Mekong Delta, 1945–2010," *Modern Asian Studies* 47 (2013), especially 516–21.

[39] "Khmer Krom and Others Resistance Activities in Hau Giang Province (DOI : 1975 – August 1979) – August 1, 1979." Folder 08, Box 22, Douglas Pike Collection: Unit 06 – Democratic Republic of Vietnam, The Vietnam Archive, Texas Tech University. Digital copy accessed October 25, 2008. The document presumably comes from a US intelli-gence agency.

[40] SHD. 10 H 282. Les minorités Khmeres au Sud Viet-Nam. January, 1954.

they had their interests at heart, but this early violence made the task difficult.

4.2 The Breakdown of Order in the Countryside: Vietnamese and French Challenges

While the French were breaking apart Việt Minh forces in 1945 and 1946, the Việt Minh itself, weak and poorly linked, was undergoing internal turmoil. As the Việt Minh leader Trần Văn Trà has written:

> After our Front was destroyed, our armed forces dispersed to areas that were still secure, the bases at Đồng Tháp Mười and U Minh [Forest], while villages continued guerrilla warfare. The government at all levels was set up but was not yet consolidated... The Party and government base in many areas disintegrated. Coordination among provinces encountered many difficulties or broke down.[41]

By early 1946, as one recent history states, the Việt Minh in southern Vietnam "was facing difficulties, and even, at times, peril."[42] But the French, stretched too thin, could not take advantage of Vietnamese weakness. Chaos and uncertainty made it difficult for any state to exercise political authority over large swaths of the delta. The Việt Minh underwent a crisis, as revealed by this revelatory document from March 1946:

> Since the fall of Cà Mau, following the difficulty of liaisons among comrades that is a result, the bureau of the regional committee has been moved to Tran Hung Dong. Following the meeting of February 20, 1946 between the twelve delegates from different sectors, the secret committee of the General Committee was elected... *However, the secret committee in question is made up of individuals who have been judged to be unfit.* At the time of the [French] capture of Cà Mau, the internal situation of the Party was confused and liaison interrupted.[43]

Nguyễn Thanh Sơn, writing to General Nguyễn Bình three months later, reiterated the critical situation in the south, emphasizing the longstanding and "serious shortcomings of liaison, information, and discipline."[44] This criticism was key: in these early years, it was often local leaders, some of them "unfit" and undisciplined, and not top ones, who contributed indiscriminate and strategically senseless violence.

---

[41] Trần Văn Trà, "Chiến tranh," 48.
[42] Hội Đồng Chỉ Đạo Biên Soạn Lịch Sử Nam Bộ Kháng Chiến, *Lịch sử Nam bộ kháng chiến* (Hanoi: Chính trị quốc gia, 2010), Vol. 1, 274.
[43] SHD. 10H 3825. [Captured document] Regional Committee in Camau. Cà Mau, March 27, 1946. My italics.
[44] ANOM. HCI. SPCE 379. [captured and translated document] Nguyen Thanh Son au camarade Nguyen Binh, chef de Zone et aux camarades des cadres de la 7 ème zone de combat. June 23, 1946.

Despite Việt Minh weakness, the French government struggled to recruit Vietnamese for administrative positions. As a 1948 revolutionary book on the Việt Minh stated, "The puppet government of Nguyễn Văn Thịnh was established, but it could not administer at the district level... *those reactionaries who worked with the colonialists were beheaded*. In one village, the French reinstalled twelve village notables; when the French returned one morning, they found a sack that had been placed before the door of a village elder; opening it, eleven heads of village notables fell out."[45] Evidence of French failure to protect inhabitants was legion. In Sóc Trăng, the provincial administrator complained in August that the police force lacked firearms – "without which it is practically paralyzed."[46] In Cần Thơ province, administrators grumbled that prosecutors seemed more focused on "the repression of petty larceny in the city" than in cracking down on terrorism in rural areas. Outside the city limits, small bands of fifteen to twenty men roamed the countryside, engaging in "acts of banditry for which they do not even try, most of the time, to ascribe a political character... They kidnap or kill notables or, above all, demand ransom from rich landowners or well-off shopkeepers."[47]

In August 1946, the administrator of Trà Vinh province demanded to be allotted administrators for Tiểu Cần, Trà Cú, and Càng Long districts of the province. "I insist that my personnel requests be met with the shortest possible delay." A month and a half later, he reported five bodies found floating on a river, all stabbed.[48] This incident was not isolated. One recent Vietnamese history describes September and October of 1946 in the western Mekong Delta as the "high tide" of attempts to "exterminate traitors [and] wipe out puppets" when setting up revolutionary governments at the village level.[49]

Violence rose because the Việt Minh wanted to consolidate its position before the ceasefire agreement negotiated by Hồ Chi Minh and Marius Moutet went into effect on October 30. But in Cochinchina, High

---

[45] Ngo Hà, *Cách mạnh tháng tám*, 35. Is this story true? This source contains other stories that seem improbable. Nonetheless, the extent of beheadings in the delta does seem to have been substantial. Emphasis is from the original.

[46] VNA-II. PTHNV D.01 File 347, L'Administrateur Chef de la Province de Soctrang [Bartel] à M. le Commissaire de la République pour la Cochinchine. Soctrang, August 9, 1946.

[47] In VNA-II. PTHNV D.01 File 347, see Le Directeur des Affaires Politiques à M. l'Inspecteur des Affaires Politiques. October 9, 1946; [same file], L'Administrateur de Cantho à M. le Ministère de l'Intérieur. Cantho, July 23, 1946.

[48] VNA – II. PTHNV D.01 File 347. L'Administrateur en Travinh [Émiry]. Rapport politique. Travinh, August 31, 1946; [same file], L'Administrateur en Travinh [Émiry] à M. le Président. October 12, 1946.

[49] *Lịch sử Nam Bộ kháng chiến*, 288.

Commissioner for Indochina d'Argenlieu ignored the ceasefire, and allowed fighting to continue. As Lieutenant Henry-Jean Loustau wrote, "My operations continued as if nothing had happened."[50] The French military's flagrant violation of the accord telegraphed to their Vietnamese opponents that the French signed this agreement in bad faith. Indeed, the Hòa Hảo leader Huỳnh Phú Sổ, admitting the violence of some of his followers, also pointed the finger at "reactionaries in the French military ranks, who, after October 30th, in some areas, continue to terrorize us and the people."[51]

Despite such violence, French sources present the year 1946 as a qualified success: French units had driven into the Mekong Delta, dislodged and broken up Việt Minh forces, and begun to reestablish a governmental presence at the city and village level. They also began to reach out to the Khmer. At first, the French flirted with the idea of giving the Khmer minority in Cochinchina greater political power. A Vĩnh Long province military history claims that the French promised greater political representation for the Khmer of the delta, including self-rule in the framework of a country of South Vietnam. For a short time, the French allowed a Khmer Party to function in the South as a counterweight to the Việt Minh attempt to reach out to Khmer.

The French saw the Việt Minh to be in disarray by the end of 1946. Việt Minh sources confirm elements of this view but contest others. Writing to General Võ Nguyên Giáp in November 1946, the Resistance Committee for the South pointed out that the French were occupying all the major cities and transportation routes, and that the Vietnamese opposing them had very few organized military units under its direct control. In the East, the committee stated, "the soldiers are poorly clothed and lack food." Despite such challenges, it went on to state, and the fact that "finances are tight," "the morale of the troops is stable." A key problem was organizational: because of distances, it was difficult to coordinate actions in the three military sectors in the South. The Việt Minh needed to develop a general staff. Despite such problems, "the system as a whole was satisfactory." Provincial committees and armed units took less action independently of the Executive Committee. All of the provincial executive committees had been reorganized. The French controlled limited territory: they "can only reestablish their government in areas held by their troops or in large cities; in the villages, they cannot succeed." French

---

[50] Loustau, *Les deux battailons*, 126.
[51] "Ông Hồn Quyền (ở Sài Gòn) vào chiến khu phỏng vấn Đức Huỳnh Giáo chủ," in Giáo Hội Phật Giáo Hòa Hảo, *Sấm giảng thi văn toàn bộ của Đức Huỳnh Giáo chủ*, ([Saigon]: Ban Phổ Thông Giáo Lý Trung Ương, 1970), 449. This originally appeared in the *Nam Kỳ* newspaper, November 29, 1946.

success had come at a cost: "many civilians had been victims of terrorism" as well as arson.[52] The Việt Minh saw itself as battered but holding its own. This was an illusion. The year 1947 would prove formative in reordering the southern landscape.

4.3 The Reordering of Southern Politics in 1947

At the beginning of 1947, P. V. Toan, writing to his friend Nguyễn Minh Nghĩa, a pharmacy student in Paris, asked rhetorically:

What will happen in the coming year? Who will be added to the list of Vietnamese who have died? How many houses will be burned, pillaged, or destroyed? How many households will be obliterated? With the passage of time, customs will be lost. Some will cry over a spouse; others will lose a father. How many unhappy ones, because their dear ones are either killed or in prison?[53]

This Việt Minh supporter's trepidation for the future presaged the disastrous year of 1947. True, the Việt Minh had successes. It had weathered French attacks, was successfully building its institutions, such as peoples committees at the village level, and was knitting together its organizations throughout the delta. But despite such successes, the Việt Minh cracked apart in 1947, marking a critical turning point in the war for the South.

The breakdown of the Việt Minh had been brewing since 1945. Groups such as the Bình Xuyên, the Hòa Hảo, and the Cao Đài did not trust the overall military commander of the southern struggle, General Nguyễn Bình. Nguyễn Bình's failure to unify the Việt Minh military forces is intriguing. After all, in December 1946, the Party Center had specifically told its "Nam Bộ comrades" that "the most important [task], regarding religious groups, the Catholics, the Cao Đài, the Hòa Hảo, is to do one's utmost to promote unity... [and] to work to cement ties with the Democrat Party and [other] parties and factions."[54] Why, if the Party Center insisted on unity, was the result the opposite? The most compelling answer to this question is that the Party Center failed to exercise tight control over the Việt Minh in the South, a problem that endured through the first half of the war.[55] Indeed, the dynamics of civil war violence, as

[52] SHD. 10 H 603. Booklet titled T/F/E/O. 2eme Bureau. Documents vietnamiens (VM). Novembre jusqu'au 20 décembre [1946]. Intercepted, decrypted and translated telegram from Comité exécutif du Nam Bo to Vo Nguyen Giap, November 10, 1946.

[53] HCI. CP 107. [Intercepted letter from P.V. Toan., Saigon, to Nguyen Minh Nghia. Paris, January 17, 1947.]

[54] "Thư gửi các đồng chí Nam Bộ" [December 1946], quoted in Lịch sử Nam Bộ Kháng Chiến, 314.

[55] Christopher E. Goscha, Vietnam. Un État né de la guerre (Paris: Armand Colin, 2013), 83–88.

well as cleavages within the Việt Minh itself, shaped the war in the South more than Party diktat.

The shifting relationships among the French, Cao Đài, and Hòa Hảo engendered new conflicts. It is difficult to untangle all the violence that occurred in the delta in 1946 and 1947, as contestants present contending stories about what happened that year. As Guillemot notes, those Cao Đài based in Tây Ninh pursued a strategy in 1946 and into 1947 to preempt the Việt Minh from expanding in the area between their stronghold of Tây Ninh and Saigon.[56] The strains within the rickety Việt Minh coalition were so bad that leading anti-communist nationalists even challenged the Việt Minh's right to represent them. On September 21, 1946, nationalists in the Hòa Hảo established the Social-Democrat Party [Đảng Việt Nam Dân Chủ Xã Hội], which promoted "social revolutionary" goals, including democracy.[57] The party included non-Hòa Hảo like Nguyễn Văn Sâm among its leaders. The Việt Minh, angered at this threat to its authority, lashed out at its potential rivals.

At the same time, not all violence was driven by high-ranking leaders. Some welled up from below. As Huỳnh Phú Sổ admitted, referring to fights between Hòa Hảo and Việt Minh: "Past clashes are due to the resentments of some fighters whom I allowed to join the Security Forces [Bảo An Đội]... Right now, some of our troubles are due to dishonest persons who, in these tumultuous times, are pretending to act in the name of Trần Văn Soái, also known as Năm Lửa [one of Huỳnh Phú Sổ's key military aides], while plundering from the people. But Năm Lửa is trying to get rid of them."[58] Leaders, in other words, could not always control their supposed followers.

In this volatile situation, the French skillfully played on Vietnamese fears and anger. As Christopher Goscha has perceptively argued, in January 1947, Léon Pignon, the Commissioner for Political Affairs in French Indochina,

urged his superiors to 'take the dispute that we have with the Việt Minh, and displace it internally to the Annamese, while committing ourselves as little as possible to the reprisals that should be the task of the indigenous opponents of this party.' His ultimate goal was to create a non-communist and counter-revolutionary state allied with the French, thanks to which the latter could

---

[56] François Guillemot, "Autopsy of a Massacre: On a Political Purge in the Early Days of the Indochina War (Nam Bo 1947)," *European Journal of East Asian Studies* 9(2) (2010), 238.

[57] See "Tuyên Ngôn của Đảng Việt Nam Dân Chủ Xã Hội do Đức Huỳnh Thủ Lãnh công bố ngày 21–9–46" in *Sấm giảng thi văn*, 440–441.

[58] "Ông Hồn Quyên (ở Sài Gòn) vào chiến khu phỏng vấn Đức Huỳnh Giáo chủ," n Giáo Hội Phật Giáo Hòa Hảo, *Sấm giảng thi văn toàn bộ của Đức Huỳnh Giáo chủ* ([Saigon]: Ban Phổ Thông Giáo Lý Trung Ương, 1970), 449.

maintain their presence in eastern Indochina... In fact... the French directly contributed to the intensification of ethnic and civil violence of the Indochina War.[59]

As Goscha argues, the French fanned the flames of existing ethnic and civil discord and worsened divisions, all in the name of defeating the Việt Minh. But to succeed, they had to have audiences that were receptive to this message. To divide the populace, the French or their allies circulated incendiary propaganda. For example, one leaflet lit into the Việt Minh: its "[people's] committees are cruel, its dishonest police terrorize the people; its coffers are empty, and taxes heavy." Propagandists harangued the inhabitants of the delta to "overthrow the wicked Việt Minh, support the movement of the masses, and support the spirit of true democracy!"[60] Given the missteps of the Việt Minh, some Vietnamese may well have been swayed by such appeals.

In late 1946 or early 1947, Cao Đài leader Phạm Công Tắc eloquently conveyed a sense that Cao Đài followers were besieged and worlds were falling apart:

Events have gone from bad to worse, and while I preach brotherly love and the forgiveness of sins, I only see unfolding, around me, endless theft, looting, destruction, and killing. Our faithful are not spared. Anarchy brandishes its sword, terror is sown throughout the land, and Death is mowing down other innocent lives in our families that are already in mourning or suffering the disappearance of their members.

Phạm Công Tắc argued that it was time to work with the French, but with the goal of achieving "democratic freedoms" and the "fullness of sovereignty."[61] On behalf of the Cao Đài, his deputy Trần Quang Vinh signed a military agreement with the French on January 8, 1947.[62] Underlining the sensitivity of working with the French, Phạm Công Tắc both noted that Ho Chi Minh had negotiated with the French, and that he was sure that "all true patriots share my sentiments" about the need to work together against the "stealing, robbing, extortion, and assassination" that had characterized the country in the recent past. That this was a troubling yet understandable decision for Cao Đài followers is captured in this letter:

---

[59] Goscha, *Vietnam. Un état né de la guerre*, 256.
[60] VNA – II. PTHNV Box 505 File F6.27.
[61] SHD. 10 H 603. Ho Phap PHAM CONG TAC, "Au peuple Annamite de Cochinchine." [undated, translation from late 1946 or January 1947]. For context, see Jérémy Jammes, "Le Saint-Siege Caodaiste de Tây Ninh et le Médium Phạm Công Tắc (1890–1959)," *Outre-Mers* 94 (2006), 238–239.
[62] Guillemot, "Autopsy of a Massacre," 233.

Figure 4.2 Việt Minh, Cao Đài, and Hòa Hảo in the Mekong Delta, 1947
Source: Isabelle Durand, Institut d'Asie Orientale, 2010. In François
Guillemot, "Autopsy of a Massacre on a Political Purge in the Early
Days of the Indochina War (Nam Bo 1947)," *European Journal of East
Asian Studies* 9(2) (2010), 235.

You said that Uncle Ba is working for the French. That is not quite right. Arrested
by the communists, he was imprisoned for four months, even though he had fought
in their ranks. They wanted to execute him. Hearing the news, he and a bunch of
others escaped. Twenty of them were arrested again and executed because they
were not from the same Party. Uncle Ba took refuge at Tây Ninh. The communists
attacked the Cao Đài Holy See, strongly committed to killing the Cao Đài leaders,
because the latter supported the nationalist side [fighting for] independence. Many
Cao Đài followers were killed. Thus Uncle Ba and his co-religionists felt compelled
to respond with force. This sad and humiliating situation was caused by the
communists, who fight for their Party, not for the Nation.[63]

[63] ANOM. HCI. CP 107. [Intercepted letter from Tran Dinh Quan, Saigon, to Nguyen
Van Hanh, Paris. February 18, 1947].

Figure 4.3 Cao Đài leader Phạm Công Tắc, 1948
Source: Jack Birns/The LIFE Picture Collection. July 1, 1948. Getty
Image #50514137.

Figure 4.4 Hòa Hảo leader Huỳnh Phú Sổ, circa 1940
Source: Photographer unknown. From Văn Thế Vĩnh, *Phật giáo Hòa
Hảo. Đạo Phật nhập thế* (United States: self published, 2016).
Unpaginated front matter. Online at https://tuoitrephatgiaohoahao
.com/p26a902/pghh-dao-phat-nhap-the.

Phạm Công Tắc did not endorse French colonialism. Quite the contrary: he made a strategic decision to ally with the French in the short term in order to win independence for Vietnam. In return, the French armed the Cao Đài of the Tây Ninh branch in order to fight a common enemy: the Việt Minh.

The Việt Minh swiftly reacted. In February 1947, Phạm Hùng called for the "impartial" suppression of the Cao Dai "reactionaries."[64] General Nguyễn Bình, Việt Minh military commander in the South since November 1945, increasingly turned to violence. As Goscha observes, "If Nguyễn Bình's fiery approach had helped hold things together during the tense year of 1946, the following year his heavy-handed approach would see it begin to fall apart."[65] Nguyễn Bình ratcheted up the conflict with the Cao Đài and promptly attacked Cao Đài forces near Tây Ninh. The Cao Đài counterattacked, "inflicting heavy losses on the latter."[66] The level of local violence was remarkable: according to one French report, Nguyễn Bình's troops killed 300 Cao Đài in the Vĩnh Lộc and Đức Hòa region northwest of Saigon in February.[67]

Soon after the main Cao Đài forces threw in their lot with the French, they reached out to the Hòa Hảo to ally with them against the Việt Minh. The Việt Minh was in a precarious condition by March 1947: of the twenty-five regiments in the South, six to seven, many under Bình Xuyên control, were breaking with the communists. Of the fifteen regiments that were specifically in the eastern zone of the South – mostly to the east and north of Saigon – the nationalist leader Nguyễn Văn Sâm estimated that only four of fifteen regiments were controlled by "true communists." The rest were under "nationalist" leadership but "very infiltrated" by the Việt Minh.[68] In the western zone, on which this book centers, of the Cao Đài and Hòa Hảo had already turned against the communists in the Việt Minh.

[64] Goscha, *Vietnam: Un état né de la guerre*, 258.
[65] Christopher Goscha, "A 'Popular' Side of the Vietnamese Army: General Nguyen Bình in the South," in Christopher Goscha and Bénoît de Tréglodé, eds., *Naissance d'un État-Parti: Le Viêt Nam depuis 1945* (Paris: Les Indes Savantes, 2004), 342.
[66] Guillemot, "Autopsy of a Massacre," 234.
[67] ANOM. HCI. SPCE 379. Service de la Sûreté. Note No. 367/C.F.R. Bazin. Activités religieuses. Secte Caodaique de Tayninh. Saigon, February 13, 1947. Signé: Bazin.
[68] ANOM. SPCE 379. Extrait de la note No. 535/C.F.R. du 3 Mars 1947. Le Controleur de la Sûreté Bazin; SHD. 10 H 603. S.E.S.A.G. Bulletin de renseignement No. 12984. Saigon, March 29, 1947. Source: Annamite. Valeur: Très sure. Très secret; HCI. SPCE 379. Service de la Sûreté: "Activités religieuses. Secte Phat – Giao Hoa-Hao de Huynh Phu So." Saigon, April 9, 1947.

4.4 The Final Fractures of the Anti-French Resistance

In March 1947, the anti-French coalition definitively split apart. In that month, Hòa Hảo leader Hùynh Phú Sổ and Mười Trí (Hùynh Văn Trí, a former Bình Xuyên who was now fighting with the Hoà Hảo) began discussing an alliance with the main Cao Đài branch in Tây Ninh. They had allied in the past, so such a move was not new. In the same month, Nguyễn Văn Sâm met with a wide range of nationalist leaders, including some in the Việt Minh, to reconstitute an anti-communist, nationalist, and anti-Việt Minh movement. On March 17, Hùynh Phú Sổ, meeting with Nguyễn Văn Sâm, agreed to join this nationalist front. French intelligence also reported at this time that the nationalists had recently tried to assassinate Việt Minh leaders.[69] The same day, a meeting was held at Bình Xuyên headquarters to iron out a combined military force (involving the Bình Xuyên, the Hòa Hảo, and members of seven military units (*chi đội*)). Participants also discussed preparations to assassinate Việt Minh general Nguyễn Bình.[70] The same month, Hùynh Phú Sổ, through his intermediary Lương Trọng Tường, contacted the French for arms to defend themselves against the Việt Minh. The French agreed to this request if the Hòa Hảo broke with the Việt Minh, but did not actually transfer any weapons.[71]

Alarmed, the Việt Minh secretly began its crackdown. Troubles first seem to have flared up in Sa Đéc province in the second half of March, when the Việt Minh arrested forty-one members of the Hòa Hảo or its affiliated Social-Democrat Party. In response, the local Hòa Hảo abducted fifty-one Việt Minh. The unstable situation predictably worsened.[72] Faced with such challenges to its authority, Zone Nine of the Việt Minh prepared to repress the Hao Hao from March 20.[73] The Việt Minh had a numerical superiority in troops in Western Nam Bộ, with 2,000 to 2,200 "well armed" soldiers facing 1,200 to 1,500 poorly armed

---

[69] SHD. 10 H 603. S.E.S.A.G. Bulletin de renseignement No. 12984.Saigon, March 29, 1947. Source: Annamite. Valeur: Très sure. Très secret.

[70] ANOM. HCI. SPCE 379. Service de la Sûreté: Activités religieuses. Secte Phat – Giao Hoa-Hao de Huynh Phu So. Saigon, April 9, 1947. This information came from "Agent Lambert," who appears to have been a high-ranking Hòa Hảo cadre.

[71] SHD. 10 H 3828. Le Controleur de la Sûreté M. BAZIN, Note No. 1006/C.F.R. Arrestation de Huynh Phu So par le Comité Administratif de la Province de Longxuyen." Saigon. April 23, 1947.

[72] SHD. 10 H 4169. Commisariat de Sadec. Dissensions Hoa Hao-Viet Minh. Sadec, April 8, 1947.

[73] SHD. 10 H 4169. Deuxième Bureau. Attitude du Commandement Viet Minh en Face de la Révolte Hoa Hao. Source: Sûre. Secret. Strictement personnel. À ne pas diffuser. April 1947.

Hòa Hảo militiamen. Despite this imbalance of forces, the Hòa Hảo could bank on deep support among its followers.[74]

On March 26, the Executive Committee of the South ordered military units in Zones Eight and Nine to send reinforcements to Châu Đốc, the heartland of Hòa Hảo power. It also ordered, in case of any uprising, the arrest of Hòa Hảo leaders.[75] The Hòa Hảo did not sit still: as Nguyễn Duy Hinh, an advisor to Huỳnh Phú Sổ, wrote, apparently about this time, "In many villages, Việt Minh cadres, and those who were pro-Việt Minh, were arrested, liquidated, or expelled elsewhere [by the Hòa Hảo]. On the Việt Minh side, the gang of Bửu Vinh, Đang, and Sõi mobilized their units to encircle hamlets and villages and also arrested, shot, killed, and set fire to homes."[76]

As early as the end of March, "fierce combat" broke out between the two sides,[77] with pitched battles in the provinces of Cần Thơ, Sa Đéc, and Châu Đốc. A report from early April stated that "the Hoa Hao of the provinces of Can Tho, Sa Dec, and Vinh Long have been in open revolt since April 2."[78] Both sides resorted to kidnapping: the Hòa Hảo abducted members of the Việt Minh's Long Xuyên Executive Committee, whereas the Việt Minh arrested some Hòa Hảo on the grounds of "robbery or violation of orders." On April 11, one newspaper account goes, the Long Xuyên Executive Committee sent a letter asking for all attacks to cease, weapons returned, and members of the Executive Committee freed. It was apparently to work out some of these issues that Huỳnh Phú Sổ, leader of the Hòa Hảo Buddhists, accompanied by four guards, travelled to a rendezvous at Đốc Vàng in the Plain of Reeds to meet with the Việt Minh.

This invitation to meet was a trap: the Việt Minh used the pretext of the meeting with Trần Văn Nguyên (now with the Việt Minh, but previously a "high ranking member of the Vietnam National Independence Party") as a lure.[79] According to Phạm Bích Hợp (and many Hòa Hảo sources), Huỳnh Phú Sổ was killed around 9 p.m. on

---

[74] SHD. 10H 4167. 2ème Bureau. Situation militaire rebelle dans le pays Hoa Hao à la date du 25 mai 1947. This report describes the Hòa Hảo territory as stretching on both sides of the Bassac [i.e. the Hậu River] from Cần Thơ to the Cambodian frontier, in particular the provinces of Long Xuyên, and Châu Đốc, the western part of the provinces of Sa Đéc and Cần Thơ and in the north of the province of Rạch Giá.

[75] SHD. 10 H 4167. 2ème Bureau. Situation militaire rebelle dans le pays Hoa Hao à la date du 25 mai 1947.

[76] Cỏ Việt Từ, Vụ án Ba Cụt (Saigon: Nguyễn Duy Hinh, [1956]), 54.

[77] SHD. 10H 4167. 2ème Bureau. Situation militaire rebelle dans le pays Hoa Hao à la date du 25 mai 1947.

[78] SHD. 10H 4167. 2ème Bureau. Déclenchement d'hostillités entre Hoa Hao et V. M. dans la Zone Ouest. Saigon, April 9, 1947.

[79] Cỏ Việt Từ, Vụ án Ba Cụt, 60.

April 16 at Đốc Vàng.[80] The last hastily written note from Huỳnh Phú Sổ, dated 9:15 in the evening of April 16, noted that "something happened, and Vinh and I were nearly killed."[81] Lâm Quang Phòng, a Việt Minh military leader serving in the western Mekong Delta who would later defect, claimed that the northerner Đào Công Tâm of Military Company 66 [Đại Đội 66] killed him.[82] The French collected accounts that others of higher rank might have been responsible, including Vũ Văn Đức and Huỳnh Phan Hộ.[83] Another view is that soldiers associated with Trần Văn Nguyên, who had set up the meeting in the first place, were to blame.[84] One 1947 source suggests that Huỳnh Phú Sổ was shot at Ba Răng (Hồng Ngự), near the Cambodian border.[85] Whoever was to blame, the Việt Minh cadre Bửu Vinh appears to have been in the room negotiating with Huỳnh Phú Sổ when he was killed, apparently by others.[86]

Much ink has been spilled about Huỳnh Phú Sổ's killing and its immediate repercussions. The Communist Party has long tried to avoid the topic, refuse to take blame, or blame others.[87] Communist historians have long intimated that the execution of Huỳnh Phú Sổ was a rogue action, perhaps taken locally with no involvement of higher party members. It is worth spending some time, then, on the sequence of events that would become one of the major turning points of the war and shape Vietnamese politics up to the present.

[80] Phạm Bích Hợp, "Nhìn lại sự kiện Đốc Vàng và hệ quả tâm lý," *Xưa và nay* 296 (November 2007), 19, 38.

[81] Letter to Ông Trần Văn Soái and Nguyễn Giác Ngộ, in *Sấm Giảng thi văn*, 455.

[82] See Hứa Hoành, "Ai giết Đức Thầy Huỳnh Phú Sổ?" (1996). The author interviewed Lâm Quang Phòng. See https://hung-viet.org/a990/ai-giet-duc-thay-huynh-phu-so-theo -hua-hoanh (accessed January 8, 2017).

[83] SHD. 10 H 4169. "Compte rendu de tournée du Capitaine NOGRET du 2è Bureau du Zone Ouest." June 10 1947. But Vũ Văn Đức may have died a month earlier, and the next head of Military Zone Nine, Huỳnh Phan Hộ, died in 1947 or 1948. According to one source, Huỳnh Phan Hộ "disappeared in 1948 due to his excessively nationalist and anti-communist beliefs." See SHD. 10 H 4166. Lieutenant Lacroix, *Phật giáo Hòa Hảo (Bouddhisme de Hòa Hảo)* [unpublished report, June 1949], 17.

[84] Cồ Việt Tử, *Vụ án Ba Cụt*, 60–61. The author saw Huỳnh Phú Sổ alive the day before his presumed death.

[85] SHD. 10 H 4176. Deuxième Bureau. Rapport d'un indicateur sur les Hoa Hao. August 26, 1947. This pro-French agent, quite opposed to Hòa Hảo violence, claimed to have access to the headquarters of Trần Văn Soái, the main Hòa Hảo warlord.

[86] Lê Hiếu Liêm, *Bồ tát Huỳnh Phú Sổ và Phật giáo thời đại* ([California?]: Viện Tư Tưởng Việt Phật, 2001), Chapter 3, www.phatgiaohoahao.net/tu-sach-phat-giao-hoa-hao/bo-tat-huynh-phu-so-va-phat-giao-thoi-dhai/03–chuong-iii-cuoc-doi-cua-huynh-phu-so/g-nhung-ngay-cuoi-cung-cua-huynh-phu-so (accessed September 22, 2017).

[87] See, for example, Nguyễn Hùng, *Ung Văn Khiêm: Anh Ba nội vụ* (Ho Chi Minh City: Công An Nhân Dân, 2004), 402. The author states that the French "used the unexpected death of Huỳnh Phú Sổ to cause divisions between the Việt Minh and the Hòa Hảo."

On April 12, the Executive Committee of Nam Bộ announced de facto martial law over the South. Its order failed to reach all recipients until April 18 or possibly April 21. The directive forbade movement at night, banned all armed gatherings, and laid out methods for a broad crackdown on the Social-Democrat Party.[88] Immediately, cracks appeared in the façade of Việt Minh unity. Huỳnh Phan Hộ, the commander of Military Zone Nine and a native of Cần Thơ province, seems to have been troubled with the extent of the crackdown. He left the area for Bạc Liêu province on an "inspection" visit, but was summoned back on April 19. Meanwhile, on April 15, the order went out to the Vietnamese army and police to "ruthlessly eliminate the [Hòa Hảo] band of Luu, Anh, Dung and Hoa. You are ordered to destroy this order after reading it. Any indiscretion over this will be punished with death."[89] The Việt Minh followed these secret arrests and killings with a public political and military campaign to crush their opponent.

In this context, two different scenarios for Huỳnh Phú Sổ's killing seem possible. The first scenario is that the Executive Committee of Nam Bộ was always in charge and that his death was not accidental. In this scenario, Huỳnh Phú Sổ was arrested, lived beyond April 16, went through a formal trial where he was judged guilty, and was then executed. It is possible, in this scenario, that the central DRV government knew of this plan of action, and approved of it. The central government had heard about Huỳnh Phú Sổ's arrest: the vice-president of the Administrative Committee, Phạm Ngọc Thuân, cabled the central government on April 28, 1947 to detail the charges against Sổ and to get authorization for its actions.[90]

---

[88] SHD.10 H 3828. Deuxième Bureau. Bulletin de renseignements 3.078. April 18, 1947; SHD. 10 H 3828. Deuxième Bureau. "Mésures édictées par le Comité Exécutif de Nam Bo." April 21, 1947 [translation]. This seems to be part of the original document from April 21 (in Vietnamese), "HUẤN LỊNH GỞI CÁC CẤP HÀNH CHÁNH, QUÂN ĐỘI, CÔNG AN" [Orders sent to all administrative, military, and public security echelons], found in Nguyễn Long Thành Nam, *Phật giáo hòa hảo trong dòng lịch sử dân tộc* (S.l.: Đuốc Từ Bi, 1991), www.hoahao.org/p74a2699/2-dien-tien-bien-co-16-4-1947 (accessed February 3, 2018).

[89] SHD. 10 H 4169. Renseignement. "Conflit V.M. Cao Dai." Saigon, April 16. This mistitled file is filled with Hòa Hảo material. It was a assigned a valeur of "A/1" by the French, indicating it is an original document, here translated into French. The Vietnamese document is dated April 1.

[90] HCI. SPCE 385. Traduction d'un document du Comité Executif de Nam Bo. On the Arrest of Huynh Phu So. Signed by the Vice-President of the Comité, PHAM NGOC THUAN. April 28, 1947. Guillemot notes as well circumstantial evidence that suggests the Party Center was aware of Huỳnh Phú Sổ's arrest and eventual killing. See Guillemot, *Dai Viet: indépendance et révolution au Viêt-Nam. L'échec de la troisième voie. 1938–1955* (Paris: Les Indes Savantes, 2012), 427.

The second scenario is that higher levels of the Party did not know of Huỳnh Phú Sổ's arrest, and that he was killed "prematurely" or even accidentally sometime between his trip to meet with Việt Minh (April 15–16) and April 23 by a local Việt Minh military unit. In support of this argument of a "premature" death, two days after his last meeting with Huỳnh Phú Sổ – and thus, it seems, on the evening of April 17 – Cổ Việt Tử heard the news that the Hòa Hảo leader had been killed.[91] On April 23, a Việt Minh unit in Châu Đốc province, reporting unconfirmed news that Huỳnh Phú Sổ had been killed, "deplored the haste" of this action. It added that propaganda would have to emphasize that Huỳnh Phú Sổ was a "criminal traitor."[92] That same day, a French synthesis of intercepted Việt Minh documents stated:

On April 23rd, the Ninth Military Zone reported to the Executive Committee of Nam Bộ that according to news coming from the Eighth Military Zone, Huỳnh Phú Sổ had been killed. It asked what would be the attitude that the [Executive] Committee would take given this premature death, which would thwart any attempt to effect a reconciliation with Huỳnh Phú Sổ. It suggested that statements be made about the seriousness of his crimes, and about his death, to protect against [the appearance of] a fake Huỳnh Phú Sổ.[93]

In this second scenario, faced with this accidental death, the Executive Committee of Nam Bộ created, after the fact, a cover story to legitimate this killing. This would have entailed, then, pretending that Huỳnh Phú Sổ was put on trial, sentenced, and only then, when his guilt was established, executed. In the end, it appears, given the preponderance of the limited evidence, that this second scenario, of a precipitous killing not approved by higher echelons, is probably correct. But if the second scenario is true, the judicial process that the government carried out, and which I detail next, was a sham: it probably "happened" *after* Huỳnh Phú Sổ was killed.

So what was this "trial," and what was Huỳnh Phú Sổ's "crime"? On April 20, the Nam Bộ Executive Committee announced that it was disbanding the Social-Democrat Party, which Huỳnh Phú Sổ led, and bringing Huỳnh Phú Sổ before a military tribunal for prosecution. Its proclamation gave three reasons for the action. First, the Hòa Hảo had set up separate structures of authority. Second, they had secretly collaborated with the French. Third, they had arrested "thousands of pro-Việt

[91] Cổ Việt Tử, *Vụ án Ba Cụt*, 60.
[92] SHD. 10 H 4169. Le Chef de Bataillon Keller. Chef du 2è Bureau. Conflit Hoa Hao. April 23 1947.
[93] SHD. 10 H 4169. 2è Bureau. Attitudes du Commandement Viet-Minh en Face de la Révolte Hoa Hao. Secret. Source sûre. Strictement personnel. À ne pas diffuser. April 1947.

Minh" persons, and had even "disemboweled women" and "ripped children's bodies asunder."[94] The Việt Minh presented itself as trying to get rid of a *separatist political party*, not a religion, though the line between "religion" and "party" is hard to draw in the case of the Social-Democrat Party and the Hòa Hảo religion.

On April 24, the Việt Minh articulated a harsher message. On behalf of the Nam Bộ Executive Committee, Ung Văn Khiêm issued a "special order" that because Huỳnh Phú Sổ had engaged in treasonous acts as leader of the Social-Democrat Party, it was launching a massive crackdown: it ordered the arrest of all Social-Democrat party leaders and members and stated that "if there is time," the suspects should be brought before a tribunal. If the Social-Democrat Party leaders and members did not follow orders, they should be resolutely "eliminated."[95] The next day – two weeks after Huỳnh Phú Sổ had been arrested – the entire Administrative Committee of Nam Bộ announced the establishment of a "special court" to try Huỳnh Phú Sổ. The court accused Sổ of six crimes. In its exact words, these were:

1. Establishing a separate army, courts, and security, as if it were a government within the government.
2. Ordering the arming of members of the Social-Democrat Party and Hòa Hảo believers.
3. Ordering Social-Democrat members and Hòa Hảo believers to rise up and kill government personnel and the common people.
4. Stealthily bringing his own armed forces to the Hậu Giang [region] to encourage looting and disorder.
5. Social-Democrat Party members and Hòa Hảo believers slaughtered thousands of people in Long Xuyên, Châu Đốc, Cần Thơ, and Sa Đéc.
6. Social-Democrat Party members and the Hòa Hảo collaborated with the French army to attack our army and terrorize the people.[96]

At the trial, the Executive Committee of Nam Bộ condemned Huỳnh Phú Sổ to death. General Nguyễn Bình announced his execution on May 20, 1947, but rumors of it had been circulating much earlier.

To reiterate, the evidence would suggest that Huỳnh Phú Sổ was probably killed prematurely or even accidentally. Faced with this killing, the Executive Committee of Nam Bộ had a choice: to disown the rogue action, or to present a united front while confirming the death at the hands of the Việt Minh. It had to make this choice at a critical time, when

[94] SHD. 10 H 4169. Ủy Ban Hành Chánh Nam Bộ. Bố Cáo. April 20, 1947.
[95] SHD. 10 H 4169. UY BAN HANH CHANH NAM BO. BAN NOI VU. SO 370/NV-5. LINH DAC BIET. [Châu Đốc?]: April 21, 1947.
[96] ANOM. HCI. SPCE 385. BO CAO CUA UY BAN HANH CHANH NAM BO. VU AN HUYNH PHU SO. May 27, 1947. [Signed:] NGUYEN BINH.

the unity of the Việt Minh was being tested by rebellion. The Executive Committee of Nam Bộ, given a choice between coming across as wavering or resolute, chose to take responsibility for the killing. It left the impression that Huỳnh Phú Sổ had gone through a legal process before being executed for political, not religious, crimes. This cover story was probably a fiction, but its creation has left the impression, to this day, that the communist-led Executive Committee of Nam Bộ Việt Minh bears full responsibility for the execution of Huỳnh Phú Sổ.

The consequences of the arrest and execution of Huỳnh Phú Sổ were monumental. According to one account, after Sổ's death, the Hòa Hảo gathered believers under the slogan "Defend the Way, Oppose the Việt Minh" [*bảo vệ đạo, chống Việt Minh*].[97] The poorly armed Hòa Hảo went on a rampage, killing Việt Minh indiscriminately. French documents from this period note, with awe, the fanaticism of the Hòa Hảo, faced with a better-armed opponent. Right after Sổ's arrest, Bảy Viễn (Lê Văn Viễn), the Binh Xuyen leader, an ally of the Hoà Hảo, warned the Việt Minh leadership that "for every one of my men who is killed, I will kill ten of yours."[98] In Long Xuyên province, the poorly armed Hòa Hảo believers rose up against the Việt Minh, a pattern that would be repeated elsewhere.

The Việt Minh did not back down after killing Huỳnh Phú Sổ. It engaged in a brutal crackdown against leaders and members of the Social-Democrat Party and the Hoà Hảo. On May 7, the French Sûreté in Châu Đốc reported that "approximately one thousand Hoa Hao have been massacred; the day before yesterday, one hundred Hoa Hao were killed in Vĩnh Lộc; women were disemboweled, children were beheaded."[99] It is not clear whether these figures only applied to Châu Đốc province or to a broader area. The French intercepted one Việt Minh report from May 6 claiming that one of its military units had killed 200 to 500 Hòa Hảo at Phú Lâm and Phú An, Châu Đốc province.[100] A month after the fighting broke out, the Long Xuyên Sûreté reported that the Việt Minh had killed "five hundred families."[101] Fighting between Hòa Hảo and Việt Minh also occurred in Châu Đốc, Long Xuyên, Sa Đéc, and Cần Thơ provinces. A French report emphasized the urgent need for a response:

---

[97] Bùi Thu Hà, "Công tác Hòa Hảo vận của Đảng bộ An Giang trong hai cuộc Kháng Chiến," *Tạp chí Nghiên cứu lịch sử Đảng* 9 (1996), 30.

[98] ANOM. HCI. SPCE 379. Service de la Sûreté. Note No. 1093/C.F.R. Lutte entre Nationalistes et Communistes. Saigon, May 8, 1947.

[99] SHD. 10 H 4169. Le Commissaire de la Sûreté [Ribes] à Chaudoc à M. le Délégué de la Sûreté à Cantho. "Secte Hoa Hao." May 7, 1947.

[100] SHD. 10 H 4169. A/s Activités rebelles en Khu 8 et 9." June 29, 1947.

[101] SHD. 10 H 4169 [Telegram–Surete Longxuyen to Comité Pacification Cantho. Undated, May or June 1947].

The conflict that currently is taking place in the western provinces between Viet Minh Hoa Hao must be addressed as soon as possible. Each minute lost is important, as the killings continue unabated, day and night, and we run the risk that the Hoa Hao will become discouraged, tired of struggling unsuccessfully with machetes and spears against rifles and machine guns.[102]

A French report from May estimated that the Việt Minh had superiority in numbers and armament: approximately 2,000 to 2,3000 Việt Minh opposing 1,000 poorly armed Hòa Hảo. Furthermore, the Việt Minh had ordered 1,000 to 1,200 fighters from other zones to the western Mekong Delta to fight the Hòa Hảo.[103] A Hòa Hảo adviser in the delta at the time, Nguyễn Duy Hinh, stated that the main Hòa Hảo militia leader Trần Văn Soái had adequate weapons, but another key militia leader, Nguyễn Giác Ngộ, "only had about 200 World War I rifles, and pistols, as well as a few grenades."[104] Despite this imbalance of forces, the Hòa Hảo were particularly strong in Long Xuyên and Châu Đốc provinces. Another report from the end of May underlines the sheer brutality of the struggle: "For several weeks, Hoa Hao forces have not been retreating before the VM [Việt Minh] in the provinces of the West. In two months, roughly 4,000 Hoa Hao followers in Long Xuyen and Chau Doc have either been buried alive, decapitated, disemboweled, or shot by the VM."[105]

The killing of Huỳnh Phú Sổ, one of the major Việt Minh blunders of the war, only compounded earlier mistakes. To the Hòa Hảo, Bình Xuyên, and Cao Đài, it confirmed the mortal threat of the Việt Minh, and stiffened their resolve to constitute an anti-communist and nationalist resistance loosely affiliated with the French. Indeed, we can no longer speak of a "Việt Minh" in the same sense after the pitched battles of the spring and early summer of 1947. After this point, I speak of the "Resistance" to refer to the remaining Việt Minh, shorn of its so-called "nationalist" elements in the Bình Xuyên, Cao Đài, and Hòa Hảo, and therefore more dominated by communists.

The struggle continued into the summer. In June, the leadership of the Social-Democrat Party (associated with the Hòa Hảo) wrote that "in areas where the Cao Đài and Việt Minh are concentrated, [we should] secretly organize assassination squads to wipe out specific

---

[102] SHD. 10 H 603. Compte-Rendu. Capitaine Bertrand, Chef du 2eme Bureau. Question des Hoa Hao [undated, 1947?].
[103] Deuxième Bureau. Situation militaire rebelle dans le pays Hoa Hao à la date du 25 Mai 1947.
[104] Cò Việt Từ, *Vụ án Ba Cụt*, 55.
[105] ANOM. HCI. SPCE 385. Service de la Sûreté. G. Lavail, Le Commissaire Chef du Contrôle Fédéral des Recherches. Hostilités entre les Hoa Hao et les Viet Minh. Saigon, May 28, 1947.

leaders."[106] Yet the Hòa Hảo realized that events had spiraled out of control. The Hòa Hảo warlord Nam Lửa [Trần Văn Soái], seeing the carnage in Sa Đéc province, wrote in June 1947 that "various places have seen assassinations, looting, kidnappings, and acts of cruelty" carried out by individuals claiming to belong to the Social-Democrat Party, and stated that henceforth, the party would punish severely those who carried out such actions.[107] His words did not matter – with no effective authority, the killing continued.

Bystanders were shocked at the ferocity of the violence. In July 1947, a letter writer stated that:

In the West [of the Mekong Delta], it is an indescribable chaos; the inhabitants live in fear and anguish every hour because of the scourge of the Hoa Hao, whose partisans are engaged in a war without mercy against the Viet Minh and arrest all those who do not join the Hoa Hao religion. They torture inhumanely; with most [of their victims] thrown into pits and pounded like rice. They are disposed of in the same way one would kill chickens or ducks.[108]

A pro-French Vietnamese eyewitness to events in and around Cần Thơ echoed these comments: he scathingly attacked the "barbaric" Hòa Hảo for their massacres and brutalities toward the population of the province.[109]

Members of the Resistance soon realized that they faced a formidable enemy. Showing the depth of their animosity, one Resistance document referred to Huỳnh Phú Sổ as a "traitor," the Social-Democrat Party as a" traitorous party," and the Hòa Hảo as a "traitorous religion."[110] A 1971 Hòa Hảo report adds that in addition to these killings of followers, "communists also murdered three of So's closest disciples and two hundred and thirty-three Hòa Hảo cadres between 1945 and 1947."[111] At the beginning of August, one refugee from Long Xuyên province, a supporter of the Resistance, reported that "the Hòa Hảo are spreading sheer terror." Letting hope get the best of him, he added that the Resistance was

---

[106] SHD. 10 H 4169. Việt Nam Dân Chủ Xã Hội Đảng. Ban Chấp Hành. L. T. Miềng [sic] Tây. Số 215. Chỉ Thị. June 15, 1947.

[107] SHD. 10 H 4176. Le Commandant en Chef des Troupes de l'Ouest [Trần Văn Soái] du Nam Bộ du Parti Sociale Démocrate Vietnamien à la population [Translation from the Vietnamese]. June 17, 1947.

[108] ANOM. HCI. CP 107. [Intercepted letter from Roland to Tran Van Lai]. Translated from Vietnamese. Saigon, July 22, 1947.

[109] SHD. 10 H 4176. Rapport d'un indicateur sur les Hoa Hao. August 26, 1947.

[110] SHD. 10 H 4169 Thuong Vu Quân Bô Việt Minh Quan C. L. Thông cao. Dê muc: Phật giao Hoa Hao. In the original, without full diacritics, "môt dang phan quôc, môt tôn giao phan quôc." Signed, Thu Van. June 14, 1947.

[111] Alexander Woodside, Community and Revolution in Modern Vietnam (Boston: Houghton Mifflin, 1976), 189.

strengthening, as an army of 10,000 Vietnamese had arrived from Siam.[112] The Resistance, slow to realize the gravity of its mistake, doggedly pursued its repression. In April, a high-level informant in the Cao Đài reported that the Resistance had arrested 700 Cao Đài from four villages in Tân An province; "many of them are already dead, and the rest have been brought to the Plain of Reeds."[113]

Was the Resistance split over its strategy towards its opponents? Was it in crisis, jerking from one approach to another? It is hard to tell. In the months to come, it would pursue a dual strategy towards the Hòa Hảo, Cao Đài, and Bình Xuyên: to try to reach out and reconcile with those who were "misled," but to crush those who persisted in opposing them. Thus, Guillemot notes that "the Executive Committee of Nam Bộ decided to set up conciliation committees in each province in the west to find solutions to the conflict between the partisans of the Viet Minh and Hoa Hao."[114] A September 1947 Directive from the Party Committee of Nam Bộ forbade party members to revisit "the mistakes of the past" among those who returned to the fold.[115] The Resistance leadership clung to the hope that they could convert errant believers. One party history speaks of a Resistance mobilization campaign among Cao Đài followers in three "camps" (Bình Thành, Tân Bình Điền, and Phú Thạnh Đông) that took place in October 1947. According to this source, the enemy (apparently the French) had been trying to cause dissension between the Resistance and religious groups by claiming that the Resistance was atheist (vô thần). The French and their minions, it said, had been "kidnapping youth, killing cadres, and terrorizing the people," but after being "educated," the Cao Đài followers promised not to let the French take advantage of them.[116]

Coming on the heels of rampant violence, such "education" failed to convince many Cao Đài members. The gulf between the Resistance and its rivals deepened, as the cycle of violence continued. Noting that the situation in Long Xuyên, Châu Đốc, Cần Thơ and Tây Ninh provinces was still "confused" – a euphemism for the Resistance failure to suppress the revolt – the communist Ung Văn Khiêm stated starkly on June 30:

---

[112] HCI. CP 107. [Intercepted letter from X., Saigon, to Ho Van Truong, Toulouse. August 2, 1947.]

[113] SHD. 10 H 3822. Service de la Sûreté. Le Controleur de la Sûreté M. Bazin. "Hostilité du Viet Minh envers les Caodaistes de Tayninh. Saigon, April 23, 1947.

[114] Guillemot, "Autopsy of a Massacre," 256.

[115] SHD. 10 H 4169 [Directive of 15 September 1947 from the Nam Bộ Central Committee, promulgated on 9 October 1947 via the Tân Uyên Executive Committee, on Cao Đài and Hòa Hảo believers.]

[116] Đảng Cộng Sản Việt Nam, Lịch sử Đảng bộ tỉnh Tiền Giang ([Tiền Giang]: Ban nghiên cứu lịch sử Đảng, 1985), Vol. 1, 177–178.

After a few months of fighting the invaders from abroad, and traitors to the nation from within, we have seen that:

...During purification operations against the traitors, the National Defense Corps, the police, and self-defense troops have exposed, with praiseworthy clairvoyance, the gang of dangerous traitors to the future of the Fatherland. The superstitious population has thus been duped by them: this act of purging of traitors who incite a revolution, we do against our will, with the intention of defending the nation, and not out of personal vengeance.

...we must know at all times that among the Cao Dai and Hoa Hao, there are always sincere and innocent people without a single treacherous thought. They have acted without discernment, ensnared by the insidious words of their leaders...[117]

The anger that infuses this document is palpable. As Guillemot notes, Resistance soldiers feared the fanaticism of the Cao Đài and of the Hòa Hảo,[118] but this same fear in turn shaped Resistance practices of gratuitous violence and, at times, apocalyptic propaganda against their enemies. The extreme antagonism of many leading communists to the main Cao Đài and Hòa Hảo groups comes through again and again in memoirs and histories. These accounts repeat the same tales of supposed atrocities, such as the purported selling of human flesh at Phú Mỹ Hưng. Mai Chí Thọ, for example, who would ultimately rise to high rank in the Democratic Republic of Vietnam (DRV), writes of the "barbaric crimes" of the Hòa Hảo and Cao Đài, including the "slitting of bellies" and extracting livers.[119] This extreme view of their enemies was mirrored by their opponents: a Cao Đài member wrote to a friend, for example, that "[Resistance] tracts sent from Tonkin order the killing of all southerners in order to cede place to northerners. That is why the old and the young are not spared from the carnage." He then mentioned the pitched battles against Cao Đài forces and the Resistance, and how Resistance forces had attacked peasants and burned down their homes.[120]

Indeed, despite the Resistance's professed desire for reconciliation, violence continued. Faced with determined opponents, the Resistance resolutely hunted down "traitors." Between May and November 1947, the Resistance police condemned 968 "reactionaries," many of them from previously Cao Đài-controlled areas, to death. On October 13, 1947, over 300 of these sentences were carried out, the single most

---

[117] This key political directive is cited in Guillemot, "Autopsy of a Massacre," 248. I have made light changes to the translation.
[118] Guillemot, 254.
[119] Mai Chí Thọ, *Hồi Ức. Những mẩu chuyện đời tôi* (Ho Chi Minh City: Trẻ, 2001), 141.
[120] ANOM. HCI. CP 107. [Intercepted letter from Phan Van Dang, Tây Ninh, to Le Quang Thuong, Tarascon, France. July 14, 1947.]

lethal day of purges that year.[121] From Tây Ninh province on the Cambodian border, the provincial administrator noted that from mid-September to mid-October, "massacres continue. We have counted 300 killed or wounded in the last month."[122] The fighting earlier in the year had intensified the animosity between the Resistance and its opponents; the purges reinforced the hatred. In the process, others seemed to have fallen victim to violence as well. Take this anguished letter from a mother to her son:

> Oh son, they [the Resistance] have killed your maternal Tam with as much, if not more, cruelty as you can imagine, I've heard that they struck her with terrible blows to the head, and then when they saw that she was not dead, they finished her off with a dagger... Despite this, our Nhut continues to follow them. I have no news of him, he should be somewhere near Cai Lay. I am really troubled with him and deeply fear for his life.[123]

If Vietnamese-on-Vietnamese violence consumed the delta, the French had a hard time taking advantage of it for their own ends. By the fall of 1947, a skeletal French governing apparatus was still stretched thin across the delta. The Resistance, according to General Boyer de La Tour, had assassinated 1,000 members belonging to numerous village councils of notables,[124] advisory bodies that were an essential linchpin in the apparatus of French rule. Not surprisingly, province chiefs also felt besieged. In October, the Tây Ninh provincial administrator wrote, in overwrought prose, that most of the inhabitants of the province "suffered from lack of work, are threatened by misery and hunger, and no longer have the moral patience or physical force to endure this life of uncertainty, oppression, and hell. Chased from hamlet to hamlet, village to village, by the lack of work, by fear, they no longer know where their landholdings are, their homes, their families and parents."[125]

Violence, spiraling out of control, struck minority groups of the delta as well. The Chams and Malays of Châu Đốc province would feel the wrath of different contestants. When it attacked the town of Tây Ninh in October 1947, the Resistance burned down a village in which one thousand Chams lived; the population of Chams living in this village

---

[121] François Guillemot, "Autopsy of a Massacre," 249.
[122] VNA-II. PTHNV. Box 482, d. E.03–21. Province de Tayninh. "Rapport d'ensemble (période du 16 septembre au 15 octobre 1947)."
[123] ANOM. HCI. CP 107. [Intercepted letter from Mme. Phuong, Saigon, to Nguyen Thi Vui, Paris. May 27, 1947.]
[124] (General) Pierre Boyer de la Tour, De l'Indochine à l'Algérie: le martye de l'Armée française (Paris: Presses du Mail, 1962), 38.
[125] VNA-II. PTHNV. Box 482, d. E.03–21. Province de Tayninh. "Rapport d'ensemble du mois d'octobre 1947."

plummeted to one hundred.[126] Chinese hunkered down, and many left the delta for Saigon. The Khmer were repeatedly drawn into conflicts: once the 1945–46 Khmer-Vietnamese violence quieted down, it did not take much for it to flare up again. Multiple sources indicate that in January and February 1947, when it was still collaborating with other Việt Minh forces, Hòa Hảo units launched repeated attacks on Cambodian villages in the lower Mekong Delta. Thus:

On January 15, 1947, in Tinh Biên district (Châu Đốc), the Hòa Hảo, assisted by the Viet Minh, carried out reprisals against Cambodians in the area (setting fire to temples, houses, massacres of inhabitants). Following this, thousands of Cambodians took refuge in the *srok* of Kirivong [in Takeo province, Cambodia]).[127]

A 1947 letter speaks of how Vietnamese in Trà Vinh, threatened by both French and Khmer, were fleeing to the islets in the middle of the Hậu river.[128] Khmer also felt besieged. On January 23, 1947, French military sources reported an attack on the Cambodian village of "Nguget Sang" [*sic:* Nguyệt Lãng?] in Trà Vinh province. An estimated 100 inhabitants were massacred, the entire village went up in smoke, and 800 people were left homeless.[129] About one month later, on February 26, 1947, Việt Minh units reportedly burned down 500 dwellings in the Cambodian village of Giồng Rùm, ten miles southeast of Trà Vinh town, while also attacking the town of Nguyen Hung to the West of Trà Vinh.[130] The village of Kế Sách, in Sóc Trăng province, with its population of Khmer, Chinese, and Vietnamese, also experienced "a very difficult period between July 1946 and July 1947," apparently because of retaliatory Việt Minh attacks.[131]

In Câu Kê district, then part of Cần Thơ province, approximately fifty Cambodian families took up and left for "rebel zones" in September 1947 after Khmer Issarak in the area pressured them. "Cauke is, in effect, under siege: the rebels, many of them Issarak, with the help of bullhorns, announced that all military forces would leave Cauke and that everyone would be wiped out. The people are in fear..."[132] In October 1947, the

---

[126] Ibid.

[127] ANOM. HCI. SPCE 385. Sûreté Fédérale au Cambodge. Rapport du Police Spéciale." Phnom Penh, March 20, 1947.

[128] ANOM. HCI. CP 107 [Intercepted letter from Nguyen Kim Quyen to Nguyen Kim Chau. January 27, 1947.]

[129] SHD. 10 H 4294. [Telegram] Col 3 REI to Opium [arrived January 23, 1947].

[130] SHD. 10 H 4294. [Telegram] Expediteur : Col 3 REI. Destinaire: Opium 3 CORorient Secteur Ouest et Marine Mytho. February 26, 1947.

[131] VNA II. PTHNV E.03–23. Province de Soctrang. Rapport d'ensemble des mois d'août et septembre 1948. Soctrang, October 3, 1948.

[132] VNA-II. PTHNV Box 482 File E.03–46. Province de Cantho. Rapport d'ensemble du mois de septembre 1947.

Cambodian population of Tây Ninh province was hit hard, and withdrew into the forests.[133] On November 17, 1947, the French reported that an estimated 500 Việt Minh set fire to 150 Cambodian dwellings as well as temples "in the Chong – Graleng zone, in the village of O-Phen (Phong Thanh), Cần Thơ province.

The impact of all this violence on the Khmer community was summarized by the Province Chief of Sóc Trăng in October 1947:

Since my return to Soctrang, I have sensed a very clear and troubling hesitation on the part of the Khmers. Subject to very violent terrorism on the part of the Việt Minh, while being approached with a very skilled propaganda by the latter, some hamlets and even villages have adopted a passive attitude, refusing even to take up arms to defend themselves... It took stupid and repeated mistakes by the Việt Minh, who burned some remote villages, for the Cambodians to proclaim once again their union [with France].[134]

Violence in Vĩnh Long and Trà Vinh provinces similarly affected bystander communities. What may have appeared to its major protagonists as a political struggle between clearly defined contestants actually combined violence ordered from on high with locally generated spasms of indiscriminate killing affecting contestants and bystanders alike.

4.5 Conclusion

With the August General Uprising of 1945, the Việt Minh had hoped to unite the people and marginalize any contestants to power. In this, they failed. The failed attempt to unify the Resistance in Saigon foreshadowed the divisions in the southern countryside, where a range of contestants, including communists, Hòa Hảo, Cao Đài, and Binh Xuyên, struggled for dominance. Contemporary scholarship tends to frame the resultant struggle as a Resistance War (Kháng chiến) against the French, while mentioning in passing the struggle among Vietnamese for paramount power. It has all but ignored the Khmer Krom. But when we look at these struggles together, we can see the civil war among the Vietnamese, the ethnic conflict between Khmer and Vietnamese, and the fight between the French and their (mostly) Vietnamese opponents fractured the delta. As in many civil wars, the top-down and instrumental use of violence by clearly demarcated groups intersected with violence welling up from below, in which

---

[133] VNA-II. PTHNV Box 482 File E.03–21. Province de Tayninh. Rapport d'ensemble du mois d'octobre 1947.
[134] VNA-II. PTHNV Box 482 File E03.23. Province de Soctrang. Rapport d'ensemble. Soctrang, October 31, 1947.

a wide range of local actors contributed to the often-indiscriminate violence.

The double fracture from 1945 to 1947 may well have constituted the worst period during the entire war in terms of the extensive use of indiscriminate violence by indigenous inhabitants against fellow civilians. It was certainly the most shocking. The orgy of violence in 1947 reshaped the southern landscape, but not in the way the Việt Minh had intended. It hardened political differences and drove families apart. But it also set up an alternative path to independence: a tactical collaboration by "nationalists" with the French, leading to eventual autonomy and independence. Such, at least, was the hope of many non-communist Vietnamese. The year 1947, then, marks a turning point in the South: the end of the possibility of a unified and inclusive Resistance to French rule. How the war would then unfold and ultimately end is the topic of the rest of this book.

Part II

Disassemblage/Reassemblage, 1947–1953

When explaining major violent transitions, such as wars leading to the fall of empires and the rise of nation-states, historians like to say that out of the "ruins" of the past, the shattered "parts" are put together into a new "whole." But is this really how change occurs? The events from 1945 to the end of 1947 reordered southern politics, transforming a Vietnamese-French conflict into an overt civil war wrapped up in a conflict against France. Revolutionaries and nationalists did not completely destroy the old order: many parts of it, like how to run a bureaucracy, endured because they were useful. Indeed, a shifting assemblage of institutions broke apart and recombined. Practices were reassembled in new ways. Old and new ideas comingled, pushed together in novel fashion.

In other words, disassemblage and reassemblage occurred, in parallel, at the same time, from the level of empire down to local politics,[1] from 1947 to 1954. In Chapter 6 I use these concepts as a metaphor for the ways that ideas of race were broken apart and reassembled. In other chapters, however, I look at concrete processes and mechanisms, such as those within the French and Vietnamese states, and how they broke down and recombined at the same time. Other chapters, such as that on militias and parastates, look at the rise of social and organizational forms that are hybrids, marrying aspects of gangs with state practices like taxation or deploying armed forces. Such practices were not only found among non-communists: the communist-led Democratic Republic of Vietnam transformed French colonial state practices and perpetuated them at the same time.

These processes of change played out in rural areas during a three-cornered struggle for power from April 1947 onwards. At one pole was

---

[1] My use of "disassemblage" and "reassemblage" shares little with the debates from Deleuze and Guattari onwards (e.g. Jasbir Puar) on "assemblage theory." Rather, it draws on the strand of scholarship leading from David Stark, "Recombinant Property in East European Capitalism," *American Journal of Sociology* 101(4) (January 1996): 993–1027; and through, for example, Stan B. H. Tan, "'Dust Beneath the Mist': State and Frontier Formation in the Central Highlands of Vietnam, the 1955–61 Period" (PhD dissertation, Australian National University, 2006).

the French military and civilian state apparatus. It opposed the Resistance, wanted to extend French rule over Vietnam but, too weak to crush its opponents, was willing to accommodate itself to some "nationalists." At a second pole was the Hòa Hảo-Cao Đài-Bình Xuyên "nationalist" alliance, which wanted independence for Vietnam, strongly opposed the communist-led Resistance, but was split over whether to collaborate with the French. (The leading Hòa Hảo and Cao Đài players said yes; lesser players sometimes said no.) At the third pole was the Resistance. While it called itself "nationalist," communists increasingly dominated its ruling apparatus after 1947. It fiercely opposed the French. With the rise of the State of Vietnam from 1949, of course, this became a four-cornered struggle for power.

From the end of 1947 until late 1949, the struggle in the South transitioned into a roughly equal contest in which the French and their allied Vietnamese and Khmer forces pursued a strategy of pacification, but faced increasingly well-organized and innovative Resistance opposition. The period from the end of 1949 through 1953 marked a turning point. In 1950, France convinced the United States that Indochina was an important front in the Cold War. What had been, up to 1949, an imperial war of reconquest finally intersected with the global Cold War. American aid began to flow into Indochina, allowing the French military and its Vietnamese allies to ramp up "pacification." At the same time, the Resistance in the South hastily attempted to shift from guerrilla warfare to conventional conflict. It failed: French "pacification," combined with a food blockade and a typhoon, sent the Resistance reeling. The Resistance effectively lost the struggle for the South in these years. While the Resistance regrouped in 1953 and 1954, their losses had been so catastrophic that they could not claw back their earlier gains. Instead, the French and their Vietnamese and Khmer allies strengthened their grip over the countryside, often to the detriment of both the Resistance and the rising Vietnamese state. When France began to "downsize" in the South from 1953 onwards, this "system" would begin to fall apart.

5 Empire, Racial Survival, and Race Hatred

The Vietnamese have often shied away from the argument that race was central to the First Indochina War. In 1947, the socialist internationalist Thiếu Sơn declared: "This is a war of self-defense, not a race war; this is a war of idealism, not of xenophobia."[2] Such sentiment has percolated into Vietnamese histories of the war, which have emphasized the right-eousness of the Vietnamese struggle against the French and downplayed racial antagonisms. Precisely because of such texts, I was intrigued when, one summer afternoon, leafing through files in the French military arch-ives in Vincennes, I stumbled across an odd publication that had been collected by the French army in the Mekong Delta at the end of 1951. I was riveted by a picture of a line of shadowy figures marching into a low, black building, with others coming out the other side. The Vietnamese text beneath the picture reads as follows:

They seized them by the thousands,
    Brought them to the electric ovens, turning yellow skin into black
    Transforming them into fake "Moroccans."[3]

I was astonished and baffled. Was I reading the text correctly? I soon encountered variations of this propaganda. For example, a tract found near Vĩnh Long in December of 1951 condemned:

The barbaric act of the French
    Turning Vietnamese soldiers into black soldiers
    The French are bringing one hundred youths to the Cape to the electric ovens,
transforming them into blacks.[4]

The examples of race propaganda above are not isolated. A tract from November 1951 stated that the French had used the Buddhist Hòa Hảo

---

[2] Thiếu Sơn, *Giữa hai cuộc cách mạng 1789–1945* (Saigon: Mạch Sống, 1947), 75.
[3] SHD. 10H 5442. Thế không chết nhục [Don't die in shame], an illustrated tract.
[4] SHD. 10H 4131. "Một hành động dã man giặc Pháp." In C.F.T.S.V, Secteur de Vinh Long. 2è Bureau. Tract V.M. diffusé par la jeunesse du Salut National de la ville de Vinh Long. December 15, 1951. The "cape" mentioned was probably Cap St. Jacques.

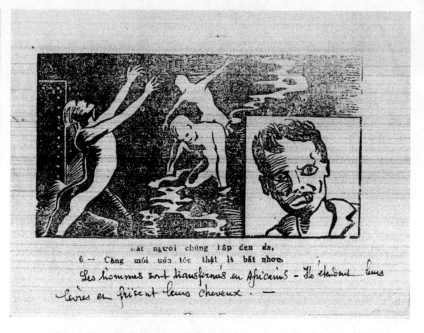

Figure 5.1 Propaganda leaflet on "cooking" people black, 1952
Source: SHD 10H 4131. Unknown creator. "Tractes rebelles."

religious sect to coerce men into serving in the armed forces; the men were being blackened in electric stoves and then sent off to northern Vietnam or Korea.[5] Another tract from January 1952 spoke of the French "seizing people and cooking them black, distending their lips and twisting their hair – it's truly savage."[6]

This propaganda recycled an old trope: even before World War II, rumors circulated among soldiers that the French would transform Vietnamese into Africans to make them more violent.[7] In 1947, members of the Social-Democrat Party, suspicious of the Cao Đài but fighting for their lives against the communist-led Resistance, issued a call to "create a movement to oppose the arrest of Democrat-Socialist [Party] soldiers to

[5] SHD. 10H 4131. Service de Sécurité du Haut Commissariat au Sud-Vietnam. "L'Histoire du nommé Trinh à Binh Thuy." Translated tract. Saigon, November 15, 1951.
[6] SHD. 10H 4131. [Tract, four pages, beginning "Thanh niên Việt Nam..." in a bundle with the note "Tracts rebelles récupérés dans le sous-secteur de Cai Be"]. January 1952.
[7] See Tạ Chí Đại Trường, Người lính thuộc địa Nam Kỳ (Hanoi: Trí Thức, 2011), 280. The author cites a 1939 newspaper. Thanks to Châu Huy Ngọc for the reference.

send to Africa, and at the same time propagandize to incite the Cao Đài to become soldiers and use the African savages to kill them."[8]

Around the same time that such texts circulated, other examples of French perfidy were noted. Some of the most surprising (and creative) were the reports of French cannibals which appeared in *National Salvation* [*Cứu Quốc*], the Liên Việt's official organ in the South, on October 10, 1951. The newspaper accused General Jean de Lattre de Tassigny, the French commander, of bringing in these "black French cannibals so that they can devour Vietnamese... These cannibals generally wear raincoats in the style that the Germans usually wear, as well as black turbans." The story elaborated that in Hanoi, one of these cannibals seized a child, ate out its insides, and sucked its blood, while another tried to eat a child but was foiled.[9]

Such propaganda and rumors remind us of a genre of colonial and postcolonial cannibal stories, similar to the accounts of blood-sucking vampires recorded by Luise White in East Africa.[10] The fact that the "cannibals" in particular were dressed in German raincoats (trench coats?) suggests a particular reading of these stories in light of World War II atrocities. Living after the Holocaust, it is hard not to associate them with tales of men marching into ovens with Auschwitz, or Treblinka, or Nazi genocide in general. The fact that some Germans in the French Foreign Legion had fought in the Waffen SS during World War II only reinforces this reading. Max Horkheimer and Theodor Adorno's 1944 critique of the Enlightenment as a stage on the path to barbarism, written in the shadow of the Holocaust, seems amply confirmed here.[11]

Seemingly confirmed as well is Franz Fanon's biting critique of the violent racism of colonial rule, a binary conflict between White and Other. In *The Wretched of the Earth*, Fanon argues that "when you examine at close quarters the colonial context, it is evident that what parcels out the world to begin with is the fact of belonging to or not belonging to a particular race."[12] He goes on: "The colonial world is a world cut in two. The dividing line, the frontiers are shown by barracks and police

---

[8] SHD. 10 H 4169. V.N.D.C.X.H.Đ. Ban Chấp Hành L.T. Miềng [*sic*] Tây. Số 215. Chỉ Thị. June 15, 1947.

[9] SHD. 10H 4131. Service de Sécurité du Haut Commissariat au Sud Vietnam. Propagande V.M. Translation from *Cứu Quốc* newspaper in Nam Bộ, no. 65, October 10, 1951. Saigon, November 21, 1951. The Liên Việt was the communist-led front organization that opposed the French.

[10] Luise White, *Speaking with Vampires: Rumor and History in Colonial Africa* (Berkeley and Los Angeles: University of California Press, 2000).

[11] See Max Horkheimer and Theodor Adorno, *Dialectic of Enlightenment* (New York: Seabury Press, 1972 [1944]), particularly the chapter on anti-Semitism.

[12] Franz Fanon, *The Wretched of the Earth* (New York: Grove Press, 1963), 40.

stations. In the colonies it is the policeman and the soldier who are the official instituted go-betweens, the spokesman of the settler and his rule of oppression."[13] Fanon's argument fits Algeria, where a white colonial administration, a large army of white French conscripts, and a significant white settler population confronted Arabs and Berbers.

Yet this reading of conflict is most assuredly wrong. It is an example of a deployment model of race thinking, focusing on European cultural practices, categories, and ideas, and the ways they frame the colonial encounter. It is hard, however, to fit the sheer complexity of race relations in the Mekong delta into such a binary frame. In the delta, a white France relied on white, Arab, African, Vietnamese, and Khmer troops to fight against Vietnamese, who themselves were trying to overcome earlier conflicts with the darker-skinned Khmer Krom of the delta. When we turn to the cannibalism and race transformation texts, it will become clear that the deployment model cannot make sense of their meaning. The fact that the propaganda stoked fear of Vietnamese being transformed into blacks, or that they might be forced to eat others, suggests that the writers of these tracts did not simply mimic French beliefs but worked within a different frame of reference.

How, then, does one interpret such texts? This chapter builds on my earlier arguments. Dynamics of violence, I have argued, shaped the very character of the war, transforming differences between groups into violent antagonisms and making political and social cleavages harden. The argument about the "double fracture," addressed in the previous chapters, is a perfect example of this process. But in this context, what exactly was the connection between race and violent action? Generally speaking, under French colonial rule, views on race shaped state and popular views and actions. But the French colonial state, and its successor Japanese state in 1945, crushed collective acts of dissent, including those inflected by race. As state institutions collapsed, and along with it the monopoly on the use of force, the key check on collective action against the state disappeared. Instead, new groups rose up to assert "locally segmented monopolies of violence,"[14] and some of these local monopolies resorted to ethnic violence. Eventually, even the weak post-1945 French state resorted to mobilizing ethnic antagonisms against its enemies.

The argument above, however, does not capture the meanings of "race" and "ethnicity" to different audiences. The war saw experimentation – dissembling of old tropes on race, and reassembling them in novel

[13] Ibid., 37–38.
[14] Stathis Kalyvas, "Wanton and Senseless? The Logic of Massacres in Algeria," *Rationality and Society* 11(3) (1999), 259.

or odd ways in a context of heightened violence. This chapter, then, examines the deployment of European beliefs on race, but stresses how ideas, foreign and familiar, are appropriated into preexisting cultural frames of reference and thus transformed in the process.[15] Vietnamese, of course, have used race and ethnicity throughout the twentieth century as markers of difference.

This chapter first addresses France's use of race in choosing the soldiers to fight on the side of France before turning to how Vietnamese racial beliefs became entangled in other ways of speaking in the world. It digs into particularly troubling texts on race and cannibalism, and the implication of such texts for understanding the war as a whole. It also shows how these texts intersect with Buddhist ones on the decay of the dharma and the coming of an apocalypse heralded by the arrival of Maitreya Buddha. Through such texts, we can shed light more broadly on the troubled politics of belonging in a time of instability, decolonization, and war.

5.1 The French Military and the Question of Race

Racial and ethnic conflict shaped colonial Vietnam before World War II. While the small French settler population was dwarfed by the large indigenous one, and most Vietnamese did not encounter French in their daily life, practices of racial discrimination had become routinized.[16] After 1945, such practices were complicated by the fact that the French military in Indochina increasingly relied on white ex-Axis soldiers (and particularly Germans) shaped by Nazi racial ideology and their practices of war as well as on dark-skinned colonial subjects from Africa and North Africa. Why, however, did France initially refuse

---

[15] For classic examples of deployment approaches, see Benedict O'Gorman Anderson, *Imagined Communities: Reflections on the Origins and Spread of Nationalism* (London: Verso, 1983), or Ann Stoler, "Sexual Affronts and Racial Frontiers: European Identities and the Cultural Politics of Exclusion in Colonial Southeast Asia," *Comparative Studies in Society and History* 34(3) (July 1992): 514–551. For approaches that focus on appropriation of outside beliefs and their refashioning, see, for example, Vicente Rafael, *Contracting Colonialism: Translation and Christian Conversion in Tagalog Society under Early Spanish Rule* (Durham, NC: Duke University Press, 1993); my own *Print and Power: Confucianism, Communism, and Buddhism in the Making of Modern Vietnam* (Honolulu: University of Hawai'i Press, 2004); and Jonathon Glassman, *War of Words, War of Stones: Racial Thought and Violence in Colonial Zanzibar* (Bloomington: Indiana University Press, 2011). Mark Bradley combines deployment and appropriation models in his *Imagining Vietnam and America: The Making of Postcolonial Vietnam, 1919–1950* (Chapel Hill: University of North Carolina Press, 2003), 6, 52.

[16] For examples, see McHale, *Print and Power*, 43–44.

to send African and Arab soldiers to Indochina? And why did it change this policy in 1947?

Questions of race profoundly shaped France's return to Indochina in 1945. Out of a sense that French prestige and whiteness were linked, France explicitly decided to send only white troops to Indochina, while keeping out African and North African colonial troops. Jean Sainteny, in a telegram to Paris on August 13, 1945, criticized the Allied decision to allow the Chinese military to occupy the northern half of Indochina as "the worst of all," as it undermined white privilege: "Believe that we should not accept silently such injustice [*iniquité*] that... will damage profoundly the prestige of the white race in the Orient."[17]

Sainteny's concern over the prestige of the white race was not isolated. The French military fretted over the racial politics of their actions. If the French military groped for information on Indochina in late summer 1945, it was sure about one thing: the expeditionary force would be all volunteer and almost completely white. General Nyo, put in charge of organizing this expeditionary force, bluntly stated that the force had to have a high proportion of whites accompanied by a token number of "Indochinese":

The reconquest of this country, [boasting an] old and refined civilization, by troops who were mostly Black, might produce an adverse reaction. And the Indochinese would not understand it if they did not take part in the liberation of their country. However, their mediocre physical strength and their inconsistent combat ability suggests that their use be limited.[18]

General Leclerc, who would lead the forces in Indochina, was even more blunt: "Unfortunately, I cannot take Blacks. This is a formal decision, following from the daily telegrams from Cédille... and the British and Annamite reactions. Sending Blacks would be a catastrophe that would risk blowing up on us [*mettre le feu aux poudres*]."[19]

Leclerc's statement drips with irony, given that non-European troops played a key role for the Allies in defeating the Japanese. East African troops – the King's African Rifles – played a minor part in the 1944 Burma campaign, in which Indian troops contributed the bulk of Allied strength. Indian troops served in the initial reoccupations of the Dutch East Indies and French Indochina in September 1945.

---

[17] Jean Sainteny, *Histoire d'une paix manquée* (Paris: A. Fayard, 1967), 61.

[18] General Nyo, quoted in Bodinier, *Le retour de la France en Indochine 1945–1946: textes et documents*, (Château de Vincennes: Service Historique de l'Armée de Terre, 1987), 28.

[19] Leclerc letter, September 24, 1945, quoted in Bodinier, *Le retour de la France en Indochine*, 66.

Nonetheless, as noted by Nyo and Leclerc, when the French were preparing their expeditionary force in 1945 to take back French Indochina, they excluded African and North African soldiers. Some authors have charged that the Americans opposed the use of black soldiers in Asia.[20] Nyo, cited above for his statement that blacks could not be used, in a different context blamed the Americans. This is a dubious claim.[21] While I have seen no proof, one possible reason for Leclerc's actions is that after the extensive rapes committed by Moroccan and Algerian soldiers in the French Expeditionary Corps fighting in Italy (1943–44), Leclerc did not want to repeat such disasters in Indochina.

Nyo's and Leclerc's mishmash of racism and sensitivity was quickly shown to be irrelevant. The first Allied troops to intervene in French Indochina to accept Japanese surrender were mostly Indian and Chinese, eventually supplemented in the South by surrendered Japanese and paramilitary Khmer. The Chinese troops occupied the North under General Lu Han. The 20th Indian Division under British General Gracey occupied Saigon and parts of the delta. Colonial authority, in other words, was reestablished using proxy troops from the British and French empires. In 1946, d'Argenlieu, the High Commissioner of Indochina, relented somewhat on the issue of using African troops – "without ignoring in any way incidents involving race, I believe that the least worst of the two solutions is to send the so-called Senegalese battalions with few Muslim elements."[22] Facing a severe recruitment crunch in France, the French soon abandoned its all-white policy and began sending Africans and North Africans to Indochina in 1947.

From 1947 on, the percentage of non-white and non-French troops would steadily rise. By 1954, French nationals formed a clear minority of soldiers. Colonial soldiers from places like Algeria, Morocco, Senegal, and Guinea came to fight in Indochina. They proved essential in suppressing challenges to imperial rule. Gregory Mann suggests that the French attracted African volunteers in particular to serve the colonial army "by high pay, aggressive recruiting tactics, and new opportunities

[20] See Henry-Jean Loustau, *Les Deux battallions: Cochinchine-Tonkin, 1945–1952* (Paris: Albin Michel, 1987), 40.
[21] For Nyo's claim about the American opposition to Africans serving in Indochina, and a rebuttal of it, see Claude Yao Kouassi, "La participation militaire de l'Afrique noire à la guerre d'Indochine (1947–1955)," doctoral thesis, Pantheon-Sorbonne University, 1986), 18–19.
[22] High Commissioner for Indochina Thierry d'Argenlieu, October 1946, quoted in Kouassi, "La participation militaire," 29. Kouassi speculates that the presence of Muslims in southern Vietnam might have affected this decision.

for advancement within the ranks."[23] One might also add that the lack of better alternatives constrained the choices made by recruits. Whatever their motives, these colonial enlistees stood on the side of colonial rule. They were reinforced by "supplétifs," or irregular self-defense and paramilitary soldiers recruited locally. The question arises: how did Vietnamese beliefs about race shape their views of these soldiers?

5.2 Vietnamese Views of Race, 1920–1954

Race talk – as an affirmation of Vietnameseness, as a tactical way to reach enemy troops, and as a depiction of the enemy's barbarism – shaped the understanding of war and violence in the Mekong delta. But where did this race talk come from? Vietnamese, like many Southeast Asians, conceptualized identity in terms of common descent. They had an origin myth of descent from a dragon and a fairy, who married, siring 100 eggs that form the basis of the Vietnamese people today. This origin myth shows up, for example, in the writings of the Hòa Hảo Prophet Huỳnh Phú Sổ and the Cao Đài Defender of the Dharma Phạm Công Tắc. It is obvious in repeated invocations of Tổ quốc, or Land of Our Ancestors, that occurred during the war.

The term for "race" used, nòi giống (also written as giống nòi), fits into this "traditional" understanding of race, summarized by the Marxist Sơn Trà in 1938 as follows: "At that time [late 1920s], we only knew of the nation [quốc gia] and compatriots [đồng bào]. In one country, from the king to the people, all people shared the same bloodline [huyết thống], were of the same race, were all brothers and sisters."[24] Such racial thinking transcended religious and political boundaries: thus, Catholics spoke of race as easily as Buddhists, conservatives used it as well as Marxists.[25] In the early twentieth century, in part as a reaction to French conquest, intellectuals also adopted a social Darwinist view of the international order, one in which Europeans and Americans temporarily occupied the top rung.[26] In the late 1920s and into the 1930s, this preexisting discourse became

---

[23] Gregory Mann, "Locating Colonial Histories: Between France and West Africa," *American Historical Review* (April 2005), 431.

[24] [Nguyễn] Sơn Trà, *Giai cấp là gì?*, quoted in McHale, *Print and Power*, 131.

[25] For a Catholic example, see Charles Keith, *Catholic Vietnam: A Church from Empire to Nation* (Berkeley: University of California Press, 2012), 172.

[26] See Bradley, *Imagining Vietnam and America*. For the Cao Đài inversion of this hierarchy, see Janet Hoskins, "'God's Chosen People': Race, Religion and Anti-Colonial Struggle in French Indochina," Asia Research Institute Working Paper 189 (September 2012).

intertwined in intellectual circles with concerns over overpopulation and racial decline.[27]

At first glance, however, the relevance of such racial thinking past 1940 might seem dubious. When we first turn to the communist-led Resistance after 1945, racialization seems to be of limited importance in defining the enemy. Communist cadres rarely invoked the concept of "race" (*nòi giống/giống nòi* or *chủng tộc*). Instead, they stressed inclusion and preferred to speak of the unity of "the people" [*dân tộc*]. For this reason, the writer Phan Khôi, a non-communist participant in the northern Resistance, would claim that during the Resistance War, the "masses" and the leadership were as one.[28] Vietnamese also embraced struggles elsewhere in the colonial world, such as the Madagascar uprisings of 1947 or the contention in North Africa in the 1940s and 1950s.

Indeed, we find clear evidence that Vietnamese in the Resistance strived to articulate a capacious, cosmopolitan, but pragmatic sense of identity. In the early years, for example, the Resistance relied on the special talents of New Vietnamese [*Việt Nam mới*]: Japanese who had deserted the Imperial Army and joined the Resistance cause in 1945. The Resistance gave these Japanese an honorary sort of Vietnameseness. German deserters played a limited role as well: some of them had technical skills prized by their new leaders. The Resistance also recruited "Volunteers of Death," or ethnic Vietnamese from Thailand, to serve the Resistance. General Nguyễn Sơn, a Vietnamese serving in China's People's Liberation Army, returned to serve the Resistance for a few years, and then went back to China. And Hồ Chí Minh even suggested that the Chinese in Vietnam organize themselves in self-rule to help the resistance, rather than just be organized by the Resistance. In Cambodia, Vietnamese and Khmer served in mixed battalions fighting for Cambodian independence.

In the end, however, Vietnamese "inclusion" had its limits. Although the use of the concept of race is scrupulously avoided in current Vietnamese historical scholarship, race talk repeatedly popped up in the South of the 1930s, 1940s and 1950s. While belief in Euro-American civilizational pre-eminence eroded in World War II, it certainly did not disappear. World War II, brutal and vicious in Asia, may have hardened Vietnamese views of race. John Dower has aptly characterized World War II as a "race war," one in which the United States and Japan each

---

[27] Thuy Linh Nguyen, "Overpopulation, Racial Degeneracy and Birth Control in French Colonial Vietnam," *Journal of Colonialism and Colonial History* 19(3) (Winter 2018), https:doi.org/10.1353/cch.2018.0024 (accessed December 26, 2018).

[28] Phan Khôi, "Phê bình lãnh đạo văn nghệ," *Giai phẩm mùa thu*, September 1956, reprinted in *Tìm hiểu sự thật* (Saigon: Nhà in Quốc gia, 195?), 9.

mobilized crude racial and ethnic stereotypes in an attempt to defeat the other.[29] Japanese propagandized their views of Asians and the "Yamato race" throughout Southeast Asia while denigrating whites.

By the 1940s, certain Vietnamese views on racial difference seem to have become entrenched. A range of writers continued to believe that certain ethnic minorities, as well as Africans, were inferior. Intellectuals across the political spectrum, even Marxists agitating for equality, sometimes adopted quite negative views of the dark-skinned. Take this comment by Đào Duy Anh, one of the best-known Marxist intellectuals of the 1930s and 1940s: "the culture of the American and European peoples is high, while the culture of the savage peoples [dân tộc mọi rợ] of Africa and Australia, just like that of the Mường, Mán, and Mọi in our country, is deficient."[30] This disdain of "savages" was enduring. A 1946 newspaper story trumpeted: "Now, no one would dare claim that the Vietnamese nation is a tribe of savages [một bộ lạc mọi rợ], since the Vietnamese people have exercised self-determination and self-rule through elections!"[31] In a 1950 story in a southern newspaper on the Elizabeth Saunders Orphanage in Japan, its director praised her five biracial orphans who had "black savage" [mọi da đen] (i.e., African-American) fathers.[32] In 1950, while making an argument about how different peoples of the world internationalize, the Hanoi journalist Phùng Tri Lai characterized African minorities in terms of their nudity, barbaric habits, and "custom" of eating human flesh.[33] Intriguingly, views of African-Americans also spilled into this debate, as when the Khmer Krom monk Trịnh Thới Cang argued that without education, "Cambodians would be practically no more than the Blacks of America."[34]

---

[29] John Dower, *War Without Mercy: Race and Power in the Pacific War* (New York: Pantheon, 1986).

[30] Đào Duy Anh, *Việt Nam văn hóa sử cương*, excerpted in Nguyễn Ngọc Thiện et al., eds, *Tuyển tập phê bình, nghiên cứu văn học Việt Nam*, Vol. 4, p. 58 (Hanoi: Văn Học, 1997). Mường refers to a particular ethnic group, and both Mán and Mọi were broader terms used to refer to "backwards" highlanders. For an extended discussion of such views of hierarchy, see Bradley, *Imagining Vietnam and America*. On the term "mọi": Oscar Salemink notes that this word "can be glossed as 'savage,' but with servile connotations added by the slave trade that was concentrated in the Highlands." See Oscar Salemink, *The Ethnography of Vietnam's Central Highlanders: A Historical Contextualization, 1850–1990* (Honolulu: Hawai'i, 2003), 28.

[31] "Trật tự mới" [A new order], *Dân sinh*, January 14, 1946, 2.

[32] "5 năm bị chiếm đóng Nhụt Bổn [sic] có thêm 40.000 đứa trẻ Nhụt lai Mỹ [sic]-Nga và mọi da đen" [The five years of the Occupation of Japan have led to 40,000 more Japanese-American, Japanese-Russian, and Japanese-black savage children] *Ánh Sáng* (Saigon), September 13, 1950, 1.

[33] Phùng Tri Lai, *Hồng Kông du ký* (Hanoi: Nhà in Vũ Hùng, 1950), 30, https://sach .nlv.gov.vn, no stable URL (accessed June 13, 2015).

[34] SHD. 10 H 4279. Subfolder "Bonze". Déclaration de M. TRINH THOI CANG. Soctrang, December 22, 1949.

Vietnamese, in other words, did not simply adopt Western racial views in toto, but also were shaped by earlier arguments over difference. Đào Duy Anh's comments above on "savages" also clues us in to the enduring prejudices, often cast in civilizational terms, about highlanders and non-Việt ethnic minorities. These groups, some darker-skinned than the ethnic Việt, were seen as culturally inferior because they did not participate in a Sinic literate culture. Other examples drive this point home. For example, after pointing out that Malays were, like the Khmer, darker than Vietnamese, one southern writer made a remarkably uninformed claim: "seen in terms of culture, Malays are very deficient. Clans are scattered all over the mountains, and they have not yet abandoned their barbaric customs [*tập tục dã man*]."[35] Writings from the 1940s into the 1960s often refer to the Khmer Krom in the Mekong delta as "*Thổ*," a term used for indigenous or tribal peoples that is now seen as derogatory. In the context of criticizing the communists, the Cao Đài leader Phạm Công Tắc explicitly articulated a notion of a hierarchy of races, and a fear of racial decline, in 1950:

Today... in the eyes of the Vietnamese race [*nòi giống*], we are moving towards independence and unification through communism. I don't reproach their struggle to create a shared happiness for the race. However... [the communists] despotically slaughter their race. I fear only one thing: that because we have been under the [French] yoke of slavery for eighty years, and our people of twenty million has not yet achieved victory, people will use foreign materialism on the Vietnamese race to drive it to ruin, turning us into [ethnic minorities like] the Mường, Mán, Mọi, or Lolo.[36]

Thus, in reaction to Japanese propaganda, French imperialism, East Asian discourses, and the violence of war, Vietnamese increasingly articulated an anticolonial nationalism with racial overtones. But it was more than a binary contest between French and Vietnamese. All kinds of others – Cham, Chinese, Khmer, and Malay, not to mention Africans and Arabs – were dragged into this war as well. The French reoccupation of their former colony set Vietnamese against the French and their troops but also Vietnamese against Vietnamese and (darker-skinned) Khmer. Thus, Vietnamese expressed anger at white French atrocities, but also fear that the Khmer would commit "*cáp duồn*," or the beheading of Vietnamese. Compounding such antagonisms, the hunt for "pro-

---

[35] Nguyễn Khắc Oanh, "Khi người Mã Lai tỉnh giác" [When the Malays awaken], *Sông Hương* [*Perfume River*] (Saigon), August 1948, 2.

[36] "Thảm trạng của quốc dân việt nam tại đại đồng xã trong dịp Tết Trung Thu, ngày rằm tháng 8 năm Canh Dần (1950)," in Phạm Công Tắc, *Lời thuyết đạo của Đức Hộ Pháp*, Vol. III (1949–1950), 172, https://tusachcaodai.files.wordpress.com/2013/05/hp-td-qiii.pdf (accessed August 1, 2018).

French" (*thân Pháp*) who were "traitors" (*Việt gian*) was particularly acute from 1945 to 1947, and persisted thereafter. This resulted in thousands of Vietnamese deaths, and also, at times, fed into the racialization of enemies.

Racialization was not linked to any particular political view or religious affiliation: the concept of an ethnonationalist purity was widely invoked. A non-communist civics handbook from 1949 defined the nation in the following manner: "A nation [*quốc gia*] is a group of people sharing the same bloodline, living in a particular territory, related to one another through race, spoken language, customs, history, geography, and culture."[37] Even communists, who at first seemed so inclusive, made similar appeals to biological essentialism. When Catholics in the Resistance appealed in 1949 to fellow Catholics who had "gone down the wrong path," they invoked the specter of racial extinction: "You cannot fold your arms and watch the enemy wipe out the race."[38]

Vietnamese commonly appealed to "compatriots [*đồng bào*, literally "those of the same womb"], those of shared "blood," or common descent. The term "compatriot," expanded, at times, to include ethnic Chinese (who often intermarried with ethnic Vietnamese in the south). It seems never to have been used, however, to refer to those from other lowland ethnic groups like the Cham, Malay, or Khmer. The common use of kin metaphors, such as speaking of the "Vietnamese family," combined with the visceral appeal to blood ties, drives this point home:

But we know that whoever is Vietnamese, and has Vietnamese blood flowing through the veins, always has in their heart a love for the Vietnamese land, the Vietnamese people, so that one day, although living in the temporarily occupied zone, you will turn towards the GREAT VIETNAMESE FAMILY.[39]

Needless to say, such race-talk would not appeal to minorities like the Cham or the Khmer Krom.

Last but not least, one cannot overlook the ubiquitous use of "*ta*" – "we" – to define an in-group against outsiders. The boundaries of "*ta*" were not always clear, but implicitly, its core were ethnic Vietnamese speaking Vietnamese. Taken together, we can see ethnic Vietnamese drawing on multiple streams of thought in defining in-groups and out-groups. These all came together amidst the violence of war, causing

[37] Nhất Hoành Sơn, *Công dân giáo dục phổ thông* (Hanoi: Ngày nay, 1949), 7.
[38] SHD. 10 H 3378. Công Giáo Kháng Chiến Nam Bộ, "Hiệu triệu toàn thể đồng bào công giáo," November 4, 1949.
[39] SHD. 10 H 4714. Subfolder "P.S." "Hiệu triêu – Hỡi các anh em Partisans, Cao Đài, Dân xã Hòa Hảo!" [Signed by Phạm Văn Bạch, UBKCNB, March 5, 1949]. Collected in Cần Thơ, May 1949.

ethnic and political boundaries to harden again and again. Racialization, one form of in-group identity, could veer into paranoia and panic, as the next section will show.

5.3 Race, Omens, Fear of the Other, and Apocalypse

The Hòa Hảo, Cao Đài, and many other southerners took prophecies seriously. The Cao Đài leader Phạm Công Tắc often communicated in séances with Victor Hugo, the great French writer. Both he and the Hòa Hảo were fond of the sixteenth-century prophet Nguyễn Bỉnh Khiêm, whose prophecies, as one 1946 book noted, were "as everyone knows, hard to understand."[40] For example, the Hòa Hảo leader Huỳnh Phú Sổ is reputed to have stated that after that Japanese coup d'état of March 1945, "the Japanese cannot eat the whole chicken" [*Nhựt Bổn ăn không hết con gà*]. This interpretation was explained thus: "the year 1945 is under the sign of the rooster (the year 'Ât Dậu' in the lunar calendar). Since the Japanese succumbed to defeat in August 1945, this means that the year 'Ât Dậu' was not completed before the fate of Japan was determined."[41] In 1946, a Vietnamese report to French intelligence (which the French labeled as of questionable reliability) stated that the Resistance had discovered in Châu Đốc Province a stone on which had been chiseled "Huỳnh Phú Sổ, Emperor of Cochinchina." According to the French, whose interpretation may be a bit suspect, the Hòa Hảo believed that "this rock seems to have fallen from the sky like a message from God."[42]

When the Hòa Hảo Prophet Huỳnh Phú Sổ was murdered in 1947, not all believers accepted the news of his death. Approximately two years later (in 1949), a story circulated that Chinese had seen Huỳnh Phú Sổ alive and well in Yunnan Province, China. French radio had supposedly announced this "news." Tracts claimed that "the Master" would return at the head of a fleet of warships.[43] Others spread the word that a new Heavenly King to Protect the Nation [*Bảo Quốc Thiên Vương*] would appear on the scene, supported by all those opposed to king Bảo Đại, a puppet installed by the French and in favor of a new religion. This may have been Resistance propaganda to divide the "nationalists": the rumor

---

[40] Nguyễn Bỉnh Khiêm, *Sấm ngữ Trạng Trình* (Hanoi: Bảo Ngọc, 1946), [1].
[41] SHD. 10 H 4167. "Origines lointaines de secte bouddhique de Hoa Hao," unsigned, undated (but probably April 1947).
[42] SHD. 10H, File 4167. Bulletin de renseignements, "A/S évolution du mouvement Hoa Hao," Saigon, October 2, 1946.
[43] SHD. 10H file 4167. Traduction d'un document récupéré le 6.2.49 au cours d'une opération dans la région de Tan Thanh (Gocong), "A/S prochain retour de Huynh Giao Chu (Huynh Phu So)," Mytho, February 21, 1949.

was accompanied by pictures of Huỳnh Phú Sổ and a prominent Cao Đài lay leader in the Resistance, Cao Triều Phát.[44]

According to one French report from 1948, a prophecy from the Way of the Strange Fragrance of the Precious Mountain [*Bửu Sơn Kỳ Hương*] suggested that at the end of one Buddhist cosmic era, Maitreya (the future Buddha) would appear in 1964. This would be part of a generalized concern among Hòa Hảo, Cao Đài, and mainstream Buddhists at this time on the end of a cycle of 2,500 years, with the Dharma decaying, strife and famine common, culminating with an apocalypse in which the future Buddha Maitreya arrives. Another Bửu Sơn Kỳ Hương prophecy that circulated in 1948 stated, in cryptic form:

Buu Son Ky Huong
   Ngoc Trung Nien Xuat
   Quan su Trang Trinh
   Minh Mang Thai [*sic*] *Sanh*
   Thien Dia Tan Tao
   Viet Nam Phuc Nghiep
   Nguyen Tien Quoc Hung

Or, as the gloss in the report put it:

Rare perfume of the precious mountain
   The Jade [Buddha?] will appear at mid-century
   The Prophet Trạng Trình [Nguyễn Binh Khiêm] [says?]
   Minh Mạng will be reborn
   To recreate all under Heaven,
   Vietnam will enter a renaissance
   A descendant of the previous *Nguyễn* [kings?] will appear.[45]

These omens drew on core Buddhist beliefs in the Mekong Delta, similar to the kinds of prophecies that have long circulated in Vietnam, about impending apocalypse. They intersected with ideas contained in the propaganda I mentioned at the very beginning of this chapter – beliefs that incited fear of and antagonism against racial others.

---

[44] SHD. 10H file 4167. A/S activité Hoa Hao, Saigon, February 24, 1949. Cao Triều Phát led a Cao Đài splinter group allied with the Resistance.

[45] SHD. 10H file 4207. "A/S activité politico-religieuse. Le Buu Son Ky Huong." Saigon, December 28, 1948. Translation of this cryptic prophecy was aided by the French gloss provided, as well as suggestions from Tuong Vu. Some of the translation is difficult, given that no diacritics were provided and the meaning of some terms is highly ambiguous. As Huỳnh Phú Sổ saw himself as a messenger of the Jade Buddha, I provisionally suggest that the reference to Jade may refer to the Jade Buddha. "Quân Sư" means "Chief Counselor" (usually referring to kings or military commanders), but it is translated here as "Prophet," which was the role in which Trạng Trình Nguyễn Binh Khiêm (1491–1585) was best known to Hòa Hảo followers. The reference to "Nguyen" most likely refers to the Nguyễn kings.

In December 1947, a news story in *Cứu Quốc* [*National Salvation*] trumpeted: "Barbaric Actions of the French – The French are Arresting Children and Extracting their Blood." The story went on to explain that two small children had subsequently died.[46] In 1948, propaganda circulated that the "barbaric" French were slipping poison into rice stocks and killing Vietnamese. The Resistance provincial committee for Trà Vinh passed along a report that ethnic Khmer in the province had poisoned Vietnamese.[47] Another tract from early 1948 added graphic detail about a powdered drug sold via the Chinese: "this drug is a violent poison: five minutes after swallowing, the sick person's heart stops beating, blood comes out of the mouth, and the sick person dies."[48]

By 1949, a generalized animosity to foreigners, sometimes articulated in racial terms, popped up in a variety of places. A January 1949 leaflet by the Committee against the Rape of the Women of the South [*Nam Bộ*] angrily spoke of the French raping females from age ten to seventy and added: "They plan to use microbial warfare to wipe out our people." After discussing this "shame… to the entire race [*giống nòi*]," the leaflet called on Vietnamese to "defend the Resistance, defend the race [*nòi giống*]."[49] A further example, this time from a publication outside the South, reinforces the idea that such rhetoric was found throughout the country, inflamed by French actions. Speaking of French rapes, killings, and destruction, the booklet stated that "the French are like animals… Our people hate them to the very marrow of their bones." [50]

Perhaps the most intriguing propaganda is that on cannibalism and race transformation that introduced this chapter. Cannibalism was usually portrayed as something that happened elsewhere: as a Saigon journalist wrote, "Hearing the three words 'Eating human flesh,' readers most certainly tremble in fright. Isn't that some savage custom found in the jungles of Africa? Or the habit of the *Mọi* [savages] in the highlands?"[51] Nonetheless, rumors of cannibalism had circulated earlier in the Mekong delta. General Trần Văn Trà has written that in Sa Đéc in early 1946, enemy troops "killed people, ripped out livers and cut [human] flesh,

---

[46] "Hành động dã man của Pháp. Pháp bắt trẻ em trích máu" [The Barbaric Actions of the French, seizing children to extract their blood], *Cứu Quốc* 770 (December 6, 1947), p. 1.
[47] , SHD. Series 10H, File 5587, "Hành-động dã man của giặc Pháp" [The Barbaric Actions of the French], Long-Châu-Tiền thông tin, December 10, 1948.
[48] VNA-II. PTHNV box 482 d. E.03.26. Province de Hatien. "Rapport d'ensemble." January 1948.
[49] SHD. 10H, File 2369, Uỷ ban chống hãm hiếp phụ nữ Nam Bộ, "Cương quyết chống nạn hãm hiếp dã man của giặc Pháp," January 1949.
[50] *Kháng chiến lâu dài và gian khổ nhưng nhất định thắng lợi* ([Northern Vietnam?]: Tổng Cục Chính Trị Cục Tuyên Quân, 1952), 4.
[51] "Ăn thịt người" [Eating human flesh], *Saigon mới*, August 21, 1948, p. 1.

forcing individuals to buy it." He adds, giving a touch of authenticity to the story, that in the Sa Đéc market and two other places, visitors "were forced to buy a kilogram [of human flesh] at the price of one đồng."[52] This market story seems to have travelled widely in the Mekong delta. In August 1947, the rumor circulated that in the Cần Thơ market, the Hòa Hảo was selling human flesh for four piastres a kilogram.[53] One letter writer emphasized of these cannibalism stories: "This is not a joke, believe me."[54] A third person, who opposed both the Resistance and the Hòa Hảo, contextualized these stories in a litany of Hòa Hảo atrocities:

massacres, assassinations, beheading innocent peasants, cutting them open to take out the heart, mixing alcohol and blood together to drink, killing children aged three to five, beheading them to scare everyone, in villages far from [Cần Thơ] town the Hòa Hảo have sliced up dead bodies and sold the flesh of victims, they even forced peasants to buy and eat human flesh and if they refused, they accused them of committing treason against the Hòa Hảo and shot them on the spot.[55]

Members of the Hòa Hảo Buddhist sect in the South had themselves criticized the French for violating bodies since the early 1940s. The Hòa Hảo leader Huỳnh Phú Sổ had accused French doctors of "opening the spleens" of individuals in order to extract silver [argent].[56] Some members of the communist-led Resistance in the South were convinced that members of religious sects had committed similar atrocities in the 1940s. The revolutionary Mai Chí Thọ, then with the Public Security forces in the western Mekong Delta, writes at length in his memoirs about the barbaric practices of "many" Hòa Hảo and Cao Đài followers, such as slitting open bellies and taking out livers. He claims that members of one of these groups stationed at a military post in Phú Mỹ (Mỹ Thọ) forced passersby to buy the flesh of dead cadres and soldiers.[57] The writer Sơn Nam, writing about his experiences in the Mekong Delta with the Resistance, claims that he knew of a case in 1947 in which soldiers linked to a religious

---

[52] Trần Văn Trà, *Miền Nam thành đồng đi trước về sau* (Hanoi: Quân đội nhân dân, 2006), 207.

[53] ANOM. HCI CP 107. [Intercepted letter from Tran Van Phu, Saigon, to Dang Ngoc Thanh. August 23, 1947].

[54] ANOM. HCI. CP 107. [Intercepted letter from Le Ba Chuc, Saigon, to Le Ba Gi, Paris. September 11, 1947].

[55] SHD. 10 H 4176. Deuxième Bureau. Rapport d'un indicateur sur les Hoa Hao en date de 26 Août 1947.

[56] ANOM. SPCE Box 385, "Secte religieuse dirigée par Huynh Pu So dit Dao Xen," Indochine, May 1, 1940.

[57] Mai Chí Thọ, *Hồi Ức. Những mẩu chuyện đời tôi* (Ho Chi Minh City: Trẻ, 2001), 141. See also Phạm Văn Bạch, "Mùa Thu nhớ mãi," in *Nam Bộ thành đồng Tổ Quốc*, (Hanoi: Chính trị Quốc gia, 1990), 92.

sect "openly sold human flesh."[58] A police agent working for the Resistance stated, in overwrought prose:

One of our agents has seen, with his own eyes, a formal order from Năm Lửa [Hòa Hảo militia leader Trần Văn Soái] asking them to arrest the two Frenchmen who are in Sau Tay's house, in order to seize their guns and kill them. Their corpses will be sliced up and sold in Cần Thơ, especially to other French, so that they will become intoxicated and kill each other.[59]

It is hard to evaluate such claims. As one essayist puts it, from late 1945 onward, "Everyone who was in the Resistance at that time in the western Mekong Delta knew of cases in which the Resistance handed down spurious verdicts about the Hòa Hảo eating human flesh."[60]

In short, claims and counterclaims about cannibalism and bodily violations were both particular to the delta as well as part of a common genre that transcends particularities of time and space. Such stories were frequently linked to race. Despite Thiếu Sơn's claim, then, the First Indochina War was a race war. But it was not like World War II, in which Japanese propagandists spoke of a "Yamato race" fighting whites in a bitter global struggle, or Nazis defined Germans as a pure Aryan "race" fighting against racial others.[61] Neither was it a Fanonian war pitting white colonialists against a darker foe. Rather, in the worst of times, Vietnamese sometimes perceived the war as a struggle for their own racial or ethnic survival against enemies, who ranged from French rapists and killers to Moroccan and Senegalese cannibals and on to Khmer Krom decapitators.

Turning back to the texts that opened this chapter, one has finally to ask: why, in a war pitting the French army against the Vietnamese, were dark-skinned soldiers vilified? One answer is simple: of the roughly 162,000 regular soldiers in the Far Eastern Expeditionary Corps as of December 1950, only 70,000 were French. Fifty thousand were North African and black African.[62] A Party history for Tiên Giang province (where some of the propaganda discussed in this chapter was found) makes repeated reference of battles against French, African, and "Thổ"

---

[58] Sơn Nam, *Hồi ký* (Ho Chi Minh City: Trẻ, 2002), Vol. 2, 130.
[59] SHD. 10 H 4169. Chef NGUYEN HUNG, "Rapport du Chef de Gendarmerie d'Assaut de Cantho envoyé au Chef de Gendarmerie Provinciale a. s. des activités Hoa hao." [Translation]. Cần Thơ, August 25, 1947.
[60] This quotation comes from Hứa Hoành, "Việt Minh giết Đức Thầy Huỳnh Phú Sổ và lãnh tụ giáo phái ở Nam Kỳ" [The Việt Minh killed the Venerable Master Huỳnh Phú Sổ and leaders of the sects in the South," www.namkyluctinh.com/a-lichsu/huahoanh/hua hoanh-vmgiethuynhphuso.htm (accessed July 7, 2020).
[61] Dower, *War Without Mercy*.
[62] For figures, see (General) Paul Simonin, *Les Berets blancs de la Légion en Indochine* (Paris: Albin Michel, 2002), 27.

(Khmer) soldiers in 1951.[63] In short, in the Mekong Delta, the literal face of the enemy was far more likely to be dark-skinned than white – and this enemy sometimes terrorized villagers.

Perhaps because these Africans and Moroccans were more alien and unfamiliar than Frenchmen, they made more convenient targets of hatred. Intriguingly, the texts conflate Moroccans and Africans as black skinned. At the same time, in parts of the Mekong Delta there was great fear of black and Moroccan soldiers because of their indiscriminate violence against civilians. This is clear in an account of a massacre in which 600 Vietnamese were purportedly killed and 1,500 houses were burned down – a massacre in which European and African troops participated.[64]

The texts on bodily violations discussed in this chapter – eating of livers, accidental ingestion of French poisons and microbes, rape, and race-transformation ovens – are of a different order than most primary texts on the war. In bringing the transgression of the Vietnamese body into the discussion, these documents convey the most troubling assaults on Vietnameseness. The embodiment of a message is its ultimate concretization. In this case, a message of anticolonial nationalism is distilled into one of maintaining the purity of the body against a barbaric enemy. The texts on race-transforming ovens are the most explicit: they stoke what Arjun Appadurai has called the "abhorrence of taxonomic hybridity."[65] That is, they make explicit what may be implicit: Vietnamese cannot be black; they should not transgress categories that should be separate.

But like all texts, these propaganda texts are polyvocal. In the propaganda on race transformation and cannibalism, the French and their soldiers are represented both as extremely powerful and as utterly despicable. The French are implicitly portrayed as hegemonic masters of modern technology as well as an enemy that can be defeated. There seems to be only one reason for the Resistance to engage in such propaganda. Many Vietnamese peasants were not taking sides for the French or for the Resistance. They were caught in between. Given the inability of the Resistance to convince some of these wavering souls of the ideological justification of their cause, they resorted to fearmongering to push these peasants over to their side.

---

[63] Đảng Cộng Sản Việt Nam, *Lịch sử Đảng bộ tỉnh Tiền Giang* ([Tiền Giang]: Ban Nghiên Cứu lịch sử Đảng, 1985), 199, 205, 206.

[64] This claim is found in *Lịch sử Công An nhân dân Bến Tre (1945–54)* (Bến tre: s. n.,1992), 1:44.

[65] Arjun Appadurai, "Dead Certainty: Ethnic Violence in an Age of Globalization," *Development and Change* 29(4) (October 1998), 910.

It is in reading such startling documents that one can, finally, under-stand the intersection of apocalyptic warnings of the end of an Age of the Decay of the Dharma with the conspiratorial language that occasionally erupts into historical accounts and memoirs in Vietnamese on the First Indochina War. These Vietnamese-language accounts attack "traitors" [*Việt gian*], "pretenders," or "fakes;" they warn of "spies" and "subver-sion;" and they disparage individuals who are "pro- French" [*thân Pháp*] but who are wearing "masks" or "disguises" [*mặt nạ*] to hide their real identities. Such language is but a trace of the fears that pervaded commu-nities during the war.

5.4 Conclusion

The history I have been narrating of violence, race-talk, and propa-ganda involving black, Arab, Vietnamese, and Khmer bodies is far outside the mainstream scholarship on the wars for Indochina. That scholarship has been deeply shaped by narratives of the Cold War and anticolonial revolutionary nationalism. Cold War scholarship today has been moving away from the view that Third World conflicts were simply proxy wars between the superpowers. But with few exceptions, this scholarship is still centered on activities of elites and capitals, not on how these wars have unfolded in the hinterlands of the affected countries. Anticolonial revolutionary nationalist narratives, while reject-ing the centrality of the superpowers as the agents of world change, also reject approaches that accentuate the significance of ethnic and reli-gious cleavages. Neither narrative helps us adequately understand the histories and texts before us.

Such criticism might suggest that postcolonial scholarship celebrating "hybridity" might provide an interpretive guide to such texts. After all, texts that refer to German trench coats, Africans, and race-transforming machines, and that circulate in an area with rich indigenous cultural streams might seem perfect exemplars of such "hybridity." This would, however, be a complete misreading of the evidence. Texts like the ones I mentioned do not illustrate the hybrid nature of the Mekong Delta. They try to convey the fear of hybridity, and the fear of bodily transform-ations that could transform the pure Vietnamese into something else.

There is a second reason to reject one form of the "hybridity" narrative in which European cultural, political, and social forces engage with local, "Third World" ones to create colonial hybridity. Steven Feierman, in an astute comment on African scholarship, notes a core problem with this approach. When one tries to combine multiple studies of particular hybridities into a broader narrative, it is difficult to find a common thread:

"The studies of commodities (or of Christian sin) in one place, and then another, and then another, can be aggregated only on the basis of their shared relationship to the relevant European category: they cannot be placed within a larger or more general African narrative. What is African inevitably appears in a form which is local and fragmented."[66]

Why, Feierman asks, should certain cultural domains "come to be understood as fragmented and partial?" The answer, he suggests, is more in the mind of the scholar than in conditions on the ground. Existing historiographical approaches, by devaluing particular local cultural practices and thus ignoring their study, have effectively made large parts of these domains "invisible." As this has happened, what is visible and remaining to the historian's eye comes to seem disjointed and unattached to a (local) macronarrative that would give it coherence.[67] To return to the histories and stories at the center of this chapter: I suspect that to most readers, they still seem a bit odd, a clear aberration from the dominant narratives of Vietnamese (and global) history. This reaction is, in part, a legacy of the fact that some of the cultural beliefs discussed in this paper have been rendered invisible in most accounts of post-1945 Vietnam.

Feierman's critique is compelling when the choice is framed as a binary between a European-defined macrohistory and a local microhistory, between the European colonizer's view and that of the colonized. But the place of other colonial subjects in Vietnam – Africans, Arabs, and Khmer – complicates this choice. For better and for worse, European colonizers were agents of a globalization that linked colonies to each other as well as to the metropole. African soldiers served in Burma. Indian police officers served in the Malay states. And Moroccan, Algerian, African, and Khmer soldiers served the French military in the Mekong Delta. The meaning of these soldiers and their representations turns out to be surprisingly contested, given the stories this chapter has discussed. At the same time that the Resistance vilified dark-skinned soldiers in this Mekong Delta propaganda, the Democratic Republic of Vietnam reached out to these same soldiers as fellow victims of French colonial rule and emphasized solidarity between colonized and oppressed peoples.

In earlier chapters, I have tried to understand the beginnings of the war from a "bottom-up" approach. The particular character of the Mekong Delta, riven by unstable and episodic violence, shaped the mental world

---

[66] Steve Feierman, "Colonizers, Scholars, and the Creation of Invisible Histories," in Victoria Bonnell and Lynn Hunt, eds., *Beyond the Cultural Turn: New Directions in the Study of Society and Culture* (Berkeley and Los Angeles: University of California Press, 1999), 185.
[67] Ibid., 186.

in which its inhabitants lived. With violence came a breakdown in trust, which in turn gave rise to an increasing propensity to believe in highly unusual rumors and stories. But this kind of explanation, in and of itself, cannot be the full story. Alone, it reminds us of reductionist explanations that assume that stresses and strains can explain away "irrational" beliefs. This bottom-up approach cannot fully explain the particular content of the propaganda I have examined.

A second approach is top-down: it involves focusing on how contestants situate themselves in local society. In particular, how did the Resistance draw on, transform, and mobilize local cultural repertoires? In these liminal times, the Resistance strived for ways to reach its audiences. The fact that it deployed race propaganda leads to the question: why did the Resistance assume such messages would be credible to its audience? Here, I would argue that it played off the very common Vietnamese (and Khmer) belief that "bad" violence gives rise to hungry and malevolent ghosts roaming the countryside:[68] perhaps propagandists hoped that at least some Vietnamese, even if skeptical, were willing to entertain the possibility of the truth of these frightening tracts. The average Vietnamese had no sense of Auschwitz, the Holocaust, or French fears of cannibals. They were receptive to these rumors because, as Luise White has commented in a different context, "the imaginary and the fantastic must be constructed out of what is socially conceivable."[69]

Many beliefs were possible in the Mekong Delta in the 1940s and 1950s. As the secular modernist Vietnamese philosopher Trần Đức Thảo suggested in 1946, "this world of possibilities forms the background on which appear perceived realities and which endow them with their meaning."[70] Like applied anthropologists, the Resistance drew on their understanding of local knowledge – this "world of possibilities" – to craft their approach to the politics of belonging. To do so, they abandoned the formulaic language of much propaganda to disassemble and reassemble new messages, ways that both built on preexisting beliefs and that added a touch of novelty (and fear) to them. Other contestants in the delta articulated a different kind of narrative: a fear of racial extinction, articulated in a context of unprecedented racial and political violence, massive migrations, and social upheaval. It was such narratives, not simply the macronarratives of Cold War, nationalism, Third Worldism, revolution,

---

[68] Such beliefs are ubiquitous. See, for example, Trần Minh Thương, "Ma quỷ trong văn hóa dân gian miền tây Nam Bộ", www.namkyluctinh.com/a-tn-ttuong/tmthuong-maquy.pdf (accessed August 6, 2020).

[69] Luise White, "Telling More: Lies, Secrets, and History," *History and Theory* 39(4) (December 2000), 14.

[70] Tran Duc Thao, "Sur L'Indochine," *Les temps modernes* 1(5) (February 1946), 881.

or modernization, that explains Vietnamese understandings of the phenomenology of decolonization. This reaction suggests, more broadly, the richness of approaches to decolonization that combine attention to transnational and global institutions, practices, and ideologies with an understanding of local worlds in crisis.

6 Contesting State and Sovereignty

As the politics of the South (Cochinchina/Nam Kỳ/Nam Bộ) fractured in 1947, the region became even more politically distinct from the rest of Vietnam. Still involved, of course, were the French, who claimed sovereignty over all of Indochina, including Vietnam, but who controlled only a minority of the population and territory. The gap between French sovereignty claims and the reality on the ground was stark. What would be the path forward? How do we understand this process in terms of the end of empire? This chapter looks at these issues at the level of empire and colony, focusing on legal and institutional issues involving the French colonial state and its Vietnamese successor. It defers until later chapters the discussion of challenges from outside the central state apparatus by other actors, including the Cao Đài and the Democratic Republic of Vietnam (DRV).

In the standard narratives of modern Vietnamese history, the double fracture of 1947 is quickly passed over. The "independence" of 1949 is seen as a sham. Instead, the DRV's military victory over France at Điện Biên Phủ in 1954, immediately followed by negotiations in Geneva, marks the key point of rupture: the collapse of the French empire in Indochina and the beginning of a new era of contested sovereignty in which two Vietnamese states vied for control of one Vietnam. What about the non-communist State of Vietnam (1949–55), which came into existence as France, struggling to hold on to its imperial possessions, was rethinking sovereignty throughout the empire? It is treated as an ersatz state, an odd legacy of French machinations, one that improbably surmounted its illegitimate birth to survive until erased by the communist victory on April 30, 1975.[1]

Within French Indochina, devolution of power stretched over more than a decade. It began inauspiciously in 1944 with the Brazzaville

---

[1] While I first presented my arguments on sovereignty in 2014, here I want to call attention to Brett Reilly's excellent article, "The Sovereign States of Vietnam, 1945–1955," *Journal of Vietnamese Studies* 11(3/4) (July 2016), 103–139. Our arguments converge in some areas, diverge in others.

Declaration. A southern Vietnamese communist dismissed this announcement out of hand in August 1945: "your Brazzaville Declaration sounded ridiculous to us. It didn't mean a thing to us. What we want is full independence."[2] The process zigged and zagged for three years, and accelerated in 1948 and 1949. The formal date of "independence" – the promised transfer of some, but not all, powers to the Bảo Đại government in 1949 – was not a blip on the radar screen, as it is often portrayed, but accelerated the demise of French sovereignty and state capacity in Indochina. In 1954, France granted full and unconditional independence to Vietnam. But *still* it tarried: South Vietnam ordered France's remaining troops to withdraw in 1956. France complied. Careful attention to this fitful process explains both the quirks of southern politics and the strange birth of a weak State of Vietnam.

France's devolution of power and sovereignty was marked by two "long partitions." Most broadly, France agreed to break up French Indochina into the three nation-states of Cambodia, Laos, and Vietnam. Second, it would eventually agree, under international auspices, to partition Vietnam itself at the 17th Parallel. Related to the first partition – and surprisingly ignored by many – after 1949, the French progressively hived off state functions to the incoming Vietnamese state. Scholars know a lot about state formation and state building – but how do we understand the *simultaneous* process of deconstructing a state and transferring its claims and its institutions, bit by bit, to another? Not well. I start with Stan B. H. Tan's argument that the state is an "assemblage of institutions" in which "recombination" is constant:

The above-proposed conception of the state suggests that it is not an already established phenomenon or an a priori finished entity. The state is always in the making. Thus said, we need to examine the process in which the effect of the state is created and sustained, both in the abstract and empirical sense, through its various agencies and by constructing a particular mode of social ordering among the population it lays claim on; or in short, the process of state formation.[3]

The same can be said of the "unmaking" of the state. "Unmaking" is not the mere deletion of parts and transfer of these parts to a new state, but a complicated process of disassembling and reassembling, with unforeseen effects. For example, one of the earliest "devolutions" of power was of all civilian rural administration. From 1949 onwards, the French

---

[2] Dr. Phạm Văn Bạch, quoted in Krull, "Dairy [*sic*], Following the Allied Occupation in September 1945." Folder 07, Box 02, Douglas Pike Collection, The Vietnam Center and Archive, Texas Tech University, 11.

[3] Stan B. H. Tan, "'Dust Beneath the Mist': State and Frontier Formation in the Central Highlands of Vietnam, the 1955–61 Period" (PhD dissertation, Australian National University, 2006), 106, 109.

civilian state progressively withdrew into urban strongholds. Understanding this process may seem simple – but this action had ripple effects, reshaping everything from the solidity of sovereignty claims to relations between the French and Vietnamese police. Institutions recombined in odd ways, and French and Vietnamese protagonists invented new ways to extend or curb power. When the military finally pulled out from rural areas, as it did in much of southern Vietnam by 1953, the light went out on the French state's pretensions of sovereign control over these areas.

As French sovereignty faded, the exact links between ethnicity and sovereignty came into question. Ethnic Vietnamese automatically assumed they that would be citizens of a new Vietnam. What about other ethnic groups that lived within the boundaries of the new territory? And what about territorial claims based on ethnicity? These were not minor questions, as the earlier discussions of Khmer-Vietnamese violence, partly rooted in arguments over who "owned" the Mekong Delta, makes clear. War also shaped the transfer of power. This fact turns out to be critical: if we often define sovereignty and its transfer in legal terms, what does it mean when the transfer of sovereignty takes place during a conflict that led to the de facto suspension of law? To understand all these issues and their historical depth, we have to start with France's nineteenth-century conquest of Indochina, which profoundly shaped the South.

6.1 The "Juridical Laboratory" of Colonialism Shapes Decolonization

France's initial colonization in the nineteenth century left a messy legacy in southern Vietnam that was hard to unravel. In the conventional view, when European powers conquered the world, and especially from the eighteenth century, new conceptions and practices of sovereignty clashed with and then displaced preexisting ones. This argument has even been extended to countries that were not conquered: thus, Thongchai Winichakul writes of an "epistemological battle" in nineteenth-century Siam in which a new (Western) conceptualization, the "geo-body," displaced old views of space and sovereignty.[4] When France seized the southern part of Vietnam, however, one conception of sovereignty did not completely replace another. Odd legacies of the past would shape imperial rule.

---

[4] Thongchai Winchakul, *Siam Mapped: A History of the Geo-body of a Nation* (Honolulu: University of Hawai'i Press, 1994), 61.

These oddities date from the initial French conquest. As Isabelle Surun has argued, the French often negotiated treaties on the ground – and far from France – creating an idiosyncratic "legal bricolage." In a path-breaking analysis of 400 treaties that the French concluded in West Africa in the nineteenth century, Surun calls attention to the myriad ways in which local representatives of the French state, none of them professional diplomats, inventively shaped their own understandings of "sovereignty" in their negotiations with local rulers, all before Europeans or others had formulated a standardized model of sovereignty in these local contexts. In these treaties, one finds:

a profusion of formulas, a legal bricolage, an indeterminacy of concepts, and internal contradictions. We thus come across "lands" [*terrains*] that turn into "territories" [*territoires*], relinquishments of sovereignty that are simultaneously affirmations of sovereignty, "annexations" that are really "protectorates" (and vice versa). We see the resurgence of an archaic [concept of] 'suzerainty' with some fleeting success, probably more appropriate to the relationship it describes than the "sovereignty" that supplants it. In highlighting discrepancies between what those texts say and the legal categories they invoke, the intent is not to disqualify the practices because of the incompetence of its actors, an incompetence often imputed to the African signatories but ultimately shared by all [actors]. Rather, it is to recognize in practice the incredible juridical laboratory that constitutes this contractual practice, which aimed to provide a framework for the appropriation of land... Treaties are the site of an erratic reinvention of territorial sovereignty in which was fully expressed the freedom and autonomy of actors prior to the rise of a standardized practice, the "colonial protectorate."[5]

The "erratic reinvention of territorial sovereignty" through "legal brico-lage" was found in southern Vietnam. The first peace treaty in 1862 between the monarch of Annam, on the one hand, and the monarchs of France and Spain, on the other, confirmed that three provinces in the south as well as the island of Poulo Condor were "completely ceded by this treaty, in full sovereignty, to His Majesty the Emperor of France." Intriguingly, the accord here is between three monarchs – the French, the Spanish, and the Vietnamese – and fits poorly into the modern under-standing that transfer of sovereignty occurs between two states. In 1864, in a surprising turn, the French *commandant* Aubaret, representing the French Emperor, signed another treaty with the king of Annam recogniz-ing the full sovereignty of Annam; he agreed "to restore [*restituer*] to His Majesty the King of Annam the Government and administration of the three provinces of Bien Hoa, Gia Dinh, and Dinh Tuong..."

---

[5] Isabelle Surun, "Une souveraineté à l'encre sympathique? Souveraineté autochtone et appropriations territoriales dans les traités franco-africains au XIXe siècle," *Annales. Histoire, Sciences Sociales* 69(2) (2014), 347.

Nonetheless, France held on to Saigon, Cholon, and a few other small pieces of territory. With the return of territory, Annam was now required to recognize the French "protectorate" over all of the six southern provinces. Remarkably, the treaty stated that "It is understood that this protectorate does not entail any notion of vassalage." Annam also agreed to give up any suzerain rights over Cambodia. France soon, and quickly and unilaterally, repudiated its own treaty, and by 1874, forced the King of Annam to recognize "the full and complete sovereignty of France over all of the territory that she actually occupies."[6] Cochinchina would exist as a French colony until World War II. But a pattern had been set in which a fickle France unilaterally came up with wildly different legal understandings of France's relationship to the Nguyễn dynasty and its territories.

France soon created a new entity – French Indochina – to incorporate its Lao, Vietnamese, and Cambodian possessions into a new whole. French Indochina became a non-national "superspace" within which multiple conceptions of sovereignty, at local, regional, and Indochinese scales of analysis could co-mingle and be accommodated. Although the Vietnamese were the dominant ethnicity in Indochina, they were still subordinate to the French colonial state, a fact that helped to keep the peace among the Khmer, Lao, and Vietnamese. Meanwhile, the status of French Indochina's internal borders was left purposefully ambiguous. This "superspace," with no exact equivalent in Southeast Asia, can be compared to British India, with its princely states and directly colonized regions.

This background helps explain two issues that would bedevil decolonization: the role of the Nguyễn dynasty in Cochinchina and the exact nature of the *Cambodian* claim over this region. The first issue seemed, at first, to have been "resolved": the Nguyễn dynasty ceded all sovereign rights to the South by 1874, making Cochinchina the only directly ruled colony in Indochina. (Tonkin, Annam, Laos, and Cambodia were, in contrast, protectorates.) But in 1949 this issue resurfaced, as France agreed to re-attach Cochinchina to the State of Vietnam, itself headed by the Nguyễn monarch Bảo Đại. (I will address this issue in more depth later in the chapter.)

The second issue, however, remained unresolved: what exactly was the relation of the Cambodian monarchy to the Khmer inhabitants of the

---

[6] The quotations are from the 1862 Traité de Paix, the 1864 Traité de Paix et d'Amitié, and the 1874 Traité de Paix et d'Amitié, all found online at the Ministère des Affaires Étrangères (France), Base des Traités et Accords et de la France https://basedoc .diplomatie.gouv.fr/exl-php/recherche/mae_internet___traites (accessed March 21, 2019).

Mekong Delta (the Khmer Krom) and their lands? In its 1863 treaty with Cambodia, France permitted Cambodians to "move, own, and settle freely" anywhere in the French empire while promising French protection for these Cambodian subjects.[7] Cambodians have also insisted that Admiral de la Grandière promised in 1864 that France would "return" the provinces of Châu Đốc, Vĩnh Long, and Hà Tiên to them,[8] and in later decades would assert special rights over the provinces of Sóc Trăng and Trà Vinh, centers of Khmer settlement. French treaties with the Nguyễn court did not clarify any of these issues. Furthermore, Cambodian uprisings in 1859–60 suggest that when the French seized the South, the Nguyễn dynasty did not have uncontested authority over the entire Mekong Delta.

Indeed, far from relinquishing its sovereign rights, Cambodia placed its claim to the Mekong Delta *in abeyance* as long as France ruled Cochinchina. Khmer Krom living in the Mekong Delta in the nineteenth and twentieth centuries continued to maintain connections to Cambodia. In a bid to "protect" the Khmer Krom minority and strengthen their level of instruction, France moved to enhance the links between Cambodia and Cochinchina in the 1930s and early 1940s. The Buddhist Institute in Phnom Penh, working closely with the colonial government and Cambodian monks, developed extensive outreach to Khmer Krom soldiers in Cochinchina and trained Khmer Krom monks from temples throughout the Mekong Delta.[9] Khmer temples in the Mekong Delta fell under the authority of the Khmer Theravada order in Cambodia, which posed no problem, except that this hierarchy was itself under the supreme authority of King Sihanouk of Cambodia. Did this mean, therefore, that French authority over Khmer monks and their temples in the Mekong Delta was subordinate to that of the Cambodian king? Such would be an affront to French sovereignty. In 1941, the French finessed this dilemma: they convinced the Cambodian monarch to agree that on Khmer Krom religious matters in the Mekong Delta, the Cambodian Buddhist order would be involved without the intervention of the

---

[7] Traité de paix et d'amitié entre la France et le Cambodge, portant établissement du protectorat français. Signed by King Norodom and Amiral de la Grandière, Gouverneur et Commandant en chef de la Cochinchine. Udon, Cambodia, August 11, 1863, https://basedoc.diplomatie.gouv.fr (Accessed August 9, 2017).

[8] The reference to de la Grandière's promise is found in Krasuong Ab'rom Jeat, *Pravautsat nii Prateeh Kampuchea, somraep t'nak thé 9, thé 8, thé 7* (Phnom Penh: s.n., 1970), 143. Thanks to Ron Leonhardt for translating this reference for me. This promise is a staple of the Cambodian claim.

[9] See, for example, NAC. RSC dossier 22328. Correspondence de l'Institut Bouddhique. 1930.

Cambodian monarch or his council of ministers.[10] This pleasant fiction left ambiguous the exact sovereign relations between Cambodia and the populations of Khmer Krom in the Mekong Delta. When the French state returned to Indochina in 1945, this and other acts of "legal bricolage" would complicate decolonization.

6.2 The Strange "Independence within Empire" from 1945 Onwards

In late 1939, the world abruptly changed. Faced with the looming threat of war, the Governor General of Indochina suspended key laws related to civil liberties, such as the rights of most newspapers to publish, and cracked down on dissent. With the Japanese invasion of Indochina in 1940, Cochinchina came under martial law. At the same time, developments within the colony during World War II would shape the struggle for independence.

In 1942, the Vichy regime banned the official use of the word "native" (*indigène*) and suggested that the term "colony" not be used: "Rightly or wrongly, the word 'colony' awakens sensitivities and should be avoided." Governor General Decoux suggested using the term "Union" instead.[11] Such language games continued into 1945 and beyond. On March 24, 1945 – only dimly aware of the Japanese *coup de force* of March 9, 1945 that ended French rule in Indochina – France issued a declaration that proposed a slight recasting of French sovereignty in Indochina. As Fredrik Logevall notes:

> The declaration announced the formation of an "Indochinese Federation" within a larger "French Union." The five "lands" of Indochina... were to be headed by a federal government composed of ministers drawn from both the Indochinese and French communities in Indochina. The Indochinese population would become eligible for a new form of imperial French citizenship, and would receive new political and electoral rights as well as unprecedented employment opportunities.[12]

As Logevall adds, this declaration was "blind to the new realities on the ground in Indochina."[13] While France made slight concessions to the Vietnamese, it made no mention of true autonomy or independence. By

---

[10] NAC. RSC Box 1658, d. 17594. "Rapport au sujet de la protection des minorités khmères de la Cochinchine. November 1941."

[11] VNA-II. II.A.45 dossier 234 (4). Le Vice-Amiral d'Escadre Jean Decoux à Messieurs les Chefs Administration locale. "Objet: usage du terme 'colonie.'" Dalat, July 3, 1942.

[12] Logevall, *Embers of War: The Fall of an Empire and the Making of America's Vietnam* (New York: Random House, 2014), 75.

[13] Ibid., 76.

August 1945, Léon Pignon was suggesting that the French at least pronounce the word "independence": "Observations resulting from various contacts with the Nationalist parties, and especially with the Viet Minh, would seem to coincide in suggesting that it is still possible to collaborate with them, as long as we can utter the word 'independence' at the right moment. No other word would do."[14]

"Independence," then, seemed to be a prop in a French magic trick: using this prop, could they *appear* to give up power without doing so? Such was the gamble. But the French trick was not convincing enough. Vietnamese wanted independence, pure and simple. From March 1945 onwards, Vietnamese were promised, granted, or asserted their independence a dizzying number of times. On March 11, 1945, Vương Hồng Sển of Sóc Trăng, ears glued to the radio, heard a stunning announcement: "the Japanese military had proclaimed to all the peoples of Indochina that they were free." But this announcement was tempered by a qualification: "what was funny was that this independence would be under the protectorate of Great Nippon/Japan!"[15] The Empire of Vietnam, under its new prime minister, Trần Trọng Kim, also announced its "independence" – although, again, under the aegis of the Japanese military. This announcement of an ersatz independence turned out to be particularly complicated for Cochinchina. In his memoirs, Sển went on to quote Vice-Governor of Cochinchina Sato:

There has been a big misunderstanding on the subject of the independence of Indochina. It is completely under the military control of Japan. The independence of the Empire of Annam and of the Kingdom of Cambodia has been announced. Cochinchina not only is under military control but is also under the Japanese military administration. Thus, no independence for Cochinchina.

Juridically, Cochinchina was a French country. Juridically, you were French. You were all French subjects, that is to say, French. There will soon be a declaration from the Commander in Chief of the Japanese Army. You will probably acquire Annamite nationality. In terms of feelings, I understand that you feel Annamite. Inhabitants can thus deck their homes in Annamite colors. For public buildings, do not display the Annamite flag. We could say that the Empire of Annam governs Cochinchina. I am not sure when that will happen. Personally, I would be happy for that, but for the present, you are under the Japanese military administration.[16]

This statement perfectly captures the oddities of sovereignty in 1945: Annamites had one previous juridical identity (as French subjects) and

---

[14] Léon Pignon, quoted in Martin Shipway, *The Road to War: France and Vietnam, 1944–1947* (Providence and Oxford: Berghahn, 1996), 140.

[15] Vương Hồng Sển, *Hơn nửa đời hư* (Westminster, CA: Văn Nghệ, 1995), 355.

[16] See the "Compte-rendu du passage de Monsieur le Vice-Gouverneur Satoh à Long Xuyen le 30 Mars 1945," reprinted in Vương Hồng Sển, *Hơn nửa đời hư*, 381–2.

a different sentimental one (as Annamites), but a third and new entity (the Empire of Annam) would rule most of the country, but not all of it, which temporarily was under the Japanese. Legal, sentimental, and *real-politik* identities clashed.

On August 12, Sển reported enthusiastically that "The good news is that the Allies will declare independence for all the countries that have been forced to be colonies of the wealthy Western powers."[17] This hope was soon dashed. This same month, however, Vietnamese took events into their own hands. A range of groups in the south, including the Cao Đài, the Trotskyists, and the Việt Minh, declared the "independence" (*độc lập*) of Vietnam, a development that we have already discussed.

By mid-September 1945, the French had established a limited presence in Saigon, and in the months to come slowly built up their armed forces and pushed the Việt Minh out of Saigon. Their colonial legal apparatus was in shambles. The French reestablished a judicial system, underlining their desire to base their return on more than pure force. From this point up to 1954, the French issued all sorts of proclamations on the autonomy or independence of Vietnam. Like the Japanese before them, the French were constantly searching for a formula that appeared to address Vietnamese demands for independence while perpetuating French control. Up to 1949, many of these formulas seemed like transparent shams. A perfect example of French prevarication was the creation of the supposedly "independent" Autonomous Republic of Cochinchina in March 1946.

The French created the Autonomous Republic of Cochinchina with French citizen Nguyễn Văn Thinh as its head in order to appeal to Vietnamese demands. On June 1, 1946, *L'Avenir*, a Saigon newspaper, announced that its inhabitants were now free: "The French Government recognizes the Republic of Cochinchina as a free State that forms part of the French Union." But then, in a strange twist of logic, the story added that "Cochinchina is French territory. Thus, Cochinchinese, whatever their particular status, possess full French nationality" [*possèdent toutes les nationalités françaises*].[18] In fact, the vast majority of Cochinchinese remained French subjects, not citizens. The Autonomous Republic of Cochinchina had a Potemkin Village quality to it, with no budget, no bureaucrats, no control of any ministries, and – tellingly – no autonomy. This strange creation was run by

[17] Vương Hồng Sển *Hơn nửa đời hư*, 355, 381.
[18] ANOM. HCI SPCE 96. Copy of *L'Avenir: Quotidien de l'Union Française* (June 1, 1946), 1.

a council dominated by naturalized French citizens of Vietnamese origin. All power rested in French hands. Eventually realizing that he had been duped, Thinh hanged himself.[19]

While the Autonomous Republic of Cochinchina was a sham, it is striking how some French could convince themselves that by rejecting the old concept of the French empire, and embedding the states of Indochina in a new French Union, they could transform sovereignty and appeal to the Vietnamese. "Empire implies the notion of authority. France no longer claims to impose its law," wrote High Commissioner Emile Bollaert. He glibly continued: "The era of the *imperium* has come to an end. That of friendship has begun." He then made a surprising claim: "You have not failed to note that the words 'dependence' and 'independence' have lost their meaning. The world no longer has truly independent states. The tendency is not towards the fragmentation of power, but towards interdependence."[20] In a startling turn, France struggled to convince Vietnamese that "independence" was meaningless and that "interdependence" was preferable. This argument flopped. As Hồ Chí Minh joked to Paul Mus about the "French Union" in 1946, "No one has really told us what it is. Is it round? Square?"[21] No one could say.

Saigon aside, what was the reality of civilian rule in the rest of the south? In small cities in the Mekong Delta like Cần Thơ, French civilian administrators fitfully reasserted control over police matters, and reestablished a court system by 1946. Yet civilian power, and the power of the judiciary in particular, had its limits: the court's authority did not go beyond the city boundaries. Vast swaths of the delta were beyond the control of the French civilian state. By 1947, a fragile civilian infrastructure was in place in urban Cochinchina, but lagged in rural areas. Civilian authority was continually circumscribed by the military, and the supposed "rule of law" often fell by the wayside. In some provinces, such as Long Xuyên, the Hòa Hảo and other politico-religious groups routinely overrode civilian authorities. In others, the French military arrogated to itself powers that were properly civilian, such as those of the police.

---

[19] For an extensive account of this "Republic," see Brett Reilly, "The Origins of the Vietnamese Civil War and the State of Vietnam" (PhD dissertation, University of Wisconsin-Madison, 2018), Chapter 2.

[20] *Le conseiller de la République Haute-Commissaire de France pour l'Indochine [Bollaert] à Messieurs les commissaires de la République [etc.]*. Saigon, May 20, 1947, in Bodinier, *Indochine 1947: règlement politique ou solution militaire?* (Vincennes: Service Historique de l'Armée de Terre, 1989), 244.

[21] Paul Mus, "L'Indochine en 1945," *Politique étrangère* (1946), 462.

One source states that Cochinchina was never formally placed under martial law (*état de siège*),[22] which would seem to underline the French desire to promote civilian rule. But this is a deceptive claim. In 1939, the Governor General of Indochina had imposed martial law, which was in force throughout World War II. In 1945 and 1946, the de Gaulle government had lifted in France the restrictive measures that had been in effect during the war with Germany. But Cochinchina remained under a form of governance "related to the circumstances of war."[23] France expressly excluded Cochinchina from the list of colonies where freedom of the press was reestablished. This legal history would seem to underline that a "state of exception" was in force, as at least some peacetime laws were suspended. In 1948, one administrator refused to accept this argument fully, but did so in a curious way: "Since then, the question has been asked: Is South Vietnam to be considered as in a state of war, to the point of justifying the maintenance of a state of affairs linked to the circumstances of war? It is difficult to say, as *juridically yes, but in fact, no*."[24] A year later, as the French were preparing to delegate some powers to a new Vietnamese government, confusion still reigned: "the juridical status of South Vietnam is not definitively and clearly established." In terms of the press, this author suggested the continuation of "exceptional means"[25] – the emergency provisions clamping down on the press from August 1939 that had become routinized in Cochinchina.

Law aside, what about practices of rule in rural areas? Reading through files from this period, it is clear that French military officers often did their best to ignore or stymie representatives of the civilian state. The same is true of members of what I will call the "parastates" in the Mekong Delta. Jean Leroy, head of a militia linked to the French military that claimed to be Catholic, ran Bến Tre as his own fiefdom, routinely flouting the authority of French judges and civilian administrators.[26] At times, the military even formally seized power: on March 29, 1948, for example, it declared a state of emergency [*état de siège*] in Long Xuyên province, took over all civilian functions, and established military tribunals to try all crime.[27] Up to 1948, the French did not cede any sovereignty to a Vietnamese civilian state. What then happened?

---

[22] Haut Commissariat de France pour l'Indochine [d'Argenlieu]. Memorandum (d'ordre politique et militaire). Saigon, February 7, 1947. Republished in Bodinier, *Indochine 1947*, 231–4.

[23] VNA-II. PTHNV D.30–502. "Note: statut de la presse en Indochine." Saigon, January 29, 1948.

[24] Ibid.

[25] VNA-II. PTHNV F.7–129. Le Sous-Sécretaire d'État à l'Information Lê Tấn Nẩm à M. le Président du Gouvernement. Saigon, January 17, 1949.

[26] Leroy, *Fils de la rizière* (Paris: R. Laffont, 1977), 95–96.

[27] VNA-II. PTHNV E.03. 18. Province de Vinhlong. Rapport d'ensemble (période du 1er au 31 mars 1948).

6.3 The "Independence" of 1949: Turning Point or Sham?

Vietnam's march to independence was filled with supposed milestones that were not milestones: a series of incremental steps whose cumulative impact, nonetheless, was the erosion of French sovereignty. From September 1945, when it returned, to its 1948 Hà Long Bay declaration, France preserved the fiction that it was the only legitimate representative of all of Indochina. In 1948, this changed. Jean Leroy, the Eurasian who ran Bến Tre province, noted an important symbolic transformation: on May 20, 1948, for the first time, the Vietnamese and French flags flew together over government buildings. That month, the Provisional Central Government of Vietnam (*Gouvernement central provisoire du Viêt Nam*) was formed, headed by General Nguyễn Văn Xuân. This provisional government irked nationalists, not least because General Xuân was a French citizen. As one report noted, "the example of the Provisional Central Government is typical: it is that of an administrative organism, formed in consultation with the French authorities, with a French general at its head, which, despite that fact, has received neither support nor money from these same authorities."[28] The utter irrelevance of the "Provisional" government is captured in this handwritten (and sometimes ungrammatical) letter sent by a group of vegetable, fruit, and fish sellers to the new "President" Xuân:

Mr. President,
    A French police officer buys, every morning, vegetables, fruit, eggs Boulevard of the Somme, but him, he pay what he wants, while we the shopkeepers we lose much money. This officer lives in the first district. Mr. President, me and my fellow vendors ask you to tell him that if he keeps on doing this, me I am not happy because lose too much money. Thank you very much, Mr. President.

[Signed,] Several shopkeepers[29]

The presidency was reduced to resolving the daily irritations of local food vendors.

Did 1949, however, mark a change? On June 14 of that year, after long negotiations, Emperor Bảo Đại returned as head of state. France signed a treaty giving "independence" to the State of Vietnam as an "Associated State" within the framework of the French Union. This odd formulation can be seen either as a sham or as a step towards true independence. Scholars have, at best, shown ambivalence about this

---

[28] ANOM. HCI SPCE 360. SESAG. "Bulletin de renseignements." Saigon, October 24, 1948.
[29] ANOM. HCI. SPCE 68. Dossier F.III.6.9. [Letter Intercepted December 24, 1948 from "X" in Saigon to Président du Gouvernement Sud Vietnam.]

early transition. Philippe Devillers called it a "turning point" (*tournant*), as it was the first time that the French had formally promised independence to the Vietnamese.[30] When Panama recognized the State of Vietnam on October 5, 1950, a journalist noted that it was the thirty-second country to do so.[31] While the French maintained control over foreign affairs and defense, they devolved some powers to the Vietnamese. Emperor Bảo Đại announced in December 1950, upon signing a military convention: "Today we turn a new page where we can inscribe at the head of the chapter: 'Vietnam, an independent State.' Henceforth, all the attributes of internal and external sovereignty are in our hands. In law as in fact, we are a free people, deciding ourselves its destiny."[32] Bảo Đại was guilty of rhetorical excess. "Independence" had its limits. France did not give up all sovereignty claims over Vietnam. Ceding some powers on paper, such as control of the municipal police and local government, the French remained the paramount power in the South, and also reserved for themselves authority over defense matters. Devillers, cited earlier, concluded that this was a "sham independence":

But this independence is only a façade. It is the independence of a satellite. All the positions and organs [of state] exist, but they are in the hands of front men or weak personalities, pliable or without ideas, from whom we have nothing to fear except their lack of initiative... and their lack of popularity. They are not markedly different in Saigon from those who are in Bucharest or Manila.[33]

Such judgments were reinforced by the men who served in these early governments, whose deep ties to France compromised their independence. Nguyễn Tôn Hoàn, the Đại Việt party leader in southern Vietnam who had pushed for independence, called it a "guinea pig government" (*gouvernement cobaye*)[34], tacitly seeing it as an experimental foray on the road to true independence. The makeup of this government supports this view. Prime Minister Trần Văn Hữu (1950–52) was a French citizen, as was his successor, Nguyễn Văn Tâm (1952–53). Nguyễn Văn Tâm's cabinet contained five French citizens; these cabinet members had three

---

[30] Philippe Devillers, *Histoire du Vietnam de 1940 à 1952* (Paris: Éditions du Seuil, 1952), 432.
[31] "Xứ Panama công nhận Việt Nam" [Panama recognizes Việt Nam] *Phục hưng* (Saigon), October 6, 1950, 1.
[32] ANOM. HCI SPCE 56. Dossier F.III.2.18.2. Article from *L'Écho du Vietnam*, "Nous ouvrons à présent une page neuve," December 11, 1950, 1.
[33] Devillers, *Histoire du Vietnam*, 446, 447.
[34] Quoted in François Guillemot, *Dai Việt: indépendance et révolution au Viêt-Nam. L'échec de la troisième voie. 1938–1955* (Paris: Les Indes Savantes, 2012), 514–515.

French wives and one Swiss wife.[35] Given such facts, it is no surprise that Logevall, following Deviller's lead, ascribes almost no significance to this "independence." Indeed, Logevall approvingly quotes John F. Kennedy's comments, made after he visited Vietnam, that the State of Vietnam "is a puppet government" with no broad support.[36] Scholars have enshrined the view that the slow devolution of power from French to Vietnamese was irrelevant, and that the only date that matters is 1954, when the French defeat in the battle of Điện Biên Phủ, followed by the signing of the Geneva Accords, forced the end of French rule over Indochina.

Given such a scholarly consensus over a sixty-year span, it may seem rash to believe that this period can tell us much about *Vietnamese* sovereignty and the state. After all, the French did not cede full control of Vietnam until 1954. But we have to pose two questions. First, how can the incremental transfer of state functions to another state, however imperfect, be inconsequential? Second, are these transfers relevant to the birth of South Vietnam? I will argue, in fact, that the slow, bumpy, halting, and twisting transfer of sovereignty was hugely significant. Two processes were at work. First, we see the slow but inexorable transfer of the civilian state apparatus, beginning in 1949, from French hands to Vietnamese ones. French civilian power hollowed out, eventually leaving only a shell of its previous self. Second, this weakening of the civilian state was initially masked by the continuing strength of the French military, which arrogated to itself many powers that in peacetime had been civilian, such as control of the countryside. The peculiarities of this transfer of sovereignty helps to explain the strangeness of the birth of South Vietnam and many of its attendant problems.

Marie Thérèse Blanchet, who has examined this transfer in legal terms, notes the conundrum facing all analysts:

Since [the 1944 Brazzaville conference], many attempts have been made to define the French Union, and, as a corollary, the status of Associated States. Sometimes, basing [the analysis] on the juridical framework established by the French Constitution, we have tried to explain it, forgetting the primacy of international law over domestic law... at other times, recognizing this primacy, we have tried to situate the Union in a classical framework governing international communities: federation, confederation. Neither one nor the other of these conceptions seems to have been very satisfactory, as we are still searching for a way to define the new Union.[37]

---

[35] ANOM. HCI SPCE 20. Direction des Services de Sécurité du Haut-Commissariat de France en Indochine. Personnalités Vietnamiennes. Le Ministère Nguyen Van Tam. June 6, 1952.

[36] Logevall, *Embers of War,* xiv.

[37] Marie-Thérèse Blanchet, *La naissance de l'état associé du Vietnam* (Paris: M.-Th. Génin, 1954), 8–9.

This conundrum was not just of interest to legal scholars: it affects how we understand arguments over Vietnamese independence. The treaties themselves put severe legal constraints on the French exercise of power. When Vietnam became an "Associated State" [*État Associé*] in 1949, it entered new legal territory. It was no longer a full dependency of France, having gained some autonomy. Neither was it fully independent. It was a novel creature, occupying a liminal space, but hard to classify.

At the same time, the creation of Vietnam as an "Associated State" of the French Union had some quirks arising out of Cochinchina's special place in Indochina: Cochinchina had been the only *colony* (meaning that it was considered an integral part of France), unlike the four protectorates of Annam, Tonkin, Laos, and Cambodia. It is worth stressing that in legal terms, Vietnamese states had previously abandoned all claims over Cochinchina, as the Nguyễn court renounced Vietnamese sovereignty over the south in 1862, 1867, and 1874.[38] This point has been ignored by the great majority of scholars. Vietnamese sovereignty over Cochinchina was only legally *reestablished* in 1949. Cochinchina's special place, and its particular history, was integral to the eventual creation of the State of Vietnam centered in the South.

Cochinchina's history shaped its legal status going forward. The break-up of French Indochina meant, of course, that the "new" countries of Cambodia, Laos, and Vietnam would no longer be under the guidance of a powerful administrator in Hanoi. There had been a High Commissioner for Indochina since 1945, but his powers were now clipped – an obvious sign of the decline of French civilian power.[39] While the Governor of Cochinchina and *Résidents supérieurs* of the other four *pays* [countries, regions] of the former French Indochina had previously exercised some autonomy, it was most marked in the only former colony, Cochinchina, which had the most robust state apparatus. This difference carried over into the post-1949 period. As Blanchet notes, "The striking features of the administrative structure of the Associated State of Viet Nam was, on the one hand, *the instability of the central administrative organization*, and on the other, regional autonomy."[40] The central administration would try to impose its will on the regions, but the regions fought back. Thus, in 1948, when the Provisional Government of Vietnam announced its intention to control the regions, the then "President" of Cochinchina Trần Văn Hữu

gave formal orders to his subordinates [in ministries] that relations with the Central Government went only through him. Mr. Tran Van Huu also let it be

---

[38] Blanchet, *La naissance*, 16–17.
[39] I thank one of my outside readers for pushing me to make this point.
[40] Blanchet, *La naissance*, 138. Author's emphasis in original.

known to General XUAN that he would allow no direct interference by Ministers of the Central Government in the affairs of South Vietnam, and that only he was qualified to transmit and apply the directives of this Government.[41]

Such clear demands for autonomy would shape southern Vietnam for the next six years and beyond.

The rising State of Vietnam slowly ate away at French state power, especially in rural areas. In the South, it blunted the appeal of the Resistance, opened a path for non-communist groups to expand their power, and would eventually marginalize the Resistance throughout much of the Mekong Delta (as I shall later show). In fact, by 1953, French control over the Mekong Delta was receding, and the growing void was filled by the rising Vietnamese state, the Cao Đài, the Hòa Hảo, the Catholic militias, the Khmer and Vietnamese militias, and the Resistance.

I am most certainly not arguing that the Vietnamese state was strong, competent, and had widespread support, or that the French immediately disappeared. Nothing could be further from the truth. South Vietnam had what Sihanouk (talking about Cambodia) referred to as "50% independence,"[42] and it is intriguing to try to understand what this phenomenon might mean. True, some writers saw the "independence" of the southern-based State of Vietnam in 1949 as a momentous event. The Sa Đéc province chief, ignoring Vietnam's lack of control over its own defense and foreign affairs, stated that "the independence of Vietnam is real, effective, and not imaginary and theoretical as opposition propaganda pretends."[43] The Hà Tiên province chief effusively stated that the new elections for communal and provincial posts have "won the admiration of the world."[44] We do not have to accept such giddy views. Nonetheless, this grant of "50% independence" marked the beginning of the erosion of control over the French colonial state apparatus, and thus slowly began to undermine French sovereignty over Vietnam.

The March 8, 1949 accords, signed by France and the new State of Vietnam, called for the transfer of government functions from France to Vietnam. France established no timetable for this transfer of power: indeed, it dragged out the process. In 1949, for example, it handed over

---

[41] ANOM. HCI SPCE 68. Le Directeur de la Police et de la Sûreté Fédérale [Perrier] à Monsieur le Conseiller Politique. Rapports entre le Gouvernement Central et le Gouvernement du Sud VIET-NAM. Saigon, August 11, 1948.

[42] Norodom Sihanouk, L'Indochine vue de Pékin (Paris: Éditions du Seuil, 1972), 43.

[43] VNA–II. PTHNV E.03–168. Province de Sadec. Rapport d'ensemble (mois de septembre 1951).

[44] VNA–II. PTHNV E.03–189. Province de Hatien. "Rapport d'ensemble d'octobre 1953."

Table 6.1 *Transfer of functions of the French colonial state to Vietnam*

Year	Function
1949	Municipal police of Hanoi, Haiphong, and Saigon
1950	Public Health, Public Works, Agriculture, Labor, Primary and Secondary Education, Immigration, parts of Justice and the National Police (Sûreté)
1951	Post and Telecommunications (PTT), Customs, Service of Mines, Conservation of Historic Monuments, Port of Saigon, Treasury
1952	Railroads
1954	Civil Aviation, Electricity, final parts of Justice, Police, and Sûreté

Sources: ANOM. HCI SPCE 60. Dossier on gouvernement de Bao Dai. Transfert des services Fédéraux; "Une page définitivement tournée," *Journal d'Extrême Orient,* September 16, 1954, 1.

control of the municipal police of Hanoi, Haiphong, and Saigon to the new Vietnamese government. Early on, France gave up control of all provincial government: the French civilian state's presence in the countryside was fading away. Table 6.1 gives a sense of this process.

This table lists the *initiation* of transfer of functions. But France dilly-dallied over ceding more sensitive national police, national defense, and internal security functions. In July 1953, pressured by the Vietnamese, French Prime Minister Laniel promised to transfer control of the remaining ministries to Vietnam. Not until 1954, however, did France finally hand over control of the last remnants of the colonial state.

Complicating the transfer of power was the "traditional" pyramidal structure of France's unitary and centralized colonial state in Cochinchina, whose institutions reached down to the village level. How exactly could one hive off the lower levels of this hierarchy without affecting the system? How, for example, could one slice off the courts in the provinces without upending the system of justice as a whole? Such dilemmas bedeviled decolonization. If such issues were real, the new Vietnamese government was irked by France's laggardly transfer of power and its casual disregard of the letter of the treaty.

In August 1950, Prime Minister Nguyễn Văn Tâm demanded that "services still in French hands be transferred to the Vietnamese 'at the earliest possible date.'"[45] The Vietnamese were particularly bothered by the French grip on many police, customs, internal security, and judicial functions. Nonetheless, despite its attempts to circumvent treaties,

---

[45] ANOM. HCI SPCE 60 [Dossier on gouvernement de Bao Dai. Transfert des services Fédéraux]. "Le gouvernement Nguyen Van Tam demande le transfer..." *Journal d'Extrême Orient,* August 19, 1953.

France increasingly found itself boxed in by the letter of the law. Here it is useful to look at some of these "micro-conflicts" between the French and Vietnamese, for they show the struggle over sovereignty at the heart of the state apparatus. This struggle, on the French side, involved what we can call "avoidance protest" from on high: the foot-dragging, evasion, and lack of cooperation that characterized the French state's actions towards its new rival.[46]

Here I will illustrate my argument by focusing on the transfer of security functions. The March 8, 1949, independence agreement was unambiguous: France was legally obligated to turn over a wide variety of police functions, ranging from local police to immigration to customs and finally, the Sûreté, or internal security, as well as "the personnel, the materiel necessary for the smooth functioning of these services, as well as the physical locations currently occupied by the regional services of the Federal Sûreté in Vietnam."[47] France reluctantly complied. The journalist Norman Lewis, for example, noted that:

A great show had been made of turning over to the Vietnamese of the Sûreté [national police] headquarters in the rue Catinat. But all the French had actually done was to leave the incoming officials an empty building and open up themselves again at another address under the title of Sûreté Fédérale. As the Sûreté Fédérale had kept all the archives, the Vietnamese organization was disabled from the start.[48]

While the French Sûreté, as suggested above, kept all its files, the Vietnamese National Police wanted them – or at least unfettered access to them. The French Sûreté, however, did not want to comply.

French foot dragging did not simply affect the central state apparatus in Saigon. When the Châu Đốc provincial office was closed in 1950, its archives were transferred to the newly renamed "Poste de Sécurité du Haut-Commissariat de Longxuyen." Moret, the head of the rebaptized Service de Sécurité du Haut-Commissariat au Sud Vietnam, realized that this closure created difficult dilemmas. Vietnamese employees who worked for the French police were now caught between loyalty to their French employer and loyalty to their new government. Informants for the French might also become endangered. Transferring highly confidential police files to the Vietnamese would "create a dangerous precedent"

---

[46] On "avoidance protest, see Michael Adas, "From Avoidance to Confrontation: Peasant Protest in Precolonial and Colonial Southeast Asia," *Comparative Studies in Society and History* 23(1) (January 1981), 217–237.

[47] *Accords Franco-vietnamien du 8 Mars 1949. Conventions d'application* (Saigon: IDEO, 1950). 258 pages. Found in ANOM. HCI SPCE 389.

[48] Norman Lewis, *A Dragon Apparent: Travels in Indochina* (London: Jonathan Cape, 1951), 175.

which the Vietnamese authorities could exploit to gain control of the "central archives of the former Federal Sûreté, which are still in our possession." Moret counseled the utmost care in providing dossiers that the Vietnamese government "wished to examine, by transmitting, through special notes, the archival information that they wish to see."[49]

A similar turf battle broke out that year between the new Vietnamese National Police and the French-controlled Customs Service [*Service des Douanes*]. Although the French had agreed to transfer most police functions to the Vietnamese, they had retained control of customs, as well as control of who entered and left the country. Irritated, the Vietnamese National Police increasingly challenged the French attempt to hold on to power. When the Vietnamese heard, from a Chinese informant, that some Chinese were traveling on an Air France flight to Hong Kong and were carrying large sums of American dollars to be used to buy arms for the Resistance, they launched an operation. They went to Tân Sơn Nhứt airport, entered the room reserved for customs, and searched the bags of about twenty Chinese. The French customs police was apoplectic: "for the harmony of relations between us and the Vietnamese Sûreté, this action was deplorable. I will go so far as to say that my own personnel were made to look ridiculous."[50] Clearly, the French colonial state was resisting, kicking and screaming, the transfer of sovereignty required by treaty. France would repeatedly face such challenges in the years to come, as their colonial state hollowed out and its powers were curbed.

Conflicts between civilian branches of the police were matched by military-civilian discord. For example, in 1951, the Vietnamese province chief of Trà Vinh complained that French military still controlled a Catholic militia, acted arbitrarily without consulting the Vietnamese government, and ran its own networks of informers. "It is not clear what limits there are on the powers of this organism. In any event, many times, not to say all, notables are arrested without advance notice being given to the province chief." The province chief repeated his complaint that the French hired defectors of dubious reliability who often falsely denounced others.[51]

As its power slowly ebbed, the French military and remnants of the French civilian state strived to maintain their influence. In 1948, the government had declared martial law in seven provinces of

---

[49] ANOM. HCI SPCE 68. Dossier F.III.6.2.2. Service de Sécurité du Haut Commisariat au Sud Vietnam. Note No. 14110/S. Saigon, August 31, 1950.

[50] ANOM. HCI SPCE 53. Le Directeur des Services de Sécurité du Haut-Commissariat en Indochine à M. le Haut-Commissariat. "Ingérence de la Sûreté Nationale Vietnamienne dans les attributions des Services Français de Sécurité.

[51] VNA-II. PTHNV E.03–170. Rapport d'ensemble de la province de Travinh. May 1951.

Cochinchina, encompassing the Transbassac or western Mekong Delta. This lasted four years, before it was lifted in all but two of these provinces.[52] By 1952, the French military recognized that "in principle," only the (supposedly independent) State of Vietnam had the right to declare martial law. In a remarkable bit of sophistry, General Bondis nonetheless argued that since this state had not yet developed a jurisprudence of martial law, the French military command still had the right to decide when to lift it! His Vietnamese counterpart pointed out that excessive accommodation along this line would simply lead to a "state of exception" to the rule of law.[53] The Vietnamese "pupil" was now schooling the former "master." In the end, the French military was forced to cede authority to the Vietnamese state. But if the French state, including the military, was retreating from the Mekong Delta, the Vietnamese state and its new army did not fill the gap.[54] Civilian authority had been weak in the provinces since 1945, and militias still dominated.

6.4 Sovereignty, Borders, and the Cambodian Question

One of the key markers of modern sovereignty is the delimitation, monitoring, and enforcement of international borders. While international borders may appear overnight, their significance has developed over time: precisely for this reason, Vazira Zamindar calls the construction of the border between India and Pakistan, and its effects on populations in both countries, the "long partition."[55] This concept applies as well to Vietnam, which experienced two "long partitions." The first debuted in 1949, when the three countries of Indochina became, by treaty, "independent" nations within the French Union. Goscha has referred to this change as the "unraveling" of French Indochina:[56] a transformation whose specific features have been little studied. Indeed, in the dominant

---

[52] "Proclamation de l'état de siège dans sept provinces de la Cochinchine," *Le monde*, April 4, 1948; "Discussions laborieuses au sein du haut comité militaire franco-vietnamien," *Le monde*, February 22, 1952; SHD. 10 H 4466. Fiche. "Au sujet de la levée de l'état de siège dans le Transbassac." April 4, 1952.

[53] See SHD. 10 H 4681. Subfolder E 31. Le Général Bondis... à Monsieur le Ministre de la Justice. Saigon, 3[?] November 1952; (in same folder) État du Vietnam. Ministre de la Justice [Le Tan Nam] à Monsieur le Général Bondis, Commissaire de la République Française et Commandant les Forces Terrestres du Sud Vietnam. Saigon, November 19, 1952.

[54] On this new army, see François Guillemot, "'Be men!': Fighting and Dying for the State of Vietnam (1951–54)," *War and Society* 31(2) (August, 2012), 184–210.

[55] Vazira Fazila-Yacoobali Zamindar, *The Long Partition* (New York: Columbia University Press, 2010).

[56] Goscha, *Vietnam or Indochina? Contesting Concepts of Space in Vietnamese Nationalism, 1887–1954* (Copenhagen: NIAS, 1995), 147–150.

post-1975 nationalist narration of Vietnamese history, this earlier partition is noted in passing, but not deeply analyzed. The second partition occurred in 1954 following the Geneva Accords, when the DRV and the State of Vietnam were temporarily divided at the Seventeenth Parallel. This 1954 partition between north and south has been extensively discussed and will not detain us here.

What about the first partition in 1949? Today, we take for granted the existence of Vietnam's national borders. But how do we understand the significance of the collapse of the larger entity of French Indochina and the creation of over 3,000 kilometers of new "international" borders? This requires a historical approach, one that addresses how Cambodia and Vietnam came to interact with one another as new nation-states. It demands that we understand the emerging meaning of these new borders on the ground, and how such borders refashioned ethnic and political identities.

As noted at the beginning of this chapter, French colonization left ambiguous the exact relationship between the Cambodian state and the Khmer Krom of the lower Mekong Delta or, conversely, the exact rights of ethnic Vietnamese in Cambodia. This ambiguity continued even when "French Indochina" became a legal reality in 1887. As Christopher Goscha has shown, "Indochina" became, in the minds of a wide range of Vietnamese, an experiential and conceptual reality: "Almost seventy years after the creation of the Indochinese Union and well after the August Revolution of 1945, both 'Vietnam' and 'Indochina' *existed* – conceptually and spatially – in communists' minds."[57] As Goscha shows, the same comment could be made about non-communist and anti-communist Vietnamese. Of all the peoples in the region, the Vietnamese had the strongest attachment to the idea of Indochina, but even Cambodians and Laotians expressed, at times, a lingering sense of its "reality."

In 1945, Vietnamese, while believing in the reality of Vietnam, did not want to abandon Indochina. Some communists, for example, imagined a Federal Indochina composed of Vietnam, Cambodia, and Laos. To ethnic Vietnamese, Vietnam was linked to wherever, in Indochina, Vietnamese were found. This formulation allowed for ambiguities: Vietnamese populations in Cambodia, for example, could participate both in the new nation of Cambodia and that of Vietnam. The Khmer Krom of the Mekong Delta faced a similar choice. Thus Son Ngoc Thanh, born in Trà Vinh, Cochinchina, made his mark in Cambodia as a Cambodian nationalist; his lesser-known brother, Sơn Thái Nguyên, participated in politics in Vietnam as a defender of the Khmer minority.

[57] Ibid., 90.

The unraveling of French Indochina gave rise to such experimentations over political representation, and created new dilemmas over how to understand the meaning of the new nation-states, their inhabitants, and their borders.

Before any of the nations of French Indochina became independent, the "national" governments began to argue over Cambodian rights in Vietnam and Vietnamese rights in Cambodia. On June 20, 1947, King Sihanouk sent a letter to the new French Commissioner to Cambodia, Léon Pignon, "setting forth, with no ambiguity, his position on the Khmer claims to the Western Mekong delta." On July 31, 1948, Cambodia restricted the right of circulation and domicile of "Indochinese" who were not considered to be the natural inhabitants [*indochinois non-régnicoles*] of the kingdom.[58] This was a major shift: Vietnamese, Chinese, Cham, and Khmer had previously flowed back and forth over the border with ease. Not only did Vietnamese in Cambodia resent such new restrictions, but they affected Vietnamese-Khmer relations in the Mekong Delta.

Among the most contentious issues facing the State of Vietnam was the role of minorities within the new borders. Cambodia had earlier resurrected its claims to parts of the delta dating from before the French conquest. In 1949, Sihanouk ordered Son San to Paris to raise this issue yet again with the Minister for Overseas Territories Coste-Floret, as well as with the French Union. Furthermore, Cambodia and the Khmers of Cochinchina specified that parts of the Mekong Delta, and particularly the provinces of Trà Vinh, Sóc Trăng, and Bạc Liêu, should belong to the Khmer. Cambodia also asserted rights to access the port of Saigon. When the French National Assembly voted to give up its colony Cochinchina and attach it to the newly "independent" Vietnam, they rejected the Cambodian claims. The Cambodian National Assembly reacted angrily. Members argued that Cochinchina was Cambodian territory, demanded that France recognize Cambodia's right to Cochinchina, asked for the Cochinchina-Cambodian border to be redrawn, lobbied for a Cambodian maritime outlet down the Mekong, and pushed to provide the Khmer minority of the Mekong Delta with a special protected status.[59] These protests failed. Cochinchina ceased being a French overseas colony and was reattached to Vietnam.[60]

---

[58] VNA-II. PTHNV E.03–231. Province de Rachgia. "Rapport d'ensemble (avril 1949)."
[59] SHD. 10 H 282. No clear author [but perhaps Direction des Services Français de Sécurité Publique en Indochine]. "Les minorités khmères au Sud Viet-Nam." January, 1954. 5–6.
[60] This was *Loi N°49–733 du 4 juin 1949 modifiant le statut de la Cochinchine dans l'Union française*, passed by the National Assembly and signed into law by Prime Minister Vincent Auriol.

With the signing of the 1949 "independence" accords for the countries of Indochina, the existing administrative boundaries separating Vietnam, Laos, and Cambodia became international ones. France slowly began the process of transferring state functions to indigenous states. From this year onwards, the "foreign affairs" of French Indochina become complicated. France accepted that Vietnam could have "foreign relations" with other countries, but tried as much as possible to arrogate to itself the right to represent Indochina in international forums. Other territorial issues, perhaps of seemingly little import at the time, also were tentatively resolved. For example, Darlac province, which had been administered through Laos in the nineteenth century, then attached administratively to Annam, was placed under the direct authority of the Crown of Annam.[61] At this point as well, for example, France apparently transferred its claim to the Paracels and the Spratlys to Vietnam.[62] Nonetheless, France kept troops on the Paracels until the end of June 1956.[63]

Vietnamese, Cambodians, and Laotians began using (and abusing) the new "international" borders in their interactions with each other. Old habits of easy travel between Vietnam and Cambodia died hard. Vietnamese, Cambodian, and French troops continually flowed across the new border: this was an enduring feature of the war. For the average resident of Vietnam or Cambodia as well, the new "international" border was meaningless. At the end of 1954, for example, despite official attempts to curb illegal trade between Cambodia and Vietnam, one could find four major unregulated markets on the Cambodian-Vietnamese border in which Vietnamese and Cambodians sold contraband goods to the other side. These markets lasted until 1967.[64]

If the average person still experienced the border as porous, the new states of Indochina now selectively invoked them as markers of sovereignty. Thus, after the birth of the new state of Vietnam, Cambodia still tried to intervene in controversies involving the Khmer Krom in the lower Mekong Delta. For example, in 1953, His Excellency Chan Nak of Cambodia complained about the poor treatment of Khmer Krom residents of Vietnam, the ill-treatment of their monks and damage to their temples, and the forced defrocking of monks and their impressment into the Vietnamese military. The Vietnamese government replied that as these disputes did not involve Cambodian citizens, Cambodia had no

---

[61] Blanchet, *Naissance*, 117–118.

[62] Ưng Trình, *Việt Nam ngoại giao sử cận đại* (Hanoi: Trí Đức Thư Xã, 1953), 136.

[63] SHD. 10 H 916., Le Général de Brigade DELTHEIL, commandant la 3è D.I.E.C. à M. Le Général de Corps d'Armée [etc]. "Implantation aux îles Paracels." June 28, 1956.

[64] Lê Hương, *Việt kiều ở Kampuchea* (Saigon: Trí Đăng, 1971), 227–229.

standing to complain.[65] Such lingering issues show how the granting of "independence" to Vietnam in 1949, albeit in the context of the French Union, set in motion a series of changes that shaped Vietnam's internal and external politics and its territorial boundaries.

6.5 Citizenship

Borders defined the cartographic limits of the new Vietnamese nation. What about the internal limits: that of citizenship? When France faced no serious challenge to its sovereignty in Indochina, this issue was irrelevant: all indigenous groups and foreigners were subordinate to French rule. When the French began to transfer power to indigenous elites, the issue of majorities and minorities suddenly became critical. Where did non-Vietnamese fit into Vietnam, and what would their rights be? What about groups that settled the South before the Vietnamese, such as the Khmer or Cham? Where did the Chinese fit in? What about the status of the Minh Hương, or Sino-Vietnamese? To address these questions, the French (as well as the Vietnamese) re-examined past practices towards majority and minority ethnic groups. In the 1949 treaties devolving sovereignty to Vietnam, Vietnam's jurisdiction was clear over ethnic Vietnamese, but was qualified when it came to non-Vietnamese, nationals of the French Union, and the Chinese.

French citizens were a special case. Clearly, the new "independent" country of Vietnam, whose prime minister was a French citizen, would not curtail the power of fellow French citizens, even if they were not ethnic Vietnamese. In the early years after 1949, then, it appears that nothing was done to scale back the privileges of French citizens. In 1954, however, French citizens in the State of Vietnam were no longer allowed to serve on municipal councils, a move that marked the beginning of the end of their colonial privileges.[66]

The burning issues involved those who were not Vietnamese or French. The "Chinese" issue was complicated, and we can distinguish between policies for longstanding communities versus recent settlers. China also made claims to the allegiance of overseas Chinese: from 1929, "the Chinese government considered as its subjects children born abroad to a Chinese father. But Cochinchina is a territory of the French Union, and

---

[65] SHD. 10 H 282. Subfolder: Minorités khmères au Sud Vietnam. Fransécur Sud Vietnam. Bulletin de renseignements. "Objet: Attitude des autorités vietnamiennes de la province de Cantho à l'égard des minorités khmères résidant dans cette région." January 26, 1954.

[66] ANOM. HCI SPCE 68. Dossier F.III.6.2. Extrait du *Bulletin Officiel du Sud Vietnam* No. 29 du 19–7–54, 527. Signé: HO QUANG HOAT.

Chinese law had no juridical standing in French territory." The Chinese claim left too many loose ends. What exactly was a Chinese father? How would one treat longstanding Chinese settlers? Some Chinese communities, such as in Mỹ Tho or Hà Tiên, predated Vietnamese settlements in the delta. The town of Hà Tiên, for example, was established by former Ming loyalists who had fled Qing China.

France, not surprisingly, partially resolved this issue by considering recent settlers, such as Chinese immigrants in the twentieth century, as "foreigners." The difficulties came with the French subjects who identified as *Minh Hương*.[67] While "*Minh Hương*" translates as "Ming incense" people, or those descended from Ming subjects who took refuge in Vietnam from Qing China, its meaning evolved over time. By the 1930s, the term had come to refer, in southern Vietnam, to those of mixed Sino-Vietnamese ancestry who still showed connections to Chinese culture. Before 1933, the French colonial state considered the *Minh Hương* to be "assimilated Asiatics" who were subject to Annamite, not French, law.[68] After that year, all *Minh Hương* born in Cochinchina became French subjects, "and could not lose this quality without first getting authorization [for so doing] through a decree of the French government."

Adjudicating the status of the *Minh Hương* meant confronting the claims by the Republic of China on the nationality of overseas Chinese. It also meant evaluating claims by some *Minh Hương* who, in order to shirk their obligations as French subjects of Cochinchina, and to profit from exemptions and advantages that foreigners enjoyed due to their privileged status, tried to pass themselves off as Chinese. Thus, some listed themselves on the registers of the Chinese congregations, or obtained, through the Consulate General of the Republic of China in Saigon, "certificates of provisional registration as Chinese." As sovereignty shifted from France to Vietnam in 1949, these earlier debates over Chineseness shaped the postcolonial debate. (By 1956, the South Vietnamese government forced all Chinese born in, and residing in, Vietnam, to take on Vietnamese citizenship.[69])

---

[67] The following section on the *Minh hương* relies on VNA-II. PTHNV D.5–567. "Qui chế của Minh Hương/ Objet: Statut des Minh Huong." Saigon, April 26, 1947. For their complex background and shifting identity, see Charles Wheeler, "Interests, Institutions, and Identity: Strategic Adaptation and the Ethno-Evolution of Minh Hương (Central Vietnam), 16th–19th Centuries," *Itinerario* 39(1) (2015), 141–166.

[68] This refers to cases that do not involve a French national, such as marriage between two non-French individuals.

[69] Bernard Fall, "La situation internationale du Sud-Vietnam" *Revue française de science politique* 8(3) (1958), 564.

The claims of those who were incontestably "indigenous" to the territory of Vietnam were the hardest to address. The case of highland minorities from central Vietnam, who had a special juridical status, is outside the scope of this book. While the Cham were indigenous to Vietnam, of course, they had no longstanding *territorial* claims to the Mekong Delta. Here we return to the Khmer Krom. In the end, if Cambodia lost the fight for territory in the Mekong Delta, Vietnam did not challenge the Khmer Krom right to live within the borders of Vietnam. But the impact of France's "slight" toward Cambodian claims in 1949 endured, leading to lasting Cambodian and Khmer Krom recriminations against France and Vietnam. At the same time, anxious about living under Vietnamese rule, many Khmer of the Mekong Delta reached out even more to the French after 1949 for protection. It would turn out to be a misguided gamble.

6.6 Conclusion

Seen from the present, Vietnamese sovereignty and the role of the state seem, in most cases, unproblematic. Vietnam has delimited most of its land borders with Cambodia, Laos, and China. Citizenship seems clear: those born within the borders of Vietnam to Vietnamese citizens are, by law, citizens of the country. The place of ethnic minorities is obvious: while symbolically important, they are bit players in a country whose political, cultural, and social life is overwhelmingly defined by ethnic Vietnamese.

At the end of the 1940s, however, little was obvious. Around the globe, decolonization was upending the imperial order, giving rise to new ways of formulating sovereignty. Shaped both by this global and imperial context, as well as the oddities of its initial colonization in the nineteenth century, Vietnam walked a twisting path to independence. Scholars, however, have almost uniformly dismissed the significance of the 1949 "independence." After all, France remained the paramount power in matters of foreign affairs and defense. It continued to meddle extensively in a supposedly "independent" country. But one French legal counsel admitted the obvious in 1953: "the French state has illegally maintained a French administrative structure parallel to that of Vietnam."[70] The inexorable increase in Vietnamese authority over their country, paralleled

---

[70] "Introduction. Deuxième partie," in Jean-Claude Devos et al., *Inventaire des Archives de l'Indochine. Sous-Série 10H* (Chateau de Vincennes: Service Historique de l'Armée de Terre, 1990), 38.

with a decline in French authority after 1949, meant that the end was foreordained, a process that we will return to in Chapter 10.

How do we theorize this process? Scholars are used to thinking about *either* the construction of states *or* their collapse. We don't usually think of these two processes *together*. States are assemblages of institutions, constantly shifting, and nowhere is this observation more relevant than in analyzing times of crisis and change. During decolonization, the "transfer" of functions from one weakening state to another expanding one was messy. When France gave up, for example, its control of provincial administration, it did not simply lose one discrete segment of the state. It lost a node in the exercise of rural power, one that linked to multiple other nodes. To continue to exercise sovereign power, it would have to compensate for such losses in tangible ways, such as by emphasizing its remaining military power.

This balancing act would turn out to be increasingly difficult. If we look at the French state from below – from the village and provincial level – France's slow loss of power and authority seems clear. Year by year, effective French sovereignty over the internal affairs of Indochina frittered away. The lights slowly went out on the French civilian administrative apparatus, leaving only the military to exercise power. By 1954, French civilian rule over Vietnam ended, and the last French military units withdrew in 1956. If French power clearly ebbed, the slack was not fully taken up by the new Vietnamese state. In rural areas, a struggle for sovereignty played out, as later chapters will show.

7   Forced Migrations and Suffering

The double fracture of 1947 transformed political, religious, and ethnic relations, shook up social norms, divided families and villages, and left the populace with a pervasive sense of unease about the future. Trust between communities plummeted. Basic concerns, such as whether to trust or fear a neighbor, could all of a sudden involve life and death. "Normal" state and village institutions could not help: they had either collapsed or been destroyed, and new ones would have to be reassembled out of the shards of old ones, or replacements found. Food insecurity dramatically increased, and parts of the delta experienced acute hunger. In this situation of radical uncertainty, people felt more vulnerable as outside forces reshaped local lives. The obvious path forward was not always clear. Most inhabitants of the Mekong Delta faced the existential dilemma: should I, and my family, stay put or flee?

This chapter is less an argument than a depiction of the upheavals in the Mekong Delta and their consequences. The lived experience discussed in these pages is the foundation for the chapters that follow. It is not that political affiliations, religious beliefs, or ethnic affiliations become unimportant: rather, fear of violence and the search for security shaped the actions of individuals and groups. Violence was not uniform across time and space: in fact, some areas would turn out to be backwaters, while others, like Trà Vinh, would see lots of contestation. That being said, huge numbers of persons would move during the war. So what exactly happened, particularly from 1947 onwards?

*

The boat followed the Mekong River, then turned into the Vàm Nao and up the Bassac River, where many convoys of cargo-laden boats moved slowly up and down the river. Sometimes they encountered Việt Minh who had set up ambushes where the river narrowed, but they suffered little harm. On both sides of the river crops grew in profusion, especially okra and sugar cane. Wherever security had returned, the riverbanks were lush with vegetation, the homes of people were scattered about, and water buffalo were common. In the areas occupied by the

Việt Minh, the vegetation was stripped bare, many homes had been set on fire, and those remaining showed signs of destruction. People and animals were completely absent.[1]

So wrote, in 1948, prominent Cao Đài leader Trần Quang Vinh, the new "Secretary of Defense" of the Provisional Central Government of Vietnam. Vinh could be expected to criticize the Resistance, which had jailed him and killed many of his fellow Cao Đài followers. But his restricted view from the river rings true. While parts of the delta had kept their population, others had drained of inhabitants. A Cao Đài from Tây Ninh reported in 1947 that "rice fields lay uncultivated, roads deserted, and homes abandoned," and added that "people have come to settle around the military posts."[2] In 1948, the Cần Thơ province chief wrote that "movement, whether by roads or by rivers, is decreasing. River convoys are rare and irregular because of the risk of a Việt Minh economic blockade. The province's economic situation is clearly declining compared to last year."[3] Echoing him, the province chief of Châu Đốc stated that "cultivated lands are largely abandoned and the rice harvest for 1947–1948 will be just barely sufficient."[4] A 1950 report summarized the impact on the southern countryside over the past four years:

the growing insecurity [since 1946] has caused an exodus of landowners to protected centers, population displacement and the desertion of some areas. There has been a gradual decrease in cultivated areas and a parallel reduction in output. For military purposes, the Viet Minh have barricaded numerous canals, cut dikes, and destroyed many bridges and structures. The surveillance and upkeep of waterways could not be carried out, and some were so clogged as to be practically useless. The specific conditions of this part of the delta are such that the network is placed under a constant threat of obstruction by a continuous process of clogging.[5]

Trần Quang Vinh's view from the river, in other words, tells only a fraction of the story. In 1952, a journalist, plunging into the depths of the western Mekong Delta, described how war had transformed the countryside:

[1] VNA-II. PTHNV. D.01–359. Cuộc Thanh Tra Các Tỉnh Miền Tây của Bộ Trưởng Bộ Quốc Phòng Chánh Phủ Trung Ương Việt Nam TRẦN QUANG VINH từ ngày 27 Juin 48 đến ngày 4 Juillet 1948.
[2] ANOM. HCI 107. [Intercepted letter from Pham Van Dang, Tayninh, to Le Quang Thuong, Tarascon, France. July 14, 1947.]
[3] VNA-II. PTHNV File E.03–46. Province de Cantho. "Rapport d'ensemble du mois de septembre 1948."
[4] VNA-II. PTHNV File E.03–283. Province de Chaudoc. "Rapport d'ensemble (février à juillet 1948."
[5] SHD. 10 H 282. Subfolder "Levée complète du blocus." "La question du Trans Bassac." June 12, 1950.

In Cần Thơ [province], the fertile fields have largely been abandoned. The grass is dense, taller than a person's head. If anyone were to plow and transplant as before, one would have to expend much money and toil to bring the field back to its previous condition. Traveling down the road to Long Xuyên and Rạch Giá, a distance of sixty-five kilometers, one comes across about fifty farming huts. This road has been long abandoned and has just been reopened; many sections are bad, with weeds growing thickly on the road.

In the old days, endlessly fertile rice fields were found on both sides of the road. Today, they lie abandoned. While the fields look immense, they are choked with weeds. From Long Xuyên to Rạch Giá, this road follows a branch of the Đào river. Scattered on the other bank of the river are several shabby thatched huts. The houses, hamlets, villages used to be strung along the road, along with crowded and bustling markets. Today, all that remains are isolated shells of houses or dwellings that have been destroyed or set on fire. Some places once had a village yet today no trace of them remains, only verdant growth.[6]

The forces of war and nature, in other words, reshaped the southern countryside. From landlords to peasants, the Mekong Delta saw social upheaval and forced migration on a scale never before experienced. Such a claim may seem perplexing: isn't it true, as I have argued earlier, that Saigon emptied its Vietnamese population into the delta right after the August Revolution of 1945? Yes. But the far bigger story is that over the war, economic uncertainty and extensive violence pushed huge numbers of rural inhabitants short distances *within* the delta, and longer distances *out* of the delta into Saigon and into Cambodia. Peasants fled danger and looked for safety. Some provinces were little touched, whereas others lost almost half their population. Scholars have ignored this massive forced migration during the First Indochina War.[7]

If we trust statistics published by the French government and its successor South Vietnamese governments, three quarters of a million individuals "go missing" from the Mekong Delta.[8] This raw number does not even take into account the expected natural increase of the population. Some of these "missing" were killed, but most probably left the delta. It is worth reflecting on this estimate: it represents nearly one in

---

[6] Nguyễn Văn Giậu published this reporter's description in Nguyễn Văn Giậu, *Việt Nam đẫm máu vì chiến tranh thực dân 1945–54* (s.l., Binh Minh, 1956), 95–96.

[7] There appears to be no study of forced migration in Vietnam during the First Indochina War. But see mentions in Andrew Hardy, *Red Hills: Migrants and the State in the Highlands of Vietnam* (Honolulu: Hawaii, 2002) and Christian C. Lentz, *Contested Territory, Điện Biên Phủ and the Making of Northwest Vietnam* (New Haven, CT: Yale University Press, 2019), which focus overwhelmingly on peacetime migration as well as on *intentional* mobilization for war. See, more broadly, Idean Salehyan, "Refugees and the Study of Civil War," *Civil Wars* 9(2) (June 2007), 130.

[8] David Biggs, perplexingly, states that "in most provinces, the area of land under cultivation fell while populations increased significantly." Biggs, *Quagmire: Nation-Building and Nature in the Mekong Delta* (Seattle: University of Washington Press, 2010), 142.

five residents of the delta provinces. If, for the sake of argument, we conjecture that 100,000 persons were killed up to 1951 in the Mekong Delta alone (which seems a very high estimate), and that the French and Vietnamese figures *overestimated* population decline in the delta provinces by 20 percent, that would still leave over 500,000 displaced persons fleeing the delta. I will use this conservative estimate of half a million displaced outside the delta in the discussion that follow.[9] Many others fled shorter distances.

Some of the "missing" from the Mekong Delta went upriver. Phnom Penh doubled in size, from 50,000 to 100,000, and some of the new arrivals were Vietnamese, who now made up roughly a third of the inhabitants of the city.[10] The monk Minh Đăng Quang did not travel so far: "In 1946, the flames of war broke out, causing widespread destruction, leaving monks with no place to live. Furthermore, looting did not allow them to support themselves at this time." He and his band of followers walked approximately forty kilometers over the Cambodian-Vietnamese border.[11] Most of the "missing," however, found their way to Saigon and Cholon. As one Trà Vinh resident wrote to an acquaintance, "All the well-off have evacuated to Saigon to look for work or live with relatives."[12] But given the sheer numbers of refugees, most migrants to the South's largest city were peasants. As the delta drained of a chunk of its population, Saigon and Cholon ballooned, tripling in size in less than a decade.

The 1951 estimates above, not based on an actual census, must be used with caution. Nonetheless, they suggest a dramatic trend. The twin cities' Vietnamese population increased by a factor of five, an extraordinary jump, while the Chinese population doubled. For the Chinese, much of this increase must have come when rural Chinese moved to Saigon and

---

[9] Historical demographers have cast doubt both on the scientific method used in population estimates and the quality of most demographic data from French Indochina. Particularly useful are Magali Barbieri, "De l'utilité des statistiques démographiques de l'Indochine française (1862–1954)," *Annales de démographie historique* 113(1) (2007), 85–126, which looks at the manner in which colonial-era population statistics were compiled; and Mak Banens, *Vietnam: A Reconstitution of its 20th Century Population History* (Tokyo: Asian Historical Statistics (AHSTAT) COE Project, Hitotsubashi University, January 2000), which models and reconstitutes population, projecting back from the 1989 census. Also of use was Paul Demeny, "Final Report: A Population Survey in Vietnam" (Report by Simulatics Submitted to the Advanced Research Project Agency; Cambridge, MA: s.n., 1967). Many thanks to Patrick Gubry for suggesting these sources.

[10] ANOM. HCI SPCE 107. Dossier "1952." Service de Sécurité du Haut-Commisssariat au Cambodge. Note pour Monsieur le Commissaire de la République au Cambodge. "Colonie Vietnamienne." Phnom Penh, July 13, 1951.

[11] Minh Đăng Quang, *Chơn lý* (Hanoi: Tôn Giáo, 2004), Vol. 3, 444–445.

[12] ANOM. HCI 107. [Letter from Huu, Saigon, to Lam Quang Khuong, Nice. October 7, 1947.]

Table 7.1 *Population of Saigon-Cholon by ethnic group, 1943–1951*

Ethnic group	1943	1951
Vietnamese	182,000	998,000
Ethnic minorities	4,000	
French	18,935	17,410
Chinese	291,957	583,000
Other foreigners	1,251	
Others		3,280
Total	498,143	1,601,690

Sources: Bộ Quốc Gia Kinh Tế, *Thống Kê Niên Giám Việt Nam/ Annuaire Statistique de l'Indochine*, Vol. 1, 1949–50 (Saigon: Viện Kinh Tế và Khảo Cứu Kinh Tế Việt Nam, 1951).

Cholon for self-protection. But Chinese migrants fleeing from China, especially from 1947 onwards, boosted the cities' population as well.[13] Unrecorded was the movement of other minorities: for example, the small Cham population of Saigon seems to date from this time, and the Khmer population increased as well. While some immigrants must have come from places to the north and east of Saigon, most must have come from the Mekong Delta, which held over two-thirds of Cochinchina's population in 1943, and nearly four-fifths of the population outside of Saigon and Cholon.

Why leave? As a member of the Cao Dài in Tây Ninh noted, your average inhabitant was caught on the horns of a dilemma:

There are few true patriots, but no lack of gangsters and thieves who inflict hardships on their compatriots. The poor unfortunates don't know what to do: houses are empty, rice paddies are abandoned. They can't work, because if they work near the French posts, they are considered traitors, while if they join the Cao Dai forces, they are seen as traitors to the fatherland. If they stay in the villages, they are forced to supply the Việt Minh, and if they don't, they'll have their heads cut off. Furthermore, if one stays in the countryside, one is at risk of being rounded up by the French, who set homes on fire and rob those suspected of being Viet Minh.[14]

Reading intercepted Vietnamese letters from 1947, one is struck by the overwhelming presence of violence. These letters provide a mind-

---

[13] See the incomplete statistics in Tsai Maw Kue, *Les Chinois du Sud-Vietnam*, quoted in Shiu Wentang, "A Preliminary Inquiry into the Wartime Material Losses of Chinese in Vietnam, 1941–1947," *Chinese Southern Diaspora Studies* 4 (2010), 118.

[14] ANOM. HCI CP 107. [Letter from Luy, Tayninh, to Vo Van Phap, Tarascon, June 10, 1947.]

numbing litany of complaints: heart-rending accounts of the death of an aunt, the destruction of a family's homes and possessions, and thousands of workers' thatched huts in Saigon going up in smoke. They include sabotage of roads, canals, bridges; destruction of rubber plantations, rice granaries, rice mills, railroad tracks and railroad stations; grenade attacks on movie theaters and buses; arson, ranging from setting buses and boats on fire to immolating entire villages; killings of individuals and massacres of groups; and the common and indiscriminate destruction wrought by the French army. The list goes on and on: violence piles upon violence so routinely that it can seem, at first, to be senseless. And with violence comes people fleeing violence, leaving homes empty and rice fields abandoned.[15] Some writers could be clinical in their observations, weighing the actions of all sides in the conflict. A somewhat pro-French letter writer captured the dilemma faced by the rural population: "In the countryside, the populace is often unhappy. It is often the victim of the Việt Minh for having supplied the inhabitants of the cities with food, and often the victim of European and Vietnamese soldiers [on the 'Government' side] who patrol during the day, and kill whomever they want, and steal all that they find in homes."[16] Another writer framed the dilemma in family terms:

Your mother is in Travinh, not daring return home, fearing both sides; if one interacts with the Việt Minh, one risks reprisals from the French, in contrast, the Việt Minh causes difficulties for those who have relations with the French. Thus, she has put the house in the hands of Du, and has come to live in Travinh [city] and cannot bring in the harvest.[17]

An angry letter writer decried the "terrible calamities in the provinces caused by the French, who are killing people as one kills ants."[18] Âu Trường Thanh wrote of the "utter brutality" of the French army.[19] "T," a full-hearted supporter of the Resistance, called French military actions "terrorist" and labeled the French actions as "massacring the

---

[15] All the examples given come from individual letters, intercepted by the French, in ANOM. HCI CP 107, spanning the very end of 1946 and through 1947. Letter writers tend to be patriotic Vietnamese: some support the Resistance, some oppose; all were writing to someone in France. Deep thanks to Charles Keith for providing this priceless resource.

[16] ANOM. HCI CP 107. [Letter from Pham Cong Binh, My Tho, to Pham Cong Chanh, Paris. January 16, 1947.]

[17] ANOM. HCI CP 107. [Letter from nephew of recipient, Saigon, to Nguyen Van Chieu, Paris, March 24, 1947.]

[18] ANOM. HCI CP 107. [Letter from M., Saigon, to Nguyen Van Khiem, Toulouse, February 22, 1947.]

[19] ANOM. HCI CP 107. [Letter from Au Truong Thanh, Saigon, to Thuong Cong Trieu, Paris, March 20, 1947.]

innocent."[20] One letter-writer, cataloguing the devastation caused by both Việt Minh and French, nonetheless stated that "the barbarism of the French troops is taken to an extreme... setting fire to homes, raping women and girls, followed by executions."[21]

Specific examples of French actions drive home these points. The letters repeatedly mention round-ups of members of the population in both Saigon and in the delta, such as in Thới Lai (near Cần Tho city). Targeted arrests occurred routinely, and routinely came with abuses. Nguyễn Quang Hòa reported arrests every night in Saigon.[22] In Phú Nhuận, outside Saigon, after arresting the wife of a *commis,* members of the French military extorted one thousand piastres to let her free.[23] In a raid on one house, a joint French-Vietnamese force hit suspects, forced their heads under water, interrogated them, then finally took them away – all while stealing typewriters and assorted other belongings.[24] A Vietnamese soldier in the French army in France began a letter: "I received the letter in which you let me know that the family home [in Bến Tre province] was burned down by the French on April 15th, 1947..."[25] In Bến Tre, one inhabitant mentioned that Cao Đài and Algerian soldiers had turned a publishing house into a prison: "one hundred persons are locked up in there, women, children, and the elderly."[26]

If some violence was targeted, much was indiscriminate. The swath of destruction that accompanied French military cannot be missed in these letters. Speaking of his family, one wrote: "Our homes and belongings have been destroyed by the French military. All of the keepsakes left behind by our ancestors and their relatives have been destroyed."[27] Another lamented that in their attacks on Bến Tre, French patrols "killed everything in their path: men, women, the elderly and the young, none were spared. Corpses floated on the rivers, reddened with blood. They

[20] ANOM. HCI CP 107. [Letter from T, Saigon, to Le Van Nghien, Paris, December 31, 1946.]

[21] ANOM. CP 107. [Letter from Be, Bien Hoa, to H.D. Pham, Paris. April 19, 1947.]

[22] ANOM. HCI CP 107. [Letter from Nguyen Quang Hoa, Saigon, to Huynh Thanh Vi, Paris, June 30, 1947.]

[23] ANOM. HCI CP 107. [Letter from "X," Saigon, to Ho Van Truong, Paris, August 2 1947.]

[24] ANOM. HCI CP 107. [Letter from The, Saigon, to Ngo Ky Hia [?], Paris, July 22, 1947.]

[25] ANOM. HCI CP 107. [Letter from Nguyen The Qui, Tarascon, France, to Mlle. Tran Kim Nguyet, Bao Huu, Ben Tre Province. July 17, 1947.]

[26] ANOM. HCI CP 107. [Letter from Quang, Ben Tre, to Mlle Vo Thi Dong, September 29, 1947.]

[27] ANOM. HCI CP 107. [Letter from "Brother", Saigon, to Vo Quang Thien, Paris. April 17, 1947.]

burned, destroyed, and pillaged everything. It was terrifying!"[28] When Tu Nga, a former employee of a French family in Vĩnh Long province who had joined the Resistance, refused to say where the Resistance had buried weapons, the French simply executed him.[29] Such was summary justice.

Where "French" violence ended and that of Vietnamese "partisans" began can be, at times, hard to untangle. Take the following petition from villagers in the area of Trảng Bàng in Tây Ninh province:

On behalf of all the honest people in the *délégation* of Trảng Bàng (Tây Ninh province), I would like to call your attention to our plight. We have undergone all sorts of miseries and now live completely terrorized, on the one hand, by pirate bands who rule the night and, on the other hand, by Partisans (former Vietnamese soldiers who have joined with the French) who sow terror in broad daylight; they arrest people and then force them to pay ransom; they engage in searches and take all that they desire, and threaten the populace.

Thus, those who have knuckled under and who have returned home to resume their lives as petty traders or farmers are subject to the arbitrary reprisals of these "partisans" and are condemned, despite giving in, to see their belongings stolen a second time. This is not to mention the other behaviors that they must endure: imprisonment and torture...These things occur in the shadows, and the French government pays no attention to them. We live in a continual state of terror.[30]

In short, the French military often used violence indiscriminately, and failed to stop its "allies" from doing the same. It is no wonder that many delta inhabitants fled their villages in search of safety.

Conflicts among Cao Đài, Hòa Hảo, Unités Mobiles de Défense de la Chrétienté (UMDC), Khmer, Resistance, and French created new refugees within the delta. Thus, when the Resistance attacked a series of villages in Tây Ninh province in September 1947, some inhabitants took flight, clustering near French posts, and others moved farther away. This reaction would be common throughout the war. One account of Tây Ninh province described: "the movement of population is much more intense than is realized. It continues since the attacks on the villages of Lôc Hung, Thanh Phuoc, Gia Binh, and An Thoi. It drives the desertion of the countryside, the abandonment of belongings and of the harvest as well as flocks. Finally, it gives rise to physical and moral hardships that

---

[28] ANOM. HCI CP 107. [Letter from Nguyen Khanh Toan, My Tho to Vo Van Anh, Paris. May 25, 1947.]

[29] ANOM. HCI CP 107. [Letter from Jean Dauplay to Mme. Nguyen Ngoc Ho, San Francisco. August 11, 1946.]

[30] ANOM. HCI SPCE 96. [Letter from Tran Van Phuoc, Thanh Phuoc village, by Tay Ninh – Godauha, Cochinchine, to Dr. Nguyen van Thinh, member of the Cochinchina Advisory Council, May 23, 1946.]

are difficult to bear."[31] Large towns and cities provided some refuge: "rural inhabitants are flowing towards the population centers, which are overcrowded."[32] A similar movement was found in other provinces. In Rạch Gía, for example, "numerous refugees from the [Hòa Hảo] sect live in the outskirts of the town, in the greatest destitution."[33] In Tây Ninh, a Cao Đài member – perhaps an officer – noted pitched battles around the Holy See, but also a tendency of the population to seek refuge around military posts.[34] A 1949 Cần Thơ report suggested that "the laboring class clings, more than ever, to the [town] centers where it feels better protected."[35]

Villagers also moved short distances within the Mekong Delta, fleeing from hotly contested zones to ones with greater security and less violence. Archival sources shed light on these great and unpredictable upheavals. As one author wrote, "the growing insecurity [in southern Vietnam since 1946] caused an exodus of landowners to protected centers, with population displacement and the desertion of some agricultural areas."[36] From 1945 to 1947, however, we have a confused view of who migrated where, as records and first-person accounts from this period are sketchy.

Refugees overwhelmingly moved by boat and by foot, as bus and car travel was unreliable and dangerous. The Resistance pulled up railroad tracks, often leaving the train from Saigon to Mỹ Tho out of service. They also sabotaged roads and bridges. Other than walking, the only transportation from Trà Vinh to Saigon in early 1947 was to take a military launch up the Mekong to Vĩnh Long, and then a bus to Saigon.[37] "For several months," one letter writer stated in March 1947, "travellers have not dared to take the bus to provinces like Sóc Trăng and Cần Thơ."[38] Sabotage aside, travelers feared attacks by brigands and other armed groups. Communication faltered as well, as the Resistance cut telegraph and phone lines and mail delivery was erratic.

[31] VNA-II. PTHNV Box 482 File E.03–21. Province de Tayninh. "Rapport d'ensemble (période du 16 septembre au 15 octobre 1947)."
[32] VNA-II. PTHNV Box 482 File E.03–281. Province de Chaudoc. "Rapport d'ensemble (février au juillet 1948)."
[33] VNA-II. PTHNV File E.03–25. Province de Rachgia. "Rapport d'ensemble (octobre 1948)."
[34] ANOM. HCI CP 107. [Letter from Phan Van Dang, Tây Ninh, to Le Quang Thung, Tarascon, France. July 14, 1947.]
[35] VNA-II. PTHNV E.03–281. Province de Cantho. "Rapport d'ensemble du mois de janvier 1949."
[36] SHD 10 H 282. "La question du Trans Bassac." June 12, 1950, 19–20.
[37] ANOM. HCI CP 107. [letter from "Nephew," Saigon, to Nguyen Van Chinh, Paris, March 24, 1947.]
[38] ANOM. HCI CP 107. [letter from Ho Thu Du, Cholon, to Phong Ho Van, Paris. April 7, 1947.]

Much movement occurred within – and not between – governmental, Resistance, or "sect" zones. In October 1948, for example, the French military moved posts in Long Mỹ and Ngã Nam, Rạch Gía province, back towards Cần Thơ province. As a result, 3,000 Vietnamese and Cambodian refugees followed troops who were withdrawing to their new post. Given that "the great majority of these refugees were bereft of any resources," the administration drew on communal funds from Ngã Nam to cover their needs.[39] Populations moved in to and out of Resistance zones, as well as towards delta towns and cities. A Châu Đốc province head stated that by 1948, "the population was tired of the unrest, of the Việt Minh, and above all of the Hòa Hảo."[40]

All this movement broke families apart, the members of which some-times lost track of each other. We can only dig up scraps from the archive on individual experiences of such calamities. Peasants, after all, often do not write; of those who do, only odd scraps of letters end up in the archives. On July 7, 1951, Lê Thị Huệ, a thirty-seven-year-old mother with six children, wrote the governor of South Vietnam. Huệ, from Thạnh Trị village in Sóc Trăng province, was anxious about the fate of her husband. He rented 320 công of land every year to cultivate, "thanks to which we avoid misery." In January of 1950, however, her "blameless" husband had been arrested by the secret police and deposited in the Sóc Trăng jail. "Until today, because of the suffering of her husband, they had to endure hardships and poverty." As for her husband: "where is he? Is he dead or alive?" she asked plaintively. A note in this file stated that he was in a military prison in Cần Thơ for Resistance activities in his village.[41]

Death of a family member gave rise to new hardships. On July 10, 1951, Trần Thị Chính "wrote" to the Governor of "Nam Việt": in other words, South Vietnam. Chính, a widow from Long Châu village in Long Xuyên province, "signed" with two fingerprints a letter that was presumably drafted on her behalf. Her husband, the Cao Đài soldier Nguyễn Trung Dù, "died in carrying out his [soldier's] duty" in January. "I beg the High Official to be magnanimous to me, to provide me with support, for I am poor and hungry, and I do not have the will to rear my young child." Interestingly enough, she was awarded $300 piastres.[42] Lê Thị Phước

[39] VNA-II. PTHNV Box 482 File E.03–25. Province de Rachgia. "Rapport d'ensemble (octobre 1948)."
[40] VNA-II. PTHNV File E.03–281. Province de Chaudoc. "Rapport d'ensemble (février à Juillet 1948)."
[41] VNA-II. PTHNV file D.7–551. [Letter from Lê Thị Huệ, Thạnh Trị village, Sóc Trăng Province, to the President.] July 7, 1951. A công is a unit of land measurement used in the western Mekong Delta, roughly one-tenth of a hectare.
[42] VNA-II. PTHNV Box 799 File T.43–456. "Hồ sơ về việc cứu giúp những góa phụ chiến binh Cao Đài." July 10, 1951.

faced a similar catastrophe. She wrote the President in September 1952 after her husband, a province chief in Cầu Ngan district in Trà Vinh province, "died in fulfilling his duty." (Trà Vinh was a brutal place to be in the war between the government and the Resistance.) Her new landlord was kicking her out of her house. "Now I am a widow, destitute, without a home in which to seek shelter. Could the government be charitable and help a widow and orphan without a home?" she beseeched. She asked for a place to stay.[43]

Others besides the Vietnamese suffered: even the French. A good case is that of Madame Faucillon and her husband in Rạch Gía, who appear to have owned a rice plantation before 1945. Their fortunes tumbled from 1945 onwards. Madame Faucillon and her husband lost all their possessions in the upheavals of 1945. By 1948, she had lost track of her husband: she had not heard from him in more than two years. To support herself, she opened a small restaurant and a small place selling drinks. She made ends meet by catering to the French and North African soldiers of the nearby military garrison. But when the French and North African battalions left, replaced by a Vietnamese one, patrons stopped coming to her shops. She was plunged into financial difficulties. At this point she petitioned the administration, now run by Vietnamese, for help. It is unclear whether her appeal succeeded.[44]

Such stories illustrate the dangers of the countryside, leading inhabitants to flee. It is true that in a few provinces, such as Vĩnh Long, population actually rose. But most provinces shed inhabitants, as the chart below indicates:

These statistics should be seen as no more than informed estimates. They might exaggerate the impact of the war on the delta. But the trends they imply are real. From 1946 to 1951 or so, the rural population dropped sharply, with those remaining in the delta concentrating in the core of government, religious, or Resistance zones. Areas close to Saigon and Cholon (like Gò Công) managed to keep the same level of population. Some provinces farther away, like Cần Thơ, managed to hold on to inhabitants quite well. Most did not. The western Mekong Delta provinces were especially hard hit, with Rạch Gíá province losing almost half its population.

War and population movement led to drops in food production, thereby increasing food precarity. While the Mekong Delta was a key source of food, rice production in the Mekong Delta had plummeted

---

[43] VNA-II. Phủ Thủ Tướng Quốc Gia Việt Nam. File 3361. [Letter From Mme. Đốc Phủ Nguyễn Văn Phước born Lê Thị Phước, September 1952.]

[44] VNA-II. PTHNV. T.43–193. Le Chef de Province à M. le Gouverneur du Sud-Vietnam. "Situation de Mme. Faucillon à Rạch Gíá." Rạch Gíá, August 10, 1950.

Table 7.2 *Population of Mekong Delta provinces, 1943 and 1951*

	1943	1951	Decrease, 1943 to 1951	Decrease (or increase)
Bạc Liêu	316,547	190,700	125,847	39.76%
Bến Tre	346,475	326,300	20,175	5.83%
Cần Thơ	440,996	385,900	55,066	12.49%
Châu Đốc	273,360	182,300	91,060	33.31%
Gò Công	119,310	119,500	-190	(0.01%)
Hà Tiên	29,691	20,600	9,091	30.62%
Long Xuyên	279,400	284, 300	-4,900	(1.75%)
Mỹ Tho	429,633	371,300	58,333	13.58%
Rạch Giá	380,959	204,200	176,759	46.4%
Sa Đéc	260,388	150,200	110,188	42.32%
Sóc Trăng	243,734	238,500	5,234	2.19%
Tân An	158,602	97,000	61,602	38.84%
Trà Vinh	285,700	211,600	74,100	25.94%
Vĩnh Long	214,708	249,700	-34,992	(16.3%)
TOTAL	3,779,503	3,032,100	747,373	19.77%

Source: Viện Tổng-kê và Khảo-cứu Kinh-tế (Vietnam), *Việt-nam niên-giám thống-kê* ([Saigon]: Viện Thống-kê và Khảo-cứu Kinh-tế Việt-nam, 1953).

during the war and many peasants were living at the edge of subsistence. The two tables below contrast rice production in the western Mekong Delta, the core of the "rice basket," in the 1943–44 and 1947–48 harvest seasons.

The harvest in 1947–48 had roughly halved compared to four years earlier. Exports crashed precipitously. Delta inhabitants were hurting from food shortages by 1948: "Destitution is common in the countryside. Everywhere, one can see the poor physical condition of most inhabitants due to poorly treated diseases and malnourishment."[45] Chapter 8 will address how the French and Resistance both used food denial as a strategy of war. Here we focus on the consequences of such a strategy, including hunger, on people's lives. As the French seized the upper hand in the early 1950s, the geography of precarity seems to have shifted. In Resistance zones, new pockets of hunger appeared in 1951, only to enlarge in 1952, as the French and their allies expanded control of the countryside. As one report noted:

The "specter of famine" threatens Việt Minh zones. In certain parts of Rạch Giá province, the populace has seized boats transporting foodstuffs for the government. In the same province, inhabitants have even tried to loot the army's stores in

[45] VNA-II. PTHNV File E.03–26. Province de Hatien. Rapport d'ensemble (février 1948).

Table 7.3 *Rice production and exports, 1943/1944 and 1947/1948*

Province	Production (tons) 1943/1944	Exports 1943/ 1944	Production 1947/ 1948	Exports 1947/ 1948
Cần Thơ	236,500	110,000	95,000	20,000
Sóc Trăng	212,500	130,000	150,000	60,000
Bạc Liêu	247,500	150,000	90,000	
Long Xuyên	234,500	140,000	90,000	10,000
Rạch Giá	275,000	150,000	?	35,000
Sa Đéc	129,000	50,000	?	0
Vĩnh Long	99,000	30,000	90,000	20,000
Trà Vinh	194,000	100,000	100,000	12,000
Total	1,628,800	860,000	615,000	157,000

Source: SHD 10 H 4466. "Possibilités de récupération de paddy en Zone Ouest."
October 23, 1948.

order to share the rice stocks. In the eastern provinces, salt and rice are scarce. The Việt Minh never has more than ten days of supplies of foodstuffs. The east of the Plain of Reeds and [the province of] Long Châu Ha [the westernmost part of the Western Mekong Delta] lacks enough rice or salt. The populace lacks adequate cloth, soap, medicines, and agricultural implements. In short, the population and the rebel units are living an 'extremely difficult' life.[46]

Hunger gnawed at those in Resistance zones. The Resistance retreated into remote regions, like the swamps of Cà Mau and the Plain of Reeds, that grew little rice. "Life in Việt Minh zones is quite difficult," a July 1951 military report noted, and "rebellions have broken out."[47] Finding food became a constant obsession. By October, the French military was reporting from Sóc Trăng province that hungry inhabitants of these zones "are making dangerous journeys to buy [rice] in Hòa Tú [near Sóc Trăng city] with Ho Chi Minh piastres. Rice prices have reached astronomical heights."[48] The situation was equally dire in nearby Bạc Liêu, where "the deep shortage of rice in the rebel zone was leading

[46] SHD. 10 H 3991. Dossier 1951–54. 2è Bureau. Bulletin de Renseignement. Situation Générale chez les V.M. Source: Vietnamnienne. Valeur: A/2. Date: 26 et 27.5.51.
[47] SHD. 10H 4280. Secteur de Soctrang. Deuxième Bureau. "Bulletin de renseignements mensuel." July 1951.
[48] SHD. 10H 4280. Secteur de Soctrang. Deuxième Bureau. "Bulletin de renseignements mensuel." October 1951.

inhabitants to defy the threats of Việt Minh leaders" and exchange goods in government-controlled markets.[49]

In 1952, the Resistance suggested to inhabitants near the Cambodian border that they travel in groups to the islands off Hòn Chông (in the Gulf of Thailand) in order to collect wild tubers.[50] In some areas, Resistance forces had to pad their food supply with potatoes, but even potatoes were in short supply, as were salt and rice.[51] In the swamps of Cà Mau, the populace "feared famine" and even those with money were having a hard time buying food.[52] The Resistance in Trà Vinh province faced both a shortage of food and, in the southeast of the province, a lack of fresh water, which they had to transport to their encampments.[53]

Despite such setbacks, peasants in the western Mekong Delta were generally better off than those in the east, or those in central Vietnam. In November 1951, reports came in that the Resistance in Tây Ninh, Thủ Dầu Một and Bà Rịa provinces (north of the Mekong Delta) "were in the grips of famine."[54] Further warnings came in from the provinces north and northeast of Saigon that "because the harvest could not be protected, there will certainly be famine next year."[55] Famine in such areas affected the western Mekong Delta as well, if only because the Resistance moved rice from the rice-surplus western Mekong Delta to rice-deficit areas in other parts of south and central Vietnam.

7.1 Conclusion

From 1946 onwards, at least half a million persons fled from dangerous parts of the delta to Saigon, Phnom Penh, or safer provinces. This statistic does not even capture all of the substantial forced migration within the

---

[49] VNA-II. PTHNV file E.03–174. Province de Baclieu. "Rapport d'ensemble." October 1951).

[50] SHD. 10 H 3991. Dossier 1952. Détachement Français de Liaison près le 3o. B.v.N. Le Capitaine Simon. A/s –Le problème du riz. S.P. 4012. November 12, 1952.

[51] Tỉnh Ủy Ban Nhân Dân tỉnh Trà Vinh, *Lịch sử tỉnh Trà Vinh* (S.l.: Ban Tư Tưởng Tỉnh Ủy Trà Vinh, 1999), Vol. 2, 143.

[52] SHD. 10 H 3991. Dossier 1951–1954. 2ème Bureau. Bulletin de Renseignements. A/S Mauvaise situation économique et politique des V.M. au Nam Bo. January 5, 1952.

[53] SHD. 10 H 3991. Dossier "1951." État-Major-2 ème Bureau. Bulletin de Renseignements. Source: Vietnamienne. November 18, 1951; (same carton) Dossier "1951–1954." 2ème Bureau. Trafic d'eau potable aux bouches du Bassac. January 22, 1952.

[54] SHD. 10 H 3991. Dossier "1951." État du Vietnam. Direction des Service de Police et de Sûreté Nationale au Sud Viet-Nam. 1ère section. Note No. 7034/IB-S. Saigon, November 9, 1951.

[55] SHD. 10 H 3991. Dossier "1951" S.D.E.C.E. No. 23.174/S/ MTR/ VR. Objet: Difficultés de ravitaillement dans la région de THUDAUMOT/ BIEN HOA. Date: 19.11.51.

delta. At the core of this movement was the search for security. Such population churn made it hard for any contestant to govern in these rural areas. The civilian state could not take up the slack, as the French military was reluctant to cede power to the French civilian state apparatus or to the rising Vietnamese central state.

As a result of this population churn, the Mekong Delta was dotted with both overcrowded towns and areas in which peasants had abandoned their villages and land. One author, Hoành Kim Anh, identified a "dead zone" as encompassing parts of the provinces of Sóc Trăng, Rạch-Gía, Bạc-Liêu, and Cà-Mau.[56] The delta had been transformed. It was only in the early 1950s that large numbers of people began to move back to abandoned parts of the delta.

In this context, France and the Resistance offered sharply different approaches to winning the war. So did the semi-autonomous parastates, militias, and strongmen. In the end, the communist-led Resistance would ultimately lose the struggle for the South. To understand this result, the book now turns to the complex local contest in rural Vietnam involving France, the Resistance, and assorted parastates, militias, and religious groups.

---

[56] Hoành Kim Anh, *9 năm kháng chiến miền tây Nam Bộ*, 38.

8 French Pacification Meets the Vietnamese Resistance

In 1955, reflecting on France's defeat, a French army captain pithily stated: "One does not go butterfly hunting with wolf traps."[1] France chose, in other words, the wrong military strategy. And the Democratic Republic of Vietnam (DRV)? We are used to reading that General Võ Nguyên Giáp's strategy of "people's war" was masterful. It was a classic form of asymmetric warfare, in which the Vietnamese strived to minimize the impact of French advantages in conventional warfare while maximizing their own strengths. "People's war" combined attention to military strategy with a broad-based political mobilization. In this view, the DRV undergirded its military strategy with "mass-regarding policies"[2] channeled through expansive and cross-cutting organizational hierarchies. This sophisticated organization mobilized the populace towards a broad-based and protracted insurgency. Success came not simply from *mobilizing* peasants, but in *representing* their interests. France, in this view, failed to understand "people's war" and failed to practice the new counterinsurgency as articulated by Hogard, Lacheroy, Galula, and Trinquier.[3] Such is the conventional view. It stresses arguments for Vietnamese strategic innovation, and accepts the critiques by French "military intellectuals" on French strategic and organizational failures. It downplays the role of experimentation from below, as well as the relevance of past colonial practices.

The arguments for the resounding success of the Resistance in central and northern Vietnam fit the Mekong Delta poorly. I will not claim that

---

[1] An unnamed Captain, quoted in Paul Ély, *Les enseignements de la guerre d'Indochine (1945–1954). Rapport du Général Ély* (Vincennes: SHD, 2011 [1955]), Vol. 1, 147.

[2] Brantly Womack, *Vietnam and China: The Politics of Asymmetry* (Cambridge: Cambridge University Press, 2006), 155.

[3] On Charles Lacheroy, see Marie-Catherine et Paul Villatoux, "Aux origines de la "guerre révolutionnaire" : le colonel Lacheroy parle," *Revue historique des armées* 268 (2012): 45–53. In this peculiar article, Lacheroy takes credit for certain innovations, like fighting at night, and the use of "quadrillage du territoire," or breaking all of the countryside into a grid to be mastered by the military. General Boyer de la Tour, however, implemented these strategies before Lacheroy arrived in Vietnam.

the French and their non-communist allies won in the South. I will argue, however, that they defeated the Resistance and established a rival state to the DRV. This chapter and the next advances this controversial argument and tries to substantiate it. How could this happen? Franco-Vietnamese "success" was born of an apparent paradox: compared to any other lowland region of Vietnam, France relied less on regular troops in the South while relying far more heavily on indigenous paramilitary forces.

Why couldn't the Resistance defeat the odd coalition of French and Vietnamese forces arrayed against it? The answer is complex. Việt Minh mistakes from August 1945 to the end of 1947 would haunt their war effort. The double fracture of 1947 reordered the politics of the Mekong Delta. France's slow and systematic implementation of what it euphemistically called "pacification," in concert with allied paramilitary forces, forced the Resistance into pivotal errors. Its attempt to mobilize the peasantry ultimately failed. Most importantly, the Resistance felt compelled to shift precipitously to conventional warfare to contest the gains of pacification. This was a fateful mistake, and the French-led forces took advantage of it. Beyond strategic arguments, one has to note that all wars with a civil war component are local as well, and local issues and animosities shaped the outcome. France's commission of war crimes in keeping food from the population, its access to increased American funding after 1949, and contingent factors (like a typhoon) also contributed to the South's different outcome. It should be clear that I am not a fan of French strategy. I am simply arguing that it worked in the South and in this war.

The texture of war varied across the South. This chapter focuses on the conflict between the Resistance and forces initially under direct French control. By "French forces," I am referring to a small number of French regular units backing up a far larger number of village self-defense forces, "commandos," and a militias under French supervision (such as the Unités Mobiles de Défense de la Chrétienté). All these groups were under the *direct* authority of France or, after 1949, the emerging State of Vietnam. In Chapter 9, I will look at a different kind of war: that between the Resistance and semi-autonomous parastates and militias, linked to confessional groups. These two wars had slightly different "logics" and it makes sense to distinguish the two.

8.1 French Pacification in Theory and Practice: The War of Posts and Towers

In the early years of the war, France cobbled together a rudimentary military strategy in Indochina. Dismissive of civilian input and lacking enough regular troops, the French military crafted a simple approach: seize the main cities and major roads, and expand control from there. Hire paramilitary forces – then, ironically, referred to as "partisans" – to supplement the small numbers of French troops and Legionnaires. Stoke dissent among members of the Resistance. Carry out lots of sweeps to destroy enemy forces. While the French did stir up divisions among members of the Resistance, its strategy flopped. By mid-1947, France faced a military and political stalemate. The French directly ruled Saigon, many of the major delta cities, and their immediate environs. Politico-religious groups and paramilitary forces such as the Cao Đài, Hòa Hảo, and Khmer controlled chunks of the countryside. Facing them was the Resistance, which controlled its own shifting patchwork of territory.

In this context of strategic stalemate, France adopted a new strategy of "pacification" in the South. Scholars have routinely dismissed this strategy as a failure. Fredrik Logevall has argued that pacification "achieved some success but tied down a lot of troops in static positions, and the posts often proved vulnerable to night-time Viet Minh attacks."[4] Logevall is correct that posts sometimes proved vulnerable. But he is hasty in dismissing the strategy, which failed in the North and Center, but succeeded in the South. General Boyer de la Tour, who took military command of this region in August 1947, was the first to articulate a truly integrated "pacification" strategy. Aided by his deputy, General Chanson (who would replace him in November 1949), Boyer de la Tour crafted an approach that relied heavily on Vietnamese and Khmer self-defense and militia units to turn the tide of the war in the South.

Before turning to Boyer de la Tour's argument, it is useful to note that the term "pacification" has no uniform meaning. It tends to involve a mix of regular and irregular forces using indiscriminate and selective violence to destroy enemy forces. Its end goal is to replace contested control over an area with a structural dominance in which one side is politically hegemonic but violence (arson, rape, killing) has vastly decreased. Violence, in this view, would return to the norm: that is, it would be primarily interpersonal, not between ethnic, religious, and political communities. Such may be the goal, but as critics have pointed out, one person's "pacification" is another person's excuse to torture civilians.[5]

Boyer de la Tour, who had spent over two decades in North Africa, resurrected classic strategies of pacification, such as those used in Morocco under Lyautey, and added some new twists. He modified the

---

[4] Logevall, *Embers of War: The Fall of an Empire and the Making of America's Vietnam* (New York: Random House, 2014), 236.
[5] Marnia Lazreg, *Torture and the Twilight of Empire: From Algiers to Baghdad* (Princeton: Princeton University Press, 2007), 87.

classic *"tache d'huile"* or "oil spot" strategy used in past colonial con-
quests, wherein the colonial army expanded political and military control
outwards from small areas to the entire countryside. Theoretically, pacification was slow, patient, and done with "strict discipline."[6] Ironically, if
French and American historians have neglected Boyer de la Tour's contribution, Vietnamese writers routinely recognize the significance – and
danger – of his strategy.[7]

The new strategy emphasized the *"quadrillage de la dissidence"*: parti-
tioning the countryside into a grid in order to monitor and quash dissent.
Initially, the French seized control of major transportation routes in order
to break the countryside into smaller pieces. Key to success was the
construction of numerous small fortified "posts" and watchtowers spaced
apart at precise distances. Paramilitary and village self-defense forces
manned these posts, monitored their immediate environs, and arrested
suspicious persons who passed through.[8] A larger "mother" post in the
area served as immediate backup, with larger and mobile French regular
forces in reserve to deploy in case of large-scale attacks.[9] As Boyer de la
Tour emphasized, this system of posts was not static defense: it was "not
a defensive means but an offensive means of monitoring dissent and of
pushing inhabitants into regions chosen by us."[10]

As pacification progressed, Boyer de la Tour argued, the military would
come to control secondary water and land routes. As it sliced the terrain
into smaller and smaller pieces, more and more of the countryside would
come under governmental or militia surveillance. With extensive use of
intelligence and nighttime patrols, Boyer de la Tour aimed to wear down,
then triumph over, the Resistance. Remarkably, this counter-insurgency
theory downplayed the need to understand revolutionary strategies,
organizational forms, use of indoctrination, or psychological warfare. It
was, as noted, the modification of tried and true colonial strategies, rather
than a novel theory of counterinsurgency against a revolutionary foe, that
subdued the Resistance in the South. Its success, of course, depended
heavily on the willingness of Vietnamese and Khmer villagers to collaborate with the French or their allies.

In practice, pacification was not as neat and systematic as Boyer de la
Tour suggested. As noted in earlier chapters, the disorganized French
military, afflicted with a small budget and insufficient resources at the
start of the war, executed its plans on the fly. Financial constraints
compelled it to rely on fewer French regular forces, which were expensive,

---

[6] Pierre Boyer de la Tour, *De l'Indochine à l'Algérie: le martye de l'Armée française* (Paris:
Presses du Mail, 1962), 326.
[7] For example, see Nguyễn Hùng, *Ung Văn Khiêm*, 437.
[8] Boyer de la Tour, *De l'Indochine à l'Algérie*, 376.   [9] Ibid., 98–104.   [10] Ibid., 377.

but expand the use of cheaper irregular militias and village self-defense forces. Given variation in the terrain, it was not always possible to space posts apart precisely. In some areas, local inhabitants collaborated with the French more than in others. Those who manned the posts sometimes defected to the Resistance with their weapons, harassed the local population, or extorted money and food from villagers. Nonetheless, pacification succeeded in denying victory to the Resistance.

The particularities of collaboration with the Cao Đài and Hòa Hảo, not directly controlled by the French, will be addressed in the Chapter 9. But what about those forces under direct French control? Here, General Boyer de la Latour improvised in a different way. In July 1947, he authorized the creation of Unités Mobiles de Défense de la Chrétienté (UMDC)[11] on the island of An Hóa, Bến Tre province. Originally, these were local Catholic brigades from Colonel Jean Leroy's home village. (Leroy, a *métis*, had a Vietnamese mother and a French father.) Acting quite autonomously, Leroy developed these brigades against the wishes of the Catholic hierarchy.[12] A similar improvisation was at the root of the arrangements with plantation owners, who paid for local "commandos" led by a French officer, or the creation of local self-defense forces, paid out of provincial budgets.[13] These "commandos" recruited Khmer and Vietnamese from all over the Mekong Delta: the provinces of Bạc Liêu and Rạch Giá "were a rich source of men."[14]

Pacification did not begin auspiciously. France struggled to extend its authority. Guy de Chaumont-Guitry, who served in the South, grumbled on June 27, 1947: "We are constantly on the defensive, nothing more. This is not how to pacify a country."[15] At the beginning of 1948, the Province Chief of Sa Đéc conveyed the beleaguered sense of many Mekong Delta administrators towards the Resistance: "Always invisible but active, these enemies of the established order continue to create a climate of permanent fear that hinders the resumption of the economic and administrative life of the province. With an extreme mobility and

---

[11] Archival sources refer to these units both as Unités Mobiles de Défense de Chrétientés and as Unités Mobiles de Défense de la Chrétienté.

[12] SHD. 10 H 283. [Report of Lieutenant Chanson, Chef de la Mission auprès des U.M.D. C. June 18, 1951.]

[13] See, for example, de la Motte, *De l'autre côté de l'eau*; SHD. 10 H 4485. 3ème Bureau. "Objet: Création des Sections de partisans de plantation. October 28, 1948."

[14] SHD. 10 H 3887. Inspection des Forces Supplétives. "Synthèse des comptes-rendus mensuels d'activité des forces supplétives du Sud Vietnam (mois de mai 1952)."

[15] June 27, 1947 entry in de Guy de Chaumont-Guitry, *Lettres d'Indochine* (Paris: Alsatia, 1951), 69.

fluidity, their armed forces do not have permanent bases and it is often difficult to track their movements."[16]

In the first half of 1948, neither side could win. Boyer de la Tour stuck with his strategy: he armed allies, slowly added more posts, and consolidated control of the population under French rule. To this incremental change, the French added information collection: they were constantly paying local inhabitants for local intelligence. Some trusted informants remained on the payroll for months at a time. The voluminous archival folders on "special accounts" [fonds spéciaux] list thousands of payments to individuals, some for as little as twenty piastres, and many in the twenty to 200 piastre range, on specific bits of intelligence that led to a result, such as the arrest of a courier or a successful ambush. Sometimes, the amounts paid were relatively large: the French paid the Đại Việt Party militant Nguyễn Hưng Khải, head of a group of "nationalists" at An Bình, 10,000 piastres in December 1948 to switch allegiance to the French side.[17]

Of all areas of Vietnam, the French seemed to have collected intelligence most extensively in the South. And the more information they had, the more they could focus on targeted – not indiscriminate – violence, and thereby minimize killing potential allies. But we must distinguish here between French regular forces, such as the often-brutal Legionnaires, and local self-defense forces. Local inhabitants, enmeshed in local kin and village networks, usually manned the posts that dotted the countryside. Their local ties may have constrained and shaped the extent of their violence. Indeed, local issues and local connections shaped the micro-dynamics of violence.

In 1949, as noted in Chapter 6, the French signed an "independence" treaty with the State of Vietnam. The state, including rural administration, slowly began to shift into Vietnamese hands, but France resisted ceding military power to the Vietnamese. In fact, after three years of limited budgets, French military outlays "skyrocketed between 1949 and 1951: 138.4 million francs in 1949, 182 million in 1950, and 322.3 million in 1951 – not including, for this last year, the delivery of American aid."[18] The slow shift in sovereignty, and flush French military budgets, would shape a pivotal period in pacification.

---

[16] VNA-II . PTHNV D.01–359. Province de Sadec. "Rapport d'ensemble (mois de janvier 1948)."

[17] See, for example, SHD. 10 H 4317, "Secteur Mékong. Dépenses. Fonds Politiques"; SHD. 10 H 4318. Folder "Mois de décembre 1948", receipt from Nguyễn Hưng Khải. For more on Nguyễn Hưng Khải and his actions in the South, see Guillemot, Dai Viet: indépendance et révolution au Viêt-Nam. L'échec de la troisième voie. 1938–1955 (Paris: Les Indes Savantes, 2012), 498–503.

[18] Hugues Tertrais, La piastre et le fusil (Paris: Comité pour l'histoire économique et financière de la France, 2002), 69.

As collaboration deepened, France and its "allies" built more posts, bringing more and more of the countryside under constant observation. Increased surveillance hampered the Resistance, which relied on stealth and freedom of movement to escape from the French forces and their allies. By late 1949, General Boyer de la Tour was arguing that the Resistance "was on the ropes."[19] This was hyperbole, but the Resistance grew alarmed. As one Vietnamese history commented about the situation from 1948 to 1950, "the enemy's new plan for pacification, the backbone of which was [General Boyer] de la Tour's system of watchtowers, caused the Resistance many difficulties. The movement declined, the revolutionary bases were caught in the pincers, and cadres and fighters were worn down by attrition."[20] These difficulties would worsen into the 1950s.

Oddly, Boyer de la Tour struggled to convince superiors to buy into his strategy. He repeatedly called for more regular troops but was rebuffed. In fact, the French military was caught in a bind. Given its success in the South, it shifted regular French units to the Center and the North to confront the Resistance there. Boyer de la Tour and his successor Chanson then made a virtue out of necessity. They increasingly relied on indigenous self-defense forces and politico-religious militias. Mobile French army units would come to their defense in case of large-scale attack. Is Logevall right, then, that this strategy of pacification "tied down a lot of troops in static positions"?[21] No. Rather than tying down French regular forces, it tied down local Khmer and Vietnamese paramilitary forces. Far from being a problem, this was an asset: overwhelmingly, these soldiers served in their own villages or districts. Being local, they picked up many of the same rumors and information as other villagers and served as the local, coercive arm of the state.

The political, religious, and ethnic complexity of the South partly explains why pacification worked there but not in other areas. Simply put, it was hard for the Resistance to mobilize such disparate groups with divergent interests. A Vietnamese military history describes, in partisan language, the forces arrayed against the Resistance in Vĩnh Long province:

By the end of 1948, the number of enemy posts had reached 128; of these, 46 were concentrated in Châu Thanh and Vĩnh Long, while 82 were found outside of these areas and in the villages of the province. Most were stationed along roads,

[19] Boyer de la Tour, *De l'Indochine à l'Algérie*, 155.
[20] Hội Đồng Chỉ Đạo Biên Soạn Lịch Sử Nam Bộ Kháng Chiến, *Lịch sử Nam Bộ Kháng chiến* (Hanoi: Chính trị quốc gia, 2010), Vol. 1, 418.
[21] Logevall, *Embers of War*, 236.

and the number of soldiers reached 3,102. These included 185 French, 509 Legionnaires, 405 Khmer, 1,187 traitorous Vietnamese partisans, 437 Cao Đài, 179 Hòa Hảo militia. (This does not include unarmed Hòa Hảo security).[22]

As the description above suggests, France cobbled together support from a motley and fractious cast. Nowhere in Indochina did France rely so heavily on paramilitary forces as in the South. The figures for the South for 1948 are startling:

As this table shows, the southern "face of battle," to borrow John Keegan's term, was non-European almost nine times out of ten. The armed forces in this region were less white than in any other part of lowland Vietnam.[23] This trend would continue. By 1953, approximately 85 percent of all French regulars were fighting vĩin central and northern Vietnam. The other 15 percent were spread around southern Vietnam, Laos, and Cambodia.[24]

Table 8.1 *French-led military forces in southern Vietnam, September/ October 1948*

GVNS [Garde du Viet Nam Sud]				10,000
Partisans [paramilitary forces]				20,000
Regular troops				38,000
–of which:	Infantry units		23,000	
	[composed of]:	Europeans (including Legionnaires)	7,000	
		North Africans	5,000	
		Senegalese	1,500	
		Indigenous (from Indochina)	9,500	
TOTAL				68,000

Source: Pierre Boyer de la Tour, *De l'Indochine à l'Algérie: Le martyr de l'armée française* (Paris: Presses du Mail, 1962), 108.

---

[22] Đảng Ủy Bộ Chỉ Huy Quân Sự Tỉnh Vĩnh Long, *Lực lương vũ trang tỉnh Vĩnh Long 30 năm kháng chiến (1945–1975)* (Hanoi: Quân Đội Nhân Dân, 1999), 93.

[23] Of the roughly 20,000 paramilitary forces in the South in November 1949, 12,000 were directly hired by the French and commanded by French officers and 6,000 were commanded by Vietnamese and received some armaments and funding from the French. Two thousand Catholics were armed by the French but supported by the Catholic Church. See Yves Gras, *Histoire de la guerre d'Indochine* (Paris: Destins Croisés, 1992), 218; see also NARA. CIA. CREST CIARDP82-00457R003600500004-7. "Vietnamese, Lao, and Cambodian Troops Under the French." November 22, 1949.

[24] Dinfreville, *L'opération Indochine* (Paris: Editions Inter-Nationales, 1953), 43–44.

The war was not, in other words, a simple contest between the "French" and the "Vietnamese." A large assemblage of ethnicities and nationalities fought alongside the French, for their own reasons, and opposed the Resistance. General Charles Chanson replaced General Boyer de la Tour in November 1949. The transition was seamless. Chanson had served two years in southern Vietnam at the beginning of the war, acting as Boyer de la Tour's deputy. Chanson would build on and improve Boyer de la Tour's strategy until a Cao Đài dissident assassinated him on July 31, 1951.[25] Chanson increased the tempo of military actions to wear down the Resistance forces. As Dominique de la Motte, who served under Chanson, put it: "Chanson was perhaps a genius, and clearly strong-willed. He decided to make the Viets die of exhaustion by carrying out constant operations in which skirmishes were rare, but which compelled the adversary to be on the move day and night."[26]

By 1950, the actors in the Franco-Vietnamese alliance manned 4,081 distinct posts that dotted the entire South (including Saigon).[27] These posts, together, created a dense web of coercive power. The "web" differed, in its constituent elements, from province to province. Thus, Trà Vinh, Sóc Trăng, and Bạc Liêu provinces, with their large Khmer populations, boasted heavy numbers of Khmer self-defense forces under provincial and French authority alongside other regular and paramilitary Vietnamese forces. In contrast, most other provinces, heavily Vietnamese in composition, had a shifting "palette" of Cao Đài, Hòa Hảo, Catholic UMDC, and regular forces. The system would endure until 1953, when it began to break down.

8.2 The Counterstrategy of the Resistance: Theory and Practice

The double fracture of 1947 had bruised the Resistance. What was to be done? In December of 1947, at a Congress of representatives of Nam Bộ party committees, these representatives assessed the state of the Resistance. In Tân An, Mỹ Tho, Gò Công, Bến Tre, and Bạc Liêu

---

[25] A declassified CIA document states that the assassin was a communist double agent named "Son" who had joined the Cao Đài. See CIA FOIA Reading room. CIA-RDP82 -00457R008300030006-5. "Connection of Assassin of General Chanson with the Thanh Nien Bao Quoc Doan." August 6, 1951, www.cia.gov/library/readingroom/docu ment/cia-rdp82-00457r008300030006-5 (accessed February 19, 2019).

[26] Dominique De la Motte, *De l'autre côté de l'eau Indochine, 1950–1952* (Paris: Tallandier, 2012), 34. Oddly, the French often referred to their allies as "Annamites" and their enemies as "Viets."

[27] "Báo cáo tình hình Nam Bộ năm 1950," in Đảng Cộng sản Việt Nam, *Văn kiện Đảng* Vol. 11 (Hanoi: Quốc Gia, 2001), http://dangcongsan.vn/tu-lieu-van-kien/van-kien-dang/va n-kien-dang-toan-tap/doc-3101420159412946.html (accessed June 21, 2016).

provinces, delegates reported that the Resistance was strong. The Bến Tre representative stated that "We have achieved complete independence. We control everything." The view was mixed in a few provinces, such as Sa Đéc and Thủ Dầu Một: in Sa Đéc, a representative said that "the Hòa Hảo cause great difficulties in one part of the province, but the rest is completely independent. All the population supports us, even the police and *partisans.*" In Trà Vinh, Vĩnh Long, Châu Đốc, Sóc Trăng, Cần Thơ, Rạch Giá, Long Xuyên, and Tây Ninh provinces, however, the Resistance faced severe difficulties. In some cases, Cambodians were the biggest challenge: Sưu from Trà Vinh province stated, paternalistically, that "The presence of many Cambodians leads to a great deal of difficulties. Economically, the situation is bad. The armed forces can do nothing, as Cambodians inform on [our] movements." In Vĩnh Long and Cần Thơ, the Hòa Hảo was the biggest obstacle, whereas in Thủ Dầu Một and Tây Ninh, it was the Cao Đài.[28]

Against this backdrop of two years of extensive violence leading to mixed results, a heated debate erupted over how the Resistance should deal with religious groups. Should they "use armed force to 'retaliate' against Cao Đài and Hòa Hảo brigands – if they burn down houses and steal water buffalo, should we respond in kind?" The majority said no: "struggle against the brigands, but respect the property of believers." Lê Duẩn reminded all gathered that these believers were peasants, victims of the ringleaders.[29] Astonishingly, antagonism against former allies had become so bitter that leaders had to warn against using indiscriminate violence against them.

In 1948, Hùng Ngôn and Bùi Đức Tịnh portrayed the Resistance struggle against the French as a great success. Nonetheless, they lamented "opportunism," "localism," "factionalism," poor organization, and excessive violence.[30] The communist Mai Chí Thọ, who had joined the Public Security forces in Cần Thơ in 1945, would later be harsher about past mistakes:

in the beginning, we relied heavily on an eye for an eye, impatiently responding with violence. Because of this immaturity, we fell into the traps of the enemy to provoke and divide us. So much blood was spilled, preconceptions hardened, hatred deepened. The front for popular unity and salvation was harmed: we gradually lost people and lost territory… especially from 1949 to 1952.[31]

[28] ANOM. HCI. SPCE 379. Réunion des chefs de province V.M. December 19, 1947. Valeur B.3

[29] Trần Bạch Đằng, *Kẻ sĩ Gia Định*, 242–243. Trần Bạch Đằng was present at this meeting.

[30] Hùng Ngôn and Bùi Đức Tịnh, *Lịch sử giải phóng Việt Nam (thời kỳ cận đại)* (Saigon: Đại Chúng, 1948), 68.

[31] Mai Chí Thọ, "Những buổi ban đầu lưu luyến ấy," in *Kỷ niệm sâu sắc trong đời Công An* (Ho Chi Minh City: Công An Nhân Dân, 1995), 12.

Despite its mistakes, the Resistance was still locked in a stalemate against the loose Franco-Vietnamese "coalition" in 1947. From 1948 onwards, the Resistance crafted a four-pronged strategy to try to win the war. First, they strengthened the communist core of the Resistance by recruiting cadres and purging "unreliable" non-communists from its ranks. Only with enough Party cadres could the communists hope to capture control of the People's Committees throughout the countryside and build mass organizations. Second, the Resistance reached out to potential allies like the Khmer and Chinese, and set up mass organizations among the populace for a variety of ends (such as recruiting Catholics and Buddhists). Third, this outreach was combined with a more skilled and nuanced political approach than before towards rivals and enemies through proselytization (*Địch vận*). As the final prong of its strategy, the Resistance strengthened its ability to engage in a repertoire of violence, ranging from intimidation to conventional warfare. Excessive violence ceded way, temporarily at least, to a more sophisticated calculus of attraction and repression. This strategy was impressive. We will now look at each of its prongs.

8.3 Rebuilding the Resistance, One Communist at a Time

At the beginning of the war, non-communists dominated the military forces and local People's Committees. Communists found this state of affairs unacceptable. They also had no choice: they lacked Party cadres. Thus, the first prong of their attempt to create an alternative revolutionary state was to recruit new members to build the Party. For Vietnamese communists, Party cells were the building blocks of its institutions, ranging from local People's Committees to national mass organizations, like those for Catholics, Buddhists, and peasants. Only with more members could communists "capture" the governing apparatus at every level. Therefore, they increased the number of party members, expanded mass organizations, and refined their ability to raise revenue to support this expansion.

The Party faced a huge challenge: the Indochinese Communist Party (ICP) had claimed to "dissolve" itself and could not publicly admit its own existence. Despite this inconvenient fiction, communists succeeded masterfully at building the Party at the national level. By the end of 1946, the ICP had 20,000 members throughout the country. A year later, it boasted 50,000; by the end of September 1948, membership had jumped to 155,000. Growth in numbers of Party cadres, however, centered on the North and the Center of the country. The ICP in the South (*Nam Bộ*) lagged badly behind. In March 1948, the South had only 9,000 communist party members. By August, this had increased to 23,000, only 15 percent of all Party members in the country. Faced with abysmal recruitment of cadres, the Party center sent representatives down south to address these "shortcomings."[32]

The shortcomings were serious. Some cadres were inept, and communists did not always trust non-communists in the Resistance. The Party opted to build a more disciplined Party core for the Resistance. Despite the severe shortage of cadres, the Party implemented the same plan in the South as in the rest of Indochina: to replace many non-communists with communists in the state and military apparatus. Tuong Vu has argued that for the DRV as a whole, 1948 was a turning point: "the coalition leading the DRV was effectively destroyed in 1948," and the rifts between so-called nationalists and communists were becoming clear at the national level.[33] Vu argues that nationalists were not being removed from their national-level positions until 1950.

The South, however, differed. Here, non-communists initially had a strong role in the Resistance. Their influence weakened markedly in 1947, when the anti-French coalition cracked apart. While the Resistance would continue to include some non-communist groups and individuals in high-ranking positions, such as Cao Triều Phát and his Cao Đài splinter group, the era of the inclusive Resistance was mostly over. As the communists in the South recruited more cadres, they solidified control over the state apparatus and its mass organizations. In 1948, the communists were ousting "nationalists" from their positions or relieving them of military command. In February 1948, the socialist newspaper *Công lý* [Justice] reported that "conflicts between nationalists and communists are spreading in the Resistance... we know that in the western Mekong and Hậu Giang areas where the Indochinese Communist Party has seized all the essential positions on the Resistance General Staff, many lower-level organs have disobeyed Resistance orders."[34] In reaction, the Bình Xuyên, patriotic outlaws, denounced General Nguyễn Bình as a "bloodthirsty dictator" who used "evil ruses to divide and massacre nationalists in the ranks of the Resistance."[35]

The French also reported conflicts between nationalists and communists in the western Mekong Delta. By mid-1948, the accumulation of

[32] "Báo cáo về tình hình Đảng năm 1948 và kế hoạch công tác nội bộ năm 1949 [Statement on the Party's situation in 1948 and internal work tasks for 1949], Đảng Cộng Sản Việt Nam, *Văn Kiện Đảng toàn tập* Vol. 10 (1949) (Hanoi: Chính Trị Quốc gia, 2001), 121–122.

[33] Tuong Vu, "'It's Time for the Indochinese Revolution to Show Its True Colours': The Radical Turn of Vietnamese Politics in 1948," *Journal of Southeast Asian Studies* 40(3) (2009), 520.

[34] "Kháng chiến quyết diệt trừ Ng. Bình?," *Công lý*, February 1–2, 1948.

[35] VNA-II. PTHNV D.05–209. *Vì sao Nguyễn Bình khủng bố Bình Xuyên?* [Why is Nguyễn Bình terrorizing the Bình Xuyên?] [tract, 1948 [?]].

evidence "confirms. . . the discontent that is one of the key preoccupations of the Nam Bộ committee." Examples included the refusal of *chi đội* [military detachments] 5 and 21 to obey the orders of the Nam Bộ committee, as well as "a real hostility between Cochinchinese and Tonkinese, military and civilian personnel, nationalists and communists."[36] Lâm Quang Phòng, formerly head of the 125th Regiment, was kicked upstairs into a "vague assignment" with Zone Nine headquarters. (He would defect to the government side in September 1948.) As the Rạch Giá province chief elaborated: "According to those who have rallied to our side, the muted contestation taking place within the Việt Minh between the democratic and communist factions has transformed into an open struggle; bitter strife has arisen between nationalists and communists. The latter have received secret orders to eliminate, during operations, nationalist leaders."[37]

A report from Hà Tiên expanded on this argument, stating that the Headquarters of Zone Nine "seems to be pursuing a systematic purging of military groups and civilian organisms," and even claimed that ideological conflicts had led to armed conflict between two Resistance units on the Cochinchina-Cambodia border. Huỳnh Phan Hộ, the former nationalist head of the Zone Nine, may have been assassinated by communists. (Contesting this view, communist sources state that he was killed in combat in Sóc Trăng in 1947.)[38] Purges reached down to administrative committees at the village level. As "nationalists" were being evicted from governing and military apparatuses, communists were taking their place.

Nonetheless, problems persisted. In evaluating accomplishments for 1950, the Party bemoaned that Zone Nine had allowed 400 "landlords" and some "spies" into the Party.[39] The purging of the Resistance would continue in the years to come. Thus, one supposed reason for the creation in 1951 of a new DRV "province" of Long-Châu-Sa out of three previous ones (Long Xuyên, Châu Đốc, and Sa Đéc) was "the purging of officials whom the DRV felt could not remain faithful to the ideal of 'bolshevization'."[40] Some non-communists, like the Resistance head in Sa Đéc, were demoted, as were members of the Democratic Party. But a cautionary

---

[36] VNA-II. PTHNV D.01–359. "Synthèse mensuelle." Saigon, July 13, 1948.
[37] VNA-II. PTHNV b. 482 d.E03-25. Province de Rachgia. Rapport d'ensemble du 1–12–47 au 31–12–48.
[38] VNA-II. PTHNV Box 482 d. E03-26. Province de Hatien. Rapport d'ensemble (août 1948).
[39] "Báo cáo tình hình Nam Bộ 1950," *Văn Kiện Đảng* Vol. 11 (1950), 726, https://tulieu vankien.dangcongsan.vn/van-kien-tu-lieu-ve-dang/book/van-kien-dang-toan-tap/van-kien-dang-toan-tap-tap-11–91 (accessed May 11, 2019).
[40] NARA. CIA. CIA-CREST 82-00457R00860034000846. "Situation in Ho Chi Minh Controlled Zones of South Vietnam." September 18 [?], 1951.

note is in order. While the numbers of non-communists in the Resistance decreased over time, some remained in high positions: for example, Diệp Ba, titular head of the Resistance Public Security services in the South from 1948 to 1954, was not a Party member.

8.4 Mobilizing Allies and Networks

The Resistance invested much energy in mobilizing potential allies, including Catholics, Buddhists, the Khmer, and the Chinese of the delta. I shall focus on the latter two categories. Both the Khmer and Chinese communities shared an odd commonality: while many were rooted in the Mekong Delta (sometimes predating the Vietnamese in the region), they were also linked to larger communities outside of southern Vietnam.

The case of the Chinese is intriguing, as the Resistance wanted to take advantage of their commercial ties, which radiated out within Vietnam as well as to Southeast Asia and to the Chinese "homeland." Not surprisingly, the Guomindang, the Chinese Communist Party, the French, and the new State of Vietnam (after 1949) also vied to control the Chinese community. As Thomas Englebert has noted, the Guomindang had set up forty-four local committees in the South and tried to establish Guomindang mass organizations controlled through their Saigon consulate. From 1945 to 1949, this led to a

tug-of-war between the GMD [Guomindang] and the French for the control of the Hoa [ethnic Chinese] [and] is one reason why the GMD was more than sympathetic to the Việt Minh armed resistance between 1945 and 1949. The two groups also shared anticolonial sentiments, and of course, there was the material gain that was to be had in the GMD's commercial dealings with the Việt Minh.[41]

While the Resistance reached out to all Chinese, it favored communists. It faced three interrelated problems with Chinese communists: unifying, organizing, and controlling them. Phạm Dân (Tương Lai), who worked on relations with overseas Chinese [Hoa kiều] in southern Vietnam from 1948, noted that unification was tricky:

In the beginning, my most difficult task was uniting the different Chinese forces. Many comrades had come from China or Malaysia. In particular, at the time, several stubborn comrades belonging to the Chinese Communist Party did not want to become Vietnamese Communist Party members. I asked "Brother Number Three" [Lê Duẩn]. He laughed. "What are you worried about?" He

---

[41] Thomas Englebert, "Vietnamese-Chinese Relations in Southern Vietnam during the First Indochina Conflict," *Journal of Vietnamese Studies* 3(3) (Fall 2008), 197–198.

continued: "if these comrades are working and fighting for the revolution, whatever Party affiliation they want is fine."[42]

In 1949, Vietnamese communists set up a special bureau in the South to watch over Chinese affairs (the Phòng Hoa Kiều Vụ), with cadres in each province and Cambodia. This bureau was linked to a range of other mass organizations focused on the Chinese. Sounding quite Maoist, the bureau stated that its aim was "to instill in Chinese nationals the idea of 'national consciousness' based on New Democracy. This means that we must lead them to fight against American imperialism and its servant, the Chinese nationalist government." Crucially, "the relationship between our Party and our Chinese comrades must be based on the following principle: "separation of Parties – unity of command." Vietnamese communists were quite willing to have Chinese communists set up their own organizations with Vietnamese assistance. "Our Chinese comrades will manage their own internal affairs and advocate for Chinese communism, as adherence to the Chinese [communist] party goes hand in hand with one's Chinese nationality."[43]

Given the Vietnamese discourse on the Chinese since 1975, it is startling to realize that during the war against the French, Vietnamese communists were happy to encourage the Chinese to become better Chinese communists: that is, oriented to their supposed homeland. Huỳnh Minh, for example, fondly remembers how the Overseas Chinese Bureau of Nam Bộ helped to organize meetings where ethnic Chinese studied the history of the Chinese Communist Party. They learned how to sing (in Chinese) "The East is Red," a song that praised Mao Zedong as the "people's savior."[44] Chinese were encouraged to join all-Chinese cells unless there were too few Chinese in an area, in which case they could join a Vietnamese cell. In mid-1952, the police of Bạc Liêu province picked up a brochure in Chinese with the slogan "Long Live Mao Zedong." The province chief suggested that it had come from Chinese communists "infiltrated" into the province.[45]

If the Resistance embrace of Chinese communist cells within Vietnam seems odd today, Vietnamese communists still worried – acutely! – that

---

[42] Phạm Dân (Tương Lai), "Công tác Hoa vận thờ chống Pháp ở Nam Bộ," *Nam Bộ thành đồng*, 299.

[43] This paragraph draws on VNA-II. PTHNV E.03.270. "Traduction de document saisi à Luong Hoa le 25/5/49," appended to "Rapport d'ensemble de la province de Travinh – mois de mai 1949."

[44] Hùynh Minh Hiền, "Những kỷ niệm sống và làm việc ở văn phòng trung ương cục miền Nam và Ủy ban Kháng chiến hành chính Nam Bộ," in *Nam Bộ thành đồng Tổ Quốc* (Hanoi: Chính trị Quốc gia, 1990), 215.

[45] VNA-II. PTHNV E.03–178. "Rapport d'ensemble (mois de juin 1952)."

the French would recruit Chinese to "infiltrate" the Resistance. Chinese spies, they warned,

infiltrate our ranks, spread rumors to discourage the population, and seek to divide Chinese and Vietnamese, using people on the move to inform the French... Their quality of being Chinese allows them to enter our ranks more easily, which neither the French nor the less skilled highlanders could do. Spies are our No. 1 enemy. They are the greatest danger to our Resistance. For this reason, counterespionage, including the extermination of spies, must be a constant preoccupation for those in charge of propagandizing the Chinese.

Indeed, the war would show that the Chinese played an essential role both for the Resistance as well as for the French.

The Resistance also reached out to the Khmer and took part in organizing them as an ally against the French. Given the significance of this issue to this book as a whole, I address it separately later in the chapter. The Resistance also struggled to recruit the Cao Đài, but only Cao Triều Phát, leader of one branch of the Cao Đài, joined their side. Phát, a Sino-Vietnamese from Bạc Liêu, had set up numerous Cao Đài oratories in seven provinces in the western Mekong Delta in the 1930s and had become "the true head of the sect" in that area, according to one account. The head of the Way of Enlightened Truth [*Minh Chơn Đạo*] branch, he organized the Unified Cao Đài [*Cao Đài Hiệp Nhứt*] to bring together Cao Đài under the Resistance umbrella.[46] In contrast, the True and Correct Way [*Ban Chinh Đạo*], a branch of the Cao Đài led by Nguyễn Ngọc Tương with 35,000 followers, shied away from politics. It was "correct" towards the French, did not join the Resistance, but allowed members of the 300 oratories to submit to local authorities,[47] including the Resistance.

Catholics were similarly split. While the Resistance had set up organizations to represent Catholics, they fretted, by 1949, that French military intelligence had "very skillfully and very secretly" penetrated these organizations, making them seem like Resistance fronts in form but in actuality not supporting the revolution. Similar fears about a Buddhist Salvation League led them to dissolve it in 1949.[48] The Lay Householder Pure

[46] ANOM. HCI SPCE 350. "Notice de renseignements concernant Cao Trieu Phat." July 1947.

[47] ANOM. HCI. SPCE 350, Paul Pujol, Secte caodaique "BAN CHINH DAO," dite secte de Bentre. August 1, 1951; ANOM. HCI. SPCE 350. "Notice de renseignements concernant M. Nguyen Ngoc Tuong chef de la secte Caodaiste dite de Bentre." [1951?].

[48] SHD. 10 H 4191. Diep Ba, Giam-Doc So Cong An Nam Bo gui Ong Uy Vien Fu Trach Noi Vu. Bao Cao Ve Tinh Hinh Thien Chua Giao. July 29, 1949. [no diacritics in original]; SHD. 10 H 4714. Subfolder "Activités V.M." U.B.K.C. H.C. Nam Bộ. Chi Thị số 36/TV-2. "Về việc giải tán Liên Đoàn Phật giáo Cứu Quốc Nam Bộ." Signed by Phạm Văn Bạch. August 22, 1949.

Land devotees [*Tịnh Độ cư sĩ*] as well as the Mendicants [*Khất Sĩ*], a new Buddhist group drawing on both Mahayana and Theravada teachings, stayed neutral. Followers of both these groups refused to bear arms, and thus were occasional targets of the Resistance, the French, or the militias.

8.5 The Use of Persuasion: The Example of Proselytization (*Địch Vận*)

Building institutions and mobilizing a base and allies were key to the Resistance and its communist leaders. To mask military weakness, the Resistance also tried to mobilize, convince, or neutralize actual or potential enemies. In the South, however, it faced a big challenge after 1947: overcoming its own mistakes. In a March 18, 1948, directive, the southern Public Security Police

noted the sinister conspiracy of French colonialism in attracting minority religious Cao Đài, Hòa Hảo and reactionaries used in the revolution against this country. . . [It] also pointed out that the purging of the Cao Đài and Hòa Hảo by armed force was a mistake. In this long struggle, we must use political education as the foundation; armed force should be combined with political work to enlighten the masses, and we must avoid conflicting with the interests of the faithful.[49]

As the quotation suggests, the Resistance hoped, from this point onwards, to pursue flexible approaches to rivals and potential allies. *Địch Vận*, or proselytization of rivals and enemies, played a key role. The Resistance had learned that abstruse ideological appeals failed to convince its peasant audience. Successful propaganda was simple, direct, and targeted at particular audiences.[50] The Resistance realized that the French commanded a heterogeneous group of fighters whose members might be convinced by a range of appeals. As a pamphlet stated:

Operations in which one does not understand the enemy will fail. One has to understand the enemy: how many of him there are, what kinds, and for each kind, how many; how they live and are treated; the petty intrigues and frictions and how they affect the morale of the enemy troops. One has to especially understand the psychology of the rank and file within the ranks of the enemy.[51]

---

[49] Bộ Nội Vụ. Viện Khoa học Công An. *Công An Nhân Dân Việt Nam. Lịch sử biên niên* (Hanoi: Công An Nhân Dân, 1994), 149–150.

[50] On pre-1945 propagandizing, see McHale, *Print and Power: Confucianism, Communism, and Buddhism in the Making of Modern Vietnam* (Honolulu: University of Hawai'i Press, 2004), Chapter 4; on post-1945 experiences, see Lê Tự, *Địch vận một nhiệm vụ chiến lược* (Liên khu III [?]: Ban Địch vận, 1950).

[51] SHD. 10 H 5442. [Pamphlet]: *Công tác Chánh trị trong Đại Đội* ([Saigon/ Cholon]: Phòng Chánh trị Khu S/C, 1949), 70–71.

Địch vận was not just the responsibility of cadres: "the entire population must engage in proselytization," a Resistance slogan trumpeted.[52] To evaluate the enemy, the Resistance involved a wide range of individuals: domestic helpers, owners of cafés, itinerant peddlers, people living around troop installations, older and younger women, even sex workers, and deserters from the French side. The French quickly became aware of these tactics. As General Lorillot stated, "I repeat that one cannot be too suspicious of 'boys' and 'congais' who are found too often in units and military establishments."[53] (The French referred to a young male servant as a *boy*. In Vietnamese, *con gái* simply means young woman, but the French often used the term to refer to a domestic helper who could be a mistress.) The French feared "false converts": individuals who pretended to rally to the French side, but who collected intelligence and proselytized for the Resistance. These "eyes and ears" picked up on the small grievances that irritated the soldiers and affected morale.

Through trial and error, the Resistance realized that it was better to take advantage of specific and concrete issues, "generally of a personal nature," than make appeals to generic ideas. For example, they would exploit "the resentment of a soldier who feels bullied or misunderstood." To take advantage of the military posts that dotted the countryside by the 1950s, the Resistance would feed off the "disdain and even hatred of the team in a tower or small post towards an incompetent leader [for] drunkenness, brutality, laziness, stupidity, women, and so on."[54] At the same time, the Resistance crafted emotional appeals to sway the populace. Targeting the Cao Đài in the French ranks, one leaflet gently suggested that "a bird always remembers its attachment to its nest. Certainly you have not forgotten your country."[55]

Địch vận was used extensively on the indigenous inhabitants of the South. But the Resistance also targeted foreign soldiers. Explaining that Vietnamese, like many Germans in the French Foreign Legion, had fought against France, it egged on Germans to disobey their French commanders.[56] Tracts even celebrated Hitler:

---

[52] SHD. 10H 3243. Commandement des Forces Terrestres du Centre Vietnam. 2ème Bureau. Le Général de Brigade Lorrillot. Directive pour la lutte contre le Dich Van. July 5, 1951. While this evidence is from central Vietnam, *Địch vận* was similar in all regions.

[53] SHD. 10H 3243. Forces Terrestres du Centre Vietnam. État-Major. Deuxième Bureau. Le Général de Brigade LORRILOT. "Objet: Lutte contre le Dich Van: Cas particulier du IV/ 2° R.E.I." [1951].

[54] SHD. 10 H 3243. Undated and unsourced document: "Buts et methodes du Service 'DICH VAN.'"

[55] SHD. 10 H 4131. Leaflet beginning "HỠI CÁC BẠN CAO ĐÀI" [1953?].

[56] Lê Tự, *Địch vận* 17.

Honor to patriots defending the Fatherland!
Honor to the valiant soldiers of the last world war.
Honor to Hitler, renovator of German youth!
Down with the colonialist sharks, who slash the throats of Vietnamese, German, and French youth!
Denounce this fratricidal war![57]

From 1947 onwards, the first Africans and North Africans deployed to Indochina. The Resistance cautiously targeted these new soldiers. The Resistance advised its soldiers to distribute tracts but to avoid firing on colonial recruits. "In situations where they imitate the French and terrorize the population, one must, for the protection of the latter, warn them. In special cases when they massacre Vietnamese soldiers, we will counterattack."[58] As more French-led soldiers deserted or were captured, the Resistance even created small European-Vietnamese, African-Vietnamese, and Euro-African-Vietnamese units with a dual propaganda and fighting capability.[59]

The Resistance exploited international events to its advantage. A 1947 leaflet, collected in Thủ Dầu Một province, targeted Malagasy and Moroccan troops: "Don't you know that the French imperialists are massacring your compatriots in Madagascar and Morocco? Your compatriots fighting for their independence and homeland share the same ideals as we Vietnamese."[60] As one Senegalese historian notes, the Việt Minh said to the Senegalese, "Tai Den, why are you on the side of the French? You're colonized like us. You should fight for your independence. Join our side, we'll treat you like friends. Follow our example.'"[61] In 1954, the Resistance incited Moroccan soldiers against the French with slogans such as "The French chased Sidi Muhammad ben Yusuf out of Morocco," and "All Moroccans who have in their veins the blood of Islam and love of country must take revenge for their brothers." Moroccans seemed keenly aware of events back home: "not only are many soldiers more or less aware in detail of the events in Morocco, but... the

---

[57] Tract quoted in VNA-II. PTHNV Box 482 dossier E03.26. Province de Hatien. "Rapport d'ensemble. November 1948.
[58] ANOM. HCI. SPCE 379. [Captured and translated document: Le Chef Du Comité Cong Tac No. 1 [Nguyen Dinh Dziem]. Comportement à l'égard des soldats marocains, algériens, et malgaches. April 27, 1947.]
[59] Lê Tự, *Địch vận*, 68.   [60] VNA-II. PTHNV F.6–28. "Propagande de l'opposition."
[61] Aissatou Diagne, "Le Sénégal et la guerre d'Indochine: Récit de vie de veterans." (MA thesis, Cheikh Anta Diop University [Senegal], 1992), 73. The author quotes Ousmane Niang, a Senegalese veteran. "Tai Den" probably refers to the Vietnamese *Tây den*, or "black French/Westerner."

subversive propaganda of the *Hizb el-Itiqlal* [Independence Party in Morocco] interests soldiers."[62]

Despite the examples above, the Resistance shied away from heavily ideological appeals to enemy troops. It recognized that in some ways, North African soldiers had a good life: "they stay in the army because life is comfortable: housing, clothing, food, enjoyments, women."[63] ("Women" here may refer to the Bordels Mobiles de Campagne, or army-supplied sex workers.) Therefore, the Resistance focused its attention on individual grievances. It also tried to instill a fear of dying in battle, and pushed soldiers to demand to be sent home.[64] Propaganda played on the national pride of Africans and North Africans and hammered away at French repression back home. This did not always work. Marc Guèye suggests one reason: the African soldiers in his regiment identified more with their ethnic groups – Agni, Baul, Bambara, Lobi, Wolof, Fula, Sara, Sarakholé, Serer, Susu, and Yoruba – than with any nation in the making.[65] Intriguingly, the Resistance noted that North Africans "were much attached to the Muslim faith" but suggested that propaganda should avoid this topic.[66]

One Vietnamese source states that from 1946 to 1954, "nearly 1,400 German Legionnaires deserted to the Việt Minh."[67] This number seems high. Despite attempts to sway enemy soldiers through proselytization, the Resistance struggled to convert them to its cause. Proselytization may, however, have eroded soldier morale, a fact reflected in very high French desertion rates. Despite such successes, the French were still seizing the strategic upper hand. The slow and inexorable expansion of posts, and thus of area under enemy control, posed a fundamental challenge to the Resistance. The Resistance would meet this challenge by deploying a repertoire of violence that ranged all the way from intimidation to conventional warfare. This strategy succeeded to a point – then failed. The next section explains why.

---

[62] SHD. 10H 3162. Commandement des Forces Terrestres du Centre Việt Nam. Affaires Militaires Musulmanes. "Note: le cessez le feu et la troupe Nord Africaine." July 31, 1954.

[63] SHD. 4131. 2ème Bureau. "Bulletin de renseignement au sujet de la propagande Dich Van." Saigon, December 19, 1950.

[64] SHD. 10H 5568. F.T.S.V. Zone Est. Quartier autonome de Thuduc. Service de Renseignements. Traduction de document V.M. récupére le 13.11.52 par le Poste de GOCONG. S.P. 50.273. November 25, 1952.

[65] Marc Guèye, *Un tirailleur sénégalais dans la guerre d'Indochine, 1953–1955: la conduite au feu du bataillon de marche du 5e R.I.* (Dakar: Presses Universitaires de Dakar, 2007), 101.

[66] See, for example, SHD. 10H 4131. Deuxième Bureau. "Bulletin de renseignements au sujet du [sic] la propagande à appliquer par le Dich Van." [Saigon?], December 23, 1950.

[67] Vũ Long, "Lính lê dương Đức trong chiến tranh Đông Dương" [German Legionnaires in the Indochinese War] *Tin Tức* [News] August 31, 2012.

8.6 Was All Revolutionary Violence Strategic?

It is striking that few scholars have looked at the variation in the use of violence in the First Indochina War in a fine-grained manner.[68] The French assuredly killed more than others, and more indiscriminately. Different sides killed in different ways: only the French, for example, bombed from airplanes. The Resistance perceived the French and its Vietnamese and Khmer allies as needlessly violent: as one member of the Resistance commented about the "Catholic" UMDC, for example: "its leaders are reactionaries, and only a minority of the soldiers are sympathetic to us; in many places, they are acting in an increasingly barbaric manner."[69] My sense, from reading the accumulated evidence, is that of the assorted Vietnamese contestants, the Hòa Hảo militias and the Catholic UMDC were the least disciplined, using violence the most, whereas the Cao Đài and the Resistance were the most disciplined.

Here I focus on the Resistance. I approach Resistance coercion in a context in which all sides contributed to a dynamic of violence. The "logic" of violence is not intuitively obvious. The revolutionary Trường Chinh initially exalted revolutionary violence and dismissed the idea that violence needed to be calibrated:

The third weak point of the August Revolution was that the revolutionary government, once established, did not resolutely get rid of the reactionary Vietnamese traitors, did not firmly deal with the French colonialists and their henchmen. The exceptions were a few places, such as Quảng Ngãi, where insurgents implemented policies of "wiping out the reactionaries" but got out of hand; elsewhere, our policies were spineless.[70]

To Trường Chinh, the only mistake in the 1945 massacres in Quảng Ngãi was their size. Others, however, argued for a disciplined use of violence. Take this 1946 commentary on the lessons of the resistance against the Japanese:

Traitors, outlaws, and especially fake Resistance endanger the movement, and we must punish them. But in punishing outlaws, we must be careful. We must know how to distinguish between the gangleaders and the "youngest brothers" who follow. Punish the leaders, persuade those lower down – that should be our policy... If we continue to hunt down outlaws too much, then someday... some

---

[68] An exception is Christopher Goscha, "La guerre par d'autres moyens: Réflexions sur la guerre du Viêt Minh dans le Sud-Vietnam de 1945 à 1951," *Guerres mondiales et conflits contemporains* 206 (2002), 27.

[69] SHD. 10 H 4191. Uy ban Khang Chien Hanh Chanh Nam Bo. Cong An Nam Bo. "BAO CAO VE TINH HINH THIEN GIAO." July 29, 1949.

[70] Trường Chinh, *Cách mạng tháng tám* (Hanoi: Sự Thật, 1955 [1946]), 37–38.

of the masses will come to hate us because they fear persecution. . . not because they have been enlightened to the revolution.[71]

The statement above suggests a sophisticated approach to balancing attraction and coercion in order to build a movement. If the Resistance had routinely followed such advice, it would have avoided some of its early difficulties.

Looking at the arc of the war, it seems clear that over time, the Resistance lessened indiscriminate violence against potential allies while continuing to use selective violence against clear enemies.[72] "Indiscriminate" here refers to two kinds of killings. First, it refers to arbitrary and random slaughter, as when one side lobs mortar shells into a village. Second, it refers to carnage emerging from blind rage, such as the cycle of Khmer-Vietnamese killings in 1945–47 in the delta, which undermined the Resistance and violated Party policy. This contrasts with selective violence, such as the targeted assassination of notables, or even the conscious targeting of a particular group or location in pursuit of political and military objectives.[73]

The first two to three years of the war were a free-for-all, when the level of violence involving Vietnamese, French, and Khmer was high and sometimes indiscriminate. From 1948 to 1950, this struggle transitioned into a roughly equal contest in which the French and their allied Vietnamese and Khmer forces tried to "pacify" the South, but faced increased – and increasingly well-organized – Resistance opposition. The Resistance calibrated its use of violence, deploying selective violence against specific targets, like village police chiefs, while also attempting to shift to conventional warfare from late 1949 on. The latter strategy resulted in heavy losses to its southern political cadres and armed forces. The years from 1950 to 1952 saw the tide turn in favor of the Franco-Vietnamese coalition opposing the Resistance. American funding allowed the French military to expand its coercive power and pulverize Resistance forces. The Resistance arguably lost the struggle for the South in these years. The partial recovery in late 1953 and 1954 never made up for earlier demoralizing losses.

In examining violence, the political scientist Stathis Kalyvas argues that "homicide does not exhaust the range of violence, but it is an

---

[71] *Quyết chiến, kinh nghiệm về cao trào Kháng Nhật cứu nước ở Việt Nam* (Hanoi: Sự Thật, 1946), 26–7. I am guessing that the phrase "*chùa chúm*" is a misprint for *chúa trùm* (gang leader).

[72] This perception mirrors the hypothesis of Stathis Kalyvas in *The Logic of Violence in Civil War* (Cambridge: Cambridge University Press, 2006), 169–171.

[73] I borrow my use of the concepts of "indiscriminate" and "selective" violence from Kalyvas, *The Logic of Violence in Civil War*.

unambiguous form that can be measured more reliably than other forms."[74] True – but to understand the narrow "logic" of violence as well as its broader social and political meaning, one has to situate violent death in a larger repertoire of coercive practices ranging from intimidation to combat. The Resistance tried to impose a political and strategic logic on its violence. Nonetheless, as Kalyvas argues, civil war violence is a "joint production" of outside political actors and local inhabitants, and the latter bring their particularistic biases, antipathies, and histories into the process. After brief comments on the patterning of violence and its strategic rationale, I will argue that civil war calls into question an excessively strategic perspective on conflict.

In what follows, I draw on a database of violence I have compiled, based on French and State of Vietnam monthly provincial reports on areas that were either under their full control or where they contested for control. (The database has little on areas under the firm control of the Resistance, the Hòa Hảo, or the Cao Đài.) The data, strong on some provinces and weak on others, only covers events from 1949 to 1952. For all these weaknesses, no other set of data exists on sub-provincial violence from the First Indochina War based on regular monthly reporting from province heads. I have recorded 2,293 acts of violence, including:

- 164 acts of arson (with many more buildings burned down);
- 471 kidnappings;
- 349 assassinations;
- 982 acts of harassment of French posts; and
- 327 attacks on posts.

In civil wars, violence varies across space, and the data shows that southern Vietnam was no exception. Some provinces, like Hà Tiên, were relatively calm whereas others, like Trà Vinh, were the site of a brutal low-level conflict. Depending on the province, the Resistance used a shifting repertoire of tactics. Let me look at each tactic in turn.

From the very beginning of the First Indochina War, the Resistance, like the French, used arson as a tactic. Its first use came in September 1945, when the Resistance forces in Saigon destroyed an electricity plant and set fire to Bến Thành market.[75] If the Resistance initially used arson to keep economic goods from the French, it was also used to deny an area to the French, control trade, instill fear in the populace, or punish French collaborators.

---

[74] Kalyvas, *The Logic of Violence in Civil War*, 20.
[75] Nguyễn Việt, *Nam Bộ và Nam Phần Trung Bộ*, 30.

Intimidation, another common Resistance tactic, is one of the hardest topics to study in wartime. The use of threats rarely leaves a record, but some traces survive. For example, in order to keep food in their own controlled zones, the Resistance forbade peasants from trading in French-controlled markets where prices were better and the currency used was the Piastre, not revolutionary money. Thus, the Resistance in Long Xuyên province in 1948 warned, in writing, that "it is expressly forbidden to go into the city or into any other area controlled by the French from 5 in the morning, March 18, until 6 in the morning, March 23, 1948. Whoever violates this order may be executed."[76] The Resistance frequently intimidated those serving the French state and its successor, the State of Vietnam. At the end of 1949, a Tây Ninh report mentioned that every administrator had received a "formal letter from Ho Chi Minh" calling on them to abandon their jobs. "They are not afraid," the report added, with a touch of bravado.[77]

When intimidation failed, the Resistance sometimes ramped up pressure by kidnapping opponents. On November 10, 1947, a reported 300 Resistance fighters attacked the An Biên Three market in Rạch Gía province, set fire to parts of it, and spirited away forty-eight hostages. Two weeks later, the Resistance took away eighty-two persons from the same market. Such mass abductions, however, were quite rare. More often, the Resistance kidnapped individuals connected to village administrations. In 1952, for example, it seized five men from Nhơn Hưng hamlet in Châu Đốc province: all five had been proposed to serve on their hamlet's council of notables. The abduction worked: it "made it impossible to reconstitute the Council of Notables in the village."[78]

Assassination was a last resort, used against those working for the enemy state as well their close collaborators. The "logic" of killing government officials seems clear: to deprive the French, then the State of Vietnam, of their "eyes and ears" on the ground, to make government fail, and to warn villagers of the consequences of collaboration with the enemy.[79] Of the forty persons listed as assassinated in Trà Vinh province in 1949, seventeen (or nearly half) were clearly linked to the state. Most of them were village police officers or local notables, though hamlet and

---

[76] SHD. 10H 4909. Comité Résistance/Executif. Délégation de Vinh Long. "Interdiction de pénétrer dans la ville de Vinh Long du 12 Mars." March 17, 1948. [translated document]

[77] VNA – II. PTHNV. E.03 dossier 268. Le Chef de la Province de Tayninh. Rapport d'ensemble pour le mois de décembre 1949.

[78] VNA – II. PTHNV. D.30–680. Le Chef de la Province de Chaudoc [Dang Van Ly] à M. le Gouverneur du Sud-Vietnam. Chaudoc, July 2, 1952.

[79] VNA – II. PTHNV. E.03–208. Province de Soc Trang. "Rapport d'ensemble (du mois de juillet 1950)."

village chiefs, teachers, and militia members also were targets. A perusal of those killed in Bến Tre province in 1951 shows a similar pattern: twelve out of thirty-nine, or a third, were clearly linked to the state.[80]

The Resistance also targeted traditional leaders of communities, such as Chinese heads of congregations or Vietnamese and Khmer monks who had collaborated with the French or their Vietnamese state successors. In February 1951, the Resistance killed Thạch Keo, head of the district of Định Chí, "one of the most active collaborators of the Government and the military authorities." As the Province Chief wrote, "his loss was deeply felt by all of those who knew him and held him in high regard for his dynamism, intelligence, and complete devotion [to the government]."[81]

The Resistance was hypervigilant about defectors and punished them harshly. In April of 1952, for example, the Resistance had placed a 20,000 piastre price on the head of defector Nguyễn Hoàng Lâm in Châu Đốc province. He had absconded with a rifle and then revealed to governmental authorities the site of a Resistance munitions and arms factory.[82] And when the Resistance killed informers for the French or State of Vietnam, it warned the populace against committing treason. When the police found Hoàng Anh Kiệt's corpse six kilometers outside of Cần Thơ city, the killer had attached a note. "Independence Freedom Happiness," it oddly began, invoking the DRV's official motto, then attacked the victim as a "despicable person" and "number one reactionary" who had "collaborated with the French." It concluded with "Cordial Greetings and Death to the Enemy!"[83] The Resistance occasionally killed persons who committed minor transgressions, but who, if copied, would cause the Resistance serious headaches in controlling their population. Thus, in November 1950, the Resistance beheaded three individuals in Sóc Trăng province who had left the Resistance zone to sell pigs and duck eggs in a zone controlled by the State of Vietnam. The offenders' heads were found in jute bags, with a note attached saying why they had been condemned to death.[84]

[80] VNA – II. PTHNV. E.03–270. Province de Travinh. Rapport d'ensemble [monthly, 1949].
[81] VNA – II. PTHNV E.03–213. Province de Soctrang. Rapport d'ensemble du mois de Fevrier 1951.
[82] VNA – II. PTHNV E. 03–176. Province de Chaudoc. Rapport d' ensemble du mois d'Avril 1952.
[83] SHD 10 H 4710. [Note found on Hoàng Anh Kiệt, assassinated on May 24, 1953, Rạch Dầu Sấu, 6 km. from Cần Thơ city.]
[84] VNA – II. PTHNV d. E.03–208. Province de Soc Trang. Rapport d'ensemble (mois de novembre 1950).

When we take all the imperfect data together, can we generalize findings on the strategies of choosing the appropriate tactics for guerrilla warfare? Yes. First, because of its potentially high cost, combat was usually a last resort. Second, with the exception of the failed conventional attacks of 1949 to 1950, the Resistance chose tactics that would avoid losses while maximizing gains. Thus, they generally avoided frontal attacks on enemy forces in favor of intimidation, harassment, arson, assassination, or harassing fire on posts.

Trà Vinh province, which showed the highest levels of violence anywhere (except Tây Ninh province) from January to April 1950, showed a fascinating pattern. After conventional attacks on posts failed, all levels of violence initially decreased. While frontal attacks on posts never again recovered, the Resistance use of targeted assassination bounced back to high levels in future years. The Resistance, unwilling to suffer such high losses again, resorted to the very effective tactic of assassination to stop the expansion of the enemy state apparatus.

Despite all the examples above, violence cannot be reduced to the execution of a calibrated political strategy. Local feuds and antagonisms shaped the production of violence as well. Lingering resentments on all sides from the "double fracture" fed enduring cycles of violence. The Resistance repeatedly attempted to impose discipline in the use of such violence, as it recognized that it had often killed wrongfully and thus caused new enemies of the revolution. As Le Van Nhieu wrote in 1952:

Every time that they learn, through investigation, that a certain A or B is a servant of the enemy, that he hinders our action, our cadres [in the past] immediately thought of eliminating him without thinking of warning, of trying to convince by all possible means, of allowing him to repent and get back on the right path. *There are even times when our cadres blindly accept, without investigation, a report that could reflect subjective observations or personal grudges.*[85]

Indeed, the determination of who to kill or what to destroy could be intensely subjective. At times, the use of violence clearly violated official DRV policy. Thus Father Nguyễn Bá Sáng, a member of the Resistance, argued that the destruction of churches in 1945 and 1946 could be understood as locally generated violence. "But [the cause of] the destruction in 1947 was clear: it was caused by Government personnel [i.e., the Resistance] in localities who lacked discipline and destroyed, failing to follow orders from above." Resistance military units destroyed convents

[85] SHD 10 H 4710. [captured and translated document – Fédération syndicale ouvrière de Thu Bien. Front du Lien Viêt]. "Objet: Extermination des traitres." Le Van Nhieu, October 18, 1952. Emphasis mine.

without asking whether or not it was militarily necessary.[86] Such destruction continued past 1947, and extended to non-Catholic sites as well, such as the destruction of shrines to tutelary divinities in local temples.[87] We see a similar result in the resort to racialized propaganda discussed in an earlier chapter, an approach condemned by the DRV. At other times, local actors gave lip service to official Resistance policies while undermining them in practice. Its contradictory actions from 1945 to 1947 against particular ethnic and religious groups – such going on the warpath against the Hòa Hảo and the Tây Ninh branch of the Cao Đài, while professing to want their support – opened up spaces for local actors to "make policy" based on personal or village grievances.

During civil wars, of course, individuals use the cover of war to settle scores, or drag the innocent into minor conflicts. Examples of this appear to be legion, but it is impossible to be sure. In December 1949, for example, a Cambodian fisherman in a Trà Vinh village was shot and killed 200 meters from a bridge. Why? At other times, the Resistance blundered and killed the wrong persons. A particularly sad case came from Hà Tiên province in July 1949, where the Resistance wanted to kill members of the Lộc Trĩ self-defense post. Hearing that they were gambling at the Mayor's house, they burst into the house and killed nine persons celebrating the wedding of the Mayor's daughter. The Resistance profusely apologized for the mistake in a Khmer-language tract.[88] (The Resistance's enemies made plenty such blunders as well.) In the end, such actions, as well as those from by the French military and the rising Vietnamese state, and contingent factors, harmed the Resistance.

What really turned the tide against the Resistance was a combination of French economic warfare and failed Resistance conventional attacks. The Resistance was the first contestant to engage in economic warfare. At the core of the struggle for the South was control of the rich rice-producing zones of the western Mekong Delta, the "rice basket" of the South. As one Resistance document noted, "the western Mekong Delta is, of all the South [Nam Bộ], the most fertile, the most populous, and the richest region. For us as well as the enemy, only the occupation of the western

---

[86] SHD. 10 H 4191. Ban Dieu Tra Cac Nha Tho Bi Pha Hoai. [Untitled letter from a committee in the Southern Resistance on DRV policy on destruction of religious property]. October 6, 1947. Also see Decrees 34 and 45, signed by Võ Nguyên Giáp and Hồ Chí Minh; Lê Cung, Lê Thành Nam, Hồ Hải Hưng, Nguyễn Minh Phương, and Nguyễn Trung Triều, *Tinh thần nhập thể của Phật giáo Việt Nam (1945–1975)* (Ho Chi Minh City: Tổng Hợp, 2018), 40.

[87] For an example from Thới Thạnh Ha village (near Ô Môn in Cần Thơ province), see VNA-II. PTHNV. E.03–30. Province de Cantho. "Rapport d'ensemble du mois de novembre 1947."

[88] VNA-II. PTHNV. E.03–285. Province de Hatien. Rapport d'ensemble (Août 1949).

region allows us to hold all of the South."[89] At the beginning of the war, the Resistance worked to deny food to Saigon and Cholon in order to force inhabitants to come over to the side of the Resistance. By 1947, this food blockade had real bite, and beriberi (a sign of a lack of thiamine) appeared in Saigon.[90] But the French could always import food to Saigon, and the Resistance food blockade against the city eased over time.

As noted, the Resistance forbade farmers from selling in French-controlled zones. It reasoned that the cost of living in "puppet" zones would spike if the Resistance limited access to key foods, like rice, that were grown in Resistance zones.[91] In 1947, the Resistance tightened the economic blockade "by forbidding the transportation and selling to the enemy of local products that could be exported, [thus] causing a marked increase in the cost of living in the areas occupied by the French."[92] At the same time, the Resistance heavily taxed rice sales, a major resource for their treasury.[93]

Generals Boyer de la Tour, then Chanson, turned the tables on the Resistance, launching an all-out economic war against it. In January 1949, France imposed an economic blockade on the western-most part of the Mekong Delta. The blockade had three aims. First, the French wanted to prevent the Resistance from selling rice, other foodstuffs, and other products outside of areas under their control, as heavy "export" taxes on such sales were key to the Resistance treasury. Second, they wanted to block the Resistance from sending rice from the rich, food-surplus zones of the western Mekong Delta to the rice-deficit Resistance zones in the eastern Mekong Delta or central Vietnam. Finally, the French aimed to keep key products – such as salt – from getting to the Resistance.[94] The French also destroyed stocks of rice in Resistance-controlled zones, sometimes by bombing. This strategy, along with the introduction of fake Ho Chi Minh banknotes into Resistance zones, caused food shortages, reduced Resistance purchasing power, and severely hurt the Resistance

---

[89] SHD. 10 H 5097. Folder "Traduction de Documents Viet Minh. Situation dans le Sud Indochinois et dans la région 'Ouest'" [1952].

[90] ANOM. HCI. CP 107. [Intercepted letter from Nam, Saigon, to Nguyen Van Le, New York. February 17,1947].

[91] SHD. 10 H 3991. Dossier "Économie V.M. année 1947." Comité Executif de Nam Bo. Service de Finance. Circulaire No. 112/ TC 2.

[92] SHD. 10 H 3991. Dossier "Économie V.M. année 1947." Comité Executif de Nam Bo. Service de Finance. Circulaire No. 112/ TC 2 [translation].

[93] SHD. 10 H 282. Subfolder "Levée complète du blocus." "La question du Trans Bassac." June 12, 1950.

[94] For a product list, see SHD. 10 H 4681. 2e Bureau. Blocus du Transbassac. S.P. 51.121. October 21, 1949.

economy.[95] The French use of induced famine as a weapon was a war crime.[96]

This economic boycott, combined with progress in pacification, hit the Resistance hard. The Resistance feared that the French were trying to "catch [the Resistance] in a spider's web" by increasing the numbers of self-defense posts. It correctly deduced that this strategy would slice the liberated zones into smaller and smaller pieces as the French zones got progressively larger. This explains the premature attempt by General Nguyễn Bình, Commander in Chief of Resistance military forces in Nam Bộ, to shift from guerrilla to conventional warfare.[97] He thus worked to mold popular militia forces [dân quân tự vệ] into conventional forces.

Nguyễn Bình wagered that the posts the French were constructing across the delta, usually manned by poorly trained and ill-paid self-defense forces, could be overwhelmed by large and well-trained units. Starting in December 1949, the Resistance launched attacks on a scale never before seen in the South. The result was disastrous for the Resistance, as French and allied forces beat back the attacks. Understanding the significance of this turning point is not easy if one relies on Vietnamese histories, which downplay setbacks. While speaking glowingly of Resistance success in Trà Vinh and Vĩnh Long provinces in this time, however, one Vietnamese book soberly concluded: "Our Resistance encountered difficulty after difficulty."[98]

This Resistance failure would have long-term impacts. The battle for Trà Vinh province, central to Resistance objectives in the western Mekong Delta, illustrates this failure. In Trà Vinh, the posts were primarily manned by Khmer soldiers, with some Vietnamese Catholics as well. They were backed up by mobile French regular forces. One Party source calls the first battle of Cầu Kè (from December 7, 1949 to January 16, 1950) a "resounding victory." It called the Battle of Trà Vinh (from March 25 to May 8, 1950) "a great victory." A Resistance communication during that battle noted that seven French officers were killed, and some of the Moroccan troops lacked spirit and surrendered as soon as

---

[95] See Tertrais, *Le piastre et le fusil*, Chapter II.

[96] French practice violated the fourth Geneva Convention of 1949, which France signed in 1949 and ratified in 1951, which addresses the rights of civilians in wartime. In particular, Article 23 states that a signatory to this convention "shall likewise permit the free passage of all consignments of essential foodstuffs, clothing and tonics intended for children under fifteen, expectant mothers and maternity cases."

[97] Christopher E. Goscha, *Vietnam: Un état né de la guerre* (Paris: Armand Colin, 2013), Chapter 3.

[98] Đảng Ủy Bộ, *Lực lượng vũ trang tỉnh Vĩnh Long*, Vol. 1, 131.

they were fired upon.[99] The French military noted that the Resistance may even have planted double agents in their intelligence services, thus leading to faulty French intelligence on the location of Resistance main force units in Trà Vinh province before the battles.[100] The Resistance claimed to have killed and wounded 1,060 enemy soldiers, taken 509 prisoners, disarmed "nearly" 4,000 members of self-defense units, and collected more than 800 guns.[101]

While recognizing that they had gone through a "difficult trial," the French military and the embryonic Vietnamese state sharply disagreed with the Resistance assessment. The province chief noted that in the first battles, the Resistance had been "seriously blunted" and "had lost many of their cadres." He claimed that in the second set of battles, the Franco-Vietnamese forces did equally well. He quoted a French military report: "We held all of our posts. All of our towers, attacked by 6,000 men over eight days, held, thanks to our parachuting food and munitions." Counterattacking, the French military inflicted heavy losses on the Resistance. "We are confident of [having achieved] an unprecedented rebel defeat."[102]

Weighing both Resistance and French perspectives, the French view seems closer to the truth. The Resistance did retain fighting strength. In October 1950, it attacked again in Cầu Ngan (Trà Vinh province) "with a violence never before equaled, but they encountered, on the part of Franco-Vietnamese troops, a vigorous response of unprecedented effectiveness."[103] After the October 4 battle south of Cầu Ngan, the French hastily counted 256 Resistance dead, and claimed that the total Resistance death toll was three times that amount. In short, this attempt at conventional war – taking the war to the French – resulted in substantial losses. As Goscha notes, the attempt to shift from guerilla to conventional warfare in the South "failed miserably," even if it showed the "extraordinary determination" of the Resistance.[104]

---

[99] SHD.10 H 5574. Quandoi quocgia Vietnam Chien Khu 8. Thong cao phong tham muu sô 175 [no diacritics in original]. March 28, 1950.

[100] SHD.10 H 4279. Forces Franco-Vietnamiennes Sud. Zone Ouest. Etat-Major. 2ᵉ Bureau. "Note d'orientation 0572/2S."

[101] Ban Tư Tưởng Tỉnh Ủy Trà Vinh, Lịch sử Tỉnh Trà Vinh (Trà Vinh [?]: Tỉnh Ủy, Ủy Ban Nhân Dân Trà Vinh, 1999), 106, 118. These numbers are suspiciously high. If they disarmed or took prisoner approximately 4,500 persons, why could they find fewer than one in five of their arms?

[102] VNA-II. PTHNV E.03–206. Province de Travinh. "Rapport d'ensemble de la province de Travinh (mois de février 1950)" and "Rapport d'ensemble (mois de mai 1950)."

[103] VNA-II. PTHNV E. 03–206. "Rapport d'ensemble de la province de Travinh (mois de septembre 1950)." This location is now written "Cầu Ngang."

[104] Goscha, Vietnam: Un état né de la guerre, 113.

These battles marked the peak of Resistance military power in Trà Vinh province. From this point onwards, the Resistance fell into a long-term decline in the province, while Franco-Vietnamese forces and the State of Vietnam expanded in influence. The Franco-Vietnamese forces expanded the territory under their control, and Resistance acts of violence declined. What was true for Trà Vinh is generally true for the delta as a whole: from 1949 through 1952, the tides of war shifted decisively in the South. As a 1952 Resistance document stated, "Thanks to skillful tactics, [the enemy] was able to concentrate his forces and intensify his activities. Instead of undertaking large-scale operations, and moving in all directions as before, it clears out small areas and annexes them at all costs, therefore keeping the tactical initiative throughout the South."[105] The struggle for Trà Vinh province, whose major cleavage was between Khmer and Vietnamese, turned out to be one of the most intense series of battles during the war.

The impact of these defeats, coupled with the French use of food denial as a strategy, pushed the populace in Việt Minh zones into dire straits. In March 1951, according to refugee reports, lots of "concentration camps" in the Resistance zone were filling with peasants "who had been imprisoned for having sold their products in [government-controlled] markets."[106] (This may have been exaggeration, but the Resistance did punish peasants who sold produce without authorization in government-controlled zones.) When rice stores in Resistance-controlled areas in the western Mekong Delta dipped low, peasants suffered. Thus, the Resistance complained that when French troops swept through the Plain of Reeds, they looted and destroyed, "using starvation as a way to attack our people and our troops." Inhabitants were reduced to mixing potatoes with their rice.[107]

Migration out of Resistance zones, clear in 1950, took off from 1951 onwards. With American funding, the French and their Vietnamese allies added military posts across the delta and stepped up sweeps and bombings. The State of Vietnam implanted itself more securely in the countryside. Bến Tre province, for example, was under the complete control of the UMDC (Jean Leroy's Catholic militias), from 1950 onwards. In 1950, the Province Chief began reporting that important population

---

[105] SHD.10 H 5097. Folder – Traduction de Documents Viet Minh. "Situation dans le Sud Indochinois et dans la région "Ouest" [1952 ?]."

[106] VNA-II. PTHNV File E.03–174. Province de Baclieu "Rapport d'ensemble du mars 1951."

[107] SHD. 10 H 3991. Dossier 1951–1954. "2ème Bureau. Document récupéré au cours de l'Opération TOURBILLON VI qui s'est déroulée en Plaine des Joncs du 20 au 27–2–1952."

centers "regained their appearance from before the war… wherever we place our [military] posts, our peasants reappear and the land is once again cultivated."[108] We should take such cheery statements with a grain of salt, as Leroy was brutal towards enemies, but the overall population shifts seem clear. Similar transformations begin to occur elsewhere. In Sóc Trăng province, for example, the province chief reported in November 1950 that [Vietnamese] Catholics "have returned in rather substantial numbers to Long Phú." This area had been the site of Khmer-Vietnamese violence in 1945 and early 1946. The Catholics "were offering to restore the Church, abandoned since the troubles of 1945."[109]

As the French and the State of Vietnam extended the reach of their "pacification," people flowed out of Resistance zones or came under central government control. In January 1951 in Bạc Liêu province, 310 refugees left Resistance zones for government ones. In March 1951 in the same province, 500 Vietnamese and 360 Khmer took refuge in the government-controlled zone.[110] More extreme population shifts happened elsewhere. For example, in December 1951, following military operations, "approximately 10,000 persons left Resistance zones to find refuge in Minh Lương," not far from the town of Rạch Gía. Eighty percent of these refugees were Cambodians, and the rest were Vietnamese. They suffered from high rates of malaria and scabies.[111] As a report from October 1951 concluded, "The exodus of inhabitants, which the Việt Minh can no longer halt, is an indication of its weakening."[112]

Shifts in Resistance control, migration, and hunger reshaped control of the delta and led to mass movements in many parts of the delta. In 1952, for example, in hotly contested Trà Vinh province, 10,878 inhabitants came under government control.[113] That this was not an isolated occurrence is shown by the province of Châu Đốc: "progress in pacification in Chaudoc is real, and the month of November was marked by important defections and by the massive exodus of peasants from areas under the grip of the Việt Minh to those under government

[108] VNA-II. PTHNV Box 482 File E.03–207. Province de Bentre "Rapport d'ensemble." August 1950.
[109] VNA-II. PTHNV Box 482 File E.03–208. Province de Soctrang. "Rapport d'ensemble." November 1950.
[110] VNA-II. PTHNV File E.03–174. Province de Baclieu. "Rapport d'ensemble." March 1951.
[111] VNA-II. PTHNV File D.5–42. Le Gouverneur du Sud-Vietnam à M. le Directeur de la Santé. Saigon, December 6, 1951.
[112] VNA-II. PTHNV File E.03–174. Province de Baclieu. "Rapport d'ensemble." October 1951.
[113] VNA-II. PTHNV File E.03–302. Province de Travinh. "Rapport d'ensemble [various months, 1952]." Note that the statistic for April was missing.

control."[114] In February 1953, 1,936 refugees fled towards government-controlled areas in Rạch Gía province.[115] Cadres and troops in Resistance zones reacted strikingly. One provincial history notes that some commanders of units, unable to stand very difficult conditions, fled the province or even moved over to the government-controlled zones.[116] "[T]he populace also has had to disperse many times, fleeing frequently to avoid the harm caused by the incredibly savage sweeps by enemy military forces."[117]

To compound the stress, the typhoon of October 20–21, 1952 hammered parts of the Resistance's Eastern Zone, northeast from the Mekong Delta. The Bé and Đồng Nai rivers rose four to five meters, overflowing the banks and causing widespread flooding. A Resistance document from an affected province reported: "many have died, disappeared, or been swept away by the currents. Homes and belongings, agricultural implements, livestock, and the harvest have all have been severely damaged or destroyed." The French and the Resistance competed to help the populace deal with this catastrophe.[118] Given the preexisting shortages of food, the Resistance struggled to meet the challenges of this latest disaster. Reports of popular dissension in Resistance-controlled zones surfaced at this time,[119] and are elliptically confirmed by Vietnamese sources. Faced with starvation, many residents fled to French or militia-controlled zones.

If hunger drove migration, so did the French use of indiscriminate aerial bombing. (They used similar tactics in the Red River Delta, even bombing dikes.) As one former Resistance member from Rạch Giá in the western Mekong Delta stated, bombings in Resistance areas became "extensive" in 1951:

Markets in Viet Minh areas were bombed many times in a month to scare the people into dispersing and returning to French-controlled zones. The bombings were also designed to destroy the economy of the liberated areas and to ruin the bountiful life of the people in Viet Minh controlled areas. The French for this reason, bombed the markets more often than the Viet Minh base camp areas.[120]

---

[114] VNA-II. PTHNV File E.03–176. Province de Chaudoc. "Rapport d'ensemble." November 1952.
[115] VNA-II. PTHNV File E.03–302. Province de Rachgia. "Rapport d'ensemble." February 1953.
[116] Tỉnh Ủy ban, *Lịch sử tỉnh Trà Vinh*, Vol. 2, 157 fn. 12.   [117] Ibid., 143.
[118] SHD. 10 H 3991. Dossier 1952. Secteur de Thudaumot. 2è Bureau. "Document récupéré le 13/11/52. Entr'aide Populaire après le typhon." Translation from Chấp Hành Đảng Bộ Tỉnh Thủ Biên].
[119] SHD. 10 H 3991. Dossier "1951" Bulletin de Renseignements No. 4331. Conditions de vie en Zone V.M. September 1951.
[120] Interrogation of Civilian Rallier. 21–23 April 1965, in *Studies of the National Liberation Front of Vietnam* (Santa Monica [?]: RAND, 1966[?]), 3.

Such French military attacks succeeded in pushing peasants in Resistance zones to flee.

The years from 1951 to 1953 were among the most trying ones the southern Resistance had ever faced. One Vietnamese military history states that 1952 "was the most difficult and brutal year" of the war.[121] With the Resistance in trouble, the delta experienced fewer attacks, more areas at peace, more reports of inhabitants coming back to the areas that had been abandoned during the war, and more people fleeing from Resistance zones. This change was exemplified by Tết 1952: the province chief of Long Xuyên province wrote that "we have not seen so many people and such a considerable display of merchandise since 1946."[122] This sentiment was echoed by the province chief of Trà Vinh, who stated that Tết unfolded peacefully "with all the splendor of the time before the war."[123] Trà Vinh and Long Xuyên were not anomalies: pacification was proceeding apace in much of the delta.

In 1953, the Resistance continued to face difficulties: "Numerous indications suggest that the V[iet] M[inh] of Nam Bộ is encountering difficulties that increase with no respite... Lacking tested leaders – lukewarm elements having being eliminated from key positions – several Executive Committees have been disbanded one after the other." In February, the Executive Committee of Rạch Giá province was eliminated, as its functions were taken over by a committee that had responsibility for multiple provinces in western Nam Bộ.[124] By March 1953, refugees from Resistance zones fleeing to Cần Thơ were reporting "economic and financial difficulties" leading to a general discouragement.[125] In Trà Vinh province, the province chief made the boldest claim about the Resistance: "it is now clear that the Resistance front in the province has completely fallen apart and, unless there is help from the outside, it will never be able to reestablish itself."[126]

While refugees flowed out of Resistance zones, they chafed under Government or militia control. Warlords and government repeatedly

---

[121] Quân Khu 7, Câu Lạc Bộ Quân Giới Nam Bộ, *Lịch sử Quân giới Nam Bộ (1945–1954)* [History of southern armaments production, 1945–1954] (Hanoi: Quân Đội Nhân Dân, 1991), 123.

[122] VNA-II. PTHNV d. E.03–177. Province de Vinhlong. "Rapport d'ensemble." January 1952.

[123] VNA-II. PTHNV d. E.03–302. Province de Travinh. "Rapport d'ensemble." February 1952.

[124] VNA-II. PTHNV Box 490 Dossier E.03–178. Province de Rachgia. "Rapport d'ensemble." February 1953.

[125] VNA-II. PTHNV d. E.03–186. Province de Cantho. "Rapport d'ensemble." March 1953.

[126] VNA-II. PTHNV d. E.03–181. Province de Travinh. "Rapport d'ensemble." March 1953.

exacted arbitrary taxes and labor from the populace, and ruled by force. These abuses continued into the early 1950s. Thus, in April 1952, approximately two-thirds of the village of Trường Long Hoa (in eastern Trà Vinh province), were reported to "have already left the village, and others will certainly follow, because they can no longer endure the regime of terror spread by the ['Catholic' UMDC] paramilitary forces." This included tortures as well as the disemboweling of two young men.[127] While we cannot speculate unduly, other sources indicate that when soldiers assigned to posts acted brutally, the residents in the area, often refugees, would pick up and flee short distances.

8.7 The "Competition" over the Khmer Krom

The chapter so far has focused on the Vietnamese and French. It has not examined, in depth, the Khmer Krom, or Khmer of the lower Mekong Delta, who played a pivotal role in the armed conflict in key provinces. From 1947 onwards, the French and the Resistance competed for Khmer Krom allegiance. Why most Khmer ultimately sided with the French and against the Resistance is key to understanding the war for the Mekong Delta. After the double fracture of the Mekong Delta, Khmer allegiance to any side was up for grabs. On October 30, 1947, the French allowed the creation, in Sóc Trăng, of a Parti Khmère. The Party stated that it would extend its "frank and sincere collaboration with any legal government that recognized its rights in practice," and that it would "defend [the community's] particular interests."[128] The Parti Khmère falls out of most primary sources after this early mention. But its existence shows how the French were trying to cater to the Khmer and wrest control of the delta from the Resistance.

The Resistance had its own plans, reaching out to the Khmer Issarak in Cambodia to develop common plans to fight the French. Who were the Issarak? Founded in Bangkok at the end of 1940 by a Cambodian monk, the Khmer Issarak Party (*Phak Khmer Issarak*) created its first military units in May 1941 under the aegis of Thai Prime Minister Phibun.[129] Many bands that opposed the French, but lacking a common leadership, called themselves "Issarak." While analysts tend to characterize the

---

[127] VNA-II. PTHNV D.7–437. Le Délégué Administratif de Caungan à M. L'Administrateur-Chef de la province de Travinh. Caungan, April 4, 1952.

[128] SHD. 10 H 282. [No author, but perhaps Direction des Services Français de Sécurité Publique en Indochine]. "Les minorités Khmères au Sud Viet-Nam." January, 1954.

[129] Christopher Goscha, "Le contexte asiatique de la guerre franco-vietnamienne: réseaux, relations, et économie (1945–1954)" (PhD dissertation, École Pratique des Hautes Études, 2000), 227.

Issarak along political lines, Michael Vickery has argued that "often the vocation of Issarak was no more than a device to give a patriotic cover to banditry, which had long been endemic in parts of rural Cambodia; and the 'bandit charisma' may have been as strong a motive as nationalism in attracting men to Issarak life."[130] Goscha notes that Dap Chhuon, an Issarak leader in Cambodia, "led a colorful but impressive crowd of men, composed of soldiers as well as arms traffickers and common criminals."[131]

Despite Issarak shortcomings, the Resistance courted them as an ally in their struggle against the French. In November 1947, the Khmer Issarak and Resistance worked out a plan to collaborate in Cambodia and in Cochinchina. In each area, Vietnamese and Khmer units chose either an Issarak or a Resistance commander. Furthermore, "the Khmer Issarak would send troops to the Cambodian zone of Cochinchina. For their part, the Resistance would be authorized to act in Cambodian territory in areas where the Annamite population was predominant." As collaboration increased, Issarak and the Resistance struggled to articulate convergent interests.

Support for Issarak groups in Cambodia, where ethnic Khmer were the majority, advanced the Resistance goal to defeat the French. But what about joining with Issarak in the lower Mekong Delta? Here the Resistance strived hard to convince Khmer that the Vietnamese-dominated Resistance would treat them fairly. No Issarak, however, wanted to replace French with Vietnamese rule. Furthermore, the Resistance continued to threaten, kidnap, and sometimes kill Khmer leaders who collaborated with the French. Engelbert quotes the intercepted letter of a Khmer from Trà Vinh, in which the father complains about Resistance exactions: "families... either [had to] pay ransom or their houses would be burnt."[132]

By 1948, the French and the Resistance were pursuing rival strategies to mobilize the Khmer. As the French military grew stronger, it was increasingly able to help defend Khmer communities in Cochinchina against the Resistance. It provided these communities with weapons for self-defense. Khmer Krom were also grossly over-represented in the ranks of "commandos" led by French officers. The Resistance claimed that the French "incited the Khmer to ethnic hatred" against the Vietnamese by spreading the belief that "Vietnamese oppressed Khmer and that only the

---

[130] Michael Vickery, *Cambodia 1975–82* (Boston: South End Press, 1984), 6.
[131] Goscha, "Le contexte asiatique de la guerre," 231.
[132] Thomas Engelbert, "Ideology and Reality," in Thomas Engelbert and Andreas Schneider, eds., *Ethnic Minorities and Nationalism in Southeast Asia* (Frankfurt: Peter lang, 2000), 129.

French would bring independence to the Khmer."[133] There is some truth to these claims. Tracts from 1948 spread by French units in Cambodia, for example, chastised some Cambodians for "handing themselves over to... your hereditary enemy" and for becoming the "valets" of the Vietnamese. Other French-sponsored tracts claimed that the Việt Minh "were progressively infiltrating your Mekong provinces, very rich areas that they covet.... The price of their aid will be your southern provinces!"[134]

Following the 1947 and 1948 agreements, Issarak units in Cambodia sent troops to the ethnic Khmer parts of the lower Mekong Delta, while Khmer Krom leaders took charge of some Issarak units within Cambodia. For example, Sangsariddha, a Khmer Krom "mestizo" from Trà Vinh, commanded a platoon in the area around Kampot (in Cambodia) in 1948; this unit had "acted in spectacular fashion."[135] Another Khmer Krom from Trà Vinh, Sovann, was reported in July 1948 to be in command of a unit of 100 Issarak that worked on the Cambodian-Vietnamese border. A Khmer Krom from Rạch Giá, Sary, commanded an Issarak unit of sixty fighters, stationed at the edge of Hà Tiên, Châu Đốc, and Rạch Giá provinces. It fell under the command of the Khmer leader Son Ngoc Minh, responsible for units in the Cambodia-Cochinchina frontier region.[136] In addition to sending troops, the Issarak engaged in heavy propagandizing, as 1948 reports from Trà Vinh and Sóc Trăng provinces show.[137]

Despite all this work, the Resistance encountered serious challenges in working with the Issarak in the Mekong Delta. Missteps continued. For example, the Resistance repeatedly expressed condescension towards Cambodians. A major Resistance document from late 1949 provides a hodge-podge of clichés about the Khmer: "The Cambodian is simple and natural. He does not think of elevated problems [and] can be tricked easily. Culturally, his level is poor and superstitious, he goes to temple, respects monks. Cambodians do not have strong will."[138]

---

[133] Đảng Ủy Bộ, *Lực lượng vũ trang tỉnh Vĩnh Long*, Vol. 1, 60.

[134] SHD. 10 H 5587, Subdossier 261. Commandement Militaire au Cambodge. Deuxième Bureau. "Tract pour Zone Sud. Soldats Khmers-Issarak." September 1948.

[135] VNA-II. PTHNV Box 482 d. E.03.26. Province de Hatien. "Rapport d'ensemble (août 1948)."

[136] SHD. 10 H 5587. "Unité mixte V.M./K.I. Région de Vinh –Gia (Frontière de la Cochinchine)"; SHD. 10 H 5587. "Cambodge-Cochinchine : A/s organisation du détachment K.I. No 302." Phnom Penh, July 20, 1948.

[137] VNA-II. PTHNV Box 482 d. E03.25. Province de Travinh. "Rapport d'ensemble (mai 1948)"; same box, Province de Soctrang. "Rapport d'ensemble des mois d'août et septembre 1948."

[138] SHD. 10 H 4714. Captured document. Assemblée Générale Territoriale Fédération Vietnamienne et Front V.M. "Décision. Programme de Démarches auprès des minorités ethniques." Translated November 17, 1949.

We can conclude that despite sincere Resistance efforts, Resistance and Khmer Issarak forces became estranged. As Khmer ethnonationalism in both Cambodia and Cochinchina increased in influence, the Resistance found it difficult to control the Khmer. Khmer saw themselves as choosing between Khmer units (including Khmer Issarak) and the French for protection. Organizational differences solidified, and Khmer realized that on certain issues, such as the fate of the provinces of Trà Vinh or Sóc Trăng in Cochinchina, they were at loggerheads with the Resistance.

On June 4, 1949, rebuffing a longstanding Cambodian territorial claim, France awarded Cochinchina to the new state of Vietnam. This act was pivotal in Khmer-Vietnamese relations. The Khmer of the Mekong Delta now became a small minority in a new entity, the state of Vietnam. While foreign affairs and defense remained in the hands of the French, domestic affairs were now under Vietnamese control. The political future of the Khmer in the new country seemed in doubt. Trịnh Thới Cang, a Khmer monk from Sóc Trăng, arrested in December 1949 on the charge that he supported the Resistance, framed the acute dilemma now facing all Khmers in southern Vietnam. His eloquent statement to the police deserves to be quoted at length:

I have always thought that the unjustified waste of our [Khmer] lifeblood was, for the Khmer minority, a slow death... but that the [Resistance-led] Revolution would bring nothing but disaster and servitude because the evolution of the Khmer was not ready for this and would lead the Khmer minority, severed from its Mother Country, to a slow death, a suicide or an irreparable disintegration.

I am loyal to the manifesto of the Parti Khmère. The experience of History is too recent, too persuasive, to imagine collaboration with communist elements, which would lead to the suppression of our freedom, our rights, and above all our religion.

...The French Parliament's ratification of the unification of southern Vietnam with the rest of Vietnam has taken away from us the last hope to be considered Cochinchinese comparable in statute to the French Canadians.... I consider this quasi-total repudiation of our rights to have been unjustly anti-Cambodian. The fatal hour has arrived whereby the Cambodians of southern Vietnam are directly in the grip of the [Vietnamese] Administration.... The Cambodians... are caught between two antagonists, both Vietnamese. If His Excellency Bao Dai succeeds in rallying all the members of the Resistance and reestablishing peace, Cambodians will have to answer to their atrocities against Vietnamese, with no distinction made between Việt Minh or [the state of] Vietnam. What will end up being our fate, the debasement... reserved for the vanquished?[139]

---

[139] SHD. 10 H 4279. Subfolder "Bonze." Déclaration de M. TRINH THOI CANG. Soctrang, December 22, 1949.

Cang's worries were quickly realized. The newly "independent" Vietnamese state moved quickly to assert power over minority groups and to replace any remaining French province chiefs with Vietnamese ones. Fear of a repetition of ethnic violence precipitated some Vietnamese actions, but the end result was to assert Vietnamese power over Khmer.

The Resistance could not take advantage of such actions, for the Issarak–Resistance alliance was fraying. As it fell apart, Resistance access to the Khmer communities suffered. In February 1950, some Issarak in Trà Vinh Province allied with French forces and turned against the Resistance. By August 1950, Issarak were spreading propaganda near Bạc Liêu and Sóc Trăng, two areas with heavy concentrations of Khmer, asking the population to remain neutral in the upcoming Resistance offensive.[140] In future years, the Resistance would continue to reach out to the Issarak in Vietnam, but with little success. The era of collaboration was coming to a close, as ethnonationalism increasingly shaped the actions of Cambodians and Vietnamese. In the process, the Khmer Krom of the lower Mekong Delta turned to the French. Increasingly, Khmer joined French commandos and local self-defense forces. A sign of this transition was that by 1953 Trà Vinh province alone boasted 5,000 to 6,000 paramilitary and self-defense troops [*supplétifs*], 90 percent of whom were ethnic Khmer.[141]

8.8 Conclusion

The struggle in the South between the French "coalition" and the Resistance was like nowhere else in Vietnam. On paper, the Resistance pursued a similar mobilizational strategy in the South as it did it the North and Center: build a communist core to the Resistance, reach out to Chinese and Khmer allies, employ *Địch vận* or proselytization, and refine the use of repertoires of violence. But the legacy of the double fracture of 1947 was hard to overcome. The Resistance also faced particular challenges in the South, with complicated religious and political diversity and entrenched rivals, that made attracting followers difficult. The premature shift to conventional warfare in 1949 and 1950, which failed, reminded the Resistance in other parts of the country that hasty actions could deeply damage the struggle. The Mekong Delta shows the limits of looking at all of Vietnam in terms of a three-stage protracted "people's war" based on

---

[140] SHD. 10 H 5574. [Deuxième Bureau]. S/ secteur de Travinh. "Période du 20 Janvier au 20 Février 1950;" SHD. 10 H 4279. 2ème Bureau. Secteur de Soctrang. "Période du 24 Août au 31 Août 1950)."
[141] ANOM. HCI. SPCE 56. Service Français de Sécurité au Sud-Vietnam. "Projet de mutinerie des Forces Supplétives à Travinh." Saigon July 27, [195]3.

extensive popular support. The war for the Mekong Delta did not fit this model well.

In the South, the Resistance struggled against the French strategy of "pacification." French pacification "worked" by slicing the countryside into smaller and smaller pieces, and then controlling these pieces. It worked through the targeted and local use of violence. It worked because irregular forces, with ethnic Khmer playing a disproportionate role, joined units that opposed the Resistance. It worked because the French were willing to commit war crimes and use food as a weapon of war, and were able to take advantage of a typhoon to defeat the Resistance. But France's direct confrontation with the Resistance is only part of the story. Perhaps more importantly, as Chapter 9 shows, the French had allied with semi-autonomous militias linked to confessional forces. To this last and central issue we now turn.

9 Alternative Trajectories: Seeing like Parastates, Militias, and Strongmen

In 1947, as the delta fractured, the French agreed to give lots of autonomy to religious groups with their own militias if they fought against the Resistance. Two agreements served as the fundamental cornerstones of this political wager. The Fray-Phạm Công Tắc "convention" of January 8, 1947, signed by a French Lieutenant-Colonel and a Cao Đài representative, initially called for the French military to arm and support 1,500 armed men. A little over four months later, on May 18, 1947, Colonel Cluset and Trần Văn Soái [Năm Lửa], the leader of the strongest Hòa Hảo military faction, signed a separate agreement that promised some autonomy for the Hòa Hảo as well as an unspecified supply of weapons and munitions.[1] These two temporary working arrangements were the shaky basis on which France built an expansive collaboration with the Cao Đài and Hòa Hảo until 1954.[2]

These agreements, and how they worked in practice, illustrate two major points. From the spring of 1947 onwards, the struggle for power in the Mekong Delta transitioned from a binary conflict pitting France against the Resistance into one defined by three poles: the French military and civilian state apparatus; the Resistance; and the Hòa Hảo-Cao Đài-Bình Xuyên "nationalist" alliance. In 1949, a new actor, the State of Vietnam, would add a fourth pole. The Cao Đài-Hòa Hảo-Bình Xuyên "alliance" was the only alternative nationalist force to the Resistance in much of the delta. These agreements, and the important role of violence in the delta, led ultimately to the militarization of Mekong Delta society as a whole.

A situational logic of alliance and opposition, understood by all participants, shaped the overarching "system."[3] Within this system, both the

---

[1] For the text of these agreements, see Bodinier, *Indochine 1947: règlement politique ou solution militaire?* (Vincennes: Service Historique de l'Armée de Terre, 1989), 461–466. Note: one can find sources using the name "Cluzet" as well as "Cluset."

[2] See SHD.10 H 3787. Commissariat de France en Indochine. Secretariat Permanent de la Défense. "Fiche concernant les rapports des Commandements Français avec les Sectes Confessionnelles du Sud-Vietnam." January 22, 1955.

[3] This strategy of alliance and opposition is clear in Resistance memoranda on proselytization and its aims. The most explicit discussion of a cold-blooded logic of shifting alliances

French and the Resistance competed to co-opt smaller groups, from parastates to local militias, to their side. The French gamed the process by repressing political parties (like the Đại Việt or the Social-Democrats) that challenged their dominance while rewarding their "allies." The Resistance played similar games. Smaller groups, in turn, attentive to the ever-shifting balance of power, carved out spaces of autonomy whenever possible. They submitted to others in exchange for favors (such as getting weapons or sources of revenue), and often collaborated with other local rivals. They defected at times as well. Thus, the militia leader Trình Minh Thế frequently threatened defection from the Tây Ninh branch of the Cao Đài; the charismatic but cruel Ba Cụt, content to control his corner of Long Xuyên province, defected numerous times from alliances with the major Hòa Hảo leader Trần Văn Soái, the French, and – eventually – the Ngô Đình Diệm government.

9.1 The Militarization of the Delta

The temple bell has fallen silent,
Transformed into bullets to kill the French enemy.

Unidentified poet[4]

As this poem from the beginning of the First Indochina War suggests, even mainstream Buddhists who sided with the Resistance were drawn into the general militarization of society. Religion, however, did not define the war. This may seem counterintuitive: didn't both the Cao Đài and Hòa Hảo share a millenarian vision that drove their actions?[5] Yes, but the situation was complicated. If a vision of the end of an age certainly shaped the Hòa Hảo and Cao Đài religions at the beginning of the war, the violence of 1947 – including the killing of Huỳnh Phú Sổ – transformed the landscape. The dynamic of violence that shaped the delta from 1945 to 1947 continued, transforming the conflict as a whole.

---

for future gain is in the May 1947 Social-Democrat Party directive that advocates a three-stage process involving shifting alliances: "First Stage: Cooperate with the Việt Minh to attack the French. Second Stage: Ally with the French to wipe out the Việt Minh and the Cao Đài (of Tây Ninh). Third Stage: Wipe out the Việt Minh, hope for sufficient military and political conditions to wipe out the French, reestablish Social-Democrat rule." See SHD.10 H 4169. Việt Nam Dân Chủ Xã Hội Đảng. Trung Ương Đảng Bộ Dân Xã gởi cho các cấp để thi hành. Chỉ Thị. May 21, 1947.

[4] Lê Cung [et al.], *Tinh thần nhập thế của Phật giáo Việt Nam (1945–1975)* (Ho Chi Minh City: Tổng Hợp, 2018), quoting a poem cited by Thích Huệ Thông, *Phật giáo Tiền Giang lược sử và những ngôi chùa*, 83.

[5] Hue Tam Ho Tai, *Millenarianism and Peasant Politics in Vietnam* (Cambridge: Harvard East Asian Studies, 1983); Jérémy Jammes, "Caodaism and its Global Networks: An Ethnological Analysis of a Vietnamese Religious Movement in Vietnam and Abroad," *Moussons* 13/14 (2009), 339–358.

Religious groups saw a growing bifurcation of authority between religious and military wings of their movements: sharp in the case of the Hòa Hảo, growing over time in the case of the Cao Đài, and mild in the case of Catholics. As the war progressed, "men of violence" and their militias increasingly came into conflict with the religious authorities they supposedly represented.

The Hòa Hảo historian Nguyễn Long Thành Nam captures this argument nicely: he argues that the entire period from 1947 to 1955 in the Mekong Delta was one of "militarization" [quân sự hoá]. By this, he means that in the wake of Huỳnh Phú Sổ's assassination, the French tried to hem in Hòa Hảo political activities, but did so by arming Hòa Hảo militias, thus militarizing the movement as a whole.[6] This argument also makes sense for Catholics, Khmer Theravada Buddhists, the Cao Đài, and those not affiliated with a particular religious group. In the Cao Đài case, while the religious leadership in Tây Ninh managed to control most of the movement for the duration of the war, its own military forces rose in power, threatening the leadership of the Tây Ninh branch of religion as a whole. These arguments parallel a communist one: communists argued that in the early part of the war, they focused too much on military solutions, not enough on politics, and lost touch with the masses.[7]

Militarization did not simply lead to the build-up of military forces on all sides. It led to the parallel collapse of the social and political institutions of the village (like councils of notables), on the one hand, and the rise of strongmen and the common use of violence to settle disputes, on the other. In short, all sides understood the danger of militarization to the Mekong Delta, but felt obligated, for self-defense, to pursue it. In the contest for survival, belonging to a well-armed group or living under its protective umbrella, submitting to such rule, or just fleeing it trumped other concerns. The result of this constant negotiation for advantage was a "stable instability": a delta in which the dominant players were clear, but in which minor players constantly played different sides off against each other.

9.2 Strongmen Politics, 1947–1953

At first, when studying the delta in the war years, the twists and turns of Mekong Delta strongmen politics boggle the mind. Alliances form, then

---

[6] Nguyễn Long Thành Nam, *Phật Giáo Hòa Hảo trong dòng lịch sử dân tộc* (S.l.: Đuốc Từ Bi, 1991), Chapter 11. On the links among war, religious groups, and institutionalization, also see Pascal Bourdeaux, "Regards sur l'autonomisation religieuse dans le processus d'indépendance du Vietnam au milieu du vingtième siècle," *French Politics, Culture & Society* 33(2) (Summer 2015), 11–32.

[7] SHD.10 H 5442. *Tu chỉnh* (nội san khu đảng bộ S.C.). no. 1 (September 23, 1949).

Figure 9.1 Hòa Hảo militia leader Trần Văn Soái, April 14, 1955
Source: Fernand Jentile. ECPAD, Ministère de la Défense, France.
File SVN 55–26 R26.

break apart; minor strongmen rise, then fall; players switch sides, then switch again. Digging into the archives, one discovers even lesser actors who come to the attention of authorities, then disappear from view. This is not to mention groups that refused to take any side in the conflict. What was going on? To understand how this war sorted itself out at the local level, it is useful to start with two key individuals in one pole of alliance in this system, the Hòa Hảo-Cao Đài-Bình Xuyên nationalist alliance. The two major players who dominated this pole outside Saigon and Cholon were the Hòa Hảo strongman Trần Văn Soái and the Cao Đài "Protector of the Dharma" Phạm Công Tắc.

"A cunning peasant, suspicious, greedy, often indecisive, violent and authoritarian; vain, he is susceptible to flattery."[8] So a French source described Trần Văn Soái, the major Hòa Hảo warlord in the delta. Of peasant stock, he was born around 1892 in Long Xuyên province. Soái was nicknamed Năm Lửa [Five Fires], because of his hot temper, and he would go by this *nom de guerre* in the first half of the war. Toward the end of the conflict, he preferred to go by his given name, Trần Văn Soái. French sources diverge on his early occupations, saying that he collected tickets on a bus and worked as a mechanic. He had no formal schooling,

---

[8] SHD.10H 3767. Haut Commissariat de France en Indochine. Commandement des Forces Terrestres du Sud Viet Nam. Cabinet du Général. Fiche concernant le Général Tran Van Soai. Saigon, July 21, 1951.

was probably illiterate, but could sign his name.[9] Hòa Hảo leader Huỳnh Phú Sổ, to whom he was very loyal, chose him as one of his major militia leaders. Photographs frequently show Trần Văn Soái in a French-style army uniform and *képi*; with his cross between a walrus and handlebar mustache, he looked like a Vietnamese version of Pétain (surprisingly popular in the Mekong Delta during World War II).[10] In the midst of the calamities of April and May 1947, when poorly armed Hòa Hảo believers had lost their prophet and faced attack after attack by the Resistance, Trần Văn Soái was bullheaded in striking back. Quick to exploit this crisis, the French armed Trần Văn Soái in this struggle. Soái would eventually become the most pro-French of all the Hòa Hảo strongmen, and – not surprisingly – the best armed.

Trần Văn Soái left behind no writings, so we cannot get inside his mind. His followers generally respected him; for one, he was a skilled fighter. As a warlord, he had established himself in Cái Vồn, on the Hậu Giang river, one of the major branches of the Mekong River, across from the city of Cần Thơ. He controlled Cần Thơ and part of Long Xuyên, one of the most fertile parts of the Mekong Delta. In concert with his entrepreneurial wife Lê Thị Gấm, he skillfully pulled in revenue from river traffic and other sources. Soái was not too worried about the religious devotion of his military lieutenants: he was more concerned with their military prowess. He thus had on his staff Văn Phú [Lý Hồng Chương], identified in one source as an "atheist Trotskyist", who yet seems to have been an anti-Stalinist socialist.[11]

In the South, the second major figure was the Cao Đài leader Phạm Công Tắc.[12] If Trần Văn Soái, of rustic peasant stock, was quite attached to his country roots, Phạm Công Tắc had an elite background. His father was Catholic, his mother Buddhist. Born in 1890 in Tân An, at the northern edge of the Mekong Delta, he was baptized as a Catholic. Significantly, if some of the early founders of the Cao Đài religion could

---

[9] SHD. 10H 4167. Le Général de LATOUR. "Le problème Hòa Hảo" Saigon, April 26, 1948; SHD.10H 3767. Haut Commissariat de France en Indochine. Commandement des Forces Terrestres du Sud Viet Nam. Cabinet du Général. Fiche concernant le Général Tran Van Soai. Saigon, July 21, 1951.

[10] Henry-Jean Lostau was startled to see, in military operations in the Plain of Reeds, "Pétain's photograph in all the Annamite houses, on the family altar to the ancestors." Lostau, *Les Deux batallions: Cochinchine-Tonkin, 1945–1952* (Paris: Albin Michel, 1987), 34–35.

[11] SHD.10H 4167. Haute Commissariat de France en Indochine. Service de Sècurité du Haut Commissariat au Sud Vietnam. "Note No. 16027. "Activités Hòa Hảo." Saigon, September 28, 1950; "The Hòa Hảo Sect and Its Social-Democrat Party (Dang Dan Chu Xa Hoi Viet Nam)" [1972?], Folder 04, Box 06, John Donnell Collection, The Vietnam Center and Archive, Texas Tech University, www.vietnam.ttu.edu/virtualarc hive/items.php?item=0720604028 (Accessed March 5, 2021).

[12] This section relies on Jérémy Jammes, *Les oracles du Cao Đài: Étude d'un mouvement réligieux et ses réseaux* (Paris: Les Indes Savantes, 2014), Chapter 4.

boast roots in Tây Ninh province and the delta, the religion itself developed in the twin cities of Saigon and Cholon. Phạm Công Tắc himself studied in Saigon's most prestigious high school, Chasseloup-Laubat, which was attended by sons of the elite from southern Vietnam and Cambodia. (The future King Sihanouk of Cambodia, for example, attended this school.) A few other early and prominent members of the Cao Đài would go here as well. After high school, Phạm Công Tắc began work for the French administration.

Caodaism was a "new religion": that is, it was born out of multiple cultural streams ranging from Western spiritism and Chinese secret societies to Chinese salvation movements. The cosmopolitan background of its founder, Ngô Văn Chiêu, as well as some its most prominent early members, shaped its eclectic theology. Phạm Công Tắc joined the religion and quickly rose in the ranks, becoming the Chief of Mediums, then Protector of the Dharma (*Hộ Pháp*) in the 1930s. When Japan "invited" itself into French Indochina in 1940, and the Cao Đài branch in Tây Ninh met Japanese representatives, the French government reacted by exiling Phạm Công Tắc for the duration of the war. In 1946 he was still under house arrest in Ambalavo, Madagascar.[13] Over the protests of the Sûreté, he was brought back to Vietnam in return for agreeing to cooperate with France in the fight against the Việt Minh.

As Janet Hoskins has aptly stated, Phạm Công Tắc "was the figure most identified with fusing nationalist and religious teachings in Vietnam. He fashioned a modernist millenarianism," one "drawing on various 'repertoires' and fusing them into an efficacious enactment of a discourse of power."[14] All true: but the war years were a challenge to this message, as well as to Phạm Công Tắc personally. Not skilled in the arts of war, he saw the use of violence in self-defense as a necessary but disliked evil. He delegated military power to his generals, some of whom were of uncertain loyalty or honesty.

The Cao Đài of Tây Ninh from 1945 to 1947 had faced an existential crisis, as the Resistance engaged in relentless military attacks and imprisoned and executed leaders. It was in this context that Phạm Công Tắc skillfully articulated, in 1947, a new Cao Đài policy: to reconcile with the French in this time of grave troubles, while pursuing, in his words, "'the unanimous desire of the Vietnamese people for the independence

---

[13] A variety of secondary sources say that Phạm Công Tắc was held on the prison island of Nosy Lava. On Ambalavo, I rely on ANOM. HCI SPCE 360. Le Directeur de la Police et de la Sureté Fédérale en Indochine à M. le Commisssaire Fédéral aux Affaires Politiques, Saigon. "Retour de PHAM CONG TAC." Saigon, May 23, 1946.

[14] Janet Hoskins, *The Divine Eye and the Diaspora: Vietnamese Syncretism Becomes Transpacific Caodaism* (Honolulu: University of Hawai'i Press, 2015), 71, 91.

and unity of the Fatherland.'"[15] This careful calibration – reaching out to the French when needed, but insisting on Cao Đài support for independence – would characterize Phạm Công Tắc's political statements for the rest of the war.

Phạm Công Tắc mostly succeeded in keeping a fractious group of "men of violence" under his control. On the surface, his chief of staff appeared to work through a clear chain of command. Appearances deceived: his top military staff engaged in constant rivalry over military and economic matters. On more than one occasion, political differences led to the assassination of fellow high-ranking officers. Top officers also competed for access to the black market.[16] Other differences were based on principle. The charismatic colonel Trình Minh Thế, who had long opposed collaboration with either the Resistance or the French, retreated into "dissidence" in June 1951,[17] one of many crises involving military leaders that would roil the Cao Đài in the years to come. (I shall discuss the crises from 1952 onwards in Chapter 10.) The constant struggle between the religious and "civilian" leadership, on one side, and the military leadership, on the other, sapped Cao Đài religious and moral authority.

Phạm Công Tắc and Trần Văn Soái were the dominant Vietnamese figures in the delta opposing the Resistance. Minor strongmen allied with these two leaders, flirted with the Resistance, or carved out autonomous spaces for themselves. The Hòa Hảo present a particularly intriguing case of how one strongman comes to dominate over others. In May 1947, Soái was but one of several heads of armed groups in the western Mekong Delta. His signing of an agreement with the French for weapons and aid "transformed a local Chief into the Commander in Chief of Hoa Hao armed forces."[18]

This agreement with the French split the Hòa Hảo. Trần Văn Soái believed that collaboration with the French was crucial for survival. Other Hòa Hảo differed. The Hòa Hảo's political wing, the Social-Democrat Party, was hit hard. Huỳnh Phú Sổ had been developing this party before his death, and it was anti-French and pro-independence. The French, acting "as if there were no Social-Democrat Party,"[19] imprisoned its

[15] ANOM. HCI SPCE 360. Le Directeur de la Police et de la Sureté Fédéral [Berque]. Note pour Monsieur le Haute Commissaire de France pour l'Indochine. "Activités du Supérieur Caodaiste PHAM CONG TAC." Saigon, August 29, [19]47.

[16] SHD. 10 H 3762. Subfolder 1948–1950. [Declaration of Nguyen Xuan Quang, November 24, 1948.]

[17] SHD. 10 H 3762. Fiche No. 11. A/S dissidence de TRINH MINH THE. Saigon, June 13, 1951.

[18] VNA-II. PTHNV E.03–262. Province de Long Xuyên. Rapport d'ensemble. February-August 1948.

[19] Nguyễn Long Thành Nam, *Phật Giáo Hòa Hảo trong dòng lịch sử dân tộc* (S.l.: Đuốc Từ Bi, 1991), Chapter 11, Section 9, "www.hoahao.org/p74a3405/chuong-11-giai-doan-quan-su-hoa (accessed March 6, 2021).

political leaders and followers. Trần Văn Soái's collaboration with the French antagonized another Hòa Hảo warlord, the Sino-Vietnamese (*Minh Hương*) Lâm Thành Nguyên (popularly referred to as Hai Ngoán), whose base of power was in Châu Đốc and most of Long Xuyên province.[20] Importantly, he had been entrusted with the leadership of the Social-Democrat Party apparatus, an alternative source of power in the Hòa Hảo universe. The French saw the struggle between Trần Văn Soái and Lâm Thành Nguyên as "a bitter conflict of sleazy interests," in which the two clashed over control of river shipping (and presumably, revenue from it) as well as over political and military control of territory.[21] The French claim was unfair, in that running militias takes money. But the conflict was also over who should represent the legacy of Hòa Hảo Buddhism's founder. Lâm Thành Nguyên, after all, claimed to possess a letter from Huỳnh Phú Sổ entrusting the leadership of the Hòa Hảo to him.

In the end, to paper over dissension, Huỳnh Phú Sổ's father, keeper of the religious legacy of his son, anointed Trần Văn Soái the leader of the Hòa Hảo army and Lâm Thành Nguyên his deputy. This solution would not last. In April 1948, despite attempts to heal emerging rifts, Lâm Thành Nguyên broke definitively with Trần Văn Soái when he "opened fire" on forces that had come to discuss issues of Hòa Hảo unity.[22] Pushed out of parts of Long Xuyên and Châu Đốc, some of Lâm Thành Nguyên's troops reestablished themselves nearby in Sa Đéc province by September 1948.[23] But Lâm Thành Nguyên had his own Achilles heel. His "Chineseness" was perceived as a source of friction: for one, Lâm Thành Nguyên supposedly gave the monopoly of the sale of rice harvested in areas under his control to his Chinese father. One Hòa Hảo military commander serving under him supposedly said that "it is incredible that a Chinese occupies such a high position in the Hòa Hảo religion." Grumbling over these issues may have led to defections from his military forces.[24]

---

[20] SHD.10H 3767. Haut Commissariat de France en Indochine. Commandement des Forces Terrestres. Note sur les Hoa Hao. Saigon, July 25, 1951.

[21] VNA-II. PTHNV E.03–262. Province de Long Xuyên. Rapport d'ensemble. February-August 1948.

[22] VNA-II. PTHNV E.03–262. Province de Longxuyen. "Rapport d'ensemble (période de février à août 1948)."

[23] VNA-II. PTHNV Box 482 d.E.03–24. Province de Sadec. "Rapport d'ensemble (septembre 1948)."

[24] ANOM. HCI. SPCE 385. Direction des Services de Sécurité du H.C. en Indochine."Activités Hòa Hảo." June 1951. Huỳnh Phú Sổ himself expressed anti-Chinese views. See his poem "Lấy chồng Chệt" [Marrying a Chinaman] in Giáo Hội Phật Giáo Hòa Hảo, *Sấm giảng thi văn toàn bộ của Đức Huỳnh Giáo chủ* ([Saigon]: Ban Phổ Thông Giáo Lý Trung Ương, 1970), 439–440.

The rivalry, then splits, between Trần Văn Soái and Lâm Thành Nguyên opened the door to other strongmen. One was Nguyễn Giác Ngô, apparently a former political prisoner on the prison island of Poulo Condor,[25] who was dominant in part of Long Xuyên province. He too claimed that Huỳnh Phú Sổ entrusted him with leading the regular army of the Hòa Hảo.[26] Nguyễn Giác Ngộ's "reputation among the Hòa Hảo for honesty [was] legendary."[27] In July 1948, he allied with Lâm Thành Nguyên, mentioned earlier, who had just split with Trần Văn Soái.[28] While the French suspected Nguyễn Giác Ngộ of being pro-Resistance, the reality was that while he strongly opposed collaboration with the French, he counselled no attacks on the Resistance unless ordered. (In fact, fighting had broken out between some "dissident" Hòa Hảo and the Resistance when these Hòa Hảo kidnapped and then probably assassinated the Resistance leader Huỳnh An in 1948.)

A final prominent and colorful Hòa Hảo leader was Lê Quang Vinh, known as Ba Cụt, or "Third Severed Finger." The French thought of him as the "enfant terrible" of the Hòa Hảo: impulsive; mercurial; allying with, then leaving, the French; but in the end always focusing on his own interests in expanding the power of his militia.[29] He was born on the Bằng Tăng canal (near Cần Thơ, in the heart of the western Mekong Delta) in 1923 or 1925, of peasant parents. Ba Cụt was one of seven children, three of whom died; he appears to have finished primary school.[30] It is said, perhaps apocryphally, that he came to the Hòa Hảo religion on reading the works of Prophet Huỳnh Phú Sổ. Ba Cụt had also studied martial arts.[31] At one point, Huỳnh Phú Sổ's father had put him in charge of the Social-Democrat Party's armed wing.[32] Ba Cụt supposedly had three "official" wives, and nine wives total.[33]

Known for his tactical skills, Ba Cụt became famous when a bullet perforated his chest, but he survived.[34] He had a reputation for

[25] SHD. 10H 4166 Lieutenant Lacroix, Chef du 2eme Bureau, Zone de l'Ouest, *Phật giáo Hòa Hảo (Le Bouddhisme Hoa Hao)* (June 1949), 32.

[26] SHD. 10H 4144. Parti Social-Democrate. Manifeste. [October] 1949.

[27] SHD. 10H 4167. Forces Franco-Vietnamiennes du Sud. 2° Bureau. Le Général de Brigade Latour. "Objet: Situation Hòa Hảo." Saigon, July 25, 1949.

[28] VNA-II. PTHNV E.03–281. Province de Chaudoc. Rapport d'ensemble (février à juillet 1948). The author mentions a "Huynh Giac Ngo," but must mean "Nguyễn Giác Ngộ."

[29] SHD. 10H 283. Deuxième Bureau. Fiche: Objet: Le Quang Vinh dit Ba Cut. April 12, 1954.

[30] Trần Thị Hoa, *Hồi ký quân sử Nghĩa Quân Cách Mạng* (Derwood, MD: Giáo Hội Phật Giáo Hải Ngoại, 2002), 14, 29. The author was the (first?) wife of Lê Quang Vinh.

[31] Cồ Việt Từ, *Vụ án Ba Cụt* (Saigon: Nguyễn Duy Hinh, [1956]), 7–8.

[32] SHD. 10H 4167. Forces Franco-Vietnamiennes du Sud. 2° Bureau. Le Général de Brigade Latour. "Objet: Situation Hoa Hao." Saigon, July 25, 1949.

[33] Cồ Việt Từ, *Vụ án Ba Cụt*, 67, 71.   [34] Ibid., 55.

plundering.[35] Showing how misguided it is to label all anti-communist contestants in the Mekong Delta struggle as "nationalists," Cồ Việt Tử argues that "the entire aspiration" of [Ba] Cụt was simply to "control several lower Mekong Delta provinces around the region of Châu Đốc, Long Xuyên, Rạch Gía, and Cần Thơ." More comfortable with the underside of society – gangsters and toughs – than the "civilized,"[36] Ba Cụt was a local outlaw strongman. He would occasionally collaborate with Trần Văn Soái, the main Hòa Hảo warlord of the delta. But he was also "a direct rival to Trần Văn Soái"[37] and, chafing under Soái's authority, sometimes withdrew into the maquis. He would end up collaborating with the French, then defecting from them, four times.[38]

The story of Hòa Hảo politics, then, was a tangled story of alliances and defections involving all sorts of twists and turns, ones that shaped the Hòa Hảo internally as well as in relations with the Resistance and French. There is no exact Cao Đài analogue to this fractious Hòa Hảo system, as the Cao Đài had, on its face, a more hierarchically structured system of authority. As we shall later see, however, the Cao Đài, while having a formal chain of religious and military command, could nonetheless still be a vipers' nest of intrigue. Despite such internal divisions, these groups tended to unite against the Resistance.

9.3 Seeing like States or Parastates? Coercion and Economic Extraction

In the contest for the delta, one group, the southern Resistance, represented a state (the Democratic Republic of Vietnam or DRV) and had a military arm unified under one commander, General Nguyễn Bình. But it might be more accurate to say that the Resistance in the Mekong Delta successfully acted as a state for long stretches, but at other times, such as at the beginning of the war (1945–46) or in times of crisis (1951–52), broke into a collection of linked parastates. A further peculiarity of the Resistance was that several semi-autonomous groups were attached to it. Of particular interest were the forces of Cao Triều Phát, who belonged to a branch of the Cao Đài that split with the Tây Ninh branch. Cao Triều Phát controlled the Unified Cao Đài [Cao Đài Hiệp Nhứt] as well as a Resistance front organization that organized Cao Đài members fighting

---

[35] SHD. 10H 4167. Forces Franco-Vietnamiennes du Sud. 2° Bureau. Le Général de Brigade Latour. "Objet: Situation Hòa Hảo." Saigon [?], July 25, 1949.

[36] Cồ Việt Tử, *Vụ án Ba Cụt*, 73.

[37] SHD. 10 H 4167. Forces Franco-Vietnamiennes du Sud. 2° Bureau. Le Général de Brigade Latour. "Objet: Situation Hòa Hảo." Saigon [?], July 25, 1949.

[38] Cồ Việt Tử, *Vụ án Ba Cụt*, 7–8.

for the salvation of the country. Although he exercised de facto autonomy in his area of operation (Bạc Liêu and Cà Mau provinces), he was a member of the Resistance.

Two groups in the delta acted consistently as parastates – the Tây Ninh branch of the Cao Đài, and Trần Văn Soái's Hòa Hảo apparatus. They, in concert with the Resistance, came to define the parameters of rule in large chunks of the delta. What, exactly, is a parastate? Parastates controlled territories with shifting, even overlapping borders. Sometimes this territory was fragmented into pieces, but they ruled over a core population. Second, parastates had access to economic resources. Third, their armed forces enforced economic and territorial claims and coerced their local populations. Most parastates were led by strongmen or, as in the case of the Cao Đài, a "Protector of the Dharma" (Hộ Pháp) who delegated military power to his "generals." Most had a rudimentary administrative apparatus. Their limited economic base made them reliant on French aid (weapons, cash), then later Vietnamese state aid, to help support their militias. This last dependency meant that they were entwined with the French state – and various forms of the Vietnamese state after 1948 – at the same time that they practiced a great deal of autonomy. Parastates were not, however, puppets of the French or Vietnamese states: they gave only limited access to state-affiliated outsiders, except designated military liaisons and invited guests, to territory under their control. Parastates were fragile: they fissured easily, and the withdrawal of French financial support threw some of them into a tailspin. No foreign state recognized their claims. Last but not least, these parastates tried to consolidate their power after 1949 by placing their representatives in the official State of Vietnam apparatus.

If the key actors listed above shaped the western Mekong Delta from mid-1947 onwards, a few actors carved out ambiguous spaces of autonomy between the French and the Resistance. Thus, Nguyễn Giác Ngộ, a secondary Hòa Hảo warlord, called for resistance to the French "to the last drop of blood." He also warned his troops in 1949 not to be hostile to the Resistance,[39] but did not join it. Trình Minh Thế, the Cao Đài militia leader, carved out his own space between the Resistance and the French. Mention has to be made of the Khmer Issarak, which initially allied with the Resistance but prized their autonomy. Finally, the Đại Việt attempted in 1948 to set up small "neutral" or "nationalist" zones independent of the Resistance or the French.

---

[39] [Translation of document: Forces Armées Nguyen Trung Truc. Commandement Suprême. Parti Social-Democrate du Vietnam. À tous les comités de commandement et combattants des forces N.T.T. No date, but after September 9, 1949.]

9.4 Institutionalizing Coercion and Economic Extraction

To win a war, all sides in this struggle needed to be better institutionalized. The Resistance, while working hard to build up membership, still
suffered from a lack of cadres. At the beginning of the conflict, most of
these cadres came from a range of non-communist backgrounds. The
main Cao Đài grouping, based in Tây Ninh, was governed through
a formal hierarchy, but one riven with tensions. It strived to build up
and control its military forces while avoiding schisms. The fractious Hòa
Hảo were the least institutionalized of any of the major contestants for
power, boasting numerous splinter groups. The Khmer, though sharing
a common ethnicity and attachment to their temples, were equally fragmented. Some Catholics organized into self-defense militias; others simply remained under parishes. The French controlled the main towns and
cities and a limited amount of the countryside. Such was the situation that
all the non-French contestants faced in 1947.

By 1953, Yves Gras estimated that 300,000 Vietnamese were deployed
in armed forces arrayed against the Resistance throughout Vietnam.[40]
Perhaps a third of these were stationed in the South. Regular soldiers
aside, I estimate that by 1953, the French and their Vietnamese allies had
over 50,000 in paramilitary, police, "commando," plantation guard, and
self-defense units in the South. Almost 35,000[41] of these were not under
direct French or Vietnamese command. Such numbers do not capture the
extent to which society had become militarized. A 1954 "accounting"
underlines this point. It set *potential* Cao Đài military strength alone at
over 64,000: over 16,000 on active duty, nearly 18,000 in reserves, and
a further 30,000 "available" [*disponible*] for military service if necessary.[42]
The Cao Đài, then, had a military "footprint" in the Mekong Delta four
times greater than the numbers of persons on active duty. Applying the
same ratio to all other paramilitary forces, we can surmise that over
120,000 in the delta were either mobilized, on reserve, or ready for call-
up as irregular forces. These individuals, whose service affected their
families, were all linked to a broader economy dominated, in their particular home regions, by militarized states, parastates, militias, and local
self-defense forces.

---

[40] Yves Gras, *Histoire de la guerre d'Indochine*, cited in François Guillemot, "'Be Men!'
Fighting and Dying for the State of Vietnam (1951–54)," *War and Society* 31(2)
(August 2012), 195.

[41] SHD. 10 3787, "Situation des effectifs des forces paramilitaires et des collectivités
armées." July 20, 1953; SHD. 10 H 3787, "État Global des Forces Paramilitaires Pour
le Sud-Vietnam à la date du 1er Septembre 1954."

[42] SHD. 10 4139. A.M. Savani, "Notes sur le Caodaisme du 1er Juin 1952 au 1er Juin
1954," 28.

While not bluntly stated in archival sources, it is obvious to anyone who examines the evidence closely that the French continued, throughout the war, to shape allegiances by offering benefits to those they preferred and withholding aid to those they did not. In 1951, for example, the French paid the salaries of one-third of all Hòa Hảo soldiers,[43] favoring those under Trần Văn Soái and Ba Cụt and neglecting the others.

By 1953, over 18,000 Hòa Hảo served in militias, with Trần Văn Soái's soldiers making up nearly two-thirds of all Hòa Hảo militia members.[44] The funding picture becomes even more complicated, as both the Vietnamese state and the French military doled out money to different warlords. Once again, Trần Văn Soái was the greatest beneficiary. But in this jerry-rigged system, nothing was simple: Nguyễn Giác Ngộ may not have received *salary* support, but did get a flat payment of 300,000 piastres a month.[45]

As the brutality of 1947 receded into the past, all sides adopted pragmatic policies on conflict. By 1949, the Cao Đài moved towards establishing a modus vivendi with the Resistance. Collaboration of the Tây Ninh sect with the French decreased in 1949, and on March 8, 1949 (the date of the France's signature of the "independence" treaty with the State of Vietnam), "Cao Đài followers stopped all acts of hostility towards the rebels," and showed possible signs of collusion (such as unconfirmed

Table 9.1 *Hòa Hảo forces as of June 1, 1951*

Commander	Soldiers paid by French	Total number of soldiers	Weapons	Posts	Towers
Trần Văn Soái	3,183	6,829	5,021	262	33
Lâm Thành Nguyên	323	2,992	1,184	51	70
Ba Gà Mỗ	180	250	246	30	0
Nguyễn Giác Ngộ		2,100	405	26	5
Ba Cụt	530	618	519	16	1
Total	4,216	12,789	7,375	385	109

Source: SHD. 10H 4166. Lieutenant Lacroix, *Phật giáo Hòa Hảo/Bouddhisme de Hòa Hảo* (June 1951), 62.

[43] SHD. 10H 4166. Lieutenant Lacroix, *Phật giáo Hòa Hảo/Bouddhisme de Hòa Hảo* (June 1951), 62.
[44] French estimates of Hòa Hảo strength fluctuate. Given that Lacroix was the head of military intelligence in the western Mekong Delta at the time he wrote the report, his detailed numbers for 1951 seem most authoritative.
[45] SHD. 10 H 283. "Tableau d'éffectifs et d'armement des Forces Hòa Hảo." June 1, 1953.

reports of selling weapons to the Resistance).[46] As with the alliance with the French, Cao Đài "accommodations" with the Resistance were localized and tactical. The Cao Đài had few illusions about Resistance aims. The Resistance, in turn, fretted that the Cao Đài aimed "to preserve and expand their economic base, to take away our agricultural resources in the region, and to use Cao Đài military forces to support Buddhism in the expansion of the religious movement."[47]

Given the killing of their prophet Huỳnh Phú Sổ, most Hòa Hảo refused to collaborate actively with the Resistance. Nonetheless, those living in areas controlled by the Resistance acquiesced to Resistance rule. And as time passed, more of them made small accommodations to local Resistance forces. Thus in 1952 the Châu Đốc province chief noted that while politico-religious groups were, in general, "observing a proper attitude towards the provincial administration," there were exceptions. One Hòa Hảo unit agreed to a "non-aggression" pact with a local Resistance unit, and another agreed to share intelligence.[48] While the Cao Đài and Hòa Hảo maintained a tight grip on their territories, the character of violence shifted. In a few provinces, such as Long Xuyên or Tây Ninh, conflicts were more likely to be among Hòa Hảo or among Cao Đài. Disputes over the edges of militia control were common.

With the exception of the large battles of 1950 and 1951, conflicts often flared up over very local issues. Often the problem was not the Resistance, but supposed allies. Peasants repeatedly complained about exactions. In 1952, a village chief angrily complained about the French stealing ducks from his village and added, referring to the fact that Vietnam was now "independent": "it's 1952, and the French army mistakenly thinks it is still 1948 or 1949!"[49] Minor tiffs could blow up because of bad blood from past conflicts. Take, for example, a ruckus over a water buffalo, belonging to a Hòa Hảo follower, that wandered into a Catholic peasant's rice paddy in August 1953. When summoned to the local paramilitary post to resolve the dispute, the water buffalo owner refused to appear, saying that soldiers had threatened him. Armed and unarmed groups then gathered, the soldiers at the post got scared, someone fired a shot, and a water buffalo was wounded. Alerted by Catholics living in the area,

[46] ANOM. HCI. SPCE 360. Le Directeur de la Police et de la Sûreté Fédérale [Perrier]. Note à Monsieur le Conseiller Politique à Saigon. "Attitude des Caodaistes de TAYNINH à l'égard des rebelles." Saigon, March 19, 1949.

[47] SHD. 10H 4207. Nguyen Truc, Truong Ty Cong An Tay Ninh, "Bao cao tinh hinh Fat giao o Huyen Chau thanh Tinh Tayninh." April 1, 1951. [no diacritics]

[48] VNA-II. PTHNV E.03–176. Province de Chaudoc. Rapport d'ensemble du mois de décembre 1952.

[49] SHD. 10 H 4872. [Letter from the village chief of Long Kiến, beginning "Kính Ngài Quận Trưởng Chợ mới." June 4, 1952.]

a lieutenant arrived and calmed everyone down, but it was an "fragile peace."[50] In the western Mekong Delta, after all, Catholic villagers often felt besieged by the numerically superior Hòa Hảo, "living under a regime of plunder, oppression, and destruction of all kinds" which had included massacres at the hands of the Hòa Hảo in 1947.[51]

The anecdotes above are suggestive, but we lack reliable statistics on violence carried out by French confessional allies. The Cao Đài, for example, did not share information on their violence against internal enemies. And a report on the Hòa Hảo in Long Xuyên province for six months of 1948 stated that they committed sixteen acts of "terrorism" (apparently assassinations), forty-four kidnappings, at least twenty-one acts of arson, and three attacks on government posts. The report added, however, that these facts, "the only ones that have come to our attention, are most certainly only a small percentage of the acts of piracy, kidnapping, and assassination committed in this period."[52]

9.5 Economics of Parastates

The Resistance and their Franco-Vietnamese coalition of opponents struggled to control economic resources. The French aimed to starve the Resistance of the food and revenue needed to support troops and buy weapons. In so doing, they undermined and helped to defeat the Resistance. The Resistance fought such attempts bitterly. In the middle were France's Vietnamese allies. They received some funding and weapons from the French to arm militias and self-defense forces. Because this funding was inadequate, they raised revenue to cover the costs of most of their soldiers. The story of the period from 1947 to 1954 is that the French, their allied parastates, and the rising Vietnamese state gradually wrested control of the Mekong Delta economy from the Resistance. But how did the parastates and their satellites raise revenue and finance themselves? "It is a great exaggeration to claim that Hòa Hảo officers are recruited from among highway robbers," Battalion Commander Fournier wrote in 1948. Nonetheless, while praising their war-fighting ability, he admitted that some minor Hòa Hảo figures were involved in rackets and extortion, and that the French had sent some to the Poulo

---

[50] SHD. 10 H 4872. Compte-rendu du Chef de Bataillion Jourdan, Commandant du Sous-Secteur de Longxuyen, concernant les incidents du 1er Août 1953 à Cu Lao Tay."

[51] SHD.10 H 4466. François Phiên, Saigon, to General Chanson. January 21, 1950; Cao Văn Việt [et al.] to General of the Franco-Vietnamese Forces. Cái Đầm, November 29, 1949.

[52] VNA-II. PTHNV E.03 262. Province de Longxuyen. Rapport d'ensemble (période de fevrier à août 1948).

Condor prison island.[53] Such conflicted comments were frequently found in French sources on the Hòa Hảo and Unités Mobiles de Défense de la Chrétienté (UMDC), and less so with the Cao Đài.

Raising revenue depended on a range of economic activities. At the beginning of the First Indochina War, the Mekong Delta was in economic crisis. Rice production dropped precipitously, as did rice exports. Landless laborers were thrown out of work. Inhabitants were forced back to the subsistence level. Contesting groups struggled to arm themselves, attract fighters to their cause, and – when possible – defend the population. This was a poor person's war. Over time, these ragtag groups expanded their access to economic resources. As French military spending took off after 1948, and particularly after 1950 when the United States provided aid, resources trickled down to parastates and smaller militias.

From 1947 onwards, the French military armed and supported the Hòa Hảo, Cao Đài, UMDC, and armed self-defense forces. Not all militias had equally good sources of alternative revenue. The Hòa Hảo leader Trần Văn Soái, for example, sitting astride a major branch of the Mekong River, could exact taxes from merchants coming down the river as well as from the fertile rice lands under their control. Those removed from major waterways or the "rice basket," like the Cao Đài of Tây Ninh, relied on a different mix of revenue to support their parastate.

The French supplemented such revenue while playing favorites with their aid. Of the soldiers under Hòa Hảo command in 1951, 60 percent received some financial support from the French.[54] The French clearly preferred the Hòa Hảo warlord Trần Văn Soái and allocated him a disproportionate share of weapons and aid. Sometimes the French military awarded extra aid in extraordinary circumstances – thus, in 1953, after the Hòa Hảo leader Nguyễn Giác Ngộ requested 550,000 piastres, they transferred 200,000 piastres to the Nguyễn Trung Trực brigades, supplementing 200,000 from the South Vietnamese government.[55]

A look at two examples – one Cao Đài, one Hòa Hảo – shows how parastate financing operated in practice. The Cao Đài centered in Tây

---

[53] Troupes Françaises en Indochine du Sud. Mission de Liaison auprès des forces Hoa Hao. Le Chef de Bataillon FOURNIER. Rapport sur le Bulletin de renseignements nr. 4.879 des T.F.I.S. en date du 21 août 1948. September 11, 1948.

[54] Source: SHD.10H 3767. HCI. Commandement des Forces Terrestres du Sud Viet Nam. Cabinet du Général. Fiche concernant le Général Tran Van Soai. Saigon, July 21, 1951.

[55] SHD.10 H 4782. Nguyen Giac Ngo, Commandant des Forces armées Nguyen Trung Truc à Monsieur le Général Bondis, May 7, 1953; Le Colonel Noblet, Commandant de la Zone Ouest, à Monsieur le Général, Commandant les Forces Terrestres du Sud-Vietnam, June 19, 1953.

Ninh relied on a combination of dues from followers, support from the Vietnamese state, skimming a portion of French-supplied soldiers' pay for state needs, and commerce.[56] The soldiers themselves relied, in part, on "living off the land," such as stealing chicken and ducks from peasants while on patrols. While the Cao Đài claimed to not extort money from anyone, they did press individuals to make "voluntary donations." This source was grossly inadequate, and the Cao Đài Holy See's budget was in "precarious" shape. After the French slowly began transferring control of the central state apparatus to the Vietnamese from 1950 onwards, the Cao Đài increasingly relied on state support. This aid was "allocated in a more or less disguised manner, such as on an important event or for a political service... and sometimes conveyed indirectly, such as an export license, easy to cash in among the rich Chinese merchants of Cholon, as well as with taxes and assessed fees in areas controlled by the Cao Đài."[57]

Were such payments a sign of increasing Vietnamese state control over the Cao Đài? No: they show the opposite. The Cao Đài, like its fellow parastates, was trying to capture a weak Vietnamese state after 1949 by putting its own leaders in state positions, and thus gaining access to resources. Many of these actions kept "the appearance of legality." The Cao Đài also relied heavily, as earlier noted, on French payments (and the supply of weapons) to support the paramilitary soldiers. These payments had begun in 1947. By December 1952, one source estimated, "over one half" of the 1,250,000 piastres a month that the French allocated for Cao Đài paramilitary salaries was siphoned off to the Cao Đài administration.[58] By the 1950s, the Cao Đài was also investing in companies, such as "a flour mill, timber harvesting, a sawmill, farming loans, the manufacture of bricks and tiles, and a pickling/brining operation."[59]

Like the Cao Đài, Hòa Hảo warlords patched together a mix of sources of revenue. Around harvest time, the different Hòa Hảo groups all tried to impose taxes on rice. They menaced cultivators that only the militias could sell the grain, and to drive the threat home, they burned stacks of rice and put out booby traps armed with grenades. They used similar tactics on fishing boats.[60] Lê Thị Gấm, wife of warlord Trần Văn Soái, was in charge of the Hòa Hảo Red Cross.[61] She quickly expanded the Red Cross, turning it into a "donation" machine with around 100 revenue

---

[56] The following section on the Cao Đài economy relies heavily on 10 H 4199. *Notes sur le Caodaisme du 1er Juin 1952 au 1er Juin 1954*, 39–40.

[57] SHD. 10 H 4199. *Notes sur le Caodaisme du 1er Juin 1952 au 1er Juin 1954*, 40.

[58] Ibid.   [59] Ibid., 41.

[60] VNA-II. PTHNV E.03–294. Province de Longxuyen. "Rapport d'ensemble." January 1952.

[61] SHD. 10 H 4176. Forces Franco-Vietnamiennes Sud. Mission de Liaison Auprès des Forces Hòa Hảo. "A/S de l'organisation des taxes sur les transports et les marchandises

agents collecting in the western Mekong Delta and as far away as Saigon. In Cần Thơ, for example, cars on the main streets would have to pay a "donation" for parking privileges. Taxes were also levied on cars going in and out of Cái Vồn, where Trần Văn Soái had his headquarters. Trucks carrying rice or fish to Saigon were charged 300 piastres; pigs, 400. Certain companies known to the Hòa Hảo paid a flat rate per truck every month.

Smaller Hòa Hảo militias used similar methods in areas under their control. Thus, Ba Cụt's militia, the Nghĩa Quân Cách Mạng, extracted 500 piastres for buses passing through its territories, with an extra payment for those carrying fish or cloth. They also collected thirty piastres a month from each home, and fifty piastres from each shop, according to one account.[62] Ba Cụt's militia intimidated landlords and government officials to pay 10,000 to 50,000 piastres, and attacked vehicles to shake down drivers and passengers for money.[63] Whether we see such payments as "voluntary contributions," "taxes," or "exactions" depends on one's viewpoint. To the French, then the Vietnamese state, Hòa Hảo were notorious for irregular exactions on the populace. Some Vietnamese agreed: a typical complaint from a Christian part of Châu Đốc stated that the Hòa Hảo had abused the population and "stolen goods, and required the donation of ducks, pigs, cows, eggs, and so on..."[64] Needless to say, some of these "exactions," while unwelcome, were a routine way for soldiers to get food.

9.6 The Complexities of Territorial Control

Maps of contestant control in the Mekong Delta during the war usually fail to capture the complexity of de facto sovereignty. The war splintered the delta into discrete as well as overlapping parts. As General Trần Văn Trà would later write, it was "a battlefield where 'canals sliced up [the terrain] like a checkerboard.'"[65] Christopher Goscha has written of the DRV's "archipelago state," one that was like a series of

---

dans le zone Hòa Hảo de Caivon." Saigon, October 24, 1953. Secret. The rest of this paragraph draws from this source.

[62] SHD. 10 H 4681. Folder F 499. Interrogatoire du 18 Avril 1954. Déclaration de NGUYEN VAN XU.

[63] SHD. 10 H 283. Deuxième Bureau. Fiche: Objet: Le Quang Vinh dit Ba Cut. April 12, 1954.

[64] SHD. 10 H 4176. Attitude hostile des Hòa Hảo à l'égard des Catholiques. Copie de la lettre du curé BINH de BEN SIEU, île de CU LAO TAY. August 11, 1947.

[65] Trần Văn Trà, *Miền nam thành đồng đi trước về sau* (Hanoi: Quân đội nhân dân, 2006), 186.

"islands" scattered across the "sea."[66] France initially occupied what looked like a series of ink-spots on the map: the cities and large towns of the delta. It expanded control outwards along roads over time. The Resistance initially occupied large zones; over time, these increasingly shrank to the periphery of the delta. Two key parastates dominated particular zones: the Cao Đài was strong in Tây Ninh province and the eastern Mekong Delta, but its forces also spilled into the western Mekong Delta. The Hòa Hảo, under warlord Trần Văn Soái, dominated much of the western Mekong Delta, the rice basket of the South. "In between" these parastates, smaller Hòa Hảo, Catholic UMDC, and Cao Đài militias carved out fragile, shifting, and overlapping pockets of control.

Local control was nested within a larger mosaic of armed conflicts. Frontiers between zones of control, and even *internal* zones of control, were constantly shifting. The struggle in one province, or even one part of a province, could differ quite radically from that in the adjoining province. For example, in Trà Vinh province the ethnic cleavage between Khmer and Vietnamese dominated politics and war, whereas in Long Xuyên province (much more heavily Vietnamese), divisions were marked along political and religious lines. In fact, in some provinces, like Long Xuyên, contestants not only controlled discrete territories, but also shared in de facto sovereignty over villages with one or two other contestants. The Mekong Delta, then, was mottled, with a wealth of different power centers whose roughly defined frontiers expanded and contracted with the fortunes of war. Some areas, with no residents, were "dead zones." Groups and individuals flowed back and forth across the essentially meaningless border between today's Cambodia and Vietnam.

Complicating territorial issues were religious ones. Spiritually potent places are found on both sides of the Cambodian-Vietnamese border. The Seven Mountains on this border has been a religiously potent area since at least the nineteenth century. Believers consider it to be "a sacred and mysterious place."[67] Huỳnh Phú Sổ, the Hòa Hảo prophet, was born nearby. The Cao Đài Holy See, technically out of the delta in Tây Ninh (and also near the Cambodian border), is another site of religious power. Last but not least, individuals from the Mekong Delta travelled to religiously potent places in Cambodia proper, including close areas such as Bokor Mountain as well as those far away, like Phnom Bakheng and

---

[66] Christopher E. Goscha, *Vietnam: Un Etat né de la guerre* (Paris: Armand Colin, 2013), 63, 64.
[67] Dật Sĩ and Nguyễn Văn Hầu, *Thất Sơn Mầu Nhiệm* (Saigon: s.n., 1972 [1955]), [i].

Phnom Krom outside of Siem Reap.[68] These sites of religious power shaped the contestation of parastates and militias.

Published and unpublished maps have a hard time capturing the fragmented and interpenetrating character of rule. Perhaps the best way to drive home the micropolitics of rivalry and alliance is to look at Long Xuyên, the most politically complicated province in southern Vietnam. At the end of 1951, the province was littered with 264 military posts and towers, staffed by 6,778 regular, paramilitary, police, and self-defense forces, representing various Hòa Hảo, Catholic, Cao Đài, Khmer, police, communal, and Vietnamese regular and auxiliary army units.[69] The Resistance also had a slight presence. Armed groups took over temples, communal houses, and churches; were located at bridges and intersections; or simply built their own fortified towers, posts, or encampments. The map below is one stab at representing this complexity.

The map shows a province with three broad "assemblages" of village rule: single militia dominance; rule fractured among two or three militias; and rule split between the government ("admin") and one or two militias.[70] In the first grouping, twenty-five villages were each under the control of one militia or parastate. Here, the "legitimate" government ruling from Saigon made claims to sovereign power, but actually had little: it had to "accommodate itself" to the dominant militia or parastate, or "submit completely" to its whims. "Some of these groups did not even want to establish communal councils, even if they could nominate the members."

In the second grouping, represented by twelve villages, the "legitimate" government failed to exert any authority at all. Here, two or even three different militias jockeyed for power. In this context, any government attempt to reach out and ally with a particular militia ran the risk of turning the other militias into enemies: "notables did not dare rely on a single grouping, for fear of being treated with bias and becoming the object of reprisals by the others." There was a twist to this complexity: because the UMDC and Cao Đài were weak in this province, which was dominated by Hòa Hảo believers, their armed militias tended to cause few problems for the dominant powers.

It was only in the third grouping, where rule was split between the "legitimate" government and a militia or parastate, that the Saigon-based

[68] NAC. RSC 4182. [Copy of Letter to Monsieur le Résident Supérieur de la République Française au Cambodge]. September 8, 1914.

[69] I calculated these statistics from the detailed listings in SHD. 10 H 4515. Plan de stationnement détaillé. Secteur de Longxuyen. 1951.

[70] VNA-II. PTHNV E.03–187. Province de Longxuyen. Rapport d'ensemble. Mois de février 1953. This and the next two paragraphs rely heavily on this source.

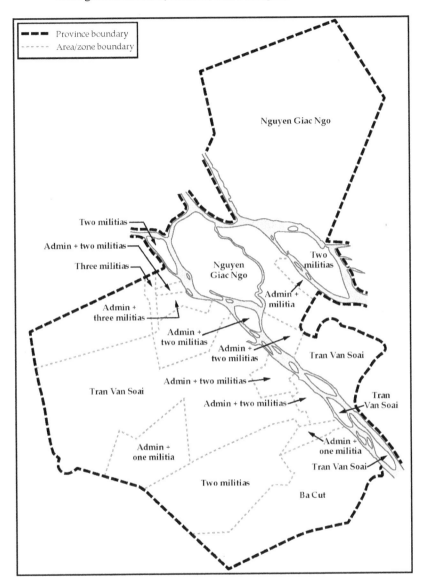

Figure 9.2 Complexities of control in Long Xuyên province, 1953
Source: Chris Robinson, 2020. Based on PTHNV E03-187. Province
de Longxuyen. "Rapport d'ensemble." Mois de fevrier 1953.

government exerted much influence. Here the administration had managed to implant itself in the villages. The apparatus of rule (e.g., administrators and police chiefs) offered protections to councils of notables, "who managed to obtain rather good results." Nonetheless, militias and the Trần Văn Soái parastate were "constantly and deliberately nibbling at" and "encroaching" on this authority.

Yet even the map above, so revelatory about the complexity of de facto sovereignty, is deceptive. Power in civil war is in the hands of those who

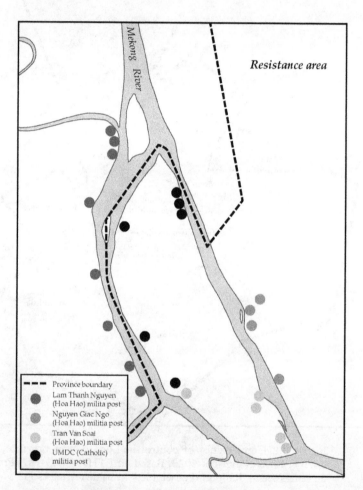

Figure 9.3 Intermingled posts, Long Xuyên/Châu Đốc provinces, 1952
Source: Chris Robinson, 2020. Based on 1952 map in Service Historique de la Défense 10 H 4466.

possess the power to kill. And here, the actual patterning of military posts and towers is key. Figure 9.3 shows the intermingling of posts, and thus of coercive force, across the landscape.

Of course, the location of posts does not always indicate the origins of villagers manning the posts. Self-defense forces lived in the villages they were defending. What about the parastates and militias allied with the French? Fragments of information suggest that recruitment was highly localized. The figure below, based on rosters of his soldiers and their villages of origin, illustrates that militia leader Ba Cụt recruited from sixty-five villages and hamlets, mostly clustered between the cities of Cần Thơ and Long Xuyên, but only eighteen of these provided

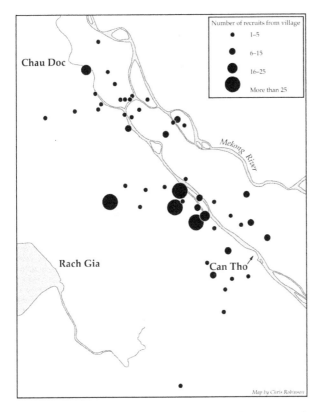

Figure 9.4 Village origin of Ba Cut's soldiers, 1953 Source: Chris Robinson, 2020. Based on 1953 data in Service Historique de la Défense 10 H 4872.

three-quarters of all recruits.[71] Village ties shaped the militia more deeply than ideology.

9.7 Conclusion

From examining in depth the role of parastates and militias, and the ways they shared control of the delta, we can conclude that the war for the Mekong Delta was truly a local series of wars, tightly linked to particular villages, in which sovereignty at the local level was often highly contested among multiple actors. These actors evolved over time: parastates, and the militias that aspired to become them, were fragile entities, prone to instability and fissures. From 1947 to 1953, external attacks and internal rivalries threatened parastate cohesion. At the same time, the complex interdependence between France, the parastates, and their satellite militias acted as a stabilizing force. These entities – all of which supported the independence of Vietnam – had come to depend unduly on the French, who provided financial support for their armed forces, gave them weapons, and took their side against the previously feckless Vietnamese state. This situation began to change after 1949 with the slow expansion of the Vietnamese state and the national army, and the French realization, by 1953, that the endgame of the war was fast arriving.

---

[71] SHD. 10 H 4872. Le Chef de Bataillon DORIN Commandant le Sous-Secteur de LONGXUYEN. A/S de la désertion du Groupement H.H./ N.Q.C.M. dans la nuit du 25 au 26–4-53.

Part III

Endgame, 1953–1956

10 The Twilight of Empire and the Strange Birth of South Vietnam

The crumbling of empires and the rise of new nation-states was, of course, one of the fundamental global transformations of the twentieth century. The First Indochina War from 1945 to 1954 has become an icon of a successful revolutionary nationalist struggle. In the usual narration, the Democratic Republic of Vietnam (DRV) and its army, confronting France, consolidated control over the upper two-thirds of Vietnam, built its mass base, and then expanded dramatically its state and military capacities. After an arduous struggle, the war came to a head in the battle of Điện Biên Phủ, where the People's Army of Vietnam defeated the French military on May 7, 1954. The DRV victory shows that communists, relying on "people's war," outsmarted the French in their protracted struggle. The legacy of this war reverberated beyond its place and time: as a model for revolutionary movements across the world, in the use of counterinsurgency in the Algerian War and the Second Indochina War (1960–75), and the subsequent Cambodian mass killings from execution and starvation under the Khmer Rouge (1975–79). It also, however, served as a signpost of Cold War conflicts.

This book fits awkwardly into this story. The arc of war in the South, and the Mekong Delta in particular, differed sharply from the North or Center. At one level, then, this book simply narrates a different story of a conflict fought according to competing political and military strategies. The war in the South, particularly after 1947, was a civil war wrapped up in a struggle for independence, one in which the non-communist contestants were relatively strong. The Resistance, misreading this situation, tried to force rivals to bend to their will. As this book has argued, the "double fracture" of 1947 reshaped the politics of the South, increased ethnic antagonisms, and weakened the Resistance.

The French threw their support behind a hodge-podge of anti-communist "nationalists" aligned against a communist-led Resistance. The Resistance then regrouped, refining its sophisticated strategy to win the war. Hemmed in, however, by French pacification, it prematurely shifted to conventional war, leading to great losses. The period from 1950 onwards would see the slow marginalization of Resistance forces in the delta. Despite the parallel retreat of the French state and military in the South, neither the de facto rulers of the countryside, ruling over balkanized fiefdoms, nor the rising State of Vietnam were able to assert authority over the whole of southern Vietnam. *As of 1953, the Resistance was on the road to defeat, but there was no overarching victor to the war*. Who would triumph? That question would have to be decided during the endgame of empire from 1953 onwards.

The above recapitulation of my book misses, of course, the core arguments of this book on sovereignty, violence, institutional collapse, reassemblage, and race. Sovereignty fragmented after 1945. The balkanized Mekong Delta became a laboratory for experimentation, backed by violence, in different practices of localized and fragmented sovereignty. The South also saw the continuous fracturing and recombination of institutions of control. In rural areas, violence – coming from on high or welling up from below – polarized allegiances and deeply shaped the nature of rule. The use of racialized rhetoric in this context only hardened boundaries between contesting groups. Violence drove a massive migration out of the delta of perhaps half a million persons, which drained many rural areas and bloated provincial cities, Phnom Penh, and Saigon. In the delta, civilian authority was weak, often replaced by either a militarized Resistance or strongmen at the heads of parastates and militias. By 1953, the "traditional" institutions of the village had, in large swaths of the delta, been destroyed, replaced by a patchwork of practices that "worked" in times of war but were not suitable in a time of peace. Seen in this light, the endgame of war would decide how to transition from war to peace, rework sovereignty claims, attenuate the impact of violence on local communities, and build new institutions. It would also decide who, exactly, would "win" the contest to rule the South.

With the 1954 victory of the DRV at Điện Biên Phủ, France resigned itself to withdrawing from Indochina. Two weeks later, on May 19, France renounced its 1947 agreements offering financial support and armaments to the Cao Đài.[1] It would later proceed to disarm all village self-defense forces, including the Khmer Krom ones.[2] (France would

---

[1] SHD. 10H 3787. Commissariat Général de la France en Indochine. Fiche concernant les rapports du Commandement Français avec les Sectes Confessionelles du Sud-Vietnam. Saigon, January 22, 1955.

[2] SHD. 10 H 4681. Sub-folder F 499. [Handwritten letter from village notables, Phu ly, My Thuan, Caivon to the Colonel Commandant de la Zone Ouest, Cantho. September 14, 1954.] The colonel jotted on this plea for arms that the Geneva Accords required all self-defense forces to be disarmed.

wait until 1955 to cut off all their aid to the Hòa Hảo.[3]) On June 4, 1954, well before the conclusion of the Geneva negotiations, France signed with the State of Vietnam (i.e., the DRV's opponent) a treaty conferring full independence on Vietnam. France "recognized Vietnam to be a State fully sovereign and independent, invested with all the powers conferred by international law."[4] France and the DRV, under international pressure, agreed at Geneva to divide Vietnam *temporarily* at the Seventeenth Parallel, with the State of Vietnam occupying the South and the DRV the North. The Accords provided for elections in 1956 to unite the country. Following the provisions of the Accords, an estimated 80,000–90,000 persons from all over the South (and some Vietnamese from Cambodia) traveled to three designated regroupment zones, then left for the North. Roughly a third of them, or 27,962, were communist party cadres and soldiers; 13,327 Party cadres, military leaders, and soldiers in four regiments came from the Mekong Delta in particular. A "not small number of relatives" and assorted others also made the trip.[5] Many cadres and soldiers, of course, stayed behind.

Scholars examining the Geneva negotiations often mention a puzzle: why did the DRV agree to divide the country, even temporarily, at the Seventeenth Parallel? Writers have argued, for example, that the Chinese pressured or strongly encouraged the Vietnamese in the DRV delegation to accept partition[6], and this move was met with dismay from the DRV negotiators. Logevall suggests that acceptance of division at the Sixteenth

---

[3] SHD. 10H 3787. Commissariat Général de la France en Indochine. Fiche concernant les rapports du Commandement Français avec les Sectes Confessionelles du Sud-Vietnam. Saigon, January 22, 1955.

[4] "Traité d'indépendance du Vietnam signé à Paris." June 4, 1954. The treaty, initialed by Prime Minister Laniel of France and Prime Minister Bửu Lộc, was not signed by the presidents of both sides. Nonetheless, it shows clear French intent before the conclusion of the Geneva negotiations. Documentation française, articles et documents, n° 67, June 15, 1954; R.G.T.F., 1ère série, Vol. VI, n° 23, 53. Online at https://basedoc .diplomatie.gouv.fr/exl-php/util/documents/accede_document.php?1597514530000 (accessed August 15, 2020).

[5] For the estimate of total numbers who went north, see Christopher E. Goscha, "Regrouping to The North (Tập Kết Ra Bắc)" in *The Indochina War 1945–1956: An Interdisciplinary Tool* (Copenhagen and Honolulu: NIAS/Hawai'i, 2011), https://indo chine.uqam.ca/en/historical-dictionary.html. See also "Giới thiệu tài liệu lưu trữ về sự kiện tập kết chuyển quân ra bắc," *Nhân Dân*, October 8, 2018, https://nhandan.com.vn /tin-tuc-su-kien/gioi-thieu-tai-lieu-luu-tru-ve-su-kien-tap-ket-chuyen-quan-ra-bac-3373 56 (accessed March 6, 2018).

[6] For a sympathetic view of the Chinese pressure argument, see Qiang Zhai, "China and the Geneva Conference of 1954," *The China Quarterly* 129 (March 1992), 112–113. For a riveting, personality-focused account that integrates some Vietnamese perspectives into analysis of Geneva, see Frederik Logevall, *Embers of War: The Fall of an Empire and the Making of America's Vietnam* (New York: Random House, 2014), Chapter 23. Christopher E. Goscha, *Vietnam. Un état né de la guerre* (Paris: Armand Colin, 2013), 407–419, is excellent. Analytically convincing is Pierre Asselin, "The Democratic

Parallel, a slightly more southern line, may have been "the real Viet Minh objective all along."[7] (French diplomats had been debating partition as a solution to the conflict for years.[8]) Another common argument is that the Geneva negotiations, focused on military matters, failed to mandate an enforceable *political* solution to division. Indeed, the State of Vietnam, not a signatory to the Geneva Accords, refused to hold the "mandated" elections in 1956. This failure, the argument goes, created the conditions for the outbreak of the Second Indochina War. The flip side of the careful attention to the climactic battle in the north, the twists and turns of the Geneva negotiations, and Saigon politics from 1954 onwards, is a general disinterest, in French, Vietnamese, and American accounts, in the topic of this book: the war for the southern countryside from 1945 to 1954. It should be obvious, however, that Resistance weakness in the South shaped both the Geneva negotiations as well as the early years of Ngô Đình Diệm's rule.

By 1953, France was haltingly recognizing that it and its allies might not defeat the Resistance, *except in southern Vietnam*, where the eventual Republic of Vietnam would emerge. As the Mekong Delta calmed down, peasants began flowing back to the countryside. Farmers brought long-abandoned areas back into cultivation. Yet the withdrawal of the French military from the Mekong Delta, obvious by 1953, and its replacement by the Vietnamese state, would give rise to new frictions. The power of the gun remained stronger than the authority of civilian government. A fundamental question remained: how would the war's endgame shape institutions and legacies long after France had left Indochina? It would make sense to assume that the main Vietnamese actors in the war for the Mekong Delta, as well as the existing power players in the southern Vietnamese state apparatus, would emerge triumphant. This failed to happen: with Ngô Đình Diệm's ascent, most of the key actors in the birth of the fully independent nation-state of South Vietnam would be the losers. Why?

10.1 Endgame: Institutional Reassemblage and Territorial Struggles

The endgame of empire and the rise of a new nation-state is not usually presented from the perspective of the inhabitants of the Mekong Delta.

Republic of Vietnam and the 1954 Geneva Conference: A Revisionist Critique," *Cold War History* 11(2) (May 2011), 155–195.

[7] Logevall, *Embers of War*, 608–609. If Vietnam had been divided at the Sixteenth Parallel, the old capital of Huế and the city of Đà Nẵng would have been included, until proposed elections in 1956, in the DRV.

[8] Denise Artaud, "La menace américaine et le règlement indochinois à la conférence de Genève," *Histoire, économie et société*, 13(1) (1994), 48–49.

The Resistance, for its part, faced trial after trial in the years from 1950 to 1953. The Communist Party in particular struggled to attract members: whereas Vietnam as a whole had over 700,000 Party members in 1952, a mere 9 percent of them, or 63,411, lived in the South.[9] This statistic is astonishing. Forced out of heavily populated areas, the Resistance took refuge in lightly populated and peripheral areas, including wetlands like the Plain of Reeds, and swampy wooded places like the U Minh Forest. Its governing apparatus was battered by internal and external challenges: "Numerous indications suggest that the V[iet] M[inh] of Nam Bộ is encountering difficulties that increase with no respite... Lacking tested leaders – lukewarm elements having being eliminated from key positions – several Executive Committees have been disbanded one after the other." Thus, in February 1953, the Executive Committee of Rạch Giá province was eliminated, as its functions were taken over by a committee overseeing multiple provinces in western Nam Bộ.[10] By March 1953, refugees from Resistance zones fleeing to Cần Thơ were reporting "economic and financial difficulties," leading to a general discouragement.[11] In Trà Vinh province, the province chief hyperbolically claimed: "it is now clear that the Resistance front in the province has completely fallen apart and, unless there is help from the outside, it will never be able to reestablish itself."[12]

Communists themselves saw the entire period from 1951 through 1953 as a great trial: "The Resistance had to overcome many difficulties and challenges. It lost land, people, and armed forces. This was partly due to the relentlessness of the enemy, its deviousness, the brutal execution of pacification, with sweeps, encroachment on territory, and the fracturing of the battlefield into smaller pieces." [13] Resistance missteps were key. In its own diagnosis, it forgot the primacy of guerrilla warfare, mistakenly concentrated armed forces, and committed serious errors in enemy-occupied areas. The Resistance attempted a comeback from the second half of 1953 onwards. The study quoted above claims that the Resistance made a remarkable turnaround, "playing an important role in the victory

---

[9] Hồ Chí Minh, *Hồ Chí Minh toàn tập: 1950–1952* (Hanoi: Chính trị quốc gia, 1995), 462; Hội Đồng Chỉ Đạo Biên Soạn Lịch Sử Nam Bộ Kháng Chiến, *Lịch sử Nam Bộ kháng chiến* (Hanoi: Chính trị quốc gia, 2010), Vol. 1, 496.

[10] VNA-II. PTHNV Box 490 Dossier E.03–178. Province de Rachgia. Rapport d'ensemble du mois de février 1953.

[11] VNA-II. PTHNV d. E.03–186. Province de Cantho. Rapport d'ensemble (mois de mars 1953).

[12] VNA-II. PTHNV d. E.03–181. Province de Travinh. Rapport d'ensemble (mois de mars 1953).

[13] *Lịch sử Nam Bộ kháng chiến*, Vol. 1, 525.

at Điện Biên Phủ."[14] In fact, the State of Vietnam was still pushing into the swamps and fields of floating rice in the Plain of Reeds, the traditional refuge for communist forces, destabilizing the Resistance.[15] The southern Resistance had become a beleaguered player in a contest defined by others.

By 1953, the *central* political struggle pitted rural parastates and militias against the rising Vietnamese state. The French military mediated among these actors. Going forward, the "solution" to ending political polarization and balkanized militia rule was unclear. Relations between the Hòa Hảo and the Tây Ninh branch of the Cao Đài, supposedly allied, began to fray once the Resistance was mostly defeated. These groups also faced their own internal conflicts, as different militias entrenched themselves in local fiefdoms. Trần Văn Soái was the dominant Hòa Hảo leader, but three other strongmen carved out spaces of autonomy, collaborated with Soái, or resisted him, as they saw fit. The French military played favorites, complicating matters further.

At first glance, the Cao Đài seem strikingly different from the Hòa Hảo. The charismatic Defender of the Dharma Phạm Công Tắc, the religious authority of the Tây Ninh branch, initially managed to rein in his military commanders. But as the war dragged on, military commanders consolidated power and defied the religious leadership, precipitating periodic crises in authority. In late 1952, the Cao Đài went through "a serious crisis, perhaps the most serious of its history,"[16] marked by assassinations of high-ranking officers and civilians. Phạm Công Tắc resolved the challenge to his authority by firing the upstart commander of the Cao Đài armed forces, General Nguyễn Văn Thành, and replacing him with Nguyễn Thành Phương. General Phương would later, as I shall discuss, precipitate an even deeper crisis within the Tây Ninh branch.[17]

The end of the war, then, was marked by great uncertainty. Just as institutional collapse and reassemblage shaped the early years of the war, they shaped the war's endgame from 1953 onwards. Three issues dominate. The first is the actual transfer of power at the central state level from

[14] *Lịch sử Nam Bộ kháng chiến*, Vol. 1, 526. Another source makes a similar argument for Trà Vinh and Vĩnh Long provinces: "From the fall of 1953, the people's movement of guerrilla war bounced back strongly after a temporary lull at the beginning of 1953." See Nguyễn Tuân Triêt and Phạm Văn Hướng, *Lịch sử tỉnh Trà Vinh* (Trà Vinh: Ban tư tưởng tỉnh uỷ Trà Vinh, 1995), Vol. 2, 171.

[15] NARA-II (College Park, MD). CIA-RDP80-00810A0035010100009-2. Central Intelligence Agency. "Activities of the Democratic Republic of Vietnam in Nambo." February 15, 1954.

[16] SHD. 10 H 4139. Commandant A.M. Savani and Lieutenant Darches, *Notes sur le Caodaisme. L'armée caodaiste* (October 1952), 68.

[17] SHD. 10 4139. A.M. Savani, "Notes sur le Caodaisme du 1er juin 1952 au 1er juin 1954," 14. [Saigon?], June 6, 1954.

France to the State of Vietnam up to 1954, and then Ngô Đình Diệm's consolidation of power into 1956. The second, no less important, is how the structure of power in the southern countryside, fashioned by Vietnamese and French contestants in a time of war, shaped this transfer. A Franco-Vietnamese "coalition" in the countryside, one in which the French played the role of dominant actor, defeated the Resistance in the South because, paradoxically, France *devolved* power to local actors like the Hòa Hảo, Cao Đài, the Unités Mobiles de Défense de la Chrétienté (UMDC), and Khmer Krom self-defense units. A third issue was the revival of religious institutions in the Mekong Delta, a development which threatened the legitimacy of strongmen acting in the name of confessional groups. We will address each of these issues in turn.

At first glance, the rising Vietnamese state may have seemed to be a weak, ineffective French "puppet." Weren't the early Prime Ministers of the State of Vietnam, like French citizen Trần Văn Hữu (1950–52), French citizen Nguyễn Văn Tâm (1952–53), and Prince Bửu Lộc (1953–54), all deferential to the French? Even the Chief of Staff of the Vietnamese armed forces, General Nguyễn Văn Hinh, was French. Many of these individuals had attended elite French schools, spent extended years abroad, and shared little with the peasants who fought the war. Unsurprisingly, historians tend to dismiss this early Vietnamese state. Their interest only perks up when France definitively loses the war in 1954 and Ngô Đình Diệm, who played no role in the conflict, assumes power.

Nonetheless, I have earlier argued that as time passed, this Vietnamese state increasingly acted independently of the French. The French civilian state shrunk after 1949 as its functions were lopped off, one by one, and handed over to the Vietnamese state. At first, French military strength masked French civilian state weakness. By 1953, however, as France grudgingly transferred more parts of its state apparatus to the Vietnamese state, the French military was downsizing in the delta. By November 1953, the French transferred all remaining police functions to the Vietnamese.

Methodically, Vietnamese bureaucrats tried to rein in French civilian power. The Vietnamese had learned well: they wielded French law like a weapon against their former masters. The Minister of Justice warned the French against "the crystallization of an emergency jurisprudence [*un régime d'exception*]" which would serve French interests, demanding instead a return to normal legal practice.[18] They pushed hard to gain

---

[18] SHD. 10 H 4681. Subfolder E 31. État du Vietnam. Ministre de la Justice [Le Tan Nam] à Monsieur le Général Bondis. Saigon, November 19, 1952.

control of all of the tools in the coercive apparatus of the state. This Vietnamese state was flexible. For example, it allowed the French military to imprison indefinitely Resistance suspects from zones not under French military or Vietnamese state control. French military tribunals had previously sentenced these individuals to fixed periods of detention.[19]

At the beginning of 1953, it may have seemed that the French and their allies had essentially defeated the Resistance in the Mekong Delta. Tết was peaceful; in Hà Tiên, the province chief stated that "inhabitants enthusiastically celebrated the Lunar New Year of the Snake which, according to local inhabitants, was the largest since 1945."[20] Similar reports came in from Cần Thơ, Vĩnh Long, and Long Xuyên provinces. Up to July 1953, the government and politico-religious groups both pushed to expand areas under their control. Efforts soon flagged: "Since this period, we have nibbled in the eastern Zone, ranging from the north of Biên Hoa to the west of Cần Thơ... Military operations to extend control practically ended after July 1953; pacification has run out of steam, then started regressing as of November; and Resistance activity has increased since December." The Vietnamese military, taking over from French units in the Mekong Delta, warned that the advances made since 1949 were now reversing.[21]

The second issue was how the structure of power in the countryside shaped the transfer of power. The rising Vietnamese state tried to turn back the last nine years of war and reestablish the traditional elite's dominance in the countryside. It gingerly inaugurated elections for village notables beginning in January 1953 in a few of the areas that had been "pacified" and turned over to its control. But only a few provinces held elections, only existing village notables could approve candidates, and most citizens could not vote. Bến Tre province led the way with ninety-four village elections involving 53,586 voters, the first in the South.[22] In south Vietnam as a whole, 4,098 candidates ran for 2,373 places. A surprising 75 percent of the former notables running won elections.

---

[19] SHD. 10 H 524. Commandant en Chef des Forces Terrestres Navales et Aeriennes. Inspection Centrale des Prisonniers and Internés Militaires. Objet Instructions relatives aux suspects arrêtés au cours d'opération et aux P.I.M. libérables de zone non-contrôlée. Saigon, December 29, 1953.

[20] VNA-II. PTHNV d. E.03–183. Province de Hatien. Rapport d'ensemble (mois de février 1953).

[21] SHD 10 H 282. État du Vietnam. Présidence du Gouvernement. État-Major Particulier. "Fiche sur les possibilités VM au Sud-Vietnam." Saigon, March 5, 1954.

[22] ANOM. HCI SPCE 28. Service de Sécurité du H.C. au S.V.N. See both "Analyse politique du scrutin." Saigon, February 17, 1953, and "Note: Elections du 25 janvier 1953."

Voters also showed some sympathy for socialists and pro-Resistance candidates.

The Vietnamese central state's key challenge was to co-opt or rein in the parastates and militias in the Mekong Delta and Tây Ninh. In late 1952, Bùi Nhung, then working for the Ministry of Modernization [*Bộ Canh Tân*], articulated the core dilemma:

In the South, we must immediately merge the "statelets" [*tiểu quốc gia*] of the Little Emperors Leroy, Ba Cụt, Bảy Viễn, Trần Văn Soái, and the larger state of Vietnam, in order to avoid [the situation] in which our compatriots, forced to reside under "statelets" in which life is filled with injustice and always full of fear, and which does not protect one's life and property, simply because the "Little Emperors" have the right of life and death in their hands. 2) [We must] request (because we would not dare require) the Commander in Chief of the French Expeditionary Forces to issue strict orders, absolutely forbidding their forces to go on sweeps against the Việt Minh, invading residential areas, pillaging villages, raping women, because in many areas the populace is a hundred times more afraid of the Expeditionary Forces than the Việt Minh.[23]

Merging what Bùi Nhung calls "statelets" was not easy. The Vietnamese state failed to push aside the de facto rulers of large chunks of the countryside. Nowhere was the challenge more acute that in Long Xuyên province, dominated by rival Hòa Hảo groups, but with a smattering of Cao Đài and Catholic militias. In 1952, the Vietnamese provincial administrator of Long Xuyên province had complained that the province, if free of the Resistance, was still a "cauldron of conflicts" in which intrigue, gangsterism, and assassination was common. The Vietnamese state stood by, impotently calling for change but failing to restore order.[24] In 1953, the province still eluded the state's grasp. As a biting evaluation put it:

the visit of high-ranking government officials, welcomed with deference by those who dictate the law [i.e., the militias linked to confessional groups] in this region, just barely reminded the population of the existence and presence of a national Government above parties and sects. Stupid incidents, due to misguided self-importance as well as habitual muddle and lack of discipline, came to the fore, showing the omnipotence of the militias who control, despite their reprehensible acts, all of the civilian and military authorities in the province.[25]

---

[23] Bùi Nhung, *Thối nát hồi ký* (Saigon: Bình Minh, 1965), 188–189. Bùi Nhung seems to have been working for the Ministry to Research Reform [*Bộ Nghiên Cứu Cải Cách*], also known as the Ministry of Modernization [*Bộ Canh Tân*].

[24] VNA-II. PTHNV E.03–294. Province de Longxuyen. Rapport d'ensemble (mois de février 1952).

[25] VNA-II. PTHNV d. E.03–187. Province de Longxuyen. Rapport d'ensemble (mois de mars 1953).

Much the same could be said about Tây Ninh province, where the Cao
Đài showed more discipline compared to their Long Xuyên compatriots.
In Tây Ninh, Cao Đài districts remained "closed" to the province chief,
who lacked the coercive muscle to enforce state rule.[26] The new
Vietnamese state struggled to assert even minimal control over much of
its claimed territory.

France remained the linchpin: it was the central node that linked all
contestants together, while keeping antagonists (like the Hòa Hảo and
Khmer) apart. The French had allies in the rural strongmen they
funded as well as in the French citizens who littered the highest
reaches of the Vietnamese state. They provided funding to contestants, supplied them with weapons, and even smoothed over disputes
among rival actors. Before mid-1953, the French military buttressed
the de facto power of the Cao Đài and Hòa Hảo, as well as the Catholic
and Khmer militias, in rural areas. If France pulled out of Vietnam
precipitously, the ruling system in rural areas would collapse. Three
possible outcomes loomed: the rural parastates and militias that dominated much of the countryside would "capture the state" and thus
expand their power; the rural parastates and their satellite militias
would fend off a weak central state and preserve their autonomy; or
the urban-based central state would consolidate power and crush its
rural rivals.

After mid-1953, the French military shifted its position. In Hòa Hảo
territories, it now "favored the implantation of the legal authority," while
advising "the most reasonable" Hòa Hảo leaders (whom it now identified
as Lâm Thành Nguyên and Nguyễn Giác Ngộ) to collaborate with the
new Vietnamese state. In return, the French military promised to support
"legitimate demands" of the Hòa Hảo.[27] The French military took
a similar attitude towards the Cao Đài. It also planned to transfer control
over the Mekong Delta to the Vietnamese state. This process began with
the thoroughly "pacified" provinces close to Saigon. But the core of the
Mekong Delta, where strongmen ruled and where confessional groups
were strongest, was tougher. The process faced a setback in 1953, when
the Vietnamese military bumbled an attempt to assassinate Trần Văn
Soái, the strongest Hòa Hảo warlord. The Hòa Hảo, getting wind of the
plot, arrested and shot the supposed assassin. Such blunders ensured that

---

[26] VNA-II. PTHNV E.03–189. Province de Tayninh. Rapport d'ensemble pour le mois de
février 1953.
[27] SHD. 10 H 283. Commandement en Chef des Forces Terrestres, [etc.]. Le Général
Commandant en Chef. Le Chef du Cabinet Militaire Farcy. Fiche au problème Hoa
Hao. June 15, 1953.

the French would delay the handover of the western Mekong Delta, originally scheduled for November 1, 1953.[28]

As the jerry-rigged system of rule in the Mekong Delta slowly collapsed, different warlords and their followers went in different directions. The Resistance struggled to claw back its influence in the Mekong Delta but had become a minor player. The Khmer Krom felt adrift: fearful of ethnic Vietnamese rule throughout the delta, their trepidation manifested itself in rumors of Khmer militia mutinies in Trà Vinh province as well as complaints from Khmer villagers in Vĩnh Long province that their self-defense weapons were being taken away from them.[29] As for the UMDC, the French relieved Jean Leroy of leadership of these Catholic militias, setting them on a path to dissolution or integration into the new Vietnamese state.

The Cao Đài of Tây Ninh and the Hòa Hảo took different paths. Cao Đài leader Phạm Công Tắc aspired to lead or shape the new Vietnamese state. He agreed to integrate some Cao Đài military units into the fledgling South Vietnamese Army while also placing Cao Đài in positions of civilian power. The Hòa Hảo militias, in contrast, were splintering: while the major militia leader Trần Văn Soái continued to consolidate authority over Hòa Hảo areas of control, less powerful militia leaders rebuffed him.

Thus, in October 1953, Long Xuyên province "went through one of the most turbulent periods it had ever known," and militia leader Ba Cụt's forces undertook "attacks on town centers, convoys, kidnappings, assassinations, robbery, [and] extortion."[30] The endgame was coming into focus, and each militia leader wanted to expand territorial control.

A challenge to strongman legitimacy and to the Vietnamese state came from an unexpected quarter: religious prophets and groups. As they reasserted themselves, they implicitly challenged the right of militia groups, generals, and bureaucrats to speak for all Vietnamese. An early example comes from 1948, when the young virtuoso Thanh Sĩ showed an ability to declaim, in rhymed poetry, for two to three hours on Buddhist topics, and attracted crowds amazed at his eloquence.[31] In the early

---

[28] SHD. 10 H 283. Fiche de renseignement. Très secret. Saigon, October 8, 1953. From textual clues, this was perhaps written by the French General in charge of French troops in the south.

[29] For example, ANOM. HCI SPCE 56. Service Français de Sécurité au Sud-Vietnam. "Projet de mutinerie des Forces Supplétives à Travinh." Saigon, July 27, [195]3; SHD GR 10 H 4681. Sub-folder F 499. [Handwritten letter from the notables of the village of Phu ly, My Thuan, Caivon to Monsieur le Colonel Commandant de la Zone Ouest, Cantho]. September 14, 1954.

[30] VNA-II. PTHNV d. E.03–187. Province de Longxuyen. Rapport d'ensemble. October 1953.

[31] Vương Kim, Tận thế và hội Long Hoa (Saigon: Long Hoa, 1953), 142–143.

1950s, religious practices, curbed by the war, seem to have come back (or at least got more reporting in the archives). In 1952, Vietnamese Theosophists and Buddhists secured a *bodhi* tree, thanks to the help of the International Theosophical Society in India. In May, in a sign of changing times, "an enormous crowd of believers," which the Province Chief in Châu Đốc estimated at 10,000 persons, gathered to witness the planting of a supposed descendant the original Bodhi tree, the one under which Gautama Buddha sat when achieving enlightenment.[32] Vietnamese were increasingly free to practice religion without interference from contestants in the war.

Nonetheless, spasms of violence interrupted the peace. For Hòa Hảo warlords like Trần Văn Soái, the absence of their founder Huỳnh Phú Sổ, assassinated by the Việt Minh in 1947, had left a void of religious leadership but had also provided opportunity. Now, as peace was returning to some parts of the delta, some residents were turning to new religious leaders and prophets. Some strongmen replied to this challenge by using the only language they knew fluently: the language of violence.[33] On the night of March 19, 1954, gunmen burst in to the Thành Hoa temple in Long Xuyên province, pulled out a submachine gun, and killed the widely popular "Reclining Monk," ông Đạo Nằm. Some followers thought that he was an incarnation of Maitreya, the future Buddha, who had come to earth to save the world. In 1953, he had expanded his temple, and thousands were coming to hear him speak. The most logical explanation for his assassination is that Trần Văn Soái saw the monk as a threat to his and the Hòa Hảo's authority.

Less than a month later, Hòa Hảo militia members halted three cars carrying monks and lay followers from the Mendicant branch [*Khất sĩ*] of Buddhism, including their founder, Minh Đăng Quang. The militia members brought them to Cái Vồn, headquarters of parastate leader Trần Văn Soái. The leader of the Mendicant Order and one other follower were apparently tortured and executed. Minh Đăng Quang was no ordinary monk. He claimed to have achieved enlightenment on Mũi

---

[32] VNA-II. PTHNV D.30–680. Le Chef de Province de Chaudoc [Đặng Văn Lý] à M. le Gouverneur du Sud-Vietnam. "Objet: Fête de l'implantation du Banian Sacrée à Chaudoc." May 12, 1952. See also "Phật tích Bồ Đề Đạo Tràng ở Châu Đốc" [The Bodhi tree Buddha relics in Châu Đốc], *Giác Ngộ* (August 6, 2010), https://giacngo.vn /tuvien/chuavntrongnuoc/2010/08/06/72F212/ (accessed September 2, 2018).

[33] These two paragraphs on ông Đạo Nam and Minh Đăng Quang rely on Thích Nữ Diệu Tâm, "Phật giáo và tín ngưỡng ở đồng bằng sông cửu long" (graduation thesis, s.l., s.n.), www.tuvienquangduc.com.au/luanvan/khoa5-26dieutam.html (accessed September 15, 2017); on ông Đạo Nằm's and Minh Đăng Quang's deaths, see SHD 10 H 283. Direction des Services Français de la Sécurité. "Activités de la secte Hoa Hao. Persécutions contre les sectes bouddhiques." Saigon, April 4, 1954, as well as Hàn Ôn, *Minh-Đăng-Quang pháp giáo* [Saigon]: [Nhà In Long Giang], [1961], 41.

Nai beach outside of Hà Tiên, on the Gulf of Thailand. A charismatic leader, he drew on both Theravada and Mahayana Buddhism and attracted both Khmer and Vietnamese followers.[34] Like Đạo Nằm, his branch of Buddhism had been expanding across the Mekong Delta and posed a challenge to Hòa Hảo authority.

Both killings, carried out by Hòa Hảo militia leaders, have fallen into oblivion. These deaths may be interpreted to suggest that the violence that had riven the delta for years was simply continuing, with the result that harmless people continued to be arbitrarily killed. In fact, the killings illustrate a different point. Paramilitary leaders like Trần Văn Soái could not adjust to changing times. Having thrived in times of war, in which control of the means of violence was key, these warlords lacked the skills to flourish in peacetime. Religious leaders and groups in the delta were re-asserting their moral and spiritual authority and, implicitly, challenging strongman rule. These killings, as well as Ngô Đình Diệm's exile of Phạm Công Tắc (to be discussed later in this chapter), underscore the importance of such religious figures to the political and social life of the South.

Against the background of such rural upheavals and instability, Ngô Đình Diệm, who had sat out the war, skillfully outmaneuvered both the de facto power brokers in the Mekong Delta as well as the existing military and civilian leaders in the Vietnamese state. Diệm spent several years outside of Vietnam in the early 1950s. Edward Miller has characterized him as "among the most prominent of Vietnam's *attentistes.*"[35] Diệm, who focused his energies on cultivating allies in high places, made his move for power at an opportune time, persuading Emperor Bảo Đại to name him Prime Minister. With American aid and his own savvy, Diệm picked off or co-opted potential rivals, starting with the smaller Cao Đài and Hòa Hảo militias, and the urban-based Bình Xuyên, before confronting the most significant and intransigent opponents in the delta and Tây Ninh.[36] This consolidation of state power lasted from July 1954 to July 1956.

I will not go into the twists and turns of Ngô Đình Diệm's rise to power, but focus instead on his problematic "resolution" of the civil war in the South. Diệm first asserted control over the urban state apparatus and the

---

[34] On Minh Đăng Quang's life, see Hàn Ôn, *Minh-Đăng-Quang pháp*; Mark McLeod, "The Way of the Mendicants: History, Philosophy, and Practice at the Central Vihara in Hồ Chí Minh City." *Journal of Vietnamese Studies* 4(2) (2009), 71–76.

[35] Edward Miller, *Misalliance: Ngo Dinh Diem, the United States, and the Fate of South Vietnam* (Cambridge: Harvard University Press, 2013), 32.

[36] For excellent accounts of Diệm's dealing with the "sects," see Miller, *Misalliance*, Chapter 3; Jessica Chapman, *Cauldron of Resistance: Ngo Dinh Diem, the United States, and 1950s Southern Vietnam* (Ithaca: Cornell University Press, 2013), particularly Chapter 4.

Vietnamese National Army (VNA), both of which had rivals to Diệm within them. (The army was initially run by Nguyễn Văn Hinh, a French citizen and son of a former Prime Minister.) Diệm then cracked down on the "outlaw partisan"[37] Bình Xuyên, which controlled the Saigon-Cholon police. It is no surprise that many writers focus on these early urban dramas. In the long run, however, Diệm knew that he would have to extend his sovereign reach over rural areas as well. He would, in other words, need to defeat or co-opt the Cao Đài and Hòa Hảo parastates and their satellite militias. He also needed to blunt the challenge of Phạm Công Tắc, the southern Cao Đài leader who posed the greatest political challenge to Diệm.

In late June 1954, when he assumed power, Diệm had little power to demand compliance and little reason to inspire loyalty. The first potential crisis arrived in August 1954. The "Nationalist Front" (the Bình Xuyên and most leaders and generals associated with the Hòa Hảo and Tây Ninh-based Cao Đài) plotted a coup d'état against Ngô Đình Diệm. They failed to agree, however, on how to divide the "spoils" of eventual victory, including leadership of the proposed government.[38] The coup fizzled. Diệm stayed in power and consolidated control.

Ngô Đình Diệm would go on to crush the Bình Xuyên in 1955 and co-opt minor Hòa Hảo and Cao Đài militia leaders like Nguyễn Giác Ngộ, Lâm Thành Nguyên, and Trình Minh Thế. American money aided the process. In the long run, a key turning point in Diệm's consolidation of power was when he convinced the formerly antagonistic Nguyễn Thành Phương, Chief of Staff of the Cao Đài army, to integrate his Cao Đài forces into the Vietnamese National Army. Ngô Đình Diệm rewarded Phương with 1 million piasters "for the maintenance of his troops," a generalship in the VNA, and a ministerial position in his September 1954 cabinet reshuffle.[39] Diệm would later get Phương to claim that the Cao Đài had operated on behalf of the French:[40] a baffling claim, given the Cao Đài record during the war, including the consideration given in 1949 by some in the Tây Ninh branch to overthrow the

---

[37] The phrase is from Kevin Li, "From Partisan to Sovereign: The Making of the Bình Xuyên," *Journal of Vietnamese Studies* 11(3/4) (2016), 143.

[38] ANOM. HCI SPCE 8. Direction des Services Français de Sécurité. "Activités politiques et gouvernementales vietnamiennes. Saigon, August 30, 1954. Ultra-secret. A French informer reported on these deliberations.

[39] SHD. 10 H 3763. Folder "Affaires Caodaistes (1954)." État du Vietnam. Sud Vietnam. Direction des Finances [Ho Quang Hoai]. [for] Le Gouverneur du Sud-Vietnam. Saigon, August 9, 1954; ANOM. HCI SPCE 8. Le Directeur des Services Français de Sécurité. "Activités politiques et gouvernementales vietnamiennes. Le Cabinet Ngo Dinh Diem remanié." September 28, 1954.

[40] Chapman, *Cauldron of Resistance*, 102.

French. The "payoff" for Diệm would come in February 1956, when he ordered General Phương to attack the Cao Đài Holy See in Tây Ninh. Perhaps mindful of the uproar that ensued when the Resistance killed Hòa Hảo prophet Huỳnh Phú Sổ in 1947, Diệm then forced Phạm Công Tắc, head of the Tây Ninh branch of the Cao Đài, into exile in Cambodia. This expulsion, a pivotal event, has been overlooked by scholars. The scholar Bernard Fall had once called Phạm Công Tắc "Vietnam's most astute politician."[41] Gone was the one confessional leader with charisma, intelligence, pretensions to national leadership, abilities to navigate national politics, and a significant southern base. His forced exile turned Cao Đài members of the Tây Ninh branch against the Diệm government.[42] As for General Phương, he had been used as a catspaw in this affair. Diệm soon turned on him. After a police investigation, the government charged Phương with several crimes. The General promptly "retired."[43] Once a powerful military leader under the Cao Đài, then Diệm, General Phương tumbled into oblivion.

Diệm similarly went after the remaining Hòa Hảo militia leaders in the western Mekong Delta who refused to join the VNA. In January 1956, Diệm launched the Nguyễn Huệ campaign in the western Mekong Delta, attacking minor Hòa Hảo strongman Ba Cụt as well as the major Hòa Hảo strongman, Trần Văn Soái. Soái wanted to preserve his parastate in the western Mekong Delta. After the collapse of Cao Đài military and political power, however, Soái caved in to Diệm's authority and integrated his troops into the national army. This result should not have been a surprise. One of the first Hòa Hảo leaders to ally with the French in 1947, Soái collaborated with former enemies when his back was against the wall.

Ba Cụt was a different story. After rallying to the Vietnamese state in November 1953, he broke with it in July 1954 and retreated to the maquis on the Vietnam-Cambodia border.[44] He refused to buckle to Ngô Đình Diệm. The VNA eventually tracked him down and arrested him in April 1956. Put on trial in Cần Thơ, the largest city in the western

---

[41] Janet Hoskins *"God's Chosen People*: Race, Religion, and the Anti-Colonial Struggle in French Indochina." Asia Research Institute Working Paper 189 (September 2012), 18, citing Fall.

[42] Diệm supporter Lê Trung Nghĩa considered the move a mistake. See Chapman, *Cauldron of Resistance*, 186. Coverage of this expulsion is spotty. Lovegall, *Embers of War*, never mentions Phạm Công Tắc, and Miller, *Misalliance*, ignores his expulsion to Cambodia.

[43] On Nguyễn Thành Phương, see Miller, *Misalliance*, 111–12, 114, 145.

[44] ANOM. HCI SPCE 56. Extrait de la note No. 7689-S/RG du 11 Juin 1954 du SFS au Sud-Vietnam; ANOM. HCI SPCE 56. Extrait de la note No. 10.089 –S/RG du 2–8-1954.

Mekong Delta, the long-haired Ba Cụt often wore a brown *áo bà ba* or pants and long tunic, as well as a checkered scarf – typical peasant garb of the delta. The trial was a sensation.[45] The military court found Ba Cụt guilty and sentenced him to death. In a symbolic end to resistance from militias, in front of a crowd, "in an atmosphere of intense emotion,"[46] Ba Cụt was guillotined in Cần Thơ at 5:40 a.m., July 13, 1956. His family requested his body for burial, but were rebuffed. Like the Hòa Hảo leader Huỳnh Phú Sổ, Ba Cụt's body "was sliced into many pieces and then scattered,"[47] perhaps in the nearby Hậu River.

The last major internal enemy to the state in the Mekong Delta was now gone. Much of the Resistance leadership had regrouped to the North. In April 1956, after France finally dissolved the French military High Command in Indochina, its last commander, General Pierre-Élie Jacquot, boarded the S.S. Cambodge with a contingent of officers and soldiers and sailed home. The war was finally over. Or so it seemed.

10.2 War and the Global Fragmentation of History and Memory

In truth, wars never end. The memory of the first war for Vietnam became fragmented across the globe, and not just in France and Vietnam. In terms of global legacies, for example, four West African dictators – Jean-Bédel Bokassa (Central African Republic), Gnassingbé Eyadéma (Togo), Aboubakar Sangoulé Lamizana (Republic of Upper Volta), and General Christophe Soglo (Dahomey/Benin) – fought in Vietnam, some in the South. Bokassa had fond memories of his time in the South: "Indochina pleased me a lot. There was true camaraderie there. I always liked the army, the French army which was my life."[48] The war enriched African foodways as well: Vietnamese wives of African soldiers popularized Vietnamese spring rolls in their new home of Senegal. Another notable legacy is the number of nationalities who would die in Vietnam: who would have guessed that an Armenian and a Palestinian would join nationals from over sixty political units in being buried in Vietnamese

[45] Bùi Văn Nhân, "Đọc 'hồi Ký Quân Sử Nghĩa Quân Cách Mạng'," *Việt Báo* May 8, 2002, https://vietbao.com/a6745/doc-hoi-ky-quan-su-nghia-quan-cach-mang (accessed September 22, 2018).

[46] Michigan State University Archives & Historical Collections. Wesley R. Fishel Papers (UA 17.95) Box 1191, Folder 22. Letter from Tieng Chuong to Wesley Fishel, July 14, 1956 (accessed online September 25, 2018).

[47] Trần Thị Hoa, *Hồi ký quân sử Nghĩa Quân Cách Mạng* (Derwood, MD: Giáo Hội Phật Giáo Hải Ngoại, 2002), 229.

[48] Brian Titley, *Dark Age: The Political Odyssey of Emperor Bokassa* (Montreal: McGill University Press, 1997), 10.

soil? Finally, some of the key French officers who fought in this war would go on to fight in Algeria, using similar methods as in Vietnam. Some, like General Massu, who served in the South, would participate in the 1961 failed putsch against de Gaulle in protest of giving up Algeria.

Within Vietnam, the role in the South of the Resistance, their Vietnamese opponents, and the Khmer Krom has been distorted by both communist and anti-communist regimes since 1954. For some Khmer Krom, one result was land dispossession in Vietnam and migration to Cambodia. Every June 4 in Phnom Penh, Khmer Krom monks and activists protest the day in 1949 when France ceded Cochinchina to the new Vietnamese state. Within Vietnam, official histories prefer to focus on the DRV's stunning victory in the Center and the North, not on the complicated results in the South. And the parastates and militias that defeated the Resistance in concert with the French? Their case is peculiar. They lost the battle to control the State of Vietnam in 1954, and thus the struggle over how this war was to be retold. The triumphant Diệm regime, anxious to burnish its own version of Vietnamese nationalism, tended to "forget" that without Khmer Krom, Cao Đài, Hòa Hảo, UMDC, African and North African soldiers fighting against the Resistance, South Vietnam would not have come into existence. On March 19, 1955, Diệm incensed Cao Đài and Hòa Hảo members of the United Nationalist Front by portraying "the nine-year struggle of the Vietnamese people amongst the political parties and religious groups as a struggle among tribes like those in Africa."[49] Diệm had racialized his bickering opponents, turning them into "less civilized" dark-skinned Africans.

Southern narratives of the war after 1954 were peculiar in another way. A surprising number of the key participants in the war had been killed, exiled, "regrouped" north to the DRV, or simply silenced. The most important architects of the communist-led August General Uprising of 1945, Trần Văn Giàu and Phạm Ngọc Thạch, were summoned north soon after the uprising and were not allowed to publish, during their lives, frank accounts of their roles in that pivotal event. (The one Cao Đài leader to join the Resistance, Cao Triều Phát, would regroup to the North, then die in 1956.). The Hòa Hảo founder Huỳnh Phú Sổ, of course, was assassinated in 1947. The most important Resistance military leader in the first half of the war, General Nguyễn Bình, was ambushed and killed in Cambodia in 1951. Trình Minh Thế, the charismatic Cao Đài militia

---

[49] ANOM. HCI SPCE 24. Folder on 1955. "Déclaration du Praesidium du Front Unifié de toutes les forces nationales au cours d'une conférence de presse tenue le 21 mars 1955 au No. 107 Bd. Tran Hung Dao."

leader, was shot and killed in 1955. While the French took credit for this death, his assassin has never been definitively identified. The Hòa Hảo militia leader Ba Cụt, of course, was guillotined in 1956. Others saw the wisdom of staying quiet. The Hòa Hảo parastate leader Trần Văn Soái buckled to Diệm, "retired," and then died in 1961. Many leaders simply left the South forcibly or of their own will. Some Khmer Krom, averse to living under ethnic Vietnamese rule, migrated across the porous Cambodia-Vietnam border. The Cao Đài leader Phạm Công Tắc, forcibly exiled to Phnom Penh, was never allowed to return. The Catholic UMDC militia leader Jean Leroy and the Bình Xuyên leader Bảy Viễn (Lê Văn Viễn) both left for France. This litany of names drives home how many of the leading individuals in the southern conflict "went missing" as prominent narrators within Vietnam of what happened.

On April 30, 1975, the DRV defeated its anti-communist opponent, the Republic of Vietnam. The losers of the First Indochina War in the South came back as the winners of the second. A second "reckoning" of the past would begin. Despite the magnitude of the 1975 victory – one in which the Army of the Republic of Vietnam utterly collapsed – the victors, concerned about perceived security threats, send many to re-education camps. Võ Văn Kiệt, a high-ranking party member, would later argue that the point was not to "take revenge" on those who had a "blood debt," but to allow those going through re-education "to see their errors, and understand that the war of the Revolution was righteous."[50] This is too pat an answer. The new government cracked down on religious organizations, throwing some Catholic priests and numerous members of the Cao Đài and Hòa Hảo in prison. The regime also settled scores with antagonists from the First Indochina War. Thus Lâm Thành Nguyên, a commander of one of the major Hòa Hảo militias during the First Indochina War, seventy-one years old in 1975, was arrested; he would die in Chí Hòa prison two years later. Trần Quang Vinh, central in Cao Đài political and military affairs in the 1940s and 1950s, seventy-eight years old in 1975, was arrested in April 1975 and never seen again. One of the most curious cases was Son Ngoc Thanh, a Khmer Krom born in Trà Vinh province, collaborator with the Việt Minh in 1945, two-time Prime Minister of Cambodia, later a collaborator with the CIA and founder of the anti-communist Khmer Serei, or Free Khmer. Arrested in the South in 1975, he was incarcerated in Saigon's Chí Hòa prison, where he would die in 1977.

---

[50] Võ Văn Kiệt, interviewed in Huy Đức, *Bên thắng cuộc* (S.l.: Smashwords Ebook, 2013), 76.

Individuals aside, religious institutions came under attack if they were considered "reactionary" (*phản động*). The communist regime seized religious property, which affected, of course, Catholics, Hòa Hảo, and Cao Đài in the delta. Every level of Hòa Hảo institutions was dissolved. Cao Đài religious practices were heavily monitored. The regime even pilloried the dead: thus, the Cao Đài defender of the Dharma Phạm Công Tắc, discussed in this book, and who had died in 1959, came under blistering attack. It is safe to say that for those groups and organizations that had joined the communist-led Việt Minh in 1945, then broken with it in 1947, the decade and a half after 1975 were filled with trials, tribulations, and bitterness.

Struggling to bring this book to a close, I realized that I faced a daunting task: the fragmentation of memory across the globe, and its maintenance by different sub-communities, has meant that for many Vietnamese (and Chinese, Khmer, Cham, and French), coming to agreement on the meaning of the war has been impossible. In the end, I would like to suggest that accounts break down into two camps. In the first are those who strive to find meaning in the violence, death and sacrifices of war. In 1982, reflecting on the conflicts that had roiled Vietnam from 1945 to 1975, General Trần Văn Trà, a southern leader in the National Liberation Front, stated:

Countless comrades, brothers, sisters, and friends have been laid to rest in the earth of the Land of our Ancestors. They came to rest so that one day we would return, representatives of those who went forth in the autumn of that year [1945], showing our compatriots that we have kept our word. Families who have experienced loss, whose loved ones left and never came back, can see that we, the children and grandchildren, brothers and sisters, will now build together the new lives that we had always hoped to build.[51]

Trần Văn Trà argues that painful sacrifices are not in vain. But what about those, whether on the "winning" side or the "losing" side, for whom the violence of war shattered their lives? While some traumas fade, others never heal. We thus end this book with the searing account of Diệp Thị Hoặc that expresses a pain that has never gone away. Her words could have been spoken by a person on the winning side, or the losing side. Hoặc, from Ấp Hòa hamlet, Phong Nẫm village, Bến Tre province, survived a 1947 massacre carried out by a French-affiliated UMDC militia under Jean Leroy. She herself lost twenty-one members of her extended family, only a fraction of the 286 village dead. Speaking in 2013 of the event that shaped her entire life, she was quoted:

---

[51] Trần Văn Trà, *Những chặng đường của B-2-Thành Đồng*. Vol. 5. *Kết thúc cuộc chiến tranh 30 năm* (Ho Chi Minh City: Văn Nghệ thành phố Hồ Chí Minh, 1982), 319.

"It was an unceasing nightmare, always tormenting me. Year after year, standing before the altar [to the ancestors], before the shared grave of twenty-one persons no longer with us – my younger brother screaming as blood gushed from his chest, head, and stomach. I will never forget the sight of my mother, her flowing hair splattered with blood. The image of my mother hugging a boy who was weeping uncontrollably, the deafening sounds of gunfire, my mother screaming then collapsing into a pool of blood, clutching her baby to her breast. My mother's body lay on top of my younger brother and her mother, younger sisters, blood flowing in streams." Wiping tears from her eyes, she choked up: "Perhaps my mother thought that the younger ones were not yet dead, so she used her body to protect them until her final breath. Remembering that day, those horrifying images come back as if it were yesterday."[52]

THE END

[52] Hà Nguyễn [and] Ngọc Lài, "Ký ức người sống sót sau vụ thảm sát ở Bến Tre," *Người đưa tin: cơ quan của Hội luật gia Việt Nam* (March 19, 2013), www.nguoiduatin.vn/ky-uc-nguoi-song-sot-sau-vu-tham-sat-o-ben-tre-a71829.html (accessed May 19, 2019).

Bibliography

Accords Franco-vietnamien du 8 Mars 1949. Conventions d'application [Franco-Vietnamese agreements of March 8, 1949. Convention on implementation]. Saigon: IDEO, 1950.

Adas, Michael. "From Avoidance to Confrontation: Peasant Protest in Precolonial and Colonial Southeast Asia." *Comparative Studies in Society and History* 23(1) (January 1981): 217–237.

Ainley, Henry. *In Order to Die: With the Foreign Legion in Indo-China*. London: Burke, 1955.

Amin, Shahid. *Event Metaphor Memory: Chauri Chaura 1922–1992*. Berkeley: California, 1995.

Anderson, Benedict O'Gorman. *Imagined Communities: Reflections on the Origins and Spread of Nationalism*. London: Verso, 1983.

Anderson, Benedict O'Gorman. *Java in a Time of Revolution*. Ithaca: Cornell, 1972.

Anderson, David. *Histories of the Hanged: The Dirty War in Kenya and the End of Empire*. New York: W. W. Norton, 2005.

Appadurai, Arjun. "Dead Certainty: Ethnic Violence in an Age of Globalization." *Development and Change* 29(4) (October 1998): 905–925.

Artaud, Denise. "La menace américaine et le règlement indochinois à la conférence de Genève" [The American threat and the settlement of the Indochina problem at the Geneva conference]. *Histoire, économie et société*, 13 (1) (1994): 47–62.

Asselin, Pierre. "The Democratic Republic of Vietnam and the 1954 Geneva Conference: A Revisionist Critique." *Cold War History* 11(2) (May 2011): 155–195.

Aymonier, Étienne. *Le Cambodge. Le groupe d'Angkor et l'histoire* [Cambodia: The Angkor complex and history]. Paris: Leroux, 1904.

Ban Chấp Hành Đảng Bộ Tỉnh Bạc Liêu. *Lịch sử Đảng bộ tỉnh Bạc Liêu (1927–1975)* [History of the party apparatus of Bạc Liêu province]. Vol. 1. Bạc Liêu: Ban Thường Vụ Tỉnh Ủy, 2002.

Ban Liên Lạc Cựu Chiến Binh Quân thời kỳ 1945-1954. *Tư liệu lịch sử Quân tình nguyện Việt Nam ở Campuchia (1945-1954)* [Historical documentation on Vietnamese volunteer troops in Kampuchea]. Cà Mau: Mũi Cà Mau, 1998.

Ban Liên Lạc Việt Kiều Campuchia Hồi Hương. *Ảnh truyền thống Việt kiều Campuchia đối với Tổ quốc (1930–1975)* [Traditional picture of Vietnamese abroad in Cambodia and their views towards the Land of the Ancestors]. Cà Mau: Mũi Cà Mau, 1998.

Banens, Mak. *Vietnam: A Reconstitution of its 20th Century Population History.* Tokyo: Asian Historical Statistics (AHSTAT) COE Project, Hitotsubashi University, January 2000.

Barbieri, Magali. "De l'utilité des statistiques démographiques de l'Indochine française (1862–1954)" [On the usefulness of demographic statistics from French Indochina]. *Annales de démographie historique* 113(1) (2007): 85–126.

Barrett, Tracy. *The Chinese Diaspora in Southeast Asia.* London: I. B. Tauris, 2012.

Bayly, Christopher and Tim Harper. *Forgotten Soldiers: The Fall of British Asia, 1941–1945.* Cambridge, MA: Harvard University Press, 2005.

Bayly, Christopher and Tim Harper. *Forgotten Wars: Freedom and Revolution in Southeast Asia.* Cambridge, MA: Harvard University Press, 2007.

Beccaria, Laurent. "Soldats perdus des guerres orphelines" [Lost soldiers of orphan wars]. *Vingtième Siècle. Revue d'histoire* 22 (April–June 1989): 103–109.

Biggs, David A. *Quagmire: Nation-Building and Nature in the Mekong Delta.* Seattle: University of Washington Press, 2010.

Blanchet, André. *Au pays des ballila jaunes: relation d'un correspondant de guerre en Indochine* [In the country of Asian fascist youth: account of a war correspondent in Indochina]. St. Étienne: Dorian, 1947.

Blanchet, Marie-Thérèse. *La naissance de l'état associé du Vietnam* [The birth of the Associated State of Vietnam]. Paris: M.-Th. Génin, 1954.

Bloch, Marc. *L'étrange défaite* [The strange defeat]. Paris: Gallimard, 1990 [1957].

Bộ Nội Vụ. Viện Khoa Học Công An. *Công An Nhân Dân Việt Nam. Lịch sử biên niên* [The public security forces of Vietnam. A historical chronicle]. Hanoi: Công An Nhân Dân, 1994.

Bộ Quốc Gia Kinh Tế. *Thống Kê Niên Giám Việt Nam/Annuaire Statistique de l'Indochine* [Indochina: Annual statistical annual]. Vol. 1, 1949–50. Saigon: Viện Kinh Tế và Khảo Cứu Kinh Tế Việt Nam, 1951.

Bộ Tư Lệnh Quân Khu 9. *Quân Khu 9 30 năm kháng chiến* [Region Nine in the thirty years of resistance]. Hanoi: Quân đội nhân dân, 1996.

Bodin, Michel. "Le combattant français du Corps Expéditionnaire en Extrême-Orient, 1945–1954" [The French soldier of the Far East Expeditionary Corps, 1945–54]. *Guerres mondiales et conflits contemporains* 168 (October 1992): 175–193.

Bodin, Michel. *Les Africains dans la guerre d'Indochine* [Africans in the Indochina War]. Paris: Harmattan, 2008.

Bodin, Michel. *La France et ses soldats, Indochine, 1945–1954* [France and its soldiers in Indochina, 1945–54]. Paris: L'Harmattan, 1996.

Bodinier, (Commandant) Gilbert. *Indochine, 1947: règlement politique ou solution militaire?* [Indochina 1947: political settlement or military solution?]. Vincennes: Service Historique de l'Armée de Terre, 1989.

Bodinier, (Commandant) Gilbert. *Le retour de la France en Indochine 1945–1946: textes et documents* [France's return to Indochina 1945–46: texts and documents]. Château de Vincennes: Service Historique de l'Armée de Terre, 1987.

Bose, Mihir Raj. *Secrets, Revolution: A Life of Subhas Chandra Bose*. London: Grice Chapman, 2004.

Bourdeaux, Pascal. "Interpretative Essay on the 'Hòa Hảo Revolution'." Unpublished paper, 2007.

Bourdeaux, Pascal. "Regards sur l'autonomisation religieuse dans le processus d'indépendance du Vietnam au milieu du vingtième siècle" [A look into the development of religious autonomy in the Vietnamese path to independence in the mid-twentieth century]. *French Politics, Culture & Society* 33(2) (Summer 2015): 11–32.

Bourdeaux, Pascal. "Approches statistiques de la communauté du bouddhisme Hòa Hảo" [Statistical approaches to the Hòa Hảo Buddhist community]. In Christopher Goscha and Benoît de Tréglodé, eds., *Naissance d'un État-Parti*. Paris: Les Indes savantes, 2004. 277–304.

Bourdieu, Pierre. *Esquisse d'une théorie de la pratique précédé de trois études d'ethnologie Kabyle* [Outline of a theory of practice, preceded by three studies of Kabyle ethnology]. Genève: Droz, 1972.

Bourdieu, Pierre. *Outline of a Theory of Practice*. Translated by Richard Nice. Cambridge: Cambridge University Press, 1977 [1972].

Boyer de la Tour, (General) Pierre. *De L'Indochine à l'Algérie: le martye de l'Armée française* [From Indochina to Algeria: the martyrdom of the French military]. Paris: Presses du Mail, 1962.

Bradley, Mark. *Imagining Vietnam and America: The Making of Postcolonial Vietnam, 1919–1950*. Chapel Hill: University of North Carolina Press, 2003.

Bradley, Mark. "Becoming Van Minh: Civilizational Discourse and Visions of the Self in Twentieth Century Vietnam." *Journal of World History* 15(1) (2004): 65–83.

Branch, Daniel. *Defeating Mau Mau, Creating Kenya: Counterinsurgency, Civil War, and Decolonization*. Cambridge: Cambridge University Press, 2009.

Brass, Paul. *The Production of Hindu-Muslim Violence in Contemporary India*. Seattle: University of Washington Press, 2003.

Brazinsky, Gregg. *Winning the Third World: Sino-American Rivalry During the Cold War*. Raleigh: University of North Carolina Press, 2017.

Brocheux, Pierre. *The Mekong Delta: Ecology, Economy, and Revolution, 1860–1960*. Madison, Wisconsin: Center for Southeast Asian Studies, 1995.

Bùi Công Đặng. "Tổng khởi nghĩa ở Lục Tỉnh" [The General Uprising in the South]. In Trần Bạch Đằng et al, eds. *Mùa Thu rồi. Ngày hăm ba* [Autumn, the twenty-third]. Hanoi: Chính trị Quốc gia, 1995. 415–460.

Bùi Nhung. *Thối nát: hồi ký* [Corruption: a memoir]. Saigon: Bình Minh, 1965.

Bùi Thu Hà. "Công tác Hòa Hảo vận của Đảng bộ An Giang trong hai cuộc Kháng Chiến" [Work of the An Giang party apparatus among the Hòa Hảo in the two Resistance wars]. *Tạp chí Nghiên cứu lịch sử Đảng* 9 (1996): 30–32.

Bùi Văn Nhân. "Đọc 'hồi Ký Quân Sử Nghĩa Quân Cách Mạng'," [Reading *A Memoir on the Righteous Revolutionary Army*]. *Việt Báo* (May 8, 2002). https://vietbao.com/a6745/doc-hoi-ky-quan-su-nghia-quan-cach-mang

Bunthorn Som. "Thach Chov: A Former Student of Khieu Samphan." *Searching for the Truth* (Phnom Penh), (First Quarter, 2010): 22–25.

Burbank, Jane and Frederick Cooper. *Empires in World History: Power and the Politics of Difference*. Princeton: Princeton University Press, 2011.

Carstensen, Martin. "Bricolage as an Analytical Lens in New Institutionalist Theory," 46–67. In Anthony Spanakos and Francisco Panizza, eds., *Conceptualizing Comparative Politics*. New York: Routledge, 2015.

Chandler, David. "Going Through the Motions: Ritual Aspects of the Reign of King Duang of Cambodia (1848–1860)." In David Chandler, ed. *Facing the Cambodian Past: Selected Essays 1971–1994*, Chiang Mai: Silkworm Books, 1996. 100–118.

Chandler, David. *The Tragedy of Cambodian History: Politics, War, and Revolution Since 1945*. New Haven: Yale University Press, 1991.

Chapman, Jessica. *Cauldron of Resistance: Ngo Dinh Diem, the United States, and 1950s Southern Vietnam*. Ithaca: Cornell University Press, 2013.

Chaumont-Guitry, Guy de. *Lettres d'Indochine* [Letters from Indochina]. Paris: Alsatia, 1951.

Chézal, Guy de. *Parachuté en Indochine* [Parachuted into Indochina]. Paris: Les Deux Sirènes, 1947.

Choi Byung Wook. *Southern Vietnam under the Reign of Minh Mạng: Central Policies and Local Response*. Ithaca, NY: Southeast Asia Program, 2004.

Cổ Việt Tử [Nguyễn Duy Hinh]. *Vụ án Ba Cụt* [The trial of Ba Cụt]. Saigon: Nguyễn Duy Hinh, [1956].

Cuộc kháng chiến thần thán của nhân dân Việt Nam. Vol. 1: từ 23 tháng chín 1945 đến tháng chạp 1947 [The sacred resistance war of the Vietnamese people. Vol. 1: From September 23, 1945 to December 1947]. Hanoi: Sự Thật, [1958?].

Đại Đạo Tam Kỳ Phổ Độ. Tòa Thánh Tây Ninh. *Lời thuyết đạo của Đức Hộ Pháp* [Sermons of the Defender of the Dharma (Phạm Công Tắc)], Vol. 3 (1949 – 1950). Tây Ninh [?]: s.n., 1974. Reprinted and reformatted as Ebook. California: Tầm Nguyên, 2013. https://tusachcaodai.files.wordpress.com/201 3/05/hp-td-qiii.pdf

Đảng Cộng Sản Việt Nam. *Lịch sử Đảng bộ tỉnh Tiền Giang* [History of the Party apparatus of Tiền Giang province]. [Tiền Giang]: Ban nghiên cứu lịch sử Đảng, 1985.

Đảng Cộng sản Việt Nam. *Văn Kiện Đảng toàn tập* [Collected Party documents]. Vol. 10 (1949). Hanoi: Chính Trị Quốc Gia, 2001. http://tulieuvankien.dangcongsan.vn/van-kien-tu-lieu-ve-dang/book/van-kien-dang-toan-tap/van-kien-dang-toan-tap-tap-10-90

Đảng Cộng sản Việt Nam. *Văn Kiện Đảng* [Party documents] Vol. 11 (1950). Hanoi: Quốc Gia, 2001. http://tulieuvankien.dangcongsan.vn/van-kien-tu-lieu-ve-dang/book/van-kien-dang-toan-tap/van-kien-dang-toan-tap-tap-11-91.

Đảng Ủy – Bộ Chỉ Huy Quân Sự Tỉnh Vĩnh Long. *Lực lượng vũ trang tỉnh Vĩnh Long 30 năm kháng chiến (1945–1975)* [Armed forces of Vĩnh Long province in the thirty years of resistance]. Hanoi: Quân Đội Nhân Dân, 1999.

Dật Sĩ and Nguyễn Văn Hầu . *Thất Sơn Mầu Nhiệm* [The mysterious Seven Mountains]. Saigon: s.n., 1972 [1955].

Decaudin, J. Un essai d'économie dirigée: le marché du paddy et le marché du riz en Cochinchine 1941–1944, *Bulletin de l'Économie Indochinois*, (Special issue,1944), Fascicules III and IV.

Delanoë, Nelcya. *Poussières d'empire* [Dust of empire]. Paris: Presses Universitaires de France, 2000.

Deleuze, Gilles and Félix Guattari. *Mille plateaux* [A thousand plateaus]. Paris: Éditions de Minuit, 1980.

Delmas, (General) Jean. "Les moyens militaires" [Military means]. In Philippe Duplay, ed., *Leclerc et l'Indochine 1945–1947: Quand se noua le destin d'un empire* [Leclerc and Indochina 1945–47: when the fate of an empire was decided]. Paris: Albin Michel, 1992. 94–105.

Delpey, Roger. *Soldats de la boue* [Soldiers in the mud]. Paris: Maison des Écrivains, 1949.

Delvert, Jean. "Quelques problèmes indochinois en 1947" [Some Indochinese challenges of 1947]. *L'information géographique* 12(2) (1948): 50–61.

Demeny, Paul. "Final Report: A Population Survey in Vietnam." Report by Simulatics Submitted to the Advanced Research Project Agency. Cambridge, MA: s.n, 1967.

Denis, Peter. *Troubled Days of Peace: Mountbatten and South East Asia Command, 1945–46*. Manchester: Manchester University Press, 1987.

Devillers, Philippe. *Histoire du Viet Nam de 1940 à 1952* [Vietnam's history, 1940–52]. Paris: Éditions du Seuil, 1952.

Devos, Jean-Claude, et al. *Inventaire des Archives de l'Indochine. Sous-Série 10 H.* [Finding Aid to the Indochina Archives]. Château de Vincennes: Service Historique de l'Armée de Terre, 1990.

Diagne, Aissatou. "Le Sénégal et la guerre d'Indochine: Récit de vie de veterans" [Senegal and the Indochina War: Veterans' life stories]. MA Thesis, Cheikh Anta Diop University [Senegal], 1992.

Diệu Tâm, Thích Nữ. "Phật giáo và tín ngưỡng ở đồng bằng sông cửu long" [Buddhism and belief in the Mekong delta]. Graduation thesis. S.l.: s.n. www .tuvienquangduc.com.au/luanvan/khoa5-26dieutam.html

Dinfreville, Jacques. *L'opération Indochine*. Paris: Editions Inter-Nationales, 1953.

Đoàn Thêm. *Hai mươi năm qua. Việc từng ngày 1945–1964.* [The past twenty years. Daily record 1945–64. [Saigon]: Nam Chi Tùng Thư, 1966.

Donnison, F. S. V. *British Military Administration in the Far East 1943–1946*. London: Her Majesty's Stationery Office, 1956.

Douglas, Mary. *How Institutions Think*. Syracuse: University of Syracuse Press, 1986.

Dower, John. *War Without Mercy: Race and Power in the Pacific War*. New York: Pantheon, 1986.

Edwards, Penny. "Making a Religion of the Nation and Its Language: The French Protectorate (1863–1954) and the Dhammakay." In John Marston and Elizabeth Guthrie, eds., *History, Buddhism, and New Religious Movements in Cambodia*. Honolulu: University of Hawai'i Press, 2004. 63–86.

Edwards, Penny. "The Tyranny of Proximity: Power and Mobility in Colonial Cambodia, 1863–1954." *Journal of Southeast Asian Studies* 37(3) (October 2006): 421–443.

Elliott, David. *The Vietnamese War: Revolution and Social Change in the Mekong Delta 1930–1975*. Armonk, NY: M. E. Sharpe, 2003.

Ély, Paul. *Les enseignements de la guerre d'Indochine (1945–1954)*. *Rapport du Général Ély* [The lessons of the Indochina War. Report of General Ély], Vol. 1. Vincennes: SHD, 2011 [1955].

Engelbert, Thomas. "Ideology and Reality: *Nationalitätenpolitik* in North and South Vietnam of the First Indochina War." In Thomas Engelbert and Andreas Schneider, eds., *Ethnic Minorities and Nationalism in Southeast Asia*. Frankfurt: Peter Lang, 2000. 105–142.

Englebert, Thomas. "Vietnamese-Chinese Relations in Southern Vietnam during the First Indochina Conflict." *Journal of Vietnamese Studies* 3(3) (Fall 2008): 191–230.

Fall, Bernard. "La situation internationale du Sud-Vietnam" [The international situation of South Vietnam]. *Revue française de science politique* 8(3) (1958): 545–575.

Fanon, Franz. *The Wretched of the Earth*. New York: Grove Press, 1963.

Feierman, Steve. "Colonizers, Scholars, and the Creation of Invisible Histories." In Victoria Bonnell and Lynn Hunt, eds., *Beyond the Cultural Turn: New Directions in the Study of Society and Culture*. Berkeley and Los Angeles: University of California Press, 1999. 182–216.

Feiertag, Olivier. "Le nerf de l'après-guerre: le financement de la reconstruction entre l'Etat et le marché (1944–1947)" [The key of the post-war period: financing reconstruction, between state and market]. *Matériaux pour l'histoire de notre temps* [Materials to understand the history of our time] 39–40 (July-December 1995): 46–51.

Félixine, Lucien. *L'Indochine livrée aux bourreaux* [Indochina handed over to executioners]. Paris: Nouvelles Éditions Latines, 1959.

Flanner, Janet. *Paris Journal 1944–1965*. New York: Harcourt Brace Jovanovitch, 1977.

Foucault, Michel. *Histoire de la folie à l'âge classique* [History of madness in the classical age]. Paris: Gallimard. 1972.

Foucault, Michel. "Nietzsche, Genealogy, History." In Michel Foucault and Donald F Bouchard, ed. *Language, Counter-Memory, Practice: Selected Essays and Interviews*, Ithaca, NY: Cornell University Press, 2012. 139–164.

Frankum, Ronald Bruce, Jr. *The Year of the Rat: Elbridge Durbrow, Ngo Đình Diệm and the Turn in U.S. Relations, 1959–1961*. Jefferson, NC: McFarland, 2014.

Gaultier, Marcel. *Prisons japonaises. Récit vécu* [Japanese prison experiences]. Monte Carlo: Regain, 1950.

Geertz, Clifford. "What Was the Third World Revolution?" *Dissent* (New York), 52(1) (Winter 2005): 35–45.

Giáo Hội Phật Giáo Hòa Hảo. *Sấm giảng thi văn toàn bô của Đức Huỳnh Giáo chủ* [Collected works of Huỳnh Phú Sổ]. [Saigon]: Ban Phổ Thông Giáo Lý Trung Ương, 1970.

Glassman, Jonathon. *War of Words, War of Stones: Racial Thought and Violence in Colonial Zanzibar*. Bloomington: Indiana University Press, 2011.

Goscha, Christopher E. "A 'Popular' Side of the Vietnamese Army: General Nguyễn Bình and the Early War in the South (1910–1951)." In Christopher

E. Goscha and Benoit deTreglodé, eds., *Naissance d'un état-parti*. Paris: Les Indes Savantes, 2004. 325–353.

Goscha, Christopher E. "Le contexte asiatique de la guerre franco-vietnamienne: Réseaux, relations, et économie (1945–1954)" [The Asian contexts of the Franco-Vietnamese war: networks, relationships, and economy]. PhD dissertation, École Pratique des Hautes Études, 2000.

Goscha, Christopher E. "La guerre par d'autres moyens: Réflexions sur la guerre du Việt Minh dans le Sud-Vietnam de 1945 à 1951" [War by other means. Reflections on Viet Minh warfighting in southern Vietnam, 1945–51]. *Guerres mondiales et conflits contemporains* 206 (2002): 29–57.

Goscha, Christopher E. *The Indochina War 1945–1956: An Interdisciplinary Tool* Copenhagen and Honolulu: NIAS/Hawai'i, 2011. https://indochine.uqam.ca/en/historical-dictionary.html

Goscha, Christopher E. *Vietnam or Indochina?: Contesting Concepts of Space in Vietnamese Nationalism, 1887–1954*. Copenhagen: NIAS, 1995.

Goscha, Christopher E. *Vietnam. Un État né de la guerre* [A state born of war]. Paris: Armand Colin, 2013.

Gourou, Pierre. "La population rurale de l'Indochine" [Indochina's rural inhabitants]. *Annales de Géographie*, 51(285) (1942): 7–25.

Gras, Yves. *Histoire de la guerre d'Indochine* [History of the Indochina War]. Paris: Destins Croisés, 1992.

Guèye, Marc. *Un tirailleur sénégalais dans la guerre d'Indochine, 1953–1955: la conduite au feu du bataillon de marche du 5e R.I.C.* [A Senegalese soldier in the Indochina War, 1953–55: conduct under fire of the fifth R.I.C.]. Dakar: Presses universitaires de Dakar, 2007.

Guiberteau, Yannick. *La Dévastation: cuirassé de rivière* [Devastation: a river gunboat]. Paris: Albin Michel, 1984.

Guillemot, François. "Autopsy of a Massacre: On a Political Purge in the Early Days of the Indochina War (Nam Bo 1947)." *European Journal of East Asian Studies* 9(2) (2010): 225–265.

Guillemot, François. "'Be men!': Fighting and Dying for the State of Vietnam (1951–54)." *War and Society* 31(2) (August 2012): 184–210.

Guillemot, François. "Au coeur de la fracture vietnamienne: l'élimination de l'opposition nationaliste et anticolonialiste dans le nord du Việt Nam (1945–1946) [At the heart of Vietnam's division: the elimination of the nationalist and anti-colonialist opposition in northern Vietnam]. In Christopher E. Goscha and Benoît de Tréglodé, eds., *Naissance d'un État-Parti: le Viêt Nam depuis 1945* [The birth of a party-state: Vietnam since 1945]. Paris: Les Indes Savantes, 2004. 175–216.

Guillemot, François. *Dai Viêt: indépendance et révolution au Viêt-Nam. L'échec de la troisième voie. 1938–1955* [Dai Viet: independence and revolution. The failure of the Third Way. 1938–55]. Paris: Les Indes Savantes. 2012.

Guillemot, François. *Viêt-Nam, fractures d'une nation. Une histoire contemporaine de 1858 à nos jours* [Vietnam, a nation divided. A contemporary history from 1858 to the present]. Paris: La Découverte, 2018.

Hàn Ôn. *Minh-Đăng-Quang pháp giáo* [Teachings of Minh Đặng Quang]. [Saigon]: [Nhà In Long Giang], [1961].

Hanley, Will. "When Did Egyptians Stop Being Ottomans? An Imperial Citizenship Case Study." In Willem Maas, ed. *Multilevel Citizenship.* Philadelphia: University of Pennsylvania Press, 2013. 89–109.

Hansen, Anne. *How to Behave: Buddhism and Modernity in Colonial Cambodia, 1860–1930.* Honolulu: University of Hawai'i Press, 2011.

Hansen, Thomas Blom and Finn Stepputat. "Sovereignty Revisited." *Annual Review of Anthropology* 35 (2006): 295–315.

Hardy, Andrew. *Red Hills: Migrants and the State in the Highlands of Vietnam.* Honolulu: University of Hawai'i Press, 2002.

Harris, Ian. *Cambodian Buddhism: History and Practice.* Honolulu: University of Hawai'i Press, 2005.

Hinton, Alexander. *Why Did They Kill? Cambodia in the Shadow of Genocide.* Berkeley: University of California Press, 2010.

Hồ Hữu Nhựt. *Trí thức Sài Gòn-Gia định, 1945–1975* [Intellectuals of Saigon and Gia Định]. Hanoi: Chính Trị Quốc gia, 2001.

Hoàng Tấn. *Nguyễn Bính: một vì sao sáng* [Nguyễn Bính: a shining star]. S.l.: Đồng Nai, 1999.

Hồ Chí Minh. *Hồ Chí Minh toàn tập: 1950–1952* [Collected works of Hồ Chí Minh, 1950–52]. Hanoi: Chính trị quốc gia, 1995.

Hồ Tấn Vinh. "Viết về Hồ Văn Ngà" [On Hồ Văn Ngà]. https://sites.google.com /site/namkyluctinhorg/tac-gia-tac-pham/e-f-g-h/ho-tan-vinh/viet-ve-ho-van-nga

Hoành Kim Anh. *9 năm kháng chiến miền tây Nam Bộ.* Saigon: s.n., 1957.

Hoàng Ngọc Thành. "Những ngày cuối cùng của nhà ái quốc Tạ Thu Thâu tại Quảng Ngãi" [The final days of the patriot Tạ Thu Thâu in Quảng Ngãi]. In Nguyễn Văn Đính, *Tạ Thu Thâu: Từ Quốc gia đến Quốc Tế* [Tạ Thu Thâu: from nationalism to internationalism]. [Amarillo, TX]: Hải Mã, [2005]. Appendix I, 99–110.

Hội Đồng Chỉ Đạo Biên Soạn Lịch Sử Nam Bộ Kháng Chiến, ed. *Lịch sử Nam bộ kháng chiến* [History of the Southern Resistance]. Vol. 1. Hanoi: Chính trị quốc gia, 2010.

Hồi ký cuộc đời Quả phụ Mục sư Triệu Ngươn Hên [Memoir of the life of the widow of Pastor Triệu Ngươn Hên]. S.l.: s.n., 2007.

Horkheimer, Max and Theodor Adorno. *Dialectic of Enlightenment.* New York: Seabury Press, 1972 [1947].

Hoskins, Janet. "'God's Chosen People': Race, Religion, and the Anti-Colonial Struggle in French Indochina." Asia Research Institute Working Paper 189 (September 2012).

Hoskins, Janet. "A Posthumous Return from Exile: The Legacy of an Anticolonial Religious Leader in Today's Vietnam." *Southeast Asian Studies* (Kyoto) 1(2) (August 2012): 213–246.

Hoskins, Janet. "Colonial Caodaists." Unpublished paper.

Hoskins, Janet. *The Divine Eye and the Diaspora: Vietnamese Syncretism Becomes Transpacific Caodaism.* Honolulu: University of Hawai'i Press, 2015.

Howell, David. *Geographies of Identity in Nineteenth-Century Japan.* Berkeley: University of California Press, 2005.

Hứa Hoành. "Ai giết Đức Thầy Huỳnh Phú Sổ?" [Who killed Huỳnh Phú Sổ?].
  1996. https://hung-viet.org/a990/ai-giet-duc-thay-huynh-phu-so-theo-hua-
  hoanh

Hùng Ngôn and Bùi Đức Tịnh. *Lịch sử giải phóng Việt Nam (thời kỳ cận đại)*
  [History of Vietnam's liberation in the modern period]. Saigon: Đại Chúng,
  1948.

Hướng Tân and Hồng Đức. *Kháng chiến Cao-Miên nhất định [The decisive
  Cambodian resistance]*. Việt Bắc [?]: Sự Thật, 1954.

Huy Đức. *Bên thắng cuộc* [The winning side]. S.l.: Smashwords Ebook, 2013.

Huỳnh Hữu Thiện. *Tiểu sử ông Huỳnh Thạnh Mậu* [Biography of Huỳnh Thạnh
  Mậu]. Liên Chính XB, 1954. https://hoahao.org/p74a4022/tieu-su-ong-huynh
  -thanh-mau.

Huỳnh Minh Hiền. "Từ Đồng Tháp Mười đến Cà Mau, hai thủ phủ của Nam
  Bộ trong Kháng Chiến chống Pháp" [From Đồng Tháp Mười to Cà Mau: the
  two capitals of the South in the Resistance War against France]. In
  Thăng Long, ed., *Nhớ Nam Bộ và cực nam Trung Bộ buổi đầu Kháng chiến
  chống Pháp* [Remembering south and south-central Vietnam at the beginning
  of the Resistance War against France]. Ho Chi Minh City: Trẻ, 1999.
  509–533.

Huỳnh Minh Hiền. "Những kỷ niệm sống và làm việc ở văn phòng trung ương
  cục miền Nam và Ủy ban Kháng chiến hành chính Nam Bộ" [Memories of
  living and working in the southern headquarters and the Resistance
  Administrative Committee of the South]. In *Nam Bộ thành đồng Tổ Quốc*
  [The South, bulwark of the land of our ancestors]. Hanoi: Chính trị Quốc
  gia, 1990. 205–229.

Jammes, Jérémy. "Le Saint-Siège Caodaiste de Tây Ninh et le Médium Phạm
  Công Tắc (1890–1959)" [The Cao Đài Holy See of Tây Ninh and the Medium
  Phạm Công Tắc]. *Outre-Mers* 94 (2006): 209–248.

Jammes, Jérémy. "Caodaism and Its Global Networks: An Ethnological Analysis
  of a Vietnamese Religious Movement in Vietnam and Abroad." *Moussons* 13
  (14) (2009): 339–358.

Jammes, Jérémy. *Les oracles du Cao Đài: Étude d'un mouvement réligieux et ses
  réseaux*. Paris: Les Indes Savantes, 2014.

Kalyvas, Stathis. *The Logic of Violence in Civil War*. Cambridge: Cambridge
  University Press, 2006.

Kalyvas, Stathis. "Wanton and Senseless? The Logic of Massacres in Algeria."
  Rationality and Society 11(3) (1999): 243–285.

Keith, Charles. *Catholic Vietnam: A Church from Empire to Nation*. Berkeley:
  University of California Press, 2012.

Keith, Charles. "Vietnamese Collaborationism in Vichy France." *Journal of Asian
  Studies* 76(4) (November 2017): 987–1008.

Kháng chiến lâu dài và gian khổ nhưng nhất định thắng lợi [The Resistance Will Be
  Long and Arduous but Will Achieve Decisive Victory]. [Northern Vietnam?]:
  Tổng Cục Chính Trị Cục Tuyên Quân, 1952.

Khin Sok, translator. *L'annexation du Cambodge par les Vietnamiens aux XIXè siècle
  d'après les deux poèmes du Vénérable Bâtum Baramey Pich* (Paris: Éditions You
  Feng, 2002).

Khmers Kampuchea Krom Federation. *The Khmer-Krom Journey to Self-Determination*. Pennsauken, NJ: Khmers Kampuchea-Krom Federation, 2009.

Khương Mễ. *Đời tôi và điện ảnh* [My life and film]. Ho Chi Minh City: Thành phố Hồ Chí Minh, 2003.

Kiernan, Ben. *How Pol Pot Came to Power: Colonialism, Nationalism, and Communism in Cambodia, 1930–1975*. New Haven: Yale University Press, 2004.

Kleinen, John. "The Dutch Diplomatic Post in Saigon: Dutch – Vietnamese relations (1945–1975)." In John Kleinen et al., *Lion and Dragon: Four Centuries of Dutch – Vietnamese Relations*. Amsterdam: Boom, 2008. 127–169.

Kouassi, Claude Yao. "La participation militaire de l'Afrique noire à la guerre d'Indochine (1947–1955)" [Black Africa's participation in the Indochina War]. Phd dissertation, Pantheon-Sorbonne University, 1986.

Krasuong Ab'rom Jeat [Department of National Education]. *Pravautsat nii Prateeh Kampuchea, somraep t'nak thé 9, thé 8, thé 7* [History of Cambodia for Grades 7, 8, and 9]. Phnom Penh: s.n., 1970.

Krull, Germaine. "Dairy [*sic*] of Saigon, Following the Allied Occupation in September 1945." Folder 07, Box 02, Douglas Pike Collection, The Vietnam Center and Archive, Texas Tech University. www.vietnam.ttu.edu/reports/im ages.php?img=/images/241/2410207001.pdf

La Gorce, Paul-Marie de. *La République et son armée* [The Republic and its army]. Paris: Fayard, 1963.

La Motte, Dominique de. *De l'autre côté de l'eau. Indochine,1950–1952* [On the other shore. Indochina, 1950–1952]. Paris: Tallandier, 2012.

Labussière, M. "Étude sur la propriété foncière rurale en Cochinchine et, particulièrement, dans l'inspection de Soctrang" [Study of rural property in Cochinchina, and particularly in Soctrang]. *Excursions et Reconnaissances* 3 (1880): 331–348.

Lacouture, Jean. "Pourquoi l'espoir? Pourquoi l'échec?" [Why hope? Why failure?]. In Philippe Duplay, ed., *Leclerc et l'Indochine 1945–1947: Quand se noua le destin d'un empire* [Leclerc and Indochina 1945–47: when empire's destiny was decided]. Paris: Albin Michel, 1992. 261–265.

Lacroix, (Lieutenant). *Phật giáo Hòa Hảo (Bouddhisme de Hòa Hảo)*. Unpublished report, June 1949.

Lagrou, Pieter. "Les guerres, les morts, et le deuil: bilan chiffré de la Seconde Guerre mondiale" [Wars, deaths, and mourning: an accounting of the Second World War]. In Stéphane Audoin-Rozeau et al., *La violence de guerre 1914–1945* [The violence of war, 1914–1945]. Paris: Éditions complexe, 2002. 313–28.

Larson, Pier. "'Capacities and Modes of Thinking': Intellectual Engagements and Subaltern Hegemony in the Early History of Malagasy Christianity." *American Historical Review* 102(4) (October 1997): 969–1002.

Lary, Diana. *The Chinese People at War. Human Suffering and Social Transformation, 1937–1945*. Cambridge: Cambridge University Press, 2010.

Lawrence, Mark Atwood. *Assuming the Burden: Europe and the American Commitment to War in Vietnam*. Berkeley: University of California Press, 2005.

Lazreg, Marnia. *Torture and the Twilight of Empire: From Algiers to Baghdad.* Princeton: Princeton University Press, 2007.

Lê Cung, Lê Thành Nam, Hồ Hải Hưng, Nguyễn Minh Phương, and Nguyễn Trung Triều. *Tinh thần nhập thế của Phật giáo Việt Nam (1945–1975)* [The spirit of worldly engagement of Vietnamese Buddhism]. Ho Chi Minh City: Tổng Hợp, 2018.

Le Gac, Julie. *Vaincre sans gloire: le Corps Expéditionnaire français en Italie (novembre 1942-juillet 1944)* [Victory without glory: the French Expeditionary Corps in Italy]. Paris: Les Belles Lettres, 2014.

Lê Hiếu Liêm. *Bồ tát Huỳnh Phú Sổ và Phật giáo thời đại* [Bodhisattva Huỳnh Phú Sổ and the Buddhist era]. [California?]: Viện Tư Tưởng Việt Phật, 1995.

Lê Hương. *Việt kiều ở Kampuchea* [The Vietnamese in Cambodia]. Saigon: Trí Đăng, 1971.

Lê Ngọc Bổn. *Biên niên sự kiện lịch sử lực lượng an ninh nhân dân (1945–1954)* [Chronicle of historical events related to the People's Public Security forces]. Hanoi: Công An Nhân Dân, 1995.

Lê Tiền Giang. *Công giáo kháng chiến Nam Bộ* [The Catholic Resistance in the South]. Saigon: Chọn, 1972.

Lê Trung Dũng. "Quá trình phân định biên giới giữa Nam Bộ Việt Nam và Campuchia" [The delimitation of the border between southern Vietnam and Cambodia]. *Nghiên cứu lịch sử* 10 (2006): 19–32.

Lê Tự. *Địch vận một nhiệm vụ chiến lược* [Proselytization: a strategic duty]. [Liên khu III ?]: Ban Địch vận, 1950.

Leclère, Adhémard. *Histoire du Cambodge depuis le 1er siecle de notre ère, d'après les inscriptions lapidaires, les annales chinoises et annamites et les documents européens des six derniers siècles* [History of Cambodia since the first century A. D. according to inscriptions, Chinese and Annamite annals, and European documents from the last six centuries]. Paris: Librairie Paul Geuthner, 1914.

Lentz, Christian C. *Contested Territory: Điện Biên Phủ and the Making of Northwest Vietnam.* New Haven, CT: Yale University press, 2019.

Leroy, Jean. *Fils de la rizière* [Son of the rice paddy]. Paris: R. Laffont, 1977.

Lévi-Straus, Claude. *La Pensée sauvage* [Wild pansy/The savage mind] Paris: Plon, 1960.

Lewis, Norman. *A Dragon Apparent: Travels in Indochina.* London: Jonathan Cape, 1951.

Li Tana. "The Water Frontier: An Introduction." In Li Tana and Nola Cooke, eds., *Water Frontier: Commerce and the Chinese in the Lower Mekong Region, 1750–1880.* Landover, MD: Rowman & Littlefield, 2004. 1–20.

Li, Kevin. "From Partisan to Sovereign: The Making of the Binh Xuyên." *Journal of Vietnamese Studies* 11(3/4) (2016): 140–187.

Lịch sử công an nhân dân Bến Tre (1945–54) [History of the Bến Tre public security forces]. Bến tre: s.n.,1992.

Lịch sử Tây Nam Bộ Kháng Chiến Tập 1 (1945–1954) [History of the Southwest Vietnam Resistance War, Vol. 1]. Nhà xuất bản Chính trị quốc gia, 2008. www .quansuvn.net/index.php?topic,24971.0

Logevall, Frederik. *Embers of War: The Fall of an Empire and the Making of America's Vietnam.* New York: Random House. 2014.

Lonsdale, John. "Authority, Gender, and Violence: The War within Mau Mau's Fight for Land and Freedom." In E. S. Atieno Odhiambo and John Lonsdale. eds., *Mau Mau and Nationhood*. Oxford: James Currey, 2003. 46–75.

Loustau, Henry-Jean. *Les deux batallions: Cochinchine-Tonkin, 1945–1952*. Paris: Albin Michel, 1987.

Lubkemann, Stephen. *Culture in Chaos: An Anthropology of the Social Condition in War*. Chicago: University of Chicago Press, 2008.

Lương Đức Thiệp. *Xã hội Việt Nam. Việt Nam tiến hóa sử* [Vietnamese society. The history of Vietnam's evolution]. Saigon: Liên Hiệp, 1950 [1944].

Lưu Khâm Hưng. "Cần Thơ trong ký ức tôi" [My memories of Cần Thơ]. https://luukhamhung.blogspot.com/2016/12/can-tho-trong-ky-uc-toi.html

Mai Chí Thọ. *Hồi Ức. Những mẩu chuyện đời tôi* [Stories of my life]. Ho Chi Minh City: Trẻ, 2001.

Mai Chí Thọ. "Những buổi ban đầu lưu luyến ấy" [Those first nostalgic memories]. In *Kỷ niệm sâu sắc trong đời Công An* [Remembrances of Public Security life]. Ho Chi Minh City: Công An Nhân Dân, 1995. 8–15.

Mann, Gregory. "Locating Colonial Histories: Between France and West Africa." *American Historical Review* (April 2005): 409–434.

Marr, David. *Vietnam 1945: The Quest for Power*. Berkeley and Los Angeles: University of California Press, 1995.

Marr, David. *Vietnam: State, War, and Revolution 1945–1946*. Berkeley: University of California Press, 2013.

Martin, Marie Alexandrine. *Cambodia: A Shattered Society*. Berkeley: California, 1994.

Mathieu, Edgar. "Le type du Cambodgien de Cochinchine" [The Cambodian of Cochinchina]. *Revue Internationale de Sociologie* 15(1) (1907): 590–596.

Mbembe, Achille. *Necropolitics*. Chapel Hill: Duke University Press, 2019.

McHale, Shawn. "Ethnicity. Violence. and Khmer-Vietnamese Relations: The Significance of the Lower Mekong Delta,1757–1954." *The Journal of Asian Studies* 72 (May 2013): 367–390.

McHale, Shawn. "Understanding the Fanatic Mind? The Việt Minh and Race Hatred in the First Indochina War." *Journal of Vietnamese Studies* 4(3) (October 2009): 98–138.

McHale, Shawn. *Print and Power: Confucianism, Communism, and Buddhism in the Making of Modern Vietnam*. Honolulu: University of Hawai'i Press, 2004.

McLeod, Mark. "The Way of the Mendicants: History, Philosophy, and Practice at the Central Vihara in Hồ Chí Minh City." *Journal of Vietnamese Studies* 4(2) (2009): 69–116.

Meysonnet, Henri and Bernard Meysonnet, ed. "Indochine 1945–1947." Unpublished manuscript, [2011?].

Michels, Eckard. "L'Allemagne et la Légion Étrangère" [Germany and the Foreign Legion]. *Cahiers du CEHD* 18 (2002): 147–173.

Miller, Edward. *Misalliance: Ngo Dinh Diem, the United States, and the Fate of South Vietnam*. Cambridge, MA: Harvard University Press, 2013.

Minh Đăng Quang. *Chơn lý*. Hanoi: Tôn Giáo, 2004.

Mus, Paul. "L'Indochine en 1945" [Indochina in 1945]. *Politique étrangère* [Foreign policy] 5 (1946): 433–464.

Mus, Paul. *Le Vietnam chez lui* [Vietnam: In country]. Paris: Centre d'Études de Politique Étrangère, 1946.

Ngô Hà. *Cách mạng tháng tám* [The August Revolution]. Bangkok: Tủ Sách Tin Việt Nam, [1948].

Ngô Văn. "Caught in a Crossfire." in *In the Crossfire: Adventures of a Vietnamese Revolutionary*. S.l: AK Press, 2010. www.bopsecrets.org/vietnam/07 .crossfire.htm

Nguyễn Bỉnh Khiêm. *Sấm ngữ Trạng Trình* [Trạng Trình's Prophecies]. Hanoi: Bảo Ngọc, 1946.

Nguyễn Hải Hàm. *Từ Yên Báy đến Côn Lôn (1930–1945). Hồi ký* [From Yên Báy to Poulo Condore: a memoir]. Falls Church: Nha Sach The He, 1995.

Nguyễn Hiến Lê. *Hồi ký Nguyễn Hiến Lê* [Memoirs of Nguyễn Hiến Lê]. Ho Chi Minh City: Văn Học, 2006.

Nguyễn Hùng. *Ung Văn Khiêm: Anh Ba nội vụ* [Ung Văn Khiêm, Brother Number Three in Internal Security Affairs]. Ho Chi Minh City: Công An Nhân Dân, 2004.

Nguyễn Long Thành Nam. *Phật giáo Hòa Hảo trong dòng lịch sử dân tộc* [Hòa Hảo Buddhism in the stream of the people's history]. S.l.: Đuốc Từ Bi, 1991 www .hoahao.org/p74a279/2/phat-giao-hoa-hao-trong-dong-lich-su-dan-toc (accessed February 3, 2018).

Nguyễn Minh Châu and Nguyễn Thanh Hà. *Báo cáo tổng hợp đấu tranh cách mạng của công nhân và công đoàn tỉnh Sóc Trăng* [Report on the revolutionary struggle of workers and unions in Soc Trang province]. Sóc Trăng: s.n., 2011.

Nguyễn Ngọc Lầu. "Tôi tham gia cách mạng tháng tám ở Hà Tiên" [I took part in the August Revolution in Hà Tiên]. In Trần Bạch Đằng et al, eds., *Mùa Thu rồi. Ngày hăm ba* [Autumn. The 23rd]. Hanoi: Chính trị Quốc gia, 1995. 398–407.

Nguyễn Ngọc Thiện et al., eds. *Tuyển tập phê bình, nghiên cứu văn học Việt Nam* [Selected readings on criticism and research on Vietnamese literature]. Vol. 4. Hanoi: Văn Học, 1997.

Nguyễn Phan Quang. *Góp thêm tư liệu Sài Gòn –Gia Định từ 1859–1945* [Contributions to the history of Saigon and Ho Chi Minh City, 1859–1945]. Hồ Chí Minh City: Trẻ, 1998.

Nguyễn Thanh Sơn. *Trọn đời theo Bác Hồ. Hồi ức của một người con đồng bằng sông Cửu Long* [All my life following Uncle Ho. Memoir of a son of the Mekong Delta]. Ho Chi Minh City: Trẻ, 2005.

Nguyen, Thuy Linh. "Overpopulation, Racial Degeneracy and Birth Control in French Colonial Vietnam." *Journal of Colonialism and Colonial History* 19(3) (Winter 2018). https://doi.org/10.1353/cch.2018.0024

Nguyễn Tuân Triêt and Phạm Văn Hướng. *Lịch sử tỉnh Trà Vinh* [History of Trà Vinh province]. Vol. 1. Trà Vinh: Ban tư tưởng tỉnh uỷ Trà Vinh, 1995.

Nguyễn Văn Giậu. *Việt Nam đẫm máu vì chiến tranh thực dân 1945–54* [A Vietnam bloodied by colonialist war]. S.l.: Bình Minh, 1956.

Nguyễn Văn Lung. "Nhớ lại trận Là Ngà" [Remembering the battle of Là Ngà]. In Võ Tấn Nhã, ed., *Kể chuyện chiến trường miền Đông Nam Bộ* [Stories from the eastern Cochinchina battlefield]. Ho Chi Minh City: Thành phố Hồ Chí Minh, 1987. 156–210.

Nguyễn Văn Trấn. *Viết cho Mẹ và Quốc Hội* [Written for my mother and the National Assembly]. Westminster, CA: Văn Nghệ, 1995.

Nguyễn Việt. *Nam Bộ và nam phần Trung Bộ trong hai năm đầu Kháng Chiến (1945–1946)* [The South and southern part of the Center in the first two years of the Resistance War]. Hanoi: Văn Sử Địa, 1957.

Nhất Hoành Sơn. *Công dân giáo dục phổ thông* [General education for citizens]. Hanoi: Ngày nay, 1949.

Paraideau, Natasha. *Mobile Citizens: French Indians in Indochina, 1858–1954.* Copenhagen: NIAS, 2016.

Phạm Bích Hợp. "Nhìn lại sự kiện Đốc Vàng và hệ quả tâm lý" [A second look at the events of Đốc Vàng and their psychological consequences]. *Xưa và nay* 296 (November 2007): 19, 38.

Phạm Công Tắc. *Lời thuyết đạo của Đức Hộ Pháp*, Vol. 3 (1949–1950). https://tusachcaodai.files.wordpress.com/2013/05/hp-td-qiii.pdf

Phạm Dân (Tương Lai). "Công tác Hoa vận thờ chống Pháp ở Nam Bộ" [Proselytization work among the Chinese during the anti-French Resistance in the South]. In *Nam Bộ thành đồng Tổ Quốc*. Hanoi: Chính trị Quốc gia, 1990. 298–302.

Phạm Duy. Chương Mười Một [Chapter 11]. In *Hồi ký* [Memoir]. Vol. 3. www.phamduy2010.com/phamduy_viethtml/hoiky/hoiky3/chuong_11.html

Phạm Văn Bạch. "Mùa Thu nhớ mãi" [An autumn forever remembered]. In *Nam Bộ thành đồng Tổ quốc*. Hanoi: Chính trị Quốc gia, 1990.

Phan Đại Doãn et al. *Một số vấn đề về quan chế triều Nguyễn* [Some issues related to the Nguyễn dynasty mandarinate]. Huế: Thuận Hóa, 1998.

Phan Khôi. *Tìm hiểu sự thật* [Understanding the truth]. Saigon: Nhà in Quốc gia, 1957.

Philpott, Daniel. *Revolutions in Sovereignty: How Ideas Shaped Modern International Relations.* Princeton: Princeton University Press, 2001.

Phùng Tri Lai. *Hồng Kông du ký* [Travels to Hong Kong]. Hanoi: Nhà in Vũ Hùng, 1950. Online at sach.nlv.gov.vn, no stable URL.

Phương Lan. *Nhà cách mạng Tạ Thu Thâu* [The revolutionary Tạ Thu Thâu]. Saigon: Khai Trí, [1972?].

Quân Khu 7. Câu Lạc Bộ Quân Giới Nam Bộ. *Lịch sử Quân giới Nam Bộ (1945–1954)* [History of southern armaments production, 1945–54]. Hanoi: Quân Đội Nhân Dân, 1991.

Quốc Sử Quán Triều Nguyễn. *Quốc Triều Chinh Biên Toát Yếu* [An abridged version of the Nguyễn dynastic annals]. Hue: Thuận Hóa, 1998.

Quyết chiến, kinh nghiệm về cao trào Kháng Nhật cứu nước ở Việt Nam [Decisive victory: experiences from the Resistance against the Japanese for the salvation of Vietnam]. Hanoi: Sự Thật, 1946.

Rafael, Vicente. *Contracting Colonialism: Translation and Christian Conversion in Tagalog Society under Early Spanish Rule.* Durham, NC: Duke University Press, 1993.

Raffin, Anne. "Youth Mobilization and Ideology: Cambodia from the Late Colonial Era to the Pol Pot Regime." *Critical Asian Studies* 44(3) (2012): 391–418.

Ramsay, Jacob. *Mandarins and Martyrs: The Church and the Nguyen Dynasty in Early Nineteenth-Century Vietnam.* Stanford: Stanford University Press, 2008.

Rand Corporation. *Studies of the National Liberation Front of South-Vietnam.* Santa Monica: s.n., [1966].

Réau, Claude. "Avec le Corps léger d'intervention de Djidjelli à Tam-Binh" [With the light intervention corps, from Djidjelli to Tam-Binh]. In Jean Clauzel, ed., *La France d'Outre-Mer 1930–1960: témoignages d'administrateurs et de magistrats* [Overseas France, 1930–60: accounts of administrators and judges]. Paris: Karthala, 2004. 524–533.

Reddi, V. M. *A History of the Cambodian Independence Movement 1863–1955.* Tirupati: Sri Venkatteswara University, 1970.

Reilly, Brett. "The Origins of the Vietnamese Civil War and the State of Vietnam." PhD dissertation, University of Wisconsin–Madison, 2018.

Reilly, Brett. "The Sovereign States of Vietnam, 1945–1955." *Journal of Vietnamese Studies,* 11(3–4) (2016): 103–39.

Research and Analysis Branch, Office of Strategic Services. *Programs of Japan in Indo-China With Index to Biographical Data. Assemblage #56.* Honolulu: Office of Strategic Services, August 10, 1945.

Robinson, Geoffrey. *The Killing Season: A History of the Indonesian Massacres, 1965–66.* Princeton, NJ: Princeton University Press, 2018.

Salehyan, Idean. "Refugees and the Study of Civil War." *Civil Wars* 9(2) (June 2007): 127–141.

Salemink, Oscar. *The Ethnography of Vietnam's Central Highlanders: A Historical Contextualization, 1850–1990.* Honolulu: University of Hawai'i Press, 2003.

Sainteny, Jean, *Histoire d'une paix manquée* [The tale of a forsaken peace]. Paris: Fayard, 1967.

Savani, A. M. *Notes sur le Caodaisme* [Notes on Caodaism]. [Saigon]: s.n., 1954).

Schendel, Willem van. "Geographies of Knowing, Geographies of Ignorance: Jumping Scale in Southeast Asia." In P. Kratoska, R. Raben, and H. Nordholt, eds., *Locating Southeast Asia: Geographies of Knowledge and Politics of Space.* Singapore: Singapore University Press, 2005. 275–307.

Schendel, Willem van. "Stateless in South Asia: The Making of the India-Bangladesh Enclaves." *Journal of Asian Studies* 61(1) (February 2002): 115–147.

Schütte, Heinz. "Les Doktors germaniques dans le Viet Minh" [German doctors in the Viet Minh]. *Aséanie* 15 (2005): 61–85.

Scott, James. *The Art of Not Being Governed: An Anarchist History of Upland Southeast Asia.* New Haven & London: Yale University Press, 2009.

Shipway, Martin. *The Road to War: France and Vietnam, 1944–1947.* Providence and Oxford: Berghahn, 1996.

Shiraishi Masaya. "Présences japonaises" [The Japanese role]. In Fondation Maréchal Leclerc de Hauteclocque, *Leclerc et l'Indochine.* 37–46.

Shiu Wentang. "A Preliminary Inquiry into the Wartime Material Losses of Chinese in Vietnam, 1941–1947." *Chinese Southern Diaspora Studies* 4 (2010): 117–128.

Sihanouk, Norodom. *L'Indochine vue de Pékin* [Indochina, seen from Beijing]. Paris: Éditions du Seuil, 1972.

Simonin, (General) Paul. *Les Berets blancs de la Légion en Indochine* [The Legion's White Berets in Indochina]. Paris: Albin Michel, 2002.

Sơn Nam. *Hồi ký* [Memoirs]. Vol. 2. Ho Chi Minh City: Trẻ, 2002.

Spector, Ronald. *In the Ruins of Empire: The Japanese Surrender and the Battle for Postwar Asia*. New York: Random House, 2008.

Stark, David. "Recombinant Property in East European Capitalism." *American Journal of Sociology* 101(4)(January 1996): 993–1027.

Stepputat, Finn. "State/Violence and 'Fragmented Sovereignties'." *Etnofoor* 24 (1) (2012): 117–121.

Stoler, Ann. "Sexual Affronts and Racial Frontiers: European Identities and the Cultural Politics of Exclusion in Colonial Southeast Asia." *Comparative Studies in Society and History* 34(3) (July 1992): 514–551.

Surun, Isabelle. "Une souveraineté à l'encre sympathique? Souveraineté auto-chtone et appropriations territoriales dans les traités franco-africains au XIXe siècle." [A sovereignty claim in invisible ink? Indigenous sovereignty and terri-torial appropriation in franco-african treaties of the nineteenth century] *Annales. Histoire, Sciences Sociales* 69(2)(2014): 313–48.

Tạ Chí Đại Trường. *Người lính thuộc địa Nam Kỳ* [Colonial soldiers of Nam Kỳ]. Hanoi: Trí Thức, 2011.

Tạ Chí Đại Trường. *Lịch sử nội chiến ở Việt Nam từ 1771 đến 1802 [The history of Vietnam's civil war, 1771–1802]. [Saigon]: Văn Sử Học, 1973.*

Tai, Hue Tam Ho. *Millenarianism and Peasant Politics in Vietnam*. Cambridge: Harvard East Asian Studies, 1983.

Tam Ích. *Cuộc cách mạng Việt Nam thành công chăng và thành công cách nào?* [Will the Vietnamese revolution succeed and how?]. Saigon: Nam Việt, 1947.

Tan, Stan B. H. "Dust Beneath the Mist: State and Frontier Formation in the Central Highlands of Vietnam. the 1955–61 period." PhD dissertation, Australian National University, 2011.

Taunton, Doidge Estcourt interview for "Vietnam: A Television History." https://openvault.wgbh.org/catalog/V_FFA5A0F537504A9A9945BF9EC7CC22FE

Taylor, Philip. "Losing the Waterways: The Displacement of Khmer Communities from the Freshwater Rivers of the Mekong Delta, 1945–2010." *Modern Asian Studies* 47 (2013): 500–541.

Taylor, Philip. *The Khmer Lands of Vietnam: Environment, Cosmology, and Sovereignty*. Singapore: NUS Press, 2014.

Tenenbaum, Élie. "Une Odysée subversive: la circulation des savoirs stratégiques irrégulières en Occident France. Grande-Bretagne. États-Unis. de 1944 à 1972" [A subversive quest: the circulation of strategic knowledge on irregular warfare in the West: France, Britain, and the United States from 1944 to 1972]. Doctoral dissertation, Paris Institute of Political Studies, 2015.

Tertrais, Hugues. *Le piastre et le fusil* [The piaster and the gun]. Paris: Comité pour l'histoire économique et financière de la France, 2002).

Thẩm Thệ Hà. *Việt Nam trên đường cách mạng tân văn hoá* [Vietnam on the road to a new cultural revolution]. Saigon: Tân Việt Nam, 1949.

Thiếu Mai [Mrs. Vũ Bá Hùng]. *Ngược gió. Hồi ký* [Against the wind: a memoir]. Saigon: Đồng Nai, 1972.

Thiếu Sơn. *Nghệ thuật và nhân sinh* [Art and life]. Hanoi: Văn Hóa thông tin Hà Nội, 2000.

Thiếu Sơn. *Giữa hai cuộc cách mạng 1789–1945* [Between two revolutions, 1789–1945]. Saigon: Mạch Sống, 1947.

Thoumelin, Pierre. *L'ennemi utile; des vétérans de la Wehrmacht et de la Waffen-SS dans les rangs de la Légion étrangère en Indochine* [The useful enemy: Wehrmacht and Waffen-SS veterans in the Foreign Legion in Indochina. [Giel-Courteilles]: Schneider, 2013.

Tilly, Charles. *Regimes and Repertoires*. Chicago: University of Chicago Press, 2006.

Tinh Ủy Ban Nhân Dân tỉnh Trà Vinh. *Lịch sử tỉnh Trà Vinh* [History of Trà Vinh Province]. S.l.: Ban Tư Tưởng Tỉnh Ủy Trà Vinh, 1999.

Titley, Brian. *Dark Age: The Political Odyssey of Emperor Bokassa*. Montreal: McGill University Press, 1997.

Tønnesson, Stein. *Vietnam 1946: How the War Began*. Berkeley: University of California Press. 2010.

Trần Bạch Đằng. *Kẻ sĩ Gia Định* [The learned of Gia Định]. Hanoi: Quân Đội Nhân Dân, 2005.

Tran Duc Thao. "Sur L'Indochine" [On Indochina]. *Les temps modernes* [Modern Times] 1(5) (February 1946): 878–900.

Trần Ngươn Phiêu. "Nỗi lòng Huỳnh Tấn Phát" [Sentiments on Huỳnh Tấn Phát]. https://nghiencuulichsu.com/2015/03/25/noi-long-huynh-tan-phat

Trần Ngươn Phiêu. *Phan Văn Hùm: thân thế và sự nghiệp* [Phan Van Hum: his life and accomplishments]. Amarillo, TX: Hải Mã, 2003.

Trần Quang Vinh. *Hồi ký Trần Quang Vinh* [The memoirs of Tran Quang Vinh]. S.l., Thánh thất vùng Hoa Thịnh Đốn, 1997.

Trần Thị Hoa (tự Phấn). *Hồi ký quân sử Nghĩa Quân Cách Mạng* [Memoir on the Righteous Revolutionary Army]. Derwood, MD: Giáo Hội Phật Giáo Hải Ngoại, 2002.

'Trần Tây phong thổ ký': The Customs of Cambodia" [1838]. Translated by Li Tana. In *Chinese Southern Diaspora Studies*, 1 (2007): 148–157. http://chl.anu.edu.au/sites/default/files/publications/csds/csds2007/Tran_Tay.pdf

Trần Văn Giàu and Trần Bạch Đằng, eds. *Địa chí văn hóa Thành phố Hồ Chí Minh* [Geography and culture of Ho Chi Minh City]. Vol. 1. Ho Chi Minh City: Thành phố Hồ Chí Minh, 1987.

Trần Văn Quế. *Côn Lôn Quần Đảo trước ngày 9–3–1945* [Poulo Condore before March 3, 1945]. Saigon: Thanh-Hương Tùng Thư, 1961.

Trần Văn Trà. "Chiến tranh nhân dân khởi đầu từ Nam Bộ như thế" [How did people's war break out in the South?]. In *Nam Bộ thành đồng Tổ Quốc*. Hanoi: Chính trị Quốc gia, 1990. 15–73.

Trần Văn Trà. *Miền Nam thành đồng đi trước về sau* [The southern citadel, before and after]. Hanoi: Quân đội nhân dân, 2006.

Trần Văn Trà. *Những chặng đường của B-2-Thành Đồng. Volume 5. Kết thúc cuộc chiến tranh 30 năm* [The history of the Bulwark B-2 Theater. Vol. 5: The end of the thirty-year war]. Ho Chi Minh City: Văn Nghệ thành phố Hồ Chí Minh, 1982.

Trịnh Đình Thảo. *Suy nghĩ và hành động* [Reflection and action]. Ho Chi Minh City: thành phố Hồ Chí Minh, 1985.

Trường Chinh. *Ba giai đoạn trường kỳ kháng chiến* [The Three Stages of Protracted War] Saigon-Cholon: Ty Thông Tin Sài Gòn-Chợ lớn, 1949.

Trường Chinh. *Cách mạng tháng Tám* [The August Revolution]. Hanoi: Sư Thật, 1955 [1946].

Trương Dương Vũ. *Máu trở về tim. Ký sự* [Blood rushes to the heart. An account]. [S.l.: Tổng Hợp Hậu Giang, 1980.

Trương Minh Đạt. *Nghiên cứu Hà Tiên* [Hà Tiên research]. Ho Chi Minh City: Tạp chí Xưa & Nay [and] Nhà xuất bản Trẻ, 2008.

Ưng Trình. *Việt Nam ngoại giao sử cận đại* [A history of modern Vietnamese foreign policy]. Hanoi: Trí Đức Thư Xã, 1953.

Varshney, Ashutosh. *Ethnic Conflict and Civic Life: Hindus and Muslims in India.* New Haven: Yale University Press, 2002.

Vickery, Michael. *Cambodia 1975–82.* Boston: South End Press, 1984.

Việt Nam Cộng Hòa. *Địa phương chí tỉnh Vĩnh Bình* [Geography and history of Vĩnh Bình province]. S.l.: s.n.,1973.

Vigneras, Marcel. *Rearming the French* (United States Army in World War Two Special Studies). Washington, DC: Center for Military History, 1989 [1957].

Villatoux, Marie-Catherine and Paul Villatoux. "Aux origines de la 'guerre révolutionnaire': le colonel Lacheroy parle" [The origins of revolutionary war: Colonel Lacheroy speaks]. *Revue historique des armées* 268 (2012): 45–53.

Võ Nguyên Giáp. *Điện Biên Phủ, điểm hẹn lịch sử: hồi ức* [Điện Biên Phủ: memoir of an historical encounter]. Hanoi: Quân đội nhân dân, 2001.

Vũ Đình Hòe. *Hồi ký* [Memoirs]. Hanoi: Văn Hóa Thông Tin, 1994.

Vũ Đức Liêm. "Vietnam at the Khmer Frontier: Boundary Politics, 1802–1847." *Cross-Currents: East Asian History and Culture Review* 5(2) (November 2016): 534–564.

Vu Ngu Chieu. "The Other Side of the 1945 Vietnamese Revolution: The Empire of Viet-Nam (March–August 1945)." *Journal of Asian Studies* 45(2) (February 1986): 293–328.

Vu,Tuong. "'It's Time for the Indochinese Revolution to Show Its True Colours': The Radical Turn of Vietnamese Politics in 1948." *Journal of Southeast Asian Studies* 40(3) (2009): 519–542.

Vu,Tuong. "Triumphs or Tragedies: A New Perspective on the Vietnamese Revolution." *Journal of Southeast Asian Studies* 45 (2014): 236–257.

Vương Hồng Sển. *Hơn nửa đời hư* [Over half of a do-nothing life]. Westminster, CA: Văn Nghệ, 1995.

Vương Kim. *Tận thế và hội Long Hoa* [The end of the age and the dragon flower assembly]. Saigon: Long Hoa, 1953.

Vương Liêm. *Đồng quê Nam Bộ (thập niên 40)* [The southern countryside in the 1940s]. Ho Chi Minh City: Văn Nghệ Thành Phố Hồ Chí Minh, 2003.

Vương Liêm. *Huỳnh Văn Một, người con trung dũng của Đức Hòa-Chợ Lớn* [Huỳnh Văn Một, a loyal and courageous son of Đức Hòa-Chợ Lớn]. Hanoi: Quân đội nhân dân, 2006.

Walder, Andrew. *Fractured Rebellion: the Beijing Red Guard Movement*. Cambridge: Harvard University Press, 2012.

Werner, Jayne. "The Cao Dai: Politics of a Vietnamese Syncretic Religious Movement." PhD dissertation, Cornell University, 1976.

Wheatley, Natasha. "Spectral Legal Personality in Interwar International Law: On New Ways of Not Being a State." *Law & History Review* 35 (August 2017): 753–788.

Wheeler, Charles. "Re-Thinking the Sea in Vietnamese History: Littoral Society in the Integration of Thuận-Quảng, Seventeenth-Eighteenth Centuries." *Journal of Southeast Asian Studies* 37(1) (February 2006): 123–153.

Wheeler, Charles. "Interests, Institutions, and Identity: Strategic Adaptation and the Ethno-Evolution of Minh Hương (Central Vietnam), 16th–19th Centuries." *Itinerario* 39(1) (2015): 141–66.

White, Luise. *Speaking with Vampires: Rumor and History in Colonial Africa*. Berkeley and Los Angeles: University of California Press, 2000.

White, Luise. "Telling More: Lies, Secrets, and History." *History and Theory* 39 (4) (December 2000): 11–22.

Winichakul, Thongchai. *Siam Mapped: A History of the Geo-body of a Nation*. Honolulu: University of Hawai'i Press, 1994.

Womack, Brantly. *Vietnam and China: The Politics of Asymmetry*. Cambridge: Cambridge University Press, 2006.

Woodside, Alexander. *Community and Revolution in Modern Vietnam*. Boston: Houghton Mifflin, 1976.

Zamindar, Vazira Fazila-Yacoobali. *The Long Partition and the Making of Modern South Asia: Refugees, Boundaries, Histories*. New York: Columbia University Press, 2010.

Zhai Qiang. "China and the Geneva Conference of 1954." *The China Quarterly* 129 (March 1992): 103–122.

Zimmerman, Sarah. "Living Beyond Boundaries: West African Servicemen in French Colonial Conflicts, 1908–1962." Dissertation, University of California at Berkeley, 2011.

Index